D0876479

THE RETURN OF INEQUALITY

THE RETURN OF

INEQUALITY

Social Change and the Weight of the Past

MIKE SAVAGE

Harvard University Press

Cambridge, Massachusetts   London, England   2021

Copyright © 2021 by the President and Fellows of Harvard College
All rights reserved
Printed in the United States of America

First printing

Library of Congress Cataloging-in-Publication Data

Names: Savage, Michael, 1959– author.
Title: The return of inequality : social change and the
weight of the past / Mike Savage.
Description: Cambridge, Massachusetts : Harvard University Press, 2021. |
Includes bibliographical references and index.
Identifiers: LCCN 2020042444 | ISBN 9780674988071 (cloth)
Subjects: LCSH: Income distribution—History—21st century. |
Equality—21st century. | Regression (Civilization)—21st century. |
Social change—21st century.
Classification: LCC HC79.I5 S297 2021 | DDC 339.2—dc23
LC record available at https://lccn.loc.gov/2020042444

Contents

Preface

In the past decade, it has become commonplace—almost trite—to claim that inequality is the defining challenge of our time. My book reflects, from a sociological perspective, what kind of challenge this is exactly, and how best to rise to it. I offer a different approach from methods now dominating the social science agenda, which have taken advantage of new data sets and analytical frameworks to concentrate on economic measurement and the listing of the various axes on which inequality operates. Make no mistake, that work is vital, and I draw on it extensively in these pages. But empirical documentation is not, by itself, enough. We need to understand better the wider theoretical and political problems that inequality poses. We are at a crucial moment in human history, and only by grasping the nature of this moment can we realize how inequality is an even more fundamental challenge than it already seems.

My specific entry point derives from my long-term academic and political interests in studying social class as a major axis of inequality. Within the heroic pedigree of socialist politics and Marxist analysis, social class was assigned a preeminent role, not simply as a technical measurement tool but in shaping the course of history itself. I remember well the famous 1979 History Workshop symposium at Oxford, which I attended as an undergraduate history student from the University of York. On that cold, dank evening, shortly after Margaret Thatcher became the British prime minister, I witnessed the doyens of Marxism—Edward Thompson, Stuart Hall, Richard Johnson, and others—tear each other apart as they crossed swords over the virtues of structuralist approaches to class.[1] Far from being an esoteric debate, class mattered passionately to these protagonists, because it spoke to the exact historical moment—a time when the social democratic consensus that had dominated Britain since 1945 was about to be dismantled.

From this heady moment, class analysis lost the passion it enjoyed that astonishing evening in 1979. During the 1980s a consensus emerged among leading sociologists, such as Anthony Giddens (1990, 1991), Ulrich Beck (1992), and Zygmunt Bauman (2000, 2007), that social class was becoming irrelevant, a throwback to an old industrial era that was being left behind by the rapid pace of globalization, technical change, and the information society. Some "keepers of the flame" responded by insisting that if class were measured scientifically, it still shaped people's life chances in fundamental ways (Goldthorpe and Marshall 1992). This defense was effective up to a point, but it took class analysis into a specialized, technically sophisticated sideline, cut off from the wider public resonances that it used to enjoy.[2] Although I engaged with this current of research, I felt keenly that the passion of studying class, which had drawn me to it amid the political debates of the 1970s, had been lost. Methodological sophistication had come at a high price.

In the years after 2000, class analysis began to enjoy a revival in Britain, as well as in other parts of the world. By 2010, a nascent tradition of "cultural class analysis" had been identified, which was attuned to how class inequality was experienced and identified the pervasive force of cultures of stigma, shame, and entitlement (see W. Atkinson 2010). This was also part of a wider reflection on how class needed to be analyzed in their intersections, especially around gender, race, and ethnicity (for example, Skeggs 1997; Devine et al. 2005; Bennett et al. 2009; Rollock et al. 2014). Nonetheless, this revival of interest in class in no way prepared me for the remarkable public reception of the Great British Class Survey (GBCS), which attracted a storm of interest in Britain, and indeed internationally, when it was published between 2013 and 2015.[3] The intense debate that the GBCS provoked showed that class analysis was fully back in the spotlight, in public and not just in academic debate. It spoke to the huge public thirst for understanding what social class inequality meant in the early twenty-first century.

Despite—or perhaps because of—this intense interest, the GBCS turned out to be a challenging experience. I was subject to more political and academic criticism than at any previous time in my career. The GBCS had touched a sensitive nerve in two very different ways. First, it animated debate on the "stuff" of inequality, on what inequality was made of. What are social classes? How many are there? How are they measured? How do they relate to other inequalities? These issues had dominated the sociological debate—and indeed, had directed my own previous research on social class. But a second issue was rather drowned out in academic debate, though it was much more visible in the media and public reception. This concerned what the GBCS told us about "now-time." What was society in 2013? How does it compare with previous periods? What fears and anxieties should we have in the current situation? Are we more divided than ever? In short, it spoke to a pessimistic and anxious mindset that clearly had considerable resonance among the public.

Since 2013, the feeling of the urgency of inequality has gathered pace, with gender and race being major flashpoints of contention and resistance. The #MeToo movement, initially fueled by accounts of film producer Harvey Weinstein's systematic sexual abuse, mobilized millions of women determined to fight sexism and misogyny. The Black Lives Matter movement drew attention to sustained brutality against black people, not only in the United States but also around the globe. It drew attention to the enduring power of institutional racism and the long-term and persisting role of historical forces, especially the power of empire and slavery. There is something compelling about the way that, even in the much-vaunted technological and digital arena of twenty-first-century global capitalism, historical figures have taken on such symbolic power. The Victorian imperialist Cecil Rhodes, US Confederate generals, and long-dead slave traders have gained major contemporary significance.

The animating concern of my book is to take stock of this apparently inexorable rise of interest in inequality and reflect on what it tells us about social change. This requires us to downplay the significance of social class, to recognize the power of many intersecting axes of inequality—race, ethnicity, and gender being especially significant—and to place all these concerns within a long-term perspective that recognizes the renewal of longer-term historical forces that for decades have complacently been seen as relics of the past. The coronavirus pandemic of 2020 demonstrates all too clearly the need for this perspective. It is not incidental that this moment of danger has become so closely identified with the entrenchment of inequality. Shortly after the virus took hold in Europe and North America, news stories about its inegalitarian effects began appearing. Wealthy urbanites left for their second homes in the countryside, whereas poor and working-class residents were cooped up in small apartments. Domestic abuse surged. Black and ethnic minorities—who were disproportionately likely to be working on the "front line"—were more likely to suffer from both the virus itself and the economic fallout that was left in its wake. In this situation, the proliferation of inequality discourse was a means of rendering the strange familiar. It made sense of the sheer horror of the pandemic by anchoring it back to familiar discourses of inequality that are now routine. Yet it also made the familiar strange, by showing that we were in uncharted territory and lacked a clear view of the course ahead.

This book therefore explicates what it means to see inequality as a historical force—as a reflection on our "now-time." I argue against the conventional view that the power of history can be rendered in terms of its legacies, residues, or relics, or even just as some kind of backdrop. This renders history as only a context that does not directly impinge on the present. I criticize the common temptation within the social sciences to fixate on the "stuff" of inequality. Measuring any specific dimension, whether this be class, gender, race, or something else, can fragment our grasp of the historical challenge of inequality by chopping inequality into discrete boxes. I will be very clear that this "stuff" is absolutely crucial and will be a constant companion through this book. Repositioning this inquiry into a fundamentally historical register allows us to synthesize and understand social change as a whole. This is therefore a reiteration of Walter Benjamin's ringing words: "To articulate the past historically does not mean to recognize it 'the way it really was' (Ranke). It means to seize hold of a memory as it flashes up at a moment of danger." It is the sense that we are now fully in a "moment of danger" that animates my book.[4]

Our "now-time" is saturated by inequality. Only twenty years ago social class was widely seen as some kind of historical throwback. The apparent dismantling of overt racism heralded by the end of the Jim Crow regime in the United States and apartheid in South Africa had been identified by some commentators as marking the arrival of a "post-racial society." Gender discrimination was also seen to be rapidly eroding, to the extent that another leading sociologist, Manuel Castells (1997), in his sweeping overview of the rise of the global network society in the 1990s, could proclaim "the end of patriarchalism." My book is written in the sad realization that the brief optimistic moment that colored the end of the twentieth century has faded. The reception of my Great British Class Survey brought this home very clearly. Class is clearly not some old, industrial relic—a "zombie category," to use Ulrich Beck's words—but is alive and kicking, generating anger and resentment, and symptomatic of a host of dystopian problems. The revival of racism, which became especially apparent in the Islamophobic reaction by white elites to the 9/11 terror attack on the United States, and the recognition that ingrained sexism not only persisted but was taking on new and vicious forms, speak also to this new pessimistic sensibility.

This is therefore not another book documenting some underappreciated aspect of inequality. I reflect more broadly about what inequality tells us about the world we currently live in and how we are at a crucial historical turning point. To truly address the significance of inequality is to challenge the separation of the social sciences from the history that took place during the end of the nineteenth century and to reawaken a vision of historical social science. This radical rethinking of knowledge claims is a crucial step toward understanding the challenge of inequality. Social science itself is at stake.

THE RETURN OF INEQUALITY

Introduction

WHAT IS THE CHALLENGE OF INEQUALITY?

At the start of the twenty-first century, inequality was largely viewed as a minor, specialist concern. Economic growth linked to deregulation and marketization, the fall of communist regimes, globalization, the rise of digital communication, and the expansion of knowledge-based economies in the previous two decades had generated a heady millennial excitement about the promise of economic and social advance. The looming problem of climate change notwithstanding, the twenty-first century seemed to mark the arrival of the good life for many.

This optimistic world now looks very foreign. There are numerous reasons for this change of mood, ranging from intensified geopolitical tensions across the globe in the aftermath of the "war on terror,' to the intensifying climate crisis, and to declining confidence (in many parts of the world) in the robustness of democratic structures and civil society. In the past decade, the topic of inequality has become the central hook on which to hang the anxieties that this pessimistic perspective has engendered. One redolent moment was President Barack Obama's pithy rendition in 2013 of income inequality as "the defining challenge of our time." Inequality became a way of summarizing a basket of bleak problems under one banner that could link fallout from the austerity politics unleashed across the world in the aftermath of the 2008 financial crash to the sense of malaise that was provoked by entrenched and sometimes growing divisions in such areas as social mobility, health, politics, and well-being.

This book is written out of my sense that inequality does indeed open a crucial, pathbreaking agenda that speaks to the broader ills of our time. And yet, the term has also become massively overloaded, piled with more freight than it can possibly bear. We may have grasped the scale, but we have not yet understood the full nature of the challenge that inequality poses. As a label, inequality proliferates across so many axes, in such varied contexts, that it can degenerate into a relentless listing exercise. Far from being productive, this can then lead to an infinite regress toward a fatalistic pessimism: Inequality is so entrenched, it's everywhere, so what can we do about it? In this respect, as in others, it can echo the climate crisis debate. Or, in contrast, it can facilitate an overly eager set of policy tools designed to "fix" the problem—what has been identified as a nascent inequality industry. As Atossa Araxia Abrahammian (2018) put it, "since 2008, wonks, politicians, poets, and bankers have all started talking about inequality. But are they interested in making us more equal?" Has inequality simply become the latest banner around which experts can mobilize new kinds of professional skills (commanding good salaries and career prospects as they do so)? And what do we make of the fact that inequality has risen to the top of the agenda at the same time that economic growth in many parts of the world has reduced poverty to its lowest level in recorded history? Is there is a danger that inequality seems like distant and irrelevant bleating to the many people around the world whose economic and social situations have actually been improving, sometimes substantially? Is it simply the latest manifestation of a liberal elite bubble mentality—a symptom of the very problem that critics of inequality are supposed to draw attention to?

My book is animated by the view that we need a more robust sociological framing of the inequality debate to broaden our understanding of the full scale of the challenge it entails. I pursue the ambitious argument that we are witnessing the emergence of an inequality paradigm, which fundamentally unsettles long-term assumptions about the direction and nature of social change.

Truly bringing out the challenge of inequality therefore requires us to disrupt conventional paradigms—what the eminent historian of science Thomas Kuhn identified as "normal science"—by provoking a revolutionary reassessment of our overarching assumptions. In these terms, inequality can provoke a revolutionary phase that disrupts the conventional "growth" and "modernization" paradigms that have dominated social science since the Second World War.

This is how Thomas Kuhn (1977: xvii) distinguished between periods of normal science and revolution:

> Scientific development depends in part on a process of non-incremental or revolutionary change. Some revolutions are large, like those associated with the names of Copernicus, Newton, or Darwin, but most are much smaller, like the discovery of oxygen or the planet Uranus. The usual prelude to changes of this sort is, I believed, the awareness of anomaly, of an occurrence or set of occurrences that does not fit existing ways of ordering phenomena. The changes that result therefore require "putting on a different kind of thinking-cap," one that renders the anomalous lawlike but that, in the process, also transforms the order exhibited by some other phenomena, previously unproblematic.

Inequality has come to prominence precisely as the anomaly that troubles conventional social scientific models. This revolutionary moment is not only one of revelation but also is disruptive and provokes critical reactions from those wedded to conventional models. In this Introduction, I trace this revolutionary moment across three independent domains: first, the relationship between rich and poor; second, the nature of social scientific expertise; and third, the vision of progress itself. These three themes might appear to raise entirely different issues. That is my point. Inequality disrupts our perceptual frames, breaking down older silos of expertise, and encouraging surprising and unanticipated new understandings. In fact, these three themes are Russian dolls, nested inside one another. We are on an exciting journey indeed.

1: Turning the Telescope: The Rich as a Social Problem

If we are to isolate one moment when the challenge of inequality to conventional paradigms crystallized, May 2011 is a good contender. This was when the Nobel laureate economist Joe Stiglitz published his article "Of the 1%, By the 1%, For the 1%" in the magazine *Vanity Fair*. Stiglitz (2011) pulled no punches:

> Americans have been watching protests against oppressive regimes that concentrate massive wealth in the hands of an elite few. Yet in our own democracy, 1 percent of the people take nearly a quarter of the nation's income—an inequality even the wealthy will come to regret.

His article was short, sensationalist. In directing its ire against top earners, he continued a long and distinguished American muckraking tradition of castigating robber barons and selfish plutocrats. Yet the article also unsettled conventional wisdom about the nature of contemporary social problems.

Previous American efforts for social advancement had directed their energies on how to reduce poverty. Indeed, this preoccupation with diagnosing and measuring poverty had been fundamental to social policy throughout the globe since at least the eighteenth century (for example, Roy and Crane 2015). Legions of economists and social reformers have identified poverty reduction as a central policy goal, and welfare reform throughout the twentieth century had made the alleviation of poverty and deprivation their central concern. This momentum continued into the latter decades of the twentieth century. During the 1960s, President Lyndon Johnson had even declared a "war on poverty." Since the 1980s, this current had shifted into alleviating "social exclusion," as it morphed into a fixation on improving the employability and marketability of those most vulnerable in the labor market. Policy interventions across the world questioned entitlement to benefit and began to champion conditional cash transfers, such as under Clinton's "workfare" reforms of the 1990s (see Peck 2001), but extending to many parts of the globe in the first decade of the twenty-first century.[1]

But Stiglitz pivoted his telescope away from those at the bottom of the economic hierarchy and instead directed his gaze up toward the celestial constellations of the superrich. Rather than exhortations to improve the lot of those at the bottom, he offered indictments of high earners as the real problem. This switch of direction was assisted by a simple but powerful methodological tool—a new economic language of "income percentiles," which allowed him to differentiate the disproportionately high incomes of the top 1 percent of earners from those in the bottom 99 percent. Here he was following the trail blazed by Paul Krugman, Thomas Piketty, and Emmanuel Saez, who had charted how the fortunes of top earners had mushroomed in the United States in previous decades.[2] He was thereby championing a stylized fact, which came to have great resonance with fellow Americans—that there was a small wealthy elite whose fortunes were completely out of kilter with ordinary Americans who, by contrast, were struggling to get by.[3] Indeed, when visiting Edmonton in 2018, where I participated in a focus group reflecting on class divisions in Canada, I was struck by the considerable popular resonance among its participants of the theme that "1 percenters" were in a world of their own. The language of "income percentiles" had moved well away from the economists' calculations and entered popular consciousness.

A few months after Stiglitz's article, an outburst of popular protest, Occupy Wall Street, took this message of economic excess into the heart of the world's dominant financial center in New York.[4] This movement also embraced the language championed by economists, emphasizing that "we are the 99 percent." Parallel protests in leading financial centers across the globe soon followed. Gitlin (2013: 9) emphasizes the historical significance of Occupy: its "terminology ('1%,' '99%') entered into popular lore so readily because it summed up, albeit crudely, the sense that the wielders of power are at once arrogant, self-dealing, incompetent, and incapable of remedying the damage they have wrought; and that their dominance constitutes a moral crisis that can only be addressed by a moral awakening." As one Occupy slogan had it: "THE SYSTEM'S NOT BROKEN, IT'S FIXED."

This targeting of "the 1 percent" was powerful because it made inequality concrete. A small but tangible group of superrich individuals could be identified as the culprits of inequality, and by extension as responsible for social "bads" of numerous kinds. This change was important: Since the early twentieth century, economists had used the Gini coefficient as an aggregate metric that summarized inequality using a single number, usually ranging between 0.6 and 0.3.[5] But this generalized abstraction lacked a focused target. In contrast, talking about the share of income taken by the top 1 percent signaled a specific group of people comparable to the poor in previous historical periods: observable individuals whose behavior and morality is a matter of public concern. In the years since 2011, this public "naming and shaming" of highly paid individuals has become a well-worn and effective repertoire. In 2017, when British Labour Party peer Lord Adonis questioned the high fees of over £9,000 charged for undergraduate study in most British universities, he realized that the most effective way of forcing this point was by criticizing the high pay of university vice chancellors. This sparked off a media feeding frenzy identifying those who were most lavishly remunerated. The success of this approach was brought home when a proposal to reduce the defined pension benefits of academic staff in 2017 provoked an ultimately successful strike, in which the disproportionate benefits of vice chancellors became a powerful mobilizing tool to whip up anger at pension reform proposals.

Stiglitz's contribution therefore marked a fundamental reorientation. Yet he was no leftist upstart. Ostensibly, Stiglitz followed a long line of hallowed economists used to giving their expert counsel in boardrooms and council chambers (Fourcade 2009; LeBaron 2011; M. Reay 2012). This dominant culture built up over the twentieth century had come to have huge sway over government and business life to the extent that it had become completely normalized in policy-making circles. Gentlemen economists (such as John Maynard Keynes) had given way to a more technocratic formation, trained in Chicago School monetarism and its later derivatives, who devised powerful interventions across the globe.[6] Stiglitz certainly had this pedigree: He had been a chief economist at the World Bank and a chairman of President Clinton's Council of Economic Advisers. His academic prowess, with his Nobel Prize and his named professorship at Columbia University, could not have been any more stellar. And yet, by articulating ideas that resonated with growing distrust and popular protest, he was fracturing the very discipline of economics of which he was a leading champion.

Occupy Wall Street shared Stiglitz's scorn for any economic rationale that might justify the burgeoning incomes of the 1 percent. They disputed the view that very-high earners were to be understood in the way that they might think of themselves, as heroic movers and shakers of a dynamic global economy. Instead, they were viewed as a narrow and selfish group whose greed has multiple negative implications for everybody else. "But one big part of the reason we have so much inequality is that the top 1 percent want it that way," Stiglitz (2011) crisply noted, pointing to how taxation policy had been remade in their favor during Ronald Reagan's presidency. Their self-ishness, narrowness, and greed were not a private matter: it damaged social well-being at large. This reframing of inequality forced moral concerns onto the public agenda in ways that challenge the hold of purely scientific and technical expertise. Stiglitz's ideas, simply expressed in one popular article, pulled together a critique of wealthy elites as a profound dysfunctional challenge.

Since this intervention, "elite bashing" has become a major current of both academic and more popular discourses. This reversing of the telescope to look at the rich, rather than the poor, as the overwhelming social problem is of great pertinence. The rise of "elite studies," which this intervention inspired, is a major theme in recent social science and will surface time and again in my book. But this approach also opens up onto further issues. We need to open up the first Russian doll to see what lies inside.

2: The Crisis of Social Science

A profound reshaping of social scientific knowledge is currently taking place. Compared to the natural and medical sciences, the social sciences have been remarkably conservative. Whereas it is routine for natural scientists to pool their disciplinary skills to hone their capacity to address specific problems, social scientists largely default to their disciplinary homes, ultimately writing as economists, sociologists, political scientists, and so forth. Where interdisciplinary fields have emerged (such as in development studies, or in research on health, education, or social policy), they are defined as "applied" areas, which convey less status than in the "core" social science disciplines.

Playing to the comforts of one's home disciplinary audience was a powerful device when the social sciences were growing fast, as they were for much of the twentieth century. But the rise of big data and the growing interest of natural scientists in social interventions have entailed more external scrutiny of the success of social science. Massive social and technical changes of recent decades call into question the intellectual silos that were forged in the nineteenth century but still dominate universities around the globe. Would we want to retain the distinction between anthropology (originally forged to study colonial societies) and sociology (which developed rather later to study developed metropolitan nations) in these postcolonial times? Wouldn't we ideally want a closer encounter between economics and political science, given the simultaneously political and economic tumults we have lived through? Aren't all our concerns fundamentally geographical and historical to the extent that hiving these off as separate disciplines is fundamentally disabling? Why aren't there social science departments dealing explicitly with the climate crisis? Or inequality?

These silos were massively challenged by Thomas Piketty's (2014) *Capital in the Twenty-First Century.* This showed how economists such as Piketty could move out of their home discipline and encourage a broader debate between economics and the social sciences that had been largely absent in previous decades. And indeed, many social scientists have seen the issue of inequality as one that allows them to make common cause. More than any other social science issue, it has generated the kind of intense cross-disciplinary synergy that cuts into an emerging interdisciplinary space. A cursory tour of leading figures who have energized the debate on inequality would include such economists as Tony Atkinson, Amartya Sen, Joe Stiglitz and Thomas Piketty; such gender scholars as bell hooks and Dorothy Smith; such sociologists as John Goldthorpe, Pierre Bourdieu, and Michele Lamont; such legal and critical race scholars as Kimberlé Crenshaw and Patricia Williams; such epidemiologists as Michael Marmot, Richard Wilkinson, and Kate Pickett; such political scientists as Robert Putnam, Kathleen Thelen, and Paul Pierson; such geographers as Danny Dorling; and such social policy researchers as John Hills. And so on—this list is not intended to be exhaustive, and my apologies to those who are not on it. My point is that in a short period of time, the issue of inequality has come to straddle specific disciplines and has inspired social scientists to work together in an unprecedented way.

We need to contextualize the gravity of this shift in terms of the strange history of the social sciences, which during the twentieth century, came to exert huge and unprecedented authority.[7] At the end of the nineteenth century, the most powerful forms of knowledge were religion and the humanities on one hand, and the natural and medical sciences on the other. Social science departments hardly existed in any universities, though the seeds of their later development were germinating, notably in the graduate schools of American universities. Many who were later lionized as the founders of social scientific thinking—Adam Smith, John Stuart Mill, Max Weber, Auguste

Comte, W. E. B. Du Bois—actually saw themselves as working in the fields of philosophy, history, and law, whereas others (such as Karl Marx) had no academic foothold at all. Although toward the end of the nineteenth century, a few figures were beginning to argue for the need for a distinctive social science—for instance, the French champion of sociology, Emile Durkheim—these individuals remained few and far between.

Andrew Abbott (2001b) has drawn attention to the significance of "fractal divides," whereby apparently new forms of knowledge actually reproduce older axial divisions. The new is drawn from the seeds of the past. In this manner, as the social sciences took on organized disciplinary forms from the early twentieth century, they reproduced older tensions between the sciences and humanities. The two earliest disciplines, economics and anthropology, took their intellectual models from the sciences and the humanities, respectively. Thus they came to institutionalize the split between naturalist and hermeneutic perspectives. These two disciplines have proved to be most cohesive and internally closed among the social sciences. The fields of political science (sometimes referred to more amorphously as "government") and sociology developed somewhat later, and became caught in these fractal oppositions. They were characterized by endemic bitter disputes among their ranks between those championing quantitative and qualitative perspectives, a situation that has often led to chronic infighting and introspection.[8] A further twist was that social psychology increasingly abandoned its location in the social sciences and became more closely allied to the medical and natural sciences, while economic history largely folded back into the broader discipline of history.

The paradox of this disciplinary formation was that whereas social life was generally seen as necessarily embodying exchange, interaction, reflexivity and open systems, the social science disciplines themselves were singularly unable to articulate such principles between (or sometimes even among) themselves. Each discipline deferred to its own canonical thinkers, its own preferred methodological tools, and operated largely independently of one another. Each sliced the social world in its own image: economists defined, measured, and analyzed the economy, operating independently of other circuits of social life; political scientists addressed the dynamics associated with political institutions; and sociologists competed with anthropologists to address more diffuse analyses of social and cultural relations.[9]

This intellectual space was also hierarchical. During the course of the twentieth century, economics became increasingly dominant (in Paul Samuelson's words, as the "queen of the social sciences"), becoming hugely influential in governing nations, businesses, and organizations of all kinds. Pitching against this hegemonic position, other social science disciplines sniped at the limited vision of instrumental "homo economicus" that this discipline seemed to champion. They had much less success, however, in dislodging economics from its primacy.

From the latter half of the twentieth century, this tension was overlain by a further differentiation between "pure" and "applied" social sciences. As states, businesses, and organizations of all forms became increasingly complex, their demands for expertise led to the expansion of the fields of social policy, management, health, education, and development. By the later twentieth century, these fields had often dwarfed in personnel and resources the pure social sciences, testifying to their powerful role in the rise of knowledge economies—what Nigel Thrift (2003) called "knowing capitalism."[10] This put in place an intellectual pipeline in which the applied social sciences enacted the expertise, concepts, and methods that had been forged in the crucible of the pure social sciences.

This social science assemblage was remarkably successful during the twentieth century, especially its second half, but was suddenly to come under huge pressure during the early twenty-first century. In the wake of the dramatic digital advances, the beloved methodological tools that the social sciences had championed—the sample survey, ethnography, and the qualitative interview—rapidly came to look dated and arcane (see Savage and Burrows 2007; Halford and Savage 2017). Vociferous and well-funded proponents of big data claimed that social research could be done much more quickly and effectively using the digital data sources left behind by administrative and commercial records. Why bother commissioning a sample survey when you could look at your own transaction data and very quickly work out in detail what was happening? The rise of big data caused growing anxiety about the status of social scientific knowledge, compounded by well-publicized examples of natural and information sciences deciding that they could now do social science using their computational skills without the need for much social scientific intervention.

It is in the context of this challenge to their intellectual authority that the theme of inequality allowed social scientists to stage a brilliant riposte. By mobilizing a bold new stream of research that combined new forms of large-scale quantitative data analysis with qualitative theoretical insight, and yoked to a moral concern with the injustice of inequality, social scientists could seize on a big-picture story that had pretty much entirely evaded the attention of big data evangelists. The new social science of inequality trumpeted a bold, big, and commanding vision. By contrast, proponents of big data failed to deliver on the knowledge revolution that they promised, because their technically skilled findings were trivial, often defaulting to startling visual displays but with no defining narrative.[11]

This new big-picture social science provoked by inequality researchers met a huge public demand from large audiences trying to make sense of the rapidly changing world they were living in. Inequality provided the kind of overarching narrative that could string together economic boom and bust, globalization, political logjam and dysfunction, and wider feelings of malaise. The result has been a remarkable upturn of popular interest in social science. In the United Kingdom, the most prominent example is Richard Wilkinson and Kate Pickett's *The Sprit Level* (2010), which was a runaway best seller and prompted huge academic and policy debate through its message that unequal societies produced more social problems. Even though this book generated critical responses from some social scientists who saw it as too simplistic, this did not detract from its power to show that inequality mattered.

The same point became even more clear in 2013 with the publication of Thomas Piketty's *Capital in the Twenty-First Century.* A dense data-driven tome laying out long-term trends of income and wealth inequality in numerous nations was not an obvious candidate to sell two million hardbacks. Nonetheless, this book captured the public imagination to a remarkable extent and catapulted Thomas Piketty to superstar status. This was not the kind of attention that social scientists had normally enjoyed, and it easily exceeded the attention that any big data exponents were attracting.

These two books reveal the breakdown of the fractal divide that had imprisoned the social sciences since their inception. These were works of sophisticated data assemblage that demanded considerable technical skill. But they also had a clear moral tone and drew on wide-ranging theoretical, historical, and interpretative reference points. They are simultaneously quantitative, qualitative, historical, comparative, theoretical, political, and moral. They mark a profound reordering of social scientific expertise and a new urgency about how the social sciences can be publically and politically engaged.

These books are the tips of an iceberg. We can glean the size of the body of ice resting below these prominent iceberg tips by reporting the frequency of inequality terms in academic journal output. Table I.1 uses the web of knowledge to identify the frequency by which academic articles address certain core topics over the past five decades. For each topic, I have listed the name of the leading discipline that uses such terms, and the extent of the lead that this discipline enjoys over its nearest rival.

Table I.1 shows the hold of the fractal split which I have discussed above: some terms—"economic growth," "economic development," and "globalization"—are dominated by economists, whereas the competing terms "modernity" and "neoliberalism" are dominated by research in history, sociology, political science, and education. "Economic inequality" is distinctive, because it hardly existed as a topic field until 2000, and its early proponents were from the humanities and sociology.[12] However, it was economists who came to champion the concept from the early years of the twenty-first century; but even though they drove the inequality charge, their position never became as dominant as that for the topic of "economic growth." Table I.1 also shows that for every term chosen for examination, there was a decline of disciplinary dominance between 2000 and 2017. This is true for those terms (such as "economic development" or "growth") that were part of the canon of economics itself. Inequality thus appears to be a Trojan horse for a wider breakdown of disciplinary specialization in the social sciences.

This splintering of the fractal divide in the social sciences extends beyond the take-up of the topic of inequality. Central categorical divides—notably race, gender, and class—which were previously taken up mainly by those in qualitative disciplines (sociology, anthropology, history, some geography, and political science), and which stood in tension with economics, have also become increasingly frequently used across the social sciences.[13]

I don't want to overstate my case. Disciplinary framings in the social sciences remain powerful: We can see this from the rising numbers of references to such terms as "economic growth" in the web of knowledge. But the direction of traffic is nonetheless clear. So, the second element of my introduction sees the success of the inequality issue as challenging the disciplinary specialization of social scientific expertise itself.

Table I.1: Social science keyword trend in social science disciplines, 1980–2017

	1980	1990	2000	2010	2017
Economic Growth	160 Economics 50% (37%)	204 Economics 49% (36%)	1,632 Economics 37% (29%)	5,182 Economics 36% (25%)	11,586 Economics 29% (20%)
Economic Inequality	8 Humanities 33% (12%)	33 Sociology 33% (16%)	332 Economics 30% (14%)	1,054 Economics 29% (10%)	2,553 Economics 23% (12%)
Economic development	350 Economics 36% (16%)	429 Economics 34% (17%)	2,635 Economics 15% (6%)	9,282 Economics 19% (6%)	21,075 Economics 16% (7%)
Modernity	57 History 14% (2%)	212 Sociology 17% (7%)	608 History 16% (1%)	1,356 History 15% (6%)	2,509 History 15% (6%)
Neoliberalism	(1)	(3)	62 Political science 29% (10%)	446 Geography 22% (4%)	1,542 Education 15% (3%)
Globalization	(0)	39 Economics 21% (5%)	1,063 Economics 15% (3%)	3,180 Economics 15% (5%)	4,611 Economics 12% (1%)

Note: Percentage figures in parentheses represent the % lead of the dominant discipline over the nearest rival. The table presents the number of articles with stated keywords, followed by name of discipline with highest percentage of references. Source: Web of science.

We need to go a step further than this. Inequality is an anomaly that questions the core guiding values underpinning projects of modernization, growth, and development over recent decades. In this respect, it comes to dispute visions of progress and growth that have characterized both expert and popular thinking in the decades since the core values of liberal modernity became dominant. It is this which reveals the true gravity of the stakes at play. Let us now open a third layer of the Russian doll.

3: Equality as a Transcendental Ideal

Here is a puzzle. Why has inequality caught the attention of powerful and wealthy elites rather than those who are actually on its receiving end, those who are subject to the deprivation, marginalization, and economic hardship that inequality brings? For it is the "great and the good"—or at least some of them—who have nailed their colors most proudly to the inequality mast.

A few years ago, I was invited to speak at a conference of bankers and fund managers. On the plane, I reflected on the irony that I had not been invited to such events before becoming director of the International Inequalities Institute at the London School of Economics, and I was in no doubt that such invitations would stop once I stepped down. As I arrived in one of Europe's most glamorous and historical cities, I was shown to my luxurious hotel room, whose windows opened onto a stunning baroque square. The workshop began the following day in a desultory manner. By lunchtime, I had come to the view that this event was designed to be an undemanding day out for hardworking finance professionals, who could relax while indulging in low-key networking in an elegant five star hotel. And all on business expenses, of course. In the afternoon, however, the mood changed when I spoke about inequality. This was not because I said anything startling or profound. I recall with some embarrassment using the hackneyed metaphor of inequality being about whether people got a larger or smaller portion of the pie. But this did not matter. Attention pricked up. Affluent, elite, finance workers were fired up by talking about inequality, and they did so with passion, both in the session and later, when they came to talk to me about their own lives and experiences. They convinced me about the sincerity of their feelings on the topic. Not for the first time, I pondered the conundrum of why such elite people, the beneficiaries of inequality, felt so vested in the topic, which you might think they would prefer to sweep under the carpet.

On the way home, the answer came to me. Inequality mattered to this privileged audience, because it spoke to a world that they could no longer predict or control. They no longer knew what lay in store for their loved ones, what world their children would inherit, whether their best-laid plans would deliver. The rules of the game, oriented toward a market-driven business logic (and that had shaped the world since the 1980s) could no longer be taken for granted. Their familiar world was disintegrating around them.

This vignette helps make sense of why business elites seem so vested in the topic of inequality. Consider the World Economic Forum, whose annual event in Davos, Switzerland, has become the major global summit of corporate business leaders. Before 2011, its annual "Global Risks Report" focused on largely systemic issues: disease, climate change, and economic shocks.

These are not risks that these leaders can be held to be directly responsible for. Beginning in 2012, societal risks became more significant—"severe income disparity" was seen as the main risk from 2012 to 2014, which then morphed into bleak concerns with state collapse and terrorism, along with migration. By 2017, their prognostications had become yet grimmer. Inequality now played an even more central role, and the language became dystopian, citing increasing polarization, profound social instability, and no less than four kinds of governmental failure.[14] The executive summary noted that "this year's findings are testament to five key challenges that the world now faces. The first two are in the economic category, in line with the fact that *rising income and wealth disparity is rated . . . as the most important trend* in determining global developments over the next 10 years" (WEF 2017: 11). The account is littered with gloomy overtones:

> Despite unprecedented levels of peace and global prosperity, in many countries a mood of economic malaise has contributed to anti-establishment, populist politics and a backlash against globalization. The weakness of the economic recovery following the global financial crisis is part of this story, but boosting growth alone would not remedy the deeper fractures in our political economy. More fundamental reforms to market capitalism may be needed to tackle, in particular, an apparent lack of solidarity between those at the top of national income and wealth distributions and those further down.

The World Economic Forum thus took up the language of economic inequality that such economists as Stiglitz had made popular, but expanded its remit: "profound social instability" now occupies central stage in their global risk map. And this, we should remind ourselves, is the view from the world's leading business elites. But inequality also has the power to mobilize across contexts and gain buy-in from diverse agents in civil society, philanthropic, and campaigning organizations. Oxfam's 2017 briefing report, timed to influence that year's Davos meeting of the World Economic Forum, argued that "left unchecked, growing inequality threatens to pull our societies apart. It increases crime and insecurity, and undermines the fight to end poverty. It leaves more people living in fear and fewer in hope" (Hardoon 2017: 1).

The irony is that—on the face of it—popular forces appear less bothered about inequality than elites do. Populist politicians do not directly criticize economic inequality as such. Much of their ire focuses on immigration and threats to national sovereignty. And although there is an anti-elite discourse in much of populist politics, this is largely directed against political establishments, with the result that very wealthy business elites—Donald Trump in the United States, Jair Bolsonaro in Brazil, and Cyril Ramaphosa in South Africa—have become popular leaders by surfing this wave.

How do we make sense of this paradox that political protest against inequality appears to be muted at the very time when inequality has been trumpeted by elites as an entrenched social problem? The growing concern with economic inequality represents a loss of faith in the prospect of progressive social change, and this awareness is especially marked among numerous elites who previously endorsed a progressive view about the prospects for economic and social change. Its currency is thus part of a wider disenchantment with the overarching principles of modernization and growth that have guided social development over recent decades.[15] It departs from progressive, evolutionary accounts and instead offers a dystopian account of regression and the return of historical forces that had previously been seen as banished to the shadows.

It is telling that inequality, rather than equality, has become the central rallying cry. Equality is one of the major modern transcendent values that has been prized as central to the modernizing progressive vision. The historian Jürgen Osterhammel, commenting on the significance of the American Revolution of 1776 and the French Revolution of 1789, reflected that: "Almost everywhere (perhaps with the possible exception of Japan), people in all subsequent epochs have appealed to liberty, equality, self-determination and human and civil rights" (Osterhammel 2014: 532). Changing the terms of debate from "equality" to "inequality," however, abandons the prospect of equality and instead repositions thinking around limiting the damage of excessive inequality.

Deflecting attention away from equality toward inequality has been a powerful move because it can engage a wide constituency of interests. It repositions egalitarian ideals in an era when transcendental values of any kind are losing their hold. Amartya Sen's (2009) brilliant reflection of concepts of justice is a revealing pointer of this current. Sen argues that justice should be construed not in terms of overarching principles (however these might be defined) but through a comparative lens that distinguishes differences and variations among people in differing situations. He criticizes theories of justice, notably that of the eminent liberal political theorist John Rawls, who elaborates "justice as fairness," by deploying a version of transcendental social contract theory that has formed the basis of liberal thinking since Thomas Hobbes and John Locke. Rawls's version used the "original position," a thought experiment in which people in an ideal presocial state had to imagine what kind of society they would support if they did not know in advance the position they were to be allocated to within it. Rawls's argument was that people would choose a society that not only embraced freedom but also in which inequalities were not ascribed, since they would be mindful of the possibility that they might initially be placed at the bottom of any unequal social order. They would therefore support a liberal model in which there were meritocratic possibilities of social mobility.

Sen argues that this approach to justice defaults to a narrow instrumental concern with the extent to which effective procedures are in place to ensure that such transcendental principles can be enacted. The result is that it loses sight of the actual outcomes and practices that exist in specific societies. It can be maintained that this is exactly what has happened in recent decades: Formal legal procedures to deal with different aspects of discrimination are now commonplace, but attention to actual social outcomes is more muted. Sen (2009: 17) draws on Indian jurisprudence concepts of *niti* and *nyaya*:

> The former idea, that of *niti*, relates to organizational propriety as well as behavioural correctness, whereas the latter, *nyaya*, is concerned with what emerges and how, and in particular the lives that people are actually able to lead.

In pursuing this concern with *nyaya*, Sen directs attention away from abstract principles of justice (such as those of Rawls) toward a concern with identifying better and worse actual outcomes across numerous cases.[16] Sen's argument is prescient, because it is precisely in this comparative spirit that the inequality paradigm has gathered force by documenting the accumulating evidence of how people's actual lives have been blighted by forces generating inequality. By avoiding transcendental (which thereby become abstract and procedural) discussions about how equality itself should be constituted, our attention is directed to concrete and specific situations—lives as they are actually lived. Developing the concept of the "1 percent," for instance, allowed inequality to be made concrete and thus directs attention to actual specific issues rather than to general principles.

The appeal of this argument is therefore to reposition social critique on a nontranscendental basis that disputes the overarching paradigm endorsing values of modernization and growth. Rather than history being seen as a backdrop that we have somehow left behind, this allows us to recognize it as part of who we are, and where we will go. It is the social counterpart of the environmental sensitivity regarding the implications of climate change for long-term sustainability. Indeed, this highlighting of inequality leads us, above all, to a recognition of the vital need for long-term social sustainability. Intergenerational justice, as well as our commitment to the as-yet unborn, becomes the overarching political goal.

4: The Stakes of the Inequality Paradigm

I have emphasized that there is more to the inequality paradigm than meets the eye. Indeed, there is more to the inequality paradigm than inequality. This is amply clear from the two trailblazing books that introduced the significance of inequality to broader audiences. Wilkinson and Pickett (2010), and Piketty (2013) argue that inequality matters by demonstrating that social advance is *not* produced by continued economic growth. Thus, Wilkinson and Pickett emphasize that the world's most economically advanced nations do not necessarily have fewer social problems: In fact, poorer but more equal nations score more highly with respect to good health and well-being. This theme picks up on the extensively discussed "paradox of happiness" that the economist Richard Layard has made famous: Increasing prosperity does not lead to more overall happiness once a certain threshold of economic development has been reached. Piketty's argument is captured in his famous formula $r > g$, namely, that returns to capital will exceed the growth rate—and therefore, that more growth will only enhance the relative gains of those with the most capital, leading to enhanced inequality and a vicious and reinforcing circuit. The more growth there is, the more

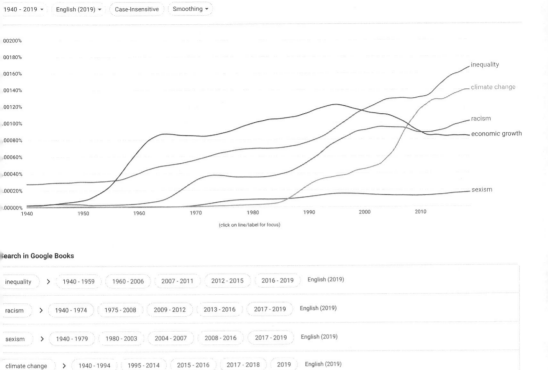

FIGURE I.I: Frequency of the terms "inequality," "racism," "sexism," "climate change," and "economic growth" in English, 1940–2019

Source: Google Ngram.

we will actually get those who are already economically privileged to do even better.

We get a sense of the stakes involved in this new framing by recognizing how inequality competes in popularity with other organizing social science terms. Here, the appeal of the inequality mantra is inversely related to beliefs in modernity, progress, and growth. Google Ngram Viewer reveals the frequency of the terms "inequality," "racism," "sexism," "climate change," and "economic growth" in English in recent decades, and the trends are revealing (see Figure I.I).

Figure I.1 shows that references to inequality are not themselves new. Indeed, from the 1940s to 1960, they easily surpassed the other terms, none of which generated much interest at all. This all changed around 1960. This was the period in which "modernization" and "development," driven by the United States and burgeoning international development bodies (such as the World Bank and the International Development Fund), was promoted as the panacea for ills of all kinds. This was the same period when the social sciences were refocused on concerns promoting growth (see, for example, Wallerstein 2000). "Economic growth" accordingly came to eclipse "inequality" in usage.

But this has changed in recent years. "Economic growth" plateaued in its significance by the 1980s and subsequently dropped off. From the 1970s, "racism" and "sexism" also became much more prominent, especially the former term, which by the later 1990s had overtaken both "inequality" and "economic growth" in its currency. From the mid-1980s, "climate change" also began its steady march to prominence. In recent years, "inequality" had resumed its appeal—and at a much higher proportional level than fifty years ago. It has become increasingly prominent at a time when racism, climate change, and (to a lesser extent) sexism have also become more marked concerns. A set of gloomy, indeed scary terms have come to the fore at the same time that economic growth has become a less dominant theme.

But the situation differs around the globe. The world's most common language, Chinese, reveals a different picture. After a brief time in the late 1960s, when inequality was much discussed, interest in it fell considerably, and concerns with economic growth were paramount. Racism and sexism hardly figure anywhere in Chinese-language discourse. Even climate change operates in a very subdued way. This is ostensibly a much more positive outlook focused on the value of economic growth—which has indeed been such a marked feature of the Chinese experience in recent decades.

Inequality and economic growth operate as mirrors of each other: where the latter dominates, the former is subdued, and vice versa. The Chinese concentration on economic growth has been at the expense of the sensitivity to inequality, which has proliferated in anglophone sources. If we compare the situation in the Spanish language, the second-most popular language in the world, we find something of a hybrid between the English and Chinese situations. Inequality did not figure as an issue at all until the 1970s, but since that time, it has dramatically increased in significance (with a dip in the early 1980s). In this respect, the theme of inequality is clearly shared with the anglophone world. However, economic growth has also been an enduring theme, rising very fast from the 1960s, and after the year 2000, it was equally as significant as the theme of inequality. Racism and sexism are also much less salient terms than in the English language, testifying to their distinctive profile within the anglophone sphere.

These simple comparisons reveal that inequality is also a geopolitical issue that plays out differently across the globe. It is most discussed in the United States in particular, as well as in Europe, rather than in those areas of the world where economic growth has been a key driver in recent decades. It is therefore, in certain ways a highly Western-centered discourse, even while it appears to be critical of the record of many Western nations. This is a paradox I will unravel further as my book progresses.

Let me pull these threads together. The inequality paradigm has come into prominence not just because inequality has somehow got inexorably worse. Or because a specialized field of research has matured. Instead, it repositions social science research in a more powerful and compelling way. It offers the promise of linking specific identifiable topics (such as the prominence of the superrich) to a bold interdisciplinary social science that breaks out of disciplinary silos and disputes the progressive modernizing agenda that has dominated academic and policy thinking since 1950. It is the challenge to progressive futuristic thinking that is of particular note. Since the eighteenth century, the dream to look toward a bold new future when past problems are left behind has been persistent and pervasive. This way of thinking is bound up with the fundamental ordering of modern conceptions of time, in which past, present, and future are ontologically distinct, so that the future is unknowable on the basis of past experience. This assumption has been the vision undergirding such diverse groups as communist revolutionaries, neoliberal free marketeers, anticolonialist movements, religious fundamentalists, and technocratic reformers. In everyday life, it is also marked in the routine hold of therapeutic and self-help repertoires on our consciousness as we routinely strive to become "better" people. Teasing out the broader significance of inequality is to depart from this kind of mundane accelerationist thinking, because it sees the build-up and accentuation of historical inequalities as marking the return of older formations into the active life of the present. The more societies appear to modernize, the more their pasts actively confront them. Inequality matters, because it carries the weight of history with it. This is the overarching theme of my book.

My argument may seem to follow a well-worn path that laments the loss of hope and certainty, but ultimately I take a very different path. Recent decades are littered with proclamations of the emergence of postindustrialism, globalization, risk society, and such like, which insist on the acceleration of our society into something new and uncertain that has broken from past moorings and become more unstable.[17] These epochalist accounts are profoundly unhelpful. Rather than moving into some brave new postindustrial and affluent era, the past is catching up with us. The bold dream of breaking free from the shackles of the past and ushering in a new dawn—the vision that has been paramount across much of the globe since the eighteenth century—is fading. Instead, we are left with a world littered by centuries of accumulated economic, social, and cultural debris, in which the power of these heaps, accretions, and wrecks has an increasing hold on the present and future. In this respect, the analogy between inequality and the climate crisis is very apt. Just as our future prospects are driven by the weight of carbon deposits and associated environmental detritus that cannot be effaced, so the true recognition of inequality forces us to acknowledge the weight of past historical social and economic forces that constrains our futures. It thus places the fundamental question of sustainability at the center of our thinking.

It is in this spirit that I will draw out the wider stakes involved with invoking inequality in order to infuse a broader sociological reflection on the course of contemporary social change. The inequality paradigm opens a dark window onto the nature of social change today. The view from this window may appear bleak: It clouds liberal progressivist ideals about the power of modernization and development to address the world's ills. But this is also a view that offers succor by suggesting new perspectives attuned to the damage caused by inequality. It champions the need for a politics of social sustainability.

5: Outline of the Book

I have endeavored to write a book that is accessible and can be read by those without prior knowledge of specific fields of study and yet also does justice to the many and varied issues challenges. It will already be clear that I dispute the view that inequality is a distinct topic that can be understood in a self-contained way. In fact, it is also about how we investigate the social world, our methods and concepts, and how we construe history and social change more broadly. If we are to understand why inequality has become such a pressing and urgent topic, we need to synthesize across many fields of study and not default back to narrow framings, measurement tools, or perspectives.

Accordingly, each chapter discusses a discrete topic and seeks to introduce key issues in recent research for a broad readership. None of the chapters can cover all the important contributions in each field, but I hope they serve as effective introductions to these topics. The originality of my book, however, lies in the way I link these topics together. Therefore, to appreciate my argument as a whole, this book needs to be read from cover to cover. Although I hope readers who want a succinct discussion of particular topics can use the index to find the where in the text where they are discussed. I would urge readers to recognize that the juxtaposition of topics rarely considered together is the most important feature of my book.

Readers should bear in mind the ordering of the chapters, which builds my argument sequentially. The first part of my book introduces the key theoretical frames that underpin my core arguments about time and historicity. My intention is both to introduce the thinking of influential theorists on inequality, ranging across such canonical figures as Thomas Piketty (Chapters 1 and 3), Pierre Bourdieu (Chapter 2), and Karl Marx (Chapter 3), but more particularly to bring their arguments into dialogue with one another. The sequencing here is not to be conflated with analytical priorities. I don't start in Chapter 1 by considering the economics of income distribution because I somehow think that this is the foundation and every other aspect of inequality is derived from it. Far from it, in fact. Instead, I start with this dimension because crucial contributions from economists help highlight why the topic of inequality has leapt to the fore, but also because of the limitations of this work. My book therefore proceeds in the manner of a Russian doll: each chapter peels away to reveal another, and each one takes us closer to the heart of the doll.

Chapters are organized in three overarching Parts. The first part excavates the main conceptual issues and lays the platform for the argument I will use in later chapters to explicate the significance of inequality. Part 1 has an overarching argument, emphasizing how inequality needs to be placed in the context of space and time (scale and history, to use alternative terms). Each chapter will add a bit more to my primary claim that we need a better appreciation of history if we are to truly recognize the challenge of inequality. I show that there has been more success in bringing out a spatializing approach to inequality—the "stuff" of inequality—and that we need to complement this with a much richer appreciation of time, temporality, and history. I show that although there is frequently a genuflection to the significance of time, this approach tends to be reduced to linear measures that ultimately limit them. I see Chapter 3, where I recapitulate the importance of the concept of capital and accumulation and the concepts of time that come with this as the intellectual crux of the book.

Part 2—on the geopolitics of contemporary inequality—offers a synthesis of global inequality. These chapters cover varied topics. These are the power of ranking procedures and the weakening of nation spaces (Chapter 4); the reemerging power of empire (Chapter 5); the muted contemporary significance of social class, the enduring power of racism and sexism, and the rise of visceral inequalities (Chapter 6 and 7); and the growing significance of cities as crucibles of inequality (Chapter 8). Chapter 9 considers the significance of technological advance and innovation. Although these topics appear diverse, I argue that we can—and must—synthesize across them to unravel the renewed power of history and forces from the past. This leads to the recognition that modernizing projects, which in the later twentieth century seemed to carry all before them, are increasingly fragile. We are witnessing the return of older historical forces.

Part 3 of my book pulls these lessons out to address the contemporary politics of inequality. I seek to broaden our understanding of the range of stakes that this requires, so that rather than focusing on policy devices, or specific campaigns or movements, we recognize better the need for an all-encompassing politics of social sustainability. Thus, Chapter 10 reflects on the weakening of policy solutions amid the decline of the national political field, and my conclusion in Chapter 11 pushes home my arguments about the need for a politics of sustainability.

My book therefore navigates a long and hazardous journey, though with a clear destination to aim for. For those who get lost along the way, I have provided two integrating devices. Readers who lose their moorings are encouraged to consult either of these compasses. First, I include a brief glossary at the end of this book. This lays out the main terms which I use in the analysis and indicates where in the book these terms are elaborated. I hope readers will be able to use this if they need advice about my underpinning arguments.

My second device is indeed a thread, along the lines of Theseus's thread when finding a way out of the Minotaur's labyrinth. I deliberately emphasize the way that inequality researchers have used innovative visualizations to make their arguments. This use of visuals is at the heart of the appeal of inequality research. In different chapters, I consider how visual motifs are central to the arguments that inequality researchers make, and that we learn a great deal by understanding the affordances that visualizations offer. I hope this will be a golden thread that offers a way through the labyrinth of issues that I discuss.

These reflections on what visualizations can and can't convey is not meant to be a presentational device, or a means to dumb down the argument. Instead, they presage a new kind of social scientific narrative that proves highly resonant. I will analytically use different kinds of visualizations to pose big issues about how time and space are treated in different schools of inequality research. Here, I take heart from the words of the great Victorian cultural critic, John Ruskin, whose own brand of Tory radicalism proved fundamental in challenging the economic logic of industrializing capitalism in the later nineteenth century: "the greatest thing a human soul ever does in this world is to *see* something, and tell what it *saw* in a plain way" (Ruskin 1856: chap. XVI). In thinking about how to elaborate the significance of the inequality paradigm, it struck me that the lever that researchers had been pulling to remarkable effect was that of the telling visualization. The differing chapters of this book show how this visual repertoire is a major and telling feature of this new social science, and I hope that readers will reflect on the power of visuals to construct this new sensitivity.

This is important, because conventional social science has characteristically downplayed the role of visualizations (see Jay 1993). Here again is a contrast with the natural sciences: in a very famous essay, Bruno Latour (1986: 21) reflected that in science, laboratory practice could be ordered

> not by looking at the scientists brains (I was forbidden access!), at the cognitive structures (nothing special) nor at the paradigms (the same for thirty years), but at the transformation of rats and chemicals into paper . . . all these inscriptions, as I called them, were combinable, superimposable and could, with only a minimum of cleaning up, be integrated as figures in the text of the articles people were writing.

It struck me that the original use of visuals has been fundamental to the success of the inequality paradigm in a way that is highly original in the social sciences, and these visuals have become the exemplars behind the forging of a new perspective. They allow us to do justice to Kuhn's insistence that older scientific paradigms are not disproved by external testing. Kuhn is clear that paradigms require exemplars that demonstrate the value of new ways of rendering the world, and powerful visual repertoires have become central motifs for researchers to show that inequality matters. They point to a way of conducting social science that deploys a "symphonic aesthetic," which replaces the linear, instrumental, and variable-centered focus of conventional perspectives. It pursues its analyses through recurring melodies—repeated motifs, deft drawing, and highly stylized narratives. As my book proceeds, I especially show how the use of lines carries enormous power. The doyen of social science visualization, Edward Tufte, has emphasized the power of "sparklines" in visualizations, and I will show how it is inequality researchers who have forced this point home. But there is more to the power of lines then skilled design principles. As Anne Seymour's foreword to the artist Richard Long's book *Walking the Line* puts it,

> Our world is made up of lines, from comet tails to DNA. Everything is connected. Everything is sequential. Everything that moves, from a snail to a lava flow leaves a line, a trace of passing. A line can be fate, a commitment, a fact, a relationship, a place. Some lines are well trodden paths, some intersect, some pass at a distance, some return to their origins. We all walk the line. We have an end and a beginning which

is joined to a much longer invisible line in the past and in the future. (Seymour 2009: 9)

The chapters in my book take up specific visualization to introduce the substantive stakes involved in thinking about inequality. Some of these use lines, but others don't: This contrast in visual repertoires will turn out to have considerable bearing on the issues revealed. "Walking the inequality line" (to coin a phrase that I will unpack in later chapters) recharges the social scientific repertoire, elaborates new synergies with researchers in the humanities and natural sciences, and appeals to a wide public audience. It leads to a politics of social sustainability. The stakes are high indeed.

PART ONE

Inequality in Time and Space

I

Turning the Telescope

THE ECONOMIC ANALYSIS OF
INCOME DISTRIBUTION

Since its inception in 2003, the motif pictured in Figure 1.1 has become the single most influential visualization to fuel inequality research.[1] It has spawned a multitude of variations. Its crispness and simplicity have become iconic.

Figure 1.1 is derived from the pioneering work of economists Thomas Piketty and Emmanuel Saez (2003) and represents the proportion of American national income that went to the top 10 percent of US earners during the long twentieth century. There is a neat story with great intuitive resonance here. Until 1940, the top 10 percent of Americans took a high proportion—between 40 and 50 percent—of total American income. However, following the New Deal and the exigencies of the Second World War, and in the context of high personal taxation rates, this share fell precipitately to about 30–35 percent between 1940 and 1980. American national income was somewhat more equally distributed as America moved forward economically during these decades, fueling the benevolent view that economic growth led to more equality. But from the early 1980s, the share of the top 10 percent rose substantially to 50 percent by the early 2000s. Inequality, by this metric, is now back to the level that it was during the early twentieth century.

FIGURE I.I: Top 10 percent income share in the United States, 1910–2010

Source: Thomas Piketty, *Capital in the Twenty-First Century* (Cambridge, MA: Harvard University Press, 2014), figure I.I. Copyright © 2014 by the President and Fellows of Harvard College. Used by permission.

Piketty and Saez (2003: 2) modestly announced: "To our knowledge, this is the first time that a homogeneous annual series of top wage shares starting before the 1950s for the United States has been produced." Since that moment, the analysis of long-term inequality trends spanning a century or more has gained a huge traction. This research mobilizes long-term historical trend data—not simply to put the record straight but also to fire contemporary debate in a way that has proved hugely influential.[2]

The power of Figure I.I lies in the fusion of technical virtuosity in data assemblage with a clear historical narrative. Piketty and Saez (2003) used evidence from American tax returns over many decades to present a long-run story that would be hard, even impossible, to glean using survey sources.[3] After a dense three-page, largely unreadable, table of income share trends (Piketty and Saez 2003: 8–11), their neat visual summary holds the imagination on a simple narrative hook: Inequality was bad a long time ago, and then it got a lot better. However, recently, economic inequality has gotten a lot worse again. Indeed, we are now back to the "bad old days," where we started out. Figure I.I is the iconic visualization of this simple—but emotive—narrative.

Today, this income-share approach has become an entirely familiar, almost banal, way of representing inequality—but this was not the case even 20 years ago. In the 1990s, the economist Paul Krugman ventured that it was the top 1 percent who had enjoyed the lion's share of economic rewards of the previous two decades of economic growth in the United States. But he had no firm evidence for this, and his claim was met with doubt, even skepticism. As Hirschmann (2016) demonstrates, it was only in 2003, when Piketty and Saez published their first influential paper, that this "stylized fact" became so widely recognized.

Why has this visual narrative become so effective? Crucial to this story is a "sparkline." This is the approach to visualization championed by the eminent methodologist Edward Tufte (2001, 2006; Tufte et al. 1990). He argues against the use of complex, fancy visualizations that seek to impress viewers through their detail, color, and flourish. Instead, Tufte champions the sparse use of trend lines, in which "the less ink, the better," thus allowing the message of any visualization to be compressed into a singular linear trace. Clarity is central. The use of lines to convey meaning is evocative: for anthropologist Timothy Ingold (2006: 162), "life . . . is not confined within points but proceeds along lines." There is no evidence that Piketty and Saez were directly influenced by Tufte, but they have nonetheless taken his message to heart.

When Piketty came to write his monumental *Capital in the Twenty-First Century,* he took this approach a stage further, marking a new phase of visual ingenuity. Tufte concentrated on how best to deploy a singular visual representation. Rather like a classic painting or photograph, the knack lies in presenting a singular, unique visual (albeit one that can be endlessly reproduced) as the hallmark of artistic originality.[4] But Piketty, probably unwittingly, takes a new tack of producing many different figures, *but each deploying the same kind of U-shaped visualizations* so that their repetition, partial variation, and extension cement the narrative.[5] We have returned to the conditions of a century or more ago.

With this deft move, Piketty uses visualizations not as singular representations, but symphonically, untangling a narrative through a core melody whose meaning is both underscored but also varied as the long text unfolds (see more generally Halford and Savage 2017). Initially the U shape is introduced as an overture in the first two tables used in the Introduction. Having established this motif early, Piketty then varies his repertoire, sometimes with an inverted-U shape, sometimes with both U and inverted-U shapes in the same diagram.[6] The motif is thereby introduced early to demonstrate his key argument; then its later variants are deployed to identify nuances in the data and enrich his argument.

Piketty is fashioning a new kind of social science that adopts the kind of narrative tools of the humanities but in a form that gives visualization a central place. He is unwittingly returning to, and renewing, John Ruskin's critical visual imagination. Although trained and adept in economic models, Piketty eschews complex algebra, equations, and models in favor of a remarkable symphonic visual performance.[7] And what a treasure trove this perspective opens on to! Piketty can extend his comparative range of national cases beyond the US model that was his starting point. This allows him to show that the very stark upturn of inequality found in the American case is not universal, and that other nations have a much more flattened U shape. In all these cases, the timeline does narrative work by delineating the variations on a core theme of the *return to the past*.

1.1: Income Distributions and the Critique of Poverty Measures

The narrative of Figure 1.1 matters, because at its heart, it tells a very different story from the commonplace liberal account of progress and social advance through economic growth. This is clear when we contrast it with Figure 1.2, which also uses a sparkline to trace the share of the world's population living in absolute poverty since the 1820s.

Figure 1.2 stretches back to the 1820s to tell an even longer-term narrative than that shown in Figure 1.1. It measures trends in "extreme poverty" using a comparative measure of the equivalence of earning (the hardly extravagant!) figure of US$1.90 per day in 2012 terms.[8] In 1820, only a small minority of people—16 percent—in the world had an income that would place them above this—very low—poverty line. Even in 1950, nearly two centuries after industrialization began in Europe, well over half of the world's population lived in extreme poverty. The second half of the twentieth century saw ac-

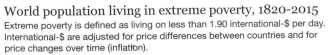

World population living in extreme poverty, 1820-2015
Extreme poverty is defined as living on less than 1.90 international-$ per day.
International-$ are adjusted for price differences between countries and for
price changes over time (inflation).

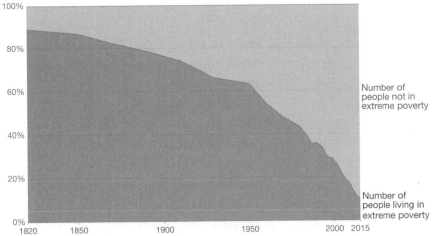

FIGURE 1.2: Share of the world population living in absolute poverty, 1820–2015

Source: Our World in Data chart based on Martin Ravallion, *The Economics of Poverty: History, Measurement, and Policy* (Oxford: Oxford University Press, 2016), figure 2.1, and updated with data from the World Bank's Povcal Net: iresearch.worldbank.org/PovcalNet/.

celerating advances, and by 1980, 68 percent of the world's population had escaped extreme poverty. And since then, the reduction of poverty has actually accelerated. By 2015, it was estimated that as much as 90 percent of the world's population lived above the threshold of $1.90 per day. Extreme poverty—measured by this metric—is now a minority experience.

Figure 1.2 also encapsulates a crisp narrative to match its sparkline. Throughout human history, dealing with scarcity has been a fundamental preoccupation for the vast majority. Working hard, the daily grind, and simply "getting by" have been the most enduring feature of the human condition over millennia. However, by the early twenty-first century, for the first time, the majority of the world's population had moved above an extreme poverty line. And the experience of spare time, leisure, and being able to buy luxury products had become mainstream, not only in the developed world of Europe, North America, and Australasia, but also in emerging economies in many parts of Asia and South America—though less so in Africa, where global poverty is increasingly concentrated.

So we now have two contrasting sparkline narratives on the table. Both are produced by expert economists whose sophisticated handling of data represents the cutting edge of their discipline. Yet their stories are very different. Figure 1.2 presents the familiar modernizing story of steady progressive advance toward increased prosperity. Yet it is Piketty's visual—and not the progressive story—that has become iconic. And with this shift, inequality rather than poverty reduction moves to center stage.

This shift is telling. In previous centuries, underlying concerns to address inequality were redirected toward those at the bottom—those whose state of poverty marked them out as lacking sufficient resources to live an adequate life.[9] There is great moral nobility in this concern to alleviate the situations of those in various states of destitution. Nonetheless, this approach leaves out one key aspect of inequality: those in poverty are not contrasted with the fortunes of the privileged, such as top earners. Rather, it is the concern with overcoming scarcity that has defined dominant social science paradigms during the twentieth century. Early social welfare measures were developed in European nations beginning in the sixteenth century to identify those in absolute poverty. And beginning in the nineteenth century, new tools of social research—the survey, interview, and observational methods—were forged specifically to understand those at the margins of society and especially those in poverty (Savage 2010).

This concern was not simply a benevolent one but also involved new modes of surveillance. In the influential thinking of Michel Foucault (1977), these interventions were bound up with new modes of power in which those identified as being "in need" became subject to surveillance, regulation, and control. Rather than direct subjugation characteristic of older regimes, new modernizing liberal regimes framed new categories of measurable "need" as a precondition to social intervention aimed at addressing these very needs.[10] During the nineteenth century and well into the twentieth, this "gaze" directed at those who were poor, destitute, or otherwise "in need" was closely affiliated with eugenic thinking, which saw such groups as biologically deficient or vulnerable, usually on racial, but also on gendered and sometimes class lines. It was in this way that the "state" of poverty became subject to scrutiny, and its delineation, containment, and limitation became identified as a crucial marker of social development.

For these reasons, defining the precise threshold at which it was meaningful to claim that someone was in a state of poverty became a crucial issue. This boundary came to have huge moral import. Where could the boundaries separating civilization from the masses be placed? Nineteenth-century British poverty researchers Charles Booth and Seebohm Rowntree (1901) were among the first to elaborate a "poverty line" in their studies of London and York. Booth was somewhat coy about how this term was defined, vaguely noting that "by the word poor I mean to describe those who have a fairly regular though bare income, such as 18s [shillings] to 21s per week for a moderate family, and by 'very poor' those who fall below this standard, whether from chronic irregularity of work, sickness, or a large number of young children."

Rowntree attempted a more precise measurement, influenced by American nutritionist Wilbur Atwater, and attempted to measure the necessary caloric intake needed for workers with different kinds of physical demands if they were to maintain a minimal level of health. But ultimately, moral judgments were smuggled in. In Booth's case, this was overt, as with the labeling of poor Londoners on his famous maps as "vicious and semi-criminal" (see the discussion in Morgan 2019). Rowntree attempted more detachment but still differentiated between those in "primary" and "secondary" poverty, with the latter having enough income in principle not to be in poverty but then allegedly squandering income on alcohol or other fripperies.

The apparently beneficent concern to delineate a clear and objective state of poverty ultimately smuggled in moralistic judgments. They thereby became implicated in a normalizing discourse in which the very idea of a civilized social body was elicited by differentiating itself from those in "abject" outsider or deviant states. Defining poverty involved an implicit judgment on those who were not poor: It entailed an inescapable relative judgment.

During the course of the twentieth century, there was an increasingly critical concern to strip away this moralism by defining poverty not as an absolute and "objective" state, but in relative terms. In these terms, poverty was demarcated as falling below a measure of what was socially acceptable according to the norms and values that were agreed on at any given point in time.[11] Therefore, as nations became wealthier, the poverty line shifted upward.

In the latter decades of the twentieth century, the European Union proved especially important in promoting this approach, inspired by economist Victor Fuchs in the 1960s, which led to relative income poverty being enshrined by Eurostat (the European Union Statistics Agency) in 2005. The European Council of Ministers defined poverty as "persons whose resources (material, cultural and social) are so limited as to exclude them from the minimum acceptable way of life in the Member State in which they live" (Council Decision, December 19, 1984).[12]

In recent decades, most nations have deployed some version of this relative definition to determine who is in need of benefits. (In the British case, those earning less than 60 percent of median income fall into this category.) Using such measures, if average income rises, so does the amount of income needed to escape poverty: The measure is thus a shifting goalpost. This relativizing measure was elaborated in the most sophisticated way by British sociologist Peter Townsend (1979: 31), whose definition of poverty came to be highly influential:

> Individuals, families and groups in the population can be said to be in poverty when they lack the resources to obtain the type of diet, participate in the activities and have the living conditions and the amenities which are customary, or at least widely encouraged or approved in the societies to which they belong. Their resources are so seriously below those commanded by the average family that they are in effect excluded from the ordinary living patterns, customs, and activities.

To grasp what activities were "widely encouraged or approved," Townsend used systematic survey evidence to carefully assess the kinds of goods and resources that Britons felt were necessary to live as a full member of society. This generated a basket of items that may not be necessary to survive in a strict biological sense but were a social necessity—such as access to a television. This relativizing move led to a more pessimistic account of sustained poverty in Britain, even as the country became more affluent overall.

The relativizing move is crucial, because it moves the focus away from poverty as a simple brute fact and situates it in a broader framework of inequality whereby its meaning and significance is associated with wider social values and expectations. However, this effort only went so far in putting inequality into view: poverty was usually defined relative to some social average or norm, not vis-à-vis other particular, more advantaged, groups. It therefore evoked a fundamental boundary between a social "mainstream" and a group whose members were in poverty—or, using a term that became increasingly common beginning in the 1980s—the "socially excluded." There was no unpacking of differential prospects and life chances within the mainstream. Therefore, this perspective did not discriminate between the differential amounts of privilege among the majority of the population who were above the relative poverty line.

In recent decades, however, measures of relative poverty have been put under increasing strain, and there has been a reversion back to absolute measures, as is evident in Figure 1.2. The reason for this shift is the difficulty of extending relative conceptions of poverty beyond the national level. As Bourguinon (2015: 24) puts it, "applying this (relative) concept to the world population and lumping together under the title 'poverty' Bolivian households whose purchasing power is only $100 per person with American households that live with $5,000 in disposable income seems senseless. In one case it is survival itself that is at stake; in others it is social status and dignity." Therefore, in trying to elaborate global measures of poverty, the pragmatic default reverts back to the kind of absolute definitions that are largely discredited in national studies. Under World Bank auspices, this approach was subtle. Relative conceptions of poverty in the world's poorest nations were taken as a benchmark of absolute poverty, which was then projected globally so that anyone earning above these levels anywhere in the world was seen not to be in poverty.[13] This broad approach was then adopted by Ravaillion et al. (1991, 2009). The impressive synthesis of Chen and Ravaillion (2013) argued that a de facto absolute poverty threshold can be set by demonstrating that because relative poverty in the world's poorest nations actually converged on the same minimum level, this provided an empirical rationale for claiming that there is a definite poverty floor below which everyone can surely agree that absolute poverty exists. This clever argument allows some kind of baseline absolute poverty threshold to be derived inductively even while recognizing theoretically that poverty is a relative construct. Nonetheless, this approach remains a theoretical fudge, because it implies that those who are above this line in richer countries, but who fall below the relative lines operating there, are not fully in extreme poverty—even though they may think otherwise.

As Jason Hickel (2017) relates, this concern to delineate global poverty rates was given huge impetus by the elaboration of the Millennium Development Goals in 2000, one of which was to halve global income poverty between 1990 and 2015.[14] This goal demanded the formulation of a metric that could assess whether such a target was being met. Accordingly, the World Bank established global poverty thresholds, with their criteria shifting from $1 a day in 1990 to $1.08 in 2001, $1.25 in 2008, and $1.90 per day in 2015 (see Ferreria et al. 2016). Through the back door, an absolute definition returned to the table, through the auspices of the World Bank.

This renewal of concerns to delineate absolute poverty rates was thereby driven by the need for metrics. Economists were well aware that it was a struggle to find a way to reconcile theoretical perspectives, oriented toward relative conceptions, and the need for metrics that could meet pragmatic demands. The impasse in linking theory and measurement was pithily recognized in 2015 by Alvaredo and Gasparino (2015: 753–754), who coyly observed: "The vast literature on poverty measurement suggests that there are neither normative nor objective arguments to set an unambiguous threshold below which everyone is poor and above which everyone is non-poor." However, they then note that the wish to address the Millennium Development Goals meant the need for "a one-dimensional, monetary, static, absolute view of poverty, that certainly has many limitations and drawbacks, but it is still the best available paradigm to summarize deprivations in the world."

This is remarkable testimony to the way that well-intentioned social scientists, who are committed to rigorous methods, end up promoting a measure that had pragmatic value, even though it was recognized to be beset by theoretical problems. It is powerful testimony to the way that target setting can push intellectual agendas. And it is interesting that this exercise becomes compelling, even when it attracts criticism. Even the anthropologist Jason Hickel, who is well aware of the problematic definition of poverty lines, ends up by claiming that income under $5 a day constitutes "debilitating poverty" (Hickel 2017: 2), thus entering into a game of contesting where the line should be drawn. It is true that if we use a more generous (but still not very generous!) definition of poverty line as those earning under $5 a day, the headcount has fallen much less steeply than in Figure 1.2: from 66 percent to 46 percent (according to the World Bank's data). Given that the world's population was growing during this time, such a reduction actually means that increasing numbers of people fall below this moderate poverty line.

Anthropologist Jason Hickel has brought another problem to the fore. When Booth and Rowntree embarked on their studies of poverty at the end of the nineteenth century, they were concerned with poverty as an over-arching human condition. But the World Bank metrics had the effect of conflating poverty with falling below a certain income threshold. However, as Hickel emphasizes, in many situations, people have had access to customary rights (for instance, the capacity to grow crops or keep livestock on common land), which could allow them to enhance their living conditions but would not be captured in an income-based denominator, such as that used by Bourguignon and Morrison (2002). If, in fact, you could supply your own food without needing to purchase it on the market, then $1 a day could leave you materially better off than $2.50 (or some other higher sum) when you are forced to buy all your necessities.[15]

These considerations indicate that the venerable tradition of poverty research has, in a very important sense, been intellectually run into the ground even though it has come to have major policy relevance. The notion that there is a global poverty line, which can be measured by some kind of cash denominator and can be projected across the earth to meaningfully systematize the proportion of people in different nations who live in "poverty," looks (and indeed is) an arbitrary and ungrounded abstraction. This does not stop it commanding great interest from policy makers intent on addressing the UN Millennium Development Goals. Pragmatic and theoretical considerations diverge. Yet, even in these policy terms, there is a further paradoxical twist. The easiest way of reducing the proportion of people under any given poverty line is to target those very slightly below it, who can thereby move to the more desirable side of the line with relatively little shift in their actual fortunes. The unintended and paradoxical consequence is that those who are most in poverty are of lesser priority if you want to reduce the poverty rate.

Poverty research has therefore become increasingly torn between a sophisticated theoretical recognition of its relative state (thereby seeing it as linked to wider systems of inequality) and the rise of global measurement benchmarks (which have pragmatically defaulted back to some kind of "absolute threshold" approach). The instability and uncertainty that this dichotomy has generated has led to major intellectual ambivalences. It is the void that this has opened up which allowed the economics of income distribution to mark a major breakthrough.

1.2: Income Distributions as Icons

Intractable problems regarding the squaring of conceptual and measurement issues around the definition of poverty have allowed a space in which a new inequality research could more easily appeal. In particular, the thorny difficulty of defining a clear poverty threshold could be bypassed by shifting attention to the distribution of income. This approach moves away from defining specific kinds of states—such as those below a specific poverty threshold—and toward an interest in broader distributional relationships. Thus, Figure 1.1 (unlike Figure 1.2) does not distinguish one key threshold but can be used much more flexibly, to examine any particular group of interest in the income distribution—the top 0.1 percent, the top 1 percent, the top 10 percent, or whatever. There is no need to conjure up a definitive "rich line" similar to a poverty line.

Figure 1.1 is also effective because it makes inequality concrete. It does this by offering an alternative to the composite measures of inequality that hitherto have dominated economic analysis. The most significant composite measure of inequality is the Gini coefficient, initially developed by the fascist Italian economist and sociologist Corrado Gini in 1912 to assess how far the distribution of income in a population deviated from perfect equality. The size of the Gini coefficient is proportional to the variation between actual measured income inequality in different societies, compared to the distribution that would exist if there is perfect equality where everyone earned the same. When these two lines are identical, the Gini coefficient is 0 (perfect equality), but when the size of the area reaches the maximum possible (where one person would have all possible income, and everyone else has nothing), the Gini coefficient is 1.

In practice, Gini coefficients for income distribution generally range between 0.2 (unusually equal) and 0.7 (extremely unequal), with most falling in the range of 0.3 to 0.5: By convention, any score above 0.5 indicates alarm-ingly high levels of inequality. The Gini coefficient is therefore a succinct metric that can be used to compare inequality across any given population, for instance, between nations at different points of time. It can readily be derived from nationally representative sample surveys asking about levels of income, or inequalities in consumption, and is therefore easy to deploy for comparative analysis as survey methods are exported across different parts of the globe. This explains why, during the twentieth century, the Gini coefficient became the main "stylized fact" summarizing the extent of in-equality in any given nation. It became part of the basket of aggregate mea-sures that were extensively deployed by governments and business after the Second World War—similar to the inflation rate, gross domestic product (GDP), and such like. It follows in the mold made famous by Belgian stat-istician Adolphe Quetelet, with his concern to unravel the norm of the "average" and its associated link to the normal distribution.[16]

But analyses using the Gini coefficient do not lend themselves to a ready narrative sparkline. In part they don't have the historical range of Figure 1.1. Because of the paucity of representative national surveys before 1950 it is difficult to plot them back into the early twentieth century, as Piketty and Saez manage to do using taxation data. Furthermore because of the limited range of the Gini coefficient, trends don't shift very dramatically when vi-sualized. Consider, for instance, Rebecca Simson's tracing back of trends in the Gini coefficient over several different parts of the world since 1980 (see Figure 1.3). If there is a narrative here, it is one of slight decline, with the Gini falling in the Middle East since 1980, Africa since the early 1990s, and South America from the early twenty-first century. But the main point is that there is no crisp narrative of the kind that Figure 1.1 shows.

The Gini coefficient gives a neat relative measure of inequality that al-lows comparison over time, but it has come under increasing criticism. In a classic paper, which laid the foundation for the resurgence of the economics of inequality, Atkinson (1970) showed how the Gini coefficient was insensi-tive because it was especially affected by (possibly marginal) shifts in the middle of the distribution rather than at the edges—and especially the top end of the distribution. An identical Gini coefficient can actually be consis-tent with significantly different income distributions, as it only measures the size of the space between the perfect distribution line and the actual

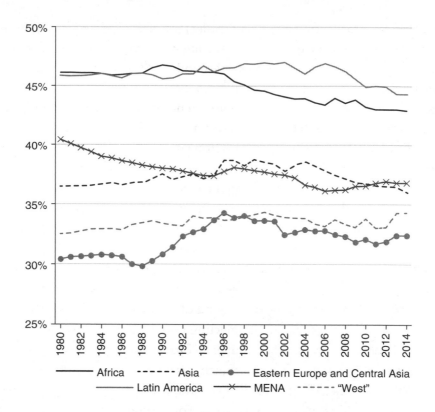

FIGURE 1.3: Shifts in Gini coefficients in selected parts of the world, 1980–2005

Note: MENA = Middle East and North Africa
Source: Reformatted from Rebecca Simpson and Mike Savage, "The Global Significance of National Inequality Decline," *Third World Quarterly* 41, no. 1 (2020): 20–41, figure 1.

income inequality line. Gini coefficients are not good at picking out the extremes—of both poverty and high income. Furthermore, because high income earners are only a small proportion of the population, it is unlikely that even soaring income shares amongst them—such as revealed by Figure 1.1—will produce a major shift in the Gini. This is one of the reasons that prompted calls for a more elaborated recognition of distributional inequality: for Piketty (2014: 266), "it is impossible to summarize a multidimensional reality with a unidimensional index without unduly simplifying things and mixing things up together that should not be treated together."

Working in Atkinson's tradition, Piketty and his colleagues thus adapted the simple idea of breaking down a population according to the income distribution and extrapolating what proportion of total income is taken by specific percentiles (or even sub-percentiles). As Piketty (2013: 266) put it: "it seemed far better to me to analyze inequalities in terms of distribution tables indicating the shares of various deciles and centiles in total income and wealth rather than using synthetic indices such as the Gini." In fact, the difference can be overstated: Income shares generally point in the same direction as the Gini (see Piketty 2013, tables 7.1 to 7.3).[17] However, in the crucial respect of being more sensitive at the "top end" of the income distribution, they can be very revealing.

Thus, this new focus on the top earners can avoid the difficulties surrounding research on the bottom (caused by the contentious discussion on poverty thresholds, which has become mired in conceptual and measurement difficulties). It is not necessary to fixate on a "rich threshold," because this can be seen entirely in relative terms. It is the top-end relativities that become crucial, reflecting the differing properties of the top and bottom of the income distribution. The bottom end of the income distribution tends to be relatively flat and uniform, reflecting not only that welfare payments generally offer some kind of a minimal income floor—but also that there is an absolute figure of zero income, which it is impossible to fall beneath. By contrast, there is no top limit to income, and so the right tail of the income distribution can be enormously spread out. For high earners, the sky is (pretty much) the limit. The result is that there is much greater discrimination at the top end than at the bottom, and much more revealing and discriminating studies unpacking this variation can become possible. This focus also marks a major break from the statistical tradition of assuming that social measures are organized around a normal distribution focused on the central tendency.

Economists have thus made major advances in distributional analysis in the past two decades. We can now see outliers—at the top rather than the bottom—without having to default to an aggregate statistic such as the Gini. The social scientific norm of rendering the "average" or aggregate has been replaced by an emphasis on the granular, concrete, and specific. The social telescope has become more focused as it has changed its direction. Whereas in previous decades, the interest had been in the poor and excluded (compared with the social "mainstream"), the gaze can now be directed toward how far top earners take a disproportionate share of national income. The top, rather than the bottom, matters.

These income distributions not only deploy a different kind of narrative, but they also embody a new kind of methodology. Calculations for the Gini coefficient typically rely on relatively small samples from nationally representative surveys that deploy methods of statistical inference to draw out findings from these small samples. On this basis, major advances were made in postwar social science, in the study of epidemiology and social mobility, for example (see Savage 2010). By contrast, Piketty and his colleagues used administrative taxation data drawn from the entire population to mine down into more granular and reliable analyses that can stretch back many decades in time.[18] It would not have been possible to differentiate respondents in a nationally representative sample survey into percentiles, because there would not have been enough cases in any specific percentile group to be confident that any findings at this level of detail would be valid. This was a particular problem at the top end. Sample surveys tend to underestimate high incomes, perhaps because high earners (perhaps unconsciously) do not fully reveal the extent of their income, and partly because they may not be sampled in sufficient numbers (for example, see Jenkins 2016). The income-shares approach therefore breaks from conventional social science both in its use of narrative visualizations and in terms of the data and methods it deploys.

What might appear to be a technical exercise, turning to look at the top rather than the bottom of the income distribution, therefore turns out to be a brilliant innovation. This also proves to be a lever to pry open much wider questions. It indirectly challenges a core tenet of social science that relies on a utilitarian view about human action. In this tradition, which underscores various kinds of rational choice theory and models assuming instrumental "homo economicus," social life is seen as undergirded by rationalizing cost-benefit calculations as people plan and go about daily life. In this utilitarian tradition, individuals seek to maximize their well-being and act accordingly, based on the constraints and opportunities of the situation they are in. In relative conceptions of inequality, such as that undergirded by income distributional analysis, this utilitarian aspect becomes more subdued. It is possible to bring out how you feel, your dignity, respect, and sense of worth vis-à-vis others when the full extent of the income distribution is revealed. Even though you may enjoy significant material resources, your emotional well-being and security can be sapped by feeling inadequate compared to those who have more, or better quality of resources, than you have.

Therefore, switching attention to inequality of income distributions away from poverty encourages a shift away from a utilitarian conception of people toward more affective accounts of human action that recognize wider emotional dynamics. We can see overtones in the work of those economists as much as those in more qualitatively oriented disciplines: for Joe Stiglitz (2012): "People are not machines. They have to be motivated to work hard. If they feel that they are being treated unfairly, it can be difficult to motivate them." A similar anti-utilitarian perspective underlies Amartya Sen's "capabilities perspective," which insists that well-being cannot be reduced to a material measure but instead depends on people's potential to flourish. Piketty himself, admittedly, remains more attuned to an instrumentalist perspective and does not draw out this potential of his work.

Piketty and Saez's apparently simple sparkline therefore turns out to have major conceptual implications. It sidesteps intractable debates about defining states and thresholds between them (which ultimately cannot be resolved) and allows a more relativist perspective on inequality to fully bite. However, it also brings with it some major limitations.

1.3: Limits of Income Distributions

Income distributions make inequality concrete and in Thomas Kuhn's terms, offer a powerful, visible exemplar of a new way of thinking—in which those at the top become the center of attention. These distributions provide a compelling narrative, based on robust, painstaking data analysis and breach the impasse that had beset poverty research. I have emphasized the pragmatic considerations that partly explain the appeal of income distribution analysis. Piketty's Figure 1.1 has more iconic power than Bourguinon's Figure 1.2, because it sidesteps intractable concerns about the definition of poverty by turning the telescope on the rich at the top. It avoids complex discussions about what a "rich threshold" might be, because it presents income distribution in purely relative terms—as the percentage of national income that is earned by top earners (which can also be sliced by differing criteria without any of them having analytical preeminence). It thus evades the thorny issue of defining a threshold, which has beset poverty researchers from the later nineteenth century to the present day.

But income distributions also have limits. By themselves, they are far too sparse and restricted to base the analysis of inequality on. There are four substantial problems leading to a major impasse, which will lead me on to my discussion in Chapter 2.

The first problem is tautologous, but it still needs to be stated. The income distributions only measure one dimension—here, income inequality. Economists are well aware that, in principle, numerous dimensions can contribute to inequality, but a concentration on income distribution has nonetheless dominated.[19] As I have shown, this focus on income distribution strategically offers a powerful way of forcing inequality issues into economic analysis (see Atkinson and Bourguignon 2000, 2015) but the relationship with other axes of inequality—for instance, gender, race, and class—are left dangling.[20] The economics of income distributions opens the door to a very large room: but in no way does it fill that room.

The second problem is that although Figure 1.1 brilliantly arrays long-term historical trends, it also ultimately restricts our understanding of history. This is because it holds economic growth constant: By benchmarking income shares of specific percentiles compared to national income as a whole, it abstracts from the historical context in which the amount of national income itself is changing. The changing absolute size of the economy is abstracted from these accounts. So too is the economic complexity, along with shifts in the industrial and occupational structure. Piketty and Saez are therefore analyzing unidimensional historical trends, but they are also controlling for history, a sceptic might suggest. One implication is that even where the income distribution is stable, if economies are getting wealthier, the absolute gap between the rich and poor gets wider—yet this will be unobserved in income distribution statistics (see Hickel 2017). More broadly, absolute historical shifts might be associated with broader social changes, such as an expanded division of labor, a complex state infrastructure, elaborated welfare provision, and so forth, which are stripped out of Piketty's income distributions. Perhaps it matters less these days that there are super-high income earners given that many—perhaps most—other employees are reasonably well paid, compared to 100 or more years ago, when these equivalent high earners stood out dramatically from the vast majority of their compatriots, who were struggling to get by. But this kind of deeper historical reflection cannot be derived from income-share analysis alone.

This kind of analysis is typical of the quantitative social science's stripping of data from historical context through the use of abstracted cross-temporal and cross-cultural measures that render social and economic change as somehow outside history (see the general arguments of Mitchell 2002). Piketty's (2020) recent analysis of historical change over an even longer duration, in *Capital and Ideology* brings home the problems of this framing even more. To be sure, it is utterly remarkable to explore inequality trends over the past two centuries across most parts of the globe, and the range and sophistication of coverage is astonishing. But Piketty's analysis proceeds by plucking historical examples of interventions that have changed the "inequality regime" in the past to argue that therefore we can remake capital today. But to render history as a vast skating rink, which expert skaters can navigate brilliantly, showing how easy it is to cover such a large expanse, renders history as "empty homogeneous time" (to use Walter Benjamin's 2010 phrase), it does not recognize that the past actually affects the present. This is a point I take up fully in Chapter 3.

The third problem is that distributional analysis proceeds by projecting exterior benchmarks to measure income inequalities—through some aggregation of percentile shares of income. An external grid of percentile divisions is laid on a variegated set of income levels. This method is very powerful and allows systematic comparison between places and over time. However, such an approach steps back from ascertaining whether any specific threshold within this percentile distribution might be socially, culturally, or politically meaningful. Does it make any real difference whether you are in the top 0.9 percent or the top 2 percent of the income distribution? A literal reading of Occupy Wall Street's campaigning would imply that the first of these percentages (but not the second) is on the wrong side of the "we are the 99 percent" slogan. But surely this boundary is also largely arbitrary, projected onto a population by the logic of imposing an external grid, measured in this case by percentiles.

Piketty does recognize this issue and occasionally considers whether it is possible to determine more salient structural boundaries within a fluid income distribution. He thus plays around with the idea that there is a lower class as the bottom 40 percent of the income distribution, a middle class lying between 50 and 90 percent, and an upper class as the top 10 percent, before shrugging his shoulders and reflecting that "I introduce these terms purely for illustrative purposes . . . and in fact they play almost no role in the analysis" (Piketty 2014: 250). However, his view that "any representation of inequality that relies on a small number of categories is doomed to be crudely schematic since the underlying social reality is always a continuous distribution" (Piketty 2013: 252) does not follow. Categories can be derived formally through some kind of cluster analysis. Nor is it self-evident that "social reality" always—or even usually—takes the form of a continuous distribution.[21] Here we see the danger of an overly economistic framing being projected too widely, without recognizing the unusual property of income as a continuous variable. We need to understand better the power of categorical, group inequalities—notably of race, gender and class. This is a topic I take up in earnest in Chapters 6 and 7.

The fourth and final problem is also important. There is an infinite regress of the right tail of the income distribution. Focusing on simply the top 1 percent may appear to allow us a very precise way of capturing the fortunes of top earners. Most of us—even if we are pretty well off—are in the 99 percent, and we may feel pleased to be able to distinguish ourselves from the truly rich elite above us. But in fact, this top 1 percent is extremely heterogeneous, to the extent that it lacks any obvious coherence. It includes very high earners, such as multi-million-dollar-salary chief executives, but also those earning income from investments who might not have any kind of job—a rentier class. Indeed, Piketty is very clear about this heterogeneity. Thus, in the American case, those at the threshold of the 1 percent are likely to get most of their income from earnings, but among the top 0.01 percent, nearly 90 percent of income is from capital investments. These are very different types of people—but both are within the "1 percent." Furthermore, the absolute gap between the upper and lower boundaries of the top 1 percent is huge. At a world scale, those earning about $51,400 are in the top 1 percent (Anand and Segal 2017). But a typical professional, such as a teacher or civil servant, earning such an income is clearly in a very different situation from a multimillion-dollar-earning CEO. And to view them as both in the same social position because they are formally in the global top 1 percent is very broadbrush indeed. In fact, it is likely that quite a few of the Occupy Wall

St. protesters who genuinely claimed that "we are the 99 percent" probably were actually in the 1 percent on this global threshold. This is not nit-picking. It points to the limits of this kind of distributional thinking.

Which leads to the fifth problem and my most fundamental epistemological issue. Distributional income analysis adopts the Kantian procedure of projecting external coordinates (in this case, differentiations into percentiles) onto complex empirical data in order to benchmark the shape of their distribution. There is a closet transcendentalism here. The resulting distributions might bear little or no resemblance to how people themselves actually conceive both their social relationships and their own specific place within them.

There is ample evidence that people's own perceptions don't map neatly— or at all—onto their placement within economists' income distributions. It is well known that those in the top of the income distribution often tend not to see themselves as occupying a very high position within it. Rachel Sherman's (2019) study of very affluent New Yorkers, all of whom would fit comfortably into the top 1 percent of earners, reveals that many of them do not feel very affluent and try to emphasize their thrift and ordinariness. Katharina Hecht's (2018) study of extremely highly paid London executives argues similarly. One explanation is that they might be deliberately disingenuous so as to downplay their privileges, but Hecht shows instead that this reflects the very heterogeneous nature of the top 1 percent. Most highly paid people can find someone even better paid than themselves to serve as their reference point for identifying what it really means to be rich.

This is only one, extreme example, which demonstrates that the relativizing push of the economics of income distribution only takes us so far. Lurking beneath this work is a largely utilitarian cost-benefit conception of human agency, which is not attuned to a fully relativizing framing in which people compare themselves with multiple others. In fact, one's location in an externally defined income distribution may not be very salient to our identities, feelings of pride, stigma, shame, and selfhood more broadly. It is well known that many extremely well-paid people can feel undervalued, marginalized, and excluded. It is also true that people who are relatively badly paid can actually feel well off and able to lead a fulfilling life. This is why distributional income analysis ultimately needs to be linked to a more thoroughgoing social analysis of how relationships become meaningful.

Conclusion

My first stylized icon—Figure 1.1—has a clear visual narrative. It tells a story of a return to the bad old days after a few decades when inequality fell. It shifts attention from the poor to "top-end outliers," the best-paid individuals who have done disproportionately well. This is a crucial platform on which to build. It has wider repercussions in directing attention away from absolute states toward visualizing relativities between groups. It is the gap between rich and poor, or between different groups (such as men and women, or racial groups) that is the crucial matter of concern. It thus takes attention away from *states and instead focuses on distributions.*

As I emphasize in this book, this shift toward distributions is far from just being stylistic or technical. By pushing toward a more relativized conception of inequality, its stakes—passions, values, identities, and recognition—are themselves up for grabs, so that it is seen to matter whether there is an unequal distribution among them. This is part of moving away from seeing categories as the basis of inequality toward a more fluid rendering of relationships. This general shift away from absolute "state"-based accounts of inequality toward relational conceptions attuned to distributions requires a fundamental rethink.

I finish by posing a puzzle. The relativity behind Figure 1.1 uses the coordinates as defined and measured by expert economists. And yet by imposing external coordinates on these relationships, it is obscure how these distributions appear to the people being analyzed themselves. This relativity is constructed from an externally projected frame of income percentiles, even though the relativist conception points toward the need to recognize how people construct their own sense of where they fit in the social body. How do we build an account of inequality that captures people's own sense of the relationships in which they live?

Time for some sociology.

Society as a Sports Field

THE CHALLENGE OF BOURDIEU

2.1: Bourdieu's *Distinction*

Figure 2.1, my second icon inequality icon, is initially mystifying. There is no crisp narrative like that of the Piketty and Saez sparkline of income distribution trends (Figure 1.1). At first glance, it is an amorphous mess of cultural labels of now largely obscure 1960s and 1970s French provenance (in gray), juxtaposed with intimidating social science labels and bar charts (in black).

And yet Figure 2.1 is the crux of unquestionably the most influential sociological research monograph to be published since the Second World War—Pierre Bourdieu's *Distinction*—published in French in 1979, and in English translation in 1984. And although the research presented is nearly fifty years old, it has in recent years inspired sociologists who have developed bold new research programs bringing out the cultural aspects of inequality.[1]

The fact that Figure 2.1 is initially illegible reflects my argument that it is only recently, driven by the crystallization of research on income distributions, that visual acuity has become central. Bourdieu was writing at a time when conventional social science took the form of literary treatises or statistical exegeses. He was unusual even at this time because of his enthusiasm for visual methods, but even so, they remained subordinate to his literary

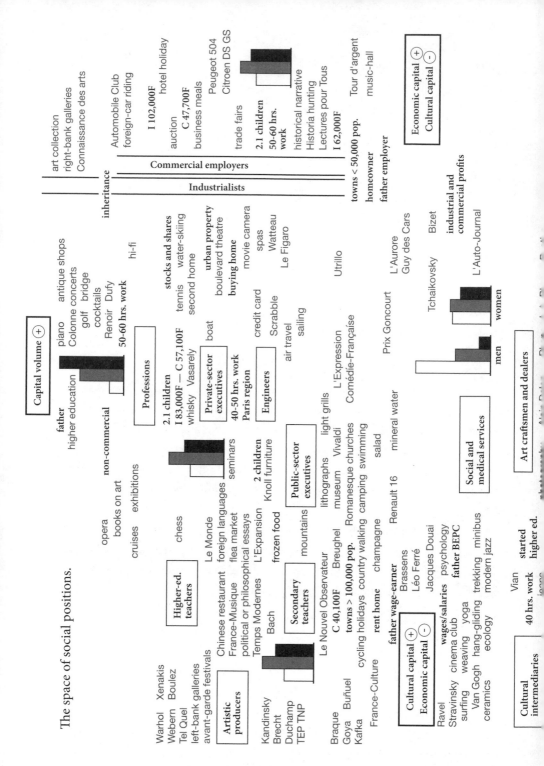

The space of social positions.

FIGURE 2.1: The French space of lifestyles, c. 1967

Source: Reformatted from Pierre Bourdieu, *Distinction: A Social Critique of the Judgement of Taste* (Cambridge, MA: Harvard University Press, 1984; Oxfordshire, UK: Routledge, 2010), figure 5. Copyright © 1984, 2010 by the President and Fellows of Harvard College and Routledge. Reproduced by permission of Taylor & Francis Group.

proclivities.[2] In fact, Figure 2.1 is buried deep in the book and is alluded to, rather than discussed directly.

In Figure 2.1, Bourdieu does not use the sparklines that Piketty and Saez employ to such great effect. Instead, there are only a series of labeled points. This is not incidental: He emphasizes space rather than time, leading him to concentrate on forces that operate diffusely through spatial fields. These forces can hardly be represented in linear form.[3] Gravity or sound waves cannot easily be represented as a singular line: by their very nature, their force is expansive, diffuse, and encroaching.

This reveals the tension between spatial and temporal axes, which lies deep within social science: It is extraordinarily difficult to address both these dimensions effectively simultaneously. Piketty and the economists of income distribution succeed in examining long-term trends but have little to say about the spatial dimension. The fully spatial sensitivity, such as Bourdieu's in Figure 2.1, is an important contrast.

Figure 2.1, through its gray labeled points, aims to represent the "space of lifestyles" in France in the 1970s. This was done through asking a representative sample of French people about their preferences for a battery of cultural producers and lifestyle indicators (artists, musicians, writers, leisure practices, and consumer items). The responses are then clustered: Without going into the mathematical principles involved, it is sufficient to note that the farther apart the points are located, the more mutually exclusive they are.[4] The more separated these labels are, the less likely that the same people engage in these different activities. Figure 2.1 thus detects the partitioning or segmentation of lifestyle activities. This is now an utterly mundane procedure in the highly profitable business of market research, which typically proceeds by segmenting consumers into clusters, so that firms can more effectively target potential customers. In the years since Bourdieu wrote, we have come to live with the endemic classification of people into myriad consumer types, from geodemographics to consumer DNA. Bourdieu was a pioneer in this approach—but distinctive because he seeks to use a similar spatializing framework to comprehend inequality.[5]

Through glasses tinted by fifty years of wear, it is now hard to see what most of these labels actually mean. This is especially true when we compare those at the top with those at the bottom. Taste for piano, opera, and concerts are at the top of the graph, while a liking for Tchaikovsky, Bizet, and modern jazz sit at the bottom. In contemporary times, we might think of all of these as part of a similar family of liking for "highbrow" classical music. Apparently, in 1960s France, they are segmented from each other. Nonetheless, we can still get a bit of sense when we see labels such as golf, cocktails, bridge, and opera at the top: These still register as distinctly upper class, even elite, tastes. And some of the labels at the bottom look much more "plebian"—for instance, driving the quintessential bargain basement car—the Citreon 2CV (until it became gentrified in the years after Bourdieu wrote).

This contrast turns out to be at the heart of Bourdieu's analytical contribution. His first vertical (y) axis—the volume of capital—distinguishes between people with greater resources (at the top) from those with fewer (at the bottom). Imagine this as a line running down the middle of Figure 2.1. On its own, this axis is rather similar to the economists' income distribution scale, with those earning the highest incomes expected to be at the top of the graph, where "capital volume" is highest. And Bourdieu thereby brings out that this axis does not simply distinguish the amount of income that you enjoy—it is also associated with distinctive lifestyle preferences. There is a cultural spillover from your level of income to your cultural and lifestyle interests.

A crucial feature of Bourdieu's use of a spatial perspective is that multiple dimensions can be rendered. Our experience of physical space is three dimensional (front-back; left-right; up-down). In a like manner, Bourdieu insists that there are several distinct dimensions segmenting lifestyle taste, which he draws out using visual representations—though flat visualizations on pages, walls, or screens are difficult to render multiple dimensions.[6]

In Figure 2.1, the second—horizontal—dimension (the x-axis) therefore offers a different perspective that is separate from capital volume. Comparing the labels on the left- and right-hand side of Figure 2.1, even fifty years later, we can make intuitive sense of the oppositions. It turns out that appreciating Citreon DS and GS cars and hotel holidays lies at the opposite edge to appreciating Kandinsky, Brecht, and other avant-garde artists. This axis still has currency today. We can easily imagine that those who like large cars, drink champagne, and supped at the Parisian Michelin three-star "Tour d'Argent" restaurant are a very different type from those who appreciate the hip cultural innovation of Pierre Boulez, Andy Warhol, or who are devotees of *Tel Quel* (the leftist literary journal that championed poststructuralism and deconstruction until its closure in 1982).[7] These reference points still evoke the very different world of hip intellectuals, committed to cutting-edge trends, standing opposed to that of extravagant diners, duly receiving their certificate for a pressed duck Michelin-starred feast at the Tour d'Argent.

This second, horizontal x-axis, became Bourdieu's hallmark. It differentiates between those who have tastes for avant-garde culture on the left-hand side, compared to those who are more attracted to lavish and expensive consumption on the right-hand side. Bourdieu describes this second axis as that of "capital composition," where those on the left have more cultural resources and know how to appreciate "high" culture, whereas those on the right are more likely to appreciate luxury and indulgence, but in a more vulgar and less discerning way. This principle is secondary and separate to that of capital volume. It therefore establishes the crucial point that not all cultural tastes can be reduced to income and economic resources alone. Here we see a dimension that the economists' income distribution graphs have not rendered.

Bourdieu's argument is intuitively easy to grasp, because it is homologous to our experience of physical space. We immediately sense the difference between going forward and sideways in any facet of daily life from riding a bike to putting the kettle on, and we can feel the pull of gravity when we climb the stairs. Similarly, we can see how inequality is not simply defined by one linear hierarchical scale but can be evident in multiple dimensions. We can also intuitively understand how such spatial dimensions are central to inequality. The geographer Steven Graham (2016) has shown how verticality is a fundamental feature of power: The height of buildings, for instance, is a testimony to the command that they can enjoy. It is not incidental that wealthy elites are drawn to the penthouses on the highest floors of glitzy urban skyscrapers.

In drawing attention to the horizontal (x-)axis—the opposition between intellectual and extravagant orientation—Bourdieu therefore insists on the cultural dimension of inequality as having some autonomy from economic inequalities. But Bourdieu also wants to relate such cultural and lifestyle differences to socioeconomic differences—and here his analysis takes a more critical flavor than the market researchers who use similar methods. Figure 2.1 thus takes the further step of superimposing (on the black labels) the occupations that respondents had, so we can inspect how they intersect with the lifestyle indicators. And it turns out that these stack neatly onto his map of lifestyles: Those in the secure and well-paid liberal professions turn out to be at the top of Figure 2.1, whereas the less well paid in the social and medical services are at the bottom. And, on the horizontal x-axis, as you might expect, cultural producers attracted to avant-garde culture stand on the left side, and industrial managers on the right side.

So Bourdieu offers a different perspective to Piketty and Saez, even though there is a crucial congruence, insofar as they agree that our economic situation (the "volume of capital") is a crucial factor in determining lifestyle and choice.[8] However, Bourdieu sees a secondary split between those with cultural capital ("intellectuals") and those without it ("industrialists"). This illuminates a crucial feature: Inequality is multidimensional and operates across several planes, it does not simply map onto income inequality, or indeed onto economic inequality more broadly. Cultural tastes, practices, and lifestyles can also be unequal.

It is important to understand what is happening here. Bourdieu is using a spatial perspective metaphorically. Figure 2.1 is not a literal representation of the separation of lifestyles across geographical space. Instead, he is seeing society as if it were a spatial configuration, as a means of bringing out the relational aspects of inequality. It is not that eating at the Tour d'Argent is inherently performing inequality. It is rather that doing so is highly exclusive and that many people can't and don't do it—whether because they can't afford it, or because they reject its commercial and elite values, or for some other reason. Bourdieu thus emphasizes how inequality is not to be defined by measures of fixed or "objective" states that we saw poverty researchers wrestling with in Chapter 1. He does not project fixed categories onto spatial coordinates, and therefore avoids the Kantian abstraction from experience that ultimately underpins income distribution approaches. Instead, the nature of these dimensions is inductively mapped.[9]

Especially since Bourdieu wrote, this use of spatial metaphors for analyzing inequality has become endemic: It has become the common sense of our time. From the inception of social science in the nineteenth century, the idea that groups take their form by being spatially demarcated—such as in the maps of British poverty researchers Booth (1889) and Rowntree (1901) or in Du Bois's (1899) mapping of racial groups in Philadelphia, or in the sociology of the Chicago School (Savage and Warde 1993)—has become utterly familiar. Even where these references do not appear to involve a direct geographical mapping, nonetheless, the conceptual language evokes spatial differentiation—such as in references to social or cultural boundaries.[10] This spatial turn is compelling, and in certain respects is a vital tool for us to unravel how inequality operates. Over the past twenty years, there has been an impressive development of sociological perspectives that have used this field analytical approach to develop a spatial approach to social structure.[11] But this framework is also limiting, as I now show by reflecting in more detail on Bourdieu's own concept of the "field."

2.2: Field Analysis

Let us reflect on the world of a newborn baby. She searches with wonder, fear, and desire for meaningful people, entities, and objects around her. She learns to identify her mother, her dog, and gradually, by navigating a process of attachment and repulsion, her world of meaning emerges. Categories such as the top 1 percent or the "poor" mean nothing to her (even if it turns out that she belongs to one of these groups), as they are too removed and abstract from her world of feeling, sentience, and perception.

Consciousness is the phenomenological world we inhabit in our day-to-day lives and where relativity truly looms large—and in a more ontologically grounded way than in the distributional analyses of economists. It does not place people in externally defined categories and expect them to act on the basis of this putative location. Instead, the sentient, feeling, and observing human is at the heart of our understanding of social relations. As we navigate our lives, we come to make judgments that involve processes of affiliation—toward objects and animals who attract us—and repulsion toward those we fear. Since Max Weber in the late nineteenth century, this phenomenological perspective has been taken up by numerous sociologists who emphasize how this pragmatic domain of social interaction gives rise to the meaning and identity that lies at the heart of our daily life. In classic sociological perspectives, this directs us to the micro-world of face-to-face interaction, most notably in the distinguished traditions of symbolic interactionism and ethnomethodology.[12] Here, social order arises out of the routine and myriad structures of small-scale communication as we learn to navigate our daily activities. In contemporary sociology, this kind of pragmatist thinking has enjoyed a recent resurgence.[13]

Pragmatist thinking, with its insistence on our immediate social situation, seems initially difficult to marry with analyses of large-scale inequalities, such as those we saw in Figure 1.1, or even Figure 2.1. But such integration is necessary if we are to force home the analysis of inequality as a fully relative process, rather than fixed states. In Chapter 1, I showed how the shift between poverty and inequality pushes this relativist perception, but the economists ultimately pull up short because of their attachment to an exterior Kantian perspective. This does not give us a handle on how inequality impinges on daily life, sentiment, and perception. Bourdieu's elaboration of field analysis is the most systematic attempt to make this link and the lessons of this important endeavor need to be brought out.

Recently, there has been a sustained attempt to champion "field analysis" as a means of linking these macro and micro dimensions of social life.[14] The American sociologist John Levi Martin (2003, 2011) has attempted to marry pragmatist psychology, physics, and the sociology of Pierre Bourdieu. His methodological insistence was that social scientists need to recover an account of the world rooted in the phenomenological reality of lived experience, rather than default to a positivist emphasis on the causal influence of discrete and abstract variables.[15] Martin notes that field theory was "developed first and most fully in the physical sciences through various attempts to comprehend how one thing could affect another without some substantive medium" (Martin and Gregg 2015: 39–40). This leads away from analyzing the interactions between fixed states toward a concern with force and flow. In understanding social relations as the product of field dynamics, he argues for a "social aesthetics," where judgment and taste drive processes of attraction and repulsion, meaning that social and personal judgments fuse. Martin thus sees social life as based on projects of organized striving, in which we share a set of passions and a common stake in the rules of the game with others in the field.

Pierre Bourdieu takes this phenomenological emphasis on relationships encountered in daily life and inflects it sociologically by infusing power, domination, and inequality into these practices.[16] He does this by drawing on the metaphor of society being akin to a sporting field, which gives a combative twist to the phenomenological approach. This metaphor sees people being located in society not through some fixed attribute but in a more dynamic way. They are no longer aloof spectators, nor boxed in neatly fenced-out pens, such as the 1 percent, but are pitched into the hurly-burly of competitive (and cooperative) life, having to make quick judgments and improvise as they are caught up in the melee of daily existence. This approach exposes the immanent relational forces as they emerge within fields themselves, rather than projecting some external grid—such as the percentile income distributions or group categories—onto them. It follows that the formation of any kind of loyalty is fraught, and that no permanent stable group is likely to emerge out of the flow of the field.

Thus, by identifying social relationships as akin to playing on a sporting field, it is identified as a fundamentally competitive space, differentiated into winner and losers. In making this assumption, Bourdieu implicitly draws on a model of modernist artistic culture as a template for field processes more generally.[17] Artistic modernism sees an endemic battle between contending artists to command pole position. He thus drew on the sense that artists, innovators, and pioneers often have of themselves that they need to compete against other players to be properly recognized. Thus, reflecting on the rise of artistic fields in the later nineteenth century, Bourdieu saw the genesis of modernist cultural fields in literature, arts, and music, whose participants all pitched against a conservative establishment as emblematic of the emergence of fields more generally. Cultural hierarchies, controlled by powerful institutional and elite forces, were challenged by new and emerging avant-gardists who had purer visions of artistic excellence. Innovative and initially shocking cultural interventions, ranging from Picasso's cubism to Proust's and Joyce's literary introspection, pitched against conservative artistic establishments, and in this process championed art for art's sake and sought to "purify" culture from the external hold of wealthy patrons.[18] By seeing conflicts such as these as emblematic of fields more widely, Bourdieu generalized from the specific case of twentieth-century modernist cultural movements to define a broader vision of social change bringing about an array of different fields, each with its own competitive, conflictual edge and its own "rules of the game."[19]

Bourdieu thus skillfully adapted older sociological thinking by Durkheim and Weber, who saw modernization as involving the differentiation and separation of spheres of social life.[20] He absorbed the sociological conventional wisdom that whereas traditional societies saw relatively muted separation of activities, these boundaries become more strongly marked as capitalist economic expansion takes place beginning in the eighteenth century. In numerous spheres, growing distinctions, such as between home and work or public and private, became marked, with boundaries between these fields being underscored by economic growth and the forces of modernization. This led to a process of differentiation and subdifferentiation of fields, in which differing spheres of social interaction become more autonomous from one another (thus, artistic value, sporting value, and so forth were not the simple reflex of economic resources, even though it might be affected by these).

I have endeavored to show how Bourdieu's thinking offers crucial resources for the inequality paradigm. It does this by taking up the phenomenological aspects of experience and perception and linking them to a relational understanding of social differentiation and inequality. In this respect, he offers a far richer human understanding of inequality than that which economists have unearthed in their distributional analyses. His spatial framing, most crisply encapsulated in his advocacy of field analysis, allows him a way of understanding how inequalities are rendered in relation to others.

But this spatial sensitivity is also an Achilles heel.

2.3: Pitfalls of Field Analysis

Bourdieu brilliantly deploys the analogy between physical and social space. In adapting the sports field as a model for what he terms "social space," he can see inequality as multidimensional: Just as our senses are inherently dimensional, so social space is not to be conflated with a single-dimensional linear distribution. Yet this is where the problem also starts. Physical space necessarily involves an aspect of mutual exclusivity, as we can't be in the same place as anyone else. It follows that fields might also be construed in these necessarily competitive terms (see notably Bourdieu 2002). This intersection becomes more explicit in his later thinking in *Pascalian Meditations*, where he notes how certain properties of social space are derived from physical space:

Just as physical space, according to Strawson, is defined by the recip-
rocal externality of positions . . . the social space is defined by the mutual exclusion, or distinction, of the positions which constitute it. . . .
Social agents, and also the things insofar as they are appropriated by
them and therefore constituted as properties, are situated in a place in
social space. (Bourdieu 2000: 134)

Here, Bourdieu invokes the irretrievably corporeal nature of both physical and social space, the way that shapes on the ground are associated with
the organization of fields and the distribution of capital.

Bourdieu has pulled off a brilliant balancing act here. He draws on a
spatial sensibility akin to that of phenomenologists, such as Martin Hei-
degger, which pushes home the nature of "being" in a more radical way than
economists, since it situates ourselves vis-à-vis others through our modes
of perception and bodily deportment. Understanding where we are placed
compared to others is not a simple ranking on a scale but locates us multi-
dimensionally. On a sporting field, we can move sideways as well as backward and forward, and we can lift the ball above our opponents.

Yet the problem is that this sociological rendering of fields as inherently
bound by conflict and structured oppositions is ultimately reductive, because
it does not adequately recognize the cooperative principles that are also essential for field relations. Sociologists are more attuned to processes of contestation, conflict, and opposition than they are to processes of attraction,
identification, and affiliation, yet both these dimensions are central to fields.
These latter features are part of the phenomenological world but are not
emphasized by sociologists. Bourdieu is having his phenomenological cake
while also eating it as sociological pie.

With this worry in mind, let us return to Figure 2.1, Bourdieu's crowning
glory. There is a major difference between Figure 1.1 and Figure 2.1: Whereas
Piketty's graph on changing income distribution examines trends over time,
Figure 2.1 is a snapshot in time. Addressing trends over time tends to abstract
from spatial relations, and Bourdieu's map of the French "space of lifestyles"
is frozen in a particular moment of history. By being necessarily dated at a
particular moment in time, Figure 2.1 lacks the narrative drive and historical dimension that makes the sparkline of Figure 1.1 so compelling. Figure 2.1
is more like a static picture.

This is not in itself an overwhelming problem. Analyses of the space of lifestyle can be updated at different intervals, so that any changes can be assessed: there is indeed an impressive body of research that has done precisely this by using repeat surveys in many European nations. These more recent studies now offer important qualifications to Bourdieu's original two-dimensional model and indicate that lifestyles and cultural relations no longer straightforwardly follow his influential account.[21] On the whole, there continues to be some kind of two-dimensional model (differentiating between capital volume and composition), but this has become much more subdued than when Bourdieu was writing. In Figure 2.1, Bourdieu's account of France in the 1960s, "legitimate" and "approved" activities were found among those individuals with lots of capital, whereas those without capital engaged in "popular" culture—such as reading car magazines but also perhaps more surprisingly appreciating Van Gogh's paintings or Tchaikovsky's music.[22] It was thus possible to distinguish different kinds of cultural engagement, distinguishing high brows from those participating in popular culture. More recent studies have shown instead that those with low levels of capital tend to be disengaged from most forms of measured cultural activity (see notably, Bennett et al. [2009] on the British case), whereas those with lots of capital are engaged in many forms of cultural activity—what has been famously labeled as "cultural omnivorousness."[23] To this extent, the divide between "high" and "popular" culture appears to have diminished, and those with little capital or resources appear to have withdrawn from many formal and public cultural activities and retreated into a world of more informal leisure, often based at home and involving social ties with kin.[24]

Furthermore, the second "capital composition" x-axis has become weaker and in some cases no longer distinguishes between the cultural avant-garde of intellectuals and luxury-oriented industrialists. The transformation of aesthetic stakes since the 1960s further backs up this observation. The modernist aesthetic assumes the centrality of sacred and legitimate historical forms that command the high ground of excellence and that avant-gardists can pitch their innovations against. Thus, it depends on the consecration of canonical cultural forms. However, these classic forms no longer appear to command such interest: Bennett et al.'s (2009) analysis of British cultural taste argues that the historical canon—such as Shakespeare's plays or classical music—no longer appeals so strongly. Even those with high educational qualifications can see this world of orchestral concerts, highbrow museums, and galleries as staid, old fashioned, and possibly even boring. These days, well-educated younger people are not that excited by (or engaged with) highbrow culture. Although classical music, for instance, is widely listened to in its more popular formats, there are very few passionate fans of Beethoven, Mahler, Stravinsky, or other canonical composers. However, more enthusiasm is shown for contemporary, cosmopolitan, and commercial forms of culture (DiMaggio and Mukhtar 2004; Bennett et al. 2009).

Furthermore, the heartland of cultural value, the "artwork" itself, is increasingly subject to economic imperatives and seen as an investment asset. Iconic works of art attract the highest possible financial returns from the highly complicit world of wealthy elites. Schimpfossl's (2018) study of the Russian superrich shows how the acquisition of art has been central to demonstrate their social ascent. Christopher Upton-Hansen's (2018) important study reviews how art has become intertwined with the dynamics of financial accumulation. Since the 1980s, metrics (notably the hedonic price model) have been developed to calculate the value of art and mark the rise to prominence of the art investment market.[25] Upton-Hansen notes the rise of art advisors in the burgeoning industry of wealth management and the role of free ports, technically located outside national jurisdictions, which store precious artworks and hence avoid national taxation: more than $125 billion worth of art was alleged to have been located in such transient locations in 2013 (Upton-Hansen 2018: 72–73). More crucially still, art prices reflect economic inequality: building a regression on the income tax data of Piketty and Saez, "'art prices rise when income inequality goes up.' A one percent increase in the share of total income earned by the top 0.1 percent triggers an increase in art prices of about 14 percent" (Goetzmann et al. 2011, quoted by Upton-Hansen 2018: 106).

Cultural value is therefore commercialized, and by being rendered for its exchange value, loses its distinctive artistic quality. The resulting weakening of the capital composition principle is amply attested through aesthetic debates about the rise of postmodern culture. These debates have questioned the separation of the aesthetic from the commercial and popular and have noted the emergence of a playful aesthetic organized around pastiche that can embrace both popular and traditional cultural motifs (Featherstone 1991). Bourdieu (1979[1984]) was skeptical of the significance of such currents, which he saw as generated by marginal "new cultural intermediaries." Working in areas such as marketing, fashion, advertising, and media, this new petite bourgeoisie—with the help of the new bourgeoisie—acts as taste makers or agents of a counterculture by pleading for a new ethics of experience and more than that, for an eclecticism in tastes. He does not really see in this something that could alter the dynamics of the field of symbolic goods or the status of highbrow culture, as the dominant class "concedes the better to conserve" (Bourdieu 1979[1984]: 371).

Starting in the 1980s, however, Featherstone (1987) and Lash and Urry (1987) argued that these cultural intermediaries have helped democratize intellectual lifestyles (and institutions) and legitimize popular genres, which altogether contribute to the postmodernist blurring, even if not the collapse of cultural hierarchies and of life and art. Self-reflective, autodidactic, and in search of new experiences, these intermediaries are receptive to postmodern principles, such as challenging conventions and social critique, that can be expressed in visual art through parody, derision, or irony. Instead of the split between cultured intellectuals and wealthy industrialists evident in Figure 2.1, recent research shows that the second dimension usually differentiates between older people more drawn to older forms of "highbrow" culture and younger groups more oriented toward commercial and contemporary culture.[26] This is an important finding, which actually underscores the arguments of economists: that economic inequality has grown in many nations at the same time that secondary inequalities between cultural and economic capital have declined.

Associated with these shifts has been the rise of a technocratic and gadget-oriented culture. When Bourdieu wrote *Distinction,* less than half of French homes had a television set, and it is therefore not surprising that Bourdieu's analysis concentrated on the differential consumption of public forms of leisure—such as in restaurants, museums, holidays, or leisure pursuits. His distinction between avant-garde artists and affluent industrialists reflected the very different kinds of public spaces that such groups inhabit: lavish restaurants compared to hip, arty galleries. In fact, even at the time he was writing, there is evidence that some well-educated individuals were drawn to more technocratic forms of activity (see Savage [2010] and Edgerton [2018] on the British case). But certainly, the explosion of electronic gadgets driven by the miniaturization of the microchip has massively extended this currency.

The rapid advance of information technology has numerous affordances, but I particularly want to emphasize its capacity to allow the accumulation of cultural references. In the case of social media, for instance, it allows the build-up of contacts that would not be possible through face-to-face, textual, or oral forms. It thus further drives the tendency for the volume of capital to take precedence over the capital composition principle. These reflections all point to an important conclusion. Bourdieu's research is couched in a very different analytical tradition from that of the economists of income distribution. Nonetheless, recent research conducted in its frame points in similar directions. The capital volume—the first horizontal y-axis of Figure 2.1—has become more important, and it demonstrates the increasing power of economic inequality to drive social divisions more broadly.[27] Compared to when Bourdieu wrote fifty years ago, the secondary distinction between intellectuals and industrialists has waned as economic inequality has increased and the capital volume axis has therefore become more drawn out.

Piketty has reflected on how the significance of growing economic inequality in the period since Bourdieu's research has changed the stakes of inequality: "we have a return of capital in the sense of financial capital, real estate capital, which is playing a very big role today, much bigger than the '50s, '60s, '70s. . . . So I think we need to think of a new paradigm to look at inequalities that combines the two (economic and cultural capital) in the order of discourse as much as in the order of economic and social relations" (Piketty 2015: 8–9, my italics). The significance of the division between intellectuals and industrialists can be expected to be much more muted when the gap between rich and poor increases. But this recognition brings with it a major problem for the conception of the field that Bourdieu uses.

I have already mentioned that we have more intuitive understanding of the tensions between those with cultural and economic capital than we have between those with differing amounts of capital. The conflicts between hip, cutting edge, cultural avant-gardes and extravagant, lavishly spending executives is very familiar. But in fact, the difference between these lifestyles appears to be fading. These days, hip artists are also effective businesspeople, while rich people are also investing heavily in the art world. The clear pulling apart of those with great amounts of economic capital and those without has the effect of eroding the very principles of field contestation that Bourdieu emphasizes. Those with large amounts of capital often don't see themselves as operating in the same social space or competing with those who are much poorer than they are. Those who are on the poorer fringes of society often see the rich as a world apart. They are no longer playing the same game. In this situation, the principles of field analysis itself, which assumes contestation, passion for the game, and excitement shared among participants, begins to fall apart. Too much inequality within a field of relations stops the game from being a compelling one to its participants.

Ultimately, for this reason, the fraught marriage of phenomenology and sociology that Bourdieu brilliantly staged now frays to the point of becoming threadbare. The burden on field analysis to link the micro and macro proves to be too great. As economic inequality increases, so fields stop being effective, because the winners and losers are too far apart and no longer see themselves as engaged in the same contest. The reasons for this become clear if we return to the sports field comparison. Any sporting contest, or any battle, depends on a degree of indeterminancy about the outcome: This is intrinsic to the passion and intensity of the field itself. No one (bar a few diehards) would turn up at a football match if it were entirely certain in advance that your team will lose. No army will choose to fight a battle that they are guaranteed to lose. (Of course, they sometimes are forced to fight battles they would rather avoid, but this is precisely the point.) By extension, construing social relations as akin to a sporting field is only convincing if a certain level of indeterminacy is evident in its social relationships. However, the recent application of Bourdieu's model of fields (and by homological extension, social space) has actually shown, time and again, the same predictable set of winners and losers. We might see this less in terms of field contestation and more through Marxist critic Walter Benjamin's terms. "Whoever until this day emerges victorious, marches in the triumphal procession in which today's rulers tread over those who are sprawled underfoot. The spoils are, as was ever the case, carried along in the triumphal procession. They are known as the cultural heritage" (Benjamin 2009: thesis 7).

In this case, the contingency and the passion bound up with the intensity of the field are bound to fade. Why should those without capital on an increasingly uneven sporting field continue to play the game when they know they are bound to be the losers? Why don't they just give up? Or, perhaps more pertinently, why don't they welcome into the field outside forces that might upset the rules of the game and disrupt the domination of those with capital within their field? Indeed, although I don't want to jump ahead, this might exactly explain the appeal of elite populist leaders such as Donald Trump, who set out their electoral appeal in terms of the challenge they will make to political elites.

At this point, followers of Bourdieu may make a neat move to find a way out of this conundrum. Rather than focus field analysis, it is possible to appeal to the concept of "capital" to offer an explanation of the systematic and predictable differentiation of winners and losers. This will be a crucial concept that I will elaborate in Chapter 3, but for now, I only want to set it alongside his field analysis. He introduces it as follows:

> The social world is accumulated history, and if it is not to be reduced to a discontinuous series of instantaneous mechanical equilibria between agents who are treated as interchangeable particles, one must reintroduce into it the notion of capital and with it, accumulation and all its effects. Capital is accumulated labour (in its materialized form or its "incorporated," embodied form) which, when appropriated on a private, i.e., exclusive, basis by agents or groups of agents, enables them to appropriate social energy in the form of reified or living labor. (Bourdieu 1986: 241)

Here, Bourdieu uses the concept of capital as part of a critical dialogue with economists, who view it as some kind of an investment that secures a return. Bourdieu's cunning ruse, however, is to appear to take this view but then twist it in two unexpected ways. First, he extends capital beyond an economic use to include cultural and social capital. His point here is that investments in certain kinds of cultural proclivities (or in your social networks) also secure some kind of return, and hence a narrow economistic perspective is misplaced.

His second move—evident in the quotation above—turns out to be even more cunning. Here he emphasizes that once capital is defined as an investment that secures a return, it can only be understood as a process that takes place over time. Thus, the importance of "accumulated history." Therefore, the kind of ahistorical analysis that reduces social exchange to game scenarios, or to some kind of neoclassical market logic, fails to grasp that the world is always in process. And this insight can be applied as much to Piketty's pirouettes around the skating rink of history as to game-theoretical models of supply and demand.

This insight is profound. I will develop it in Chapter 3, and it will under-gird all the arguments to come. However, Bourdieu does not bring out that it also undercuts his own field analysis—since these field processes can also be seen precisely in the ahistorical way that he criticizes. The metaphor of the field as a sporting contest leads itself to conceiving of a time-bounded contest, and which repeats itself on future occasions, not one which is sub-ject to the accumulation he emphasizes above.

This reflects an impasse about how the concept of capital is used in Bour-dieu's own work. He oscillates between seeing capital as a meta-historical force—just as in the passage quoted above—and seeing it as field-specific, where its valuation and propensity to accumulate is only confined to what is valued in the stakes of the specific game. Martin and Gregg (2015) demon-strate how this conflation is ultimately disabling. They rightly argue that for the principles of field analysis to be fully applied, the passions involved can only be organized around "field-specific capital" (that is, those defined by the stakes of the contest itself), and that it is inappropriate to extend the concept of capital beyond this to see it as exogeneous to the field (as a kind of external resource or asset).[28] As they put it:

> Capital must be understood as a field-specific constellation of relations. But in that case, it seems hard to imagine how there could be any cap-ital other than field position. For example, an artist might indeed have high fine motor coordination, but if no one in the field of drawing be-lieved that she was an accomplished draughtsman, it seems that it would be incorrect to say something like "despite the fact that she has a low field position, she has high artistic capital," which confuses re-source and capital, and places the capital outside the field's range of effective consecration. Accepting such a usage would be equivalent to making capital a resource as opposed to a relation. If we insist that the field is not simply the set of recognized positions but the distillation of all sets of relations that have implications for the production and expe-rience of relations, it seems that capital is redundant with field posi-tion. (Martin and Gregg 2015: 54)

Yet this is precisely how Bourdieu frequently uses the concept of capital—as a resource. He sees it as accrued by the victors in field contests, which can then be redeployed in the future to gain systematic advantages in the future—as "accumulated history," to use his memorable phrase. This also brings with it a conception of capital akin to "homo economicus" that is not so different from the economists that he criticizes. He ultimately undercuts his own spatializing field theory. The phenomenological passions and intensities of the field encounter depend on the combatants being invested in the thrill of the contest. This will be lost when the game gets too predictable. Ultimately, there is an irreconcilable tension between emphasizing capital—which conveys the "weight of history," or the spatializing and relational perspectives of field theory. At the end of the day, either the sociological emphases on power and domination or the phenomenological aspects linked to experience has to give. Bourdieu's bravura balancing act comes off the tightrope.

Conclusion

Only two visual icons, Figures 1.1 and 2.1, have already taken us on a long journey from the state of poverty to relative inequalities, from the economic to the cultural, and from the macro to the micro. This journey has revealed some common features and an increasingly clear recognition of the all-embracing nature of inequality. It also turns out that there is remarkable common cause between the recent findings of economics and sociology, even though these disciplines start from different positions.

Our first icon (Figure 1.1) sensitized us to the power of a timeline. It provided a simple but intuitively powerful narrative about how economic inequality is getting worse, and it disrupted a progressive story about modernization and progressive social change associated with the decline of scarcity and the eradication of poverty. But it focuses on only one dimension—income distribution—and gives us no way of grasping how people themselves understand their positions, defaulting instead to an external grid of percentile income shares derived from economists' expert calculations. It thus gestures toward understanding inequality as a relative state, only to pull away from a deeper hermeneutic engagement with what relativity actually entails.

Our second icon (Figure 2.1) redresses this shortcoming—up to a point. It adopts a spatializing strategy of placing relationships in graphical *n*-dimensional space. It is cross-sectional, and thereby abstracts from a time-line as a means of providing a snapshot of the phenomenal world of meaning and identity forming out of processes of repulsion and attraction at a given moment in time. By depicting the oppositions between indicators of taste and lifestyle, the economic can be distinguished from the cultural axes. This interest in fields provides a rich metaphor that allows us to conceptualize inequality as akin to a sporting contest, in which we jostle for advantage and position.

Both icons are powerful but apparently contradictory: Figure 1.1 focuses on trends in time, whereas Figure 2.1 explicates spatial relationships. In fact, their substantive findings turn out not to be so contradictory. Recent research examining lifestyles and cultural practices reveals that the second axis, which differentiates between economic and cultural capital, is receding in importance; the capital "volume" axis—the one akin to the income distribution axis—is becoming more prominent. Both icons thus turn out to be consistent in recognizing how the intensification of economic inequality is becoming a more marked feature of contemporary societies, not only in the economic realm but also through affecting lifestyle and cultural preferences.

But at the end of the day, we have rubbed up against a major obstacle to effectively combining perspectives containing both the temporal and spatial dimensions of inequality. The spatializing approach of Bourdieu, which seems to render relativity very effectively, cannot ultimately combine the phenomenological world of feeling, intensity, and passion with the structural inequalities that it readily delineates. Bourdieu's appeal to the overarching concept of capital, with its reference to the accumulation of inequality over time, cannot be accommodated without breaching the core phenomenological insights of field theory.

What we are facing is the very serious difficulty of integrating questions of both time and space into the analysis of inequality. To reflect further on how we might do this, I need to reflect further on the concept of capital, and how it might be reconciled with field analysis.

Here, we have a long and veritable body of thinking going back to Karl Marx, a story I will take up in Chapter 3.

Renewing Marx

CAPITAL ACCUMULATION AND THE
WEIGHT OF HISTORY

In Chapters 1 and 2, I have argued that we need a better understanding of historical process than is allowed in the economics of income distribution or Bourdieu's field analysis. Actually, both approaches acknowledge this when they appeal to the concept of capital. Here, they both tilt their hats to the groundbreaking analysis of Karl Marx. Ultimately, however, their interest takes a glancing form, and they are not diverted from their own projects. In this chapter, I argue there is much to be learned from returning more fully to reflect on the core insight of the Marxist tradition, of capital as a force for *accumulation*.

As before, I approach this question by reflecting on the power of a striking visual. Figure 3.1 offers a brilliant and provocative platform for considering the trajectory of capital over recent decades. It too, was produced by the economist Thomas Piketty. For, having made his name with his trailblazing work on income inequality, which I reviewed in Chapter 1, in his monumental book, *Capital in the Twenty-First Century,* he opened up a new line of inquiry—that of placing wealth inequality, and not only income inequality, fully into the picture.

Figure 3.1 shows how Piketty is measuring capital in a different way than Marx, even though he self-consciously writes in the latter's shadow.[1] For

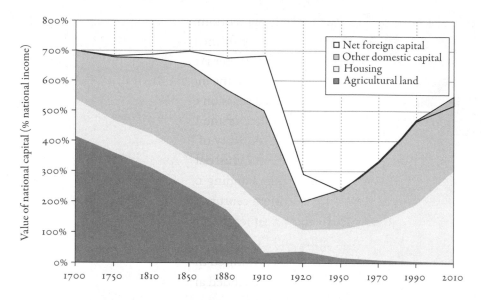

FIGURE 3.1: Capital in Britain, 1700–2010

Source: Thomas Piketty, *Capital in the Twenty-First Century* (Cambridge, MA: Harvard University Press, 2014), figure 3.1. Copyright © 2014 by the President and Fellows of Harvard College. Used by permission.

Marx, capital differs from money because of its capacity to accumulate: Capital is money put to work to generate more money. This accumulation of capital can only take place through the exploitation of workers, who produce more value through their labor than is returned to them in their wages. This exploitation therefore generates a surplus, which allows capital to reap profit and thereby accumulate. Piketty shies away from Marx's analysis of accumulation as exploitation. In his characteristic empirical style, Piketty sidesteps a theoretical definition and proffers an empirically measurable definition of capital: "all forms of wealth that individuals (or groups of individuals) can own and . . . can be transferred or traded through the market on a permanent basis" (Piketty 2013: 46). It thus includes capital tied up in owner-occupied housing, savings (such as in stocks and shares), or cash. This is capital as some kind of tradable asset rather than a dynamic process. You don't need to be a Marxist to measure capital in this way. And it is this stock of capital that Piketty measures in Figure 3.1.

The appeal of Figure 3.1 is that the same neat narrative sparkline that we saw in Figure 1.1 reappears even though the object of measurement is different. Figure 3.1 is not measuring economic inequality—but instead the stock of capital. However, the power of the symphonic aesthetic, the repetition of core motifs (discussed in Chapter 1) allows us to readily appropriate its narrative to underpin and reinforce the inequality story. It is striking that the first visual Piketty uses in his discussion of the capital / income ratio focuses on Britain (rather than France or the United States). He justifies this pragmatically because of the high-quality of British data sources. Nonetheless, as the icon of the world's first industrial nation, the British story occupies a pivotal place in our understanding of global inequality. Figure 3.1 shows that until the early twentieth century, the entire stock of tradable capital in Britain was worth about 7 times the stock of annual national income. Until the industrial revolution of the later eighteenth century, the value associated with agricultural land constituted the bulk of this capital, reflecting Britain as a society dominated by a landed aristocracy. This ratio of 7:1 persisted until the early twentieth century, though industrial capital comes to make up a bigger portion of tradable capital. However, from the First World War to the 1950s, this ratio radically fell as a result of capital depreciation both during the 1929 recession as well as during war-time destruction and appropriation. By 1920, the ratio of capital to income had slumped to only 2:1. Since this period, it has risen steadily again, and by 2010 was over five times the value of national income. The familiar U shape is back!

On the face of it, Figure 3.1 tells us nothing about wealth inequality, since it does not break down who owns what portions of the aggregate wealth reported. But in a deeper sense, it tells us a great deal about inequality at the most general level. For capital represents the hold of the old over the young, the dead over the living, and the power of existing asset holders compared to those who rely on selling their labor power today. During the middle decades of the twentieth century, capital reached its low point of relative significance. It is not incidental that a youth culture sparked in the 1960s at exactly this time. This was the moment in history when the decline of the capital / income ratio meant that young wage earners enjoyed more relative power than in previous generations.[2] However, far from the 1960s marking a new countercultural trend that would sweep all before it, Piketty shows that it was a historical blip that has now been "corrected." We have seen the return of capital assets, and thereby the power of history has itself been renewed.

Piketty's calculation of the capital / income ratio is therefore a brilliant device. It reveals that even though inequality takes numerous forms, most fundamentally of all, it is defined by the weight of the past. Figure 3.1 traces a simple sparkline, but it powerfully punctures our modernist pretensions: It is not simply measuring a distributional trend but also the differential force of history itself. Understanding inequality needs to go beyond considering the differential relationship between people at any given moment in time (as in Figures 1.1 and 2.1) but needs to acknowledge the balance of present-day actions against the weight of past forces. And whereas legions of social scientists see this historical baggage declining as societies modernize, recent trends actually mark a dramatic reverse in this decline. As we are now returning to a world with higher capital stocks, the weight of the past is returning, and along with this comes resurgent elitism, patronage, discrimination, and the entrenchment of inherited privilege. Contemporary capitalism is not new, dynamic, and turbo-charged (that is, in the terms that many of its champions position it) but is in fact marked by the increasing weight of older historical formations. Piketty links this to the return of what he calls "patrimonial capitalism," harking back to the aristocratic world of the nineteenth-century belle époque.

This brilliant move is a profound challenge to modernization theory at large but more radically to the core social science belief that we have somehow cut loose from tradition. Since the eighteenth century, we have lived in a world where it is routinely proclaimed that the past has been left behind. It was in the turbulent context of nineteenth-century industrialization, urbanization, and political revolutions that sociology emerged as a means of diagnosing the distinctive dynamics of a "modernity" that had left traditional society in its wake (Kumar 1978). The deep challenge of Piketty's work is that it urges us to examine whether the twenty-first century is now receding from this vision of modernity, and we are instead marked by a cyclical process of return as the weight of the past increases. His later *Capital and Ideology* (Piketty 2020), which asks us to learn from previous historical moment (such as taxation on high earners) to renew our current repertoires to address inequality follows this lead.

This chapter teases out the implications of this fundamental insight. I proceed initially by drawing out Piketty's findings regarding the significance of capital accumulation. Having established this beachhead, Section 3.2 reflects more broadly on how the weight of history requires us to radically question our understanding of time and historical process and hence our very conceptions of social change. It fundamentally punctures our modern temporal ontology, in which we characteristically view the past as "left behind." I also show how Bourdieu's conceptions of field analysis can be adapted to make it better able to grasp this temporality. This finally leads me to force home my critique of epochalist thinking in sociology that will provide a vital platform for the later chapters in this book. Placing inequality at the heart of our thinking allows a much richer and comprehensive theory of social change than that grounded in conventional modernist inflected versions.

3.1: Why Does Wealth Inequality Matter?

The crispest way to understand the significance of Piketty's intervention is to see it as a critical reflection on the distinctive nature of the French experience. Figure 3.2 compares the proportion of total wealth and total income held by the top 1 percent and 10 percent in France between 1975 and 2014.

On the face of it, the French vision of modernity has tended to emphasize equality. Linking back to the founding tenets of "liberty, equality, fraternity," which were trumpeted during the French Revolution, this placing of equality and solidarity alongside liberty marks a rather different inflection from the American model, which prioritized liberty alone. And indeed, even in recent decades while many other developed nations have embraced deregulation, tax cuts, and privatization, the French have held out for a strong state that has resisted market-oriented reforms. Piketty is indeed very mindful of the differences between France and the United States, and he recognizes that French political forces have prevented the explosion of top incomes so evident in the United States. But even so, his examination of trends in income and wealth inequality pulls out a striking feature of the French case.

One point is immediately clear. Even in relatively egalitarian France, there is much more inequality of wealth than of income, and this has been growing. The top 1 percent have 22 percent of total wealth compared to 12 percent of total income. This trend, for wealth inequality to be more concentrated than income inequality, is nearly universal (for example, see Chauvel et al. 2021). At the bottom of the distribution, this reflects the fact that (apart

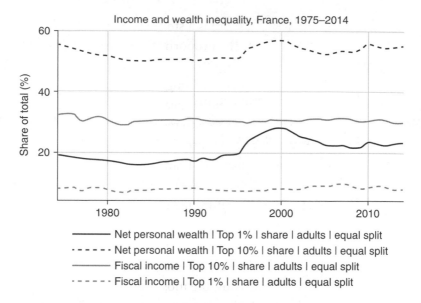

FIGURE 3.2: Comparing income and wealth inequality in France, 1975–2014

Note: Percentage of total national income and wealth taken by the top 5%.
Source: World Inequality Database.

from those relying on subsistence farming) everyone needs to earn some income to survive. Therefore, it is not possible to have zero income, but it is entirely possible to have zero wealth, or indeed, negative wealth (if you are in debt). At the top of the distribution this trend reflects that because wealth can be piled up incrementally on the basis of past assets, rather than earned on the basis of current work, it can pile up and accumulate over long periods of time.

So, even in egalitarian France, 58 percent of the wealth is owned by only 10 percent of the population: highly inegalitarian. But the second point is even more disturbing. In France, the share of national income—after tax— enjoyed by the top 10 percent and the top 1 percent hardly varies year on year. This is a massive contrast to the American case, as we saw in Chapter 1. The French 1 percent have not enjoyed the same golden summer as their American counterparts. However, when we examine equivalent trends for wealth inequality, this picture changes; the share of wealth owned by the top 1 percent and the top 10 percent rises substantially, especially for the top 1 percent. Even leaving aside the temporary wealth bubble around the turn of the millennium (presumably linked to the inflation of stock prices in the context of the dot.com boom), there is a steady increase from 15.8 percent in 1984 to 23.4 percent in 2014 of the proportion of wealth taken by the top 1 percent.

So, the French case presents an interesting puzzle. A growing concentration of wealth occurred *without a similar concentration of income,* in a nation that has remained relatively committed to redistributive taxation and social inclusion. French egalitarianism, therefore, can't be taken at face value. Even without a rise in top income shares in France, Figure 3.1 demonstrates a striking concentration of *wealth* in the form of tradable assets, such as property, savings, and cash. Piketty is committed to puncturing any French complacency that it does not have an "inequality problem."[3]

The French case is not anomalous. It is increasingly clear that focusing on wealth inequality extends and to some extent challenges accounts based purely on income distribution. Thus, the most systematic study of comparative wealth inequality reports that "many countries that we customarily describe as comparatively egalitarian following income-based comparisons—such as Scandinavian countries—can be classified as anything but in terms of their levels of wealth inequality" (Pfeffer and Waitkus 2019: 26; on Sweden, see also Lundenberg and Waldenstrom 2018). Figure 3.3 shows that only the United States stands out in having exceptionally high amounts of both income *and* wealth inequality, further testifying to its unenviable role as the global inequality icon. By contrast, Austria, Sweden, Germany, and Norway, who have the next-highest concentrations of wealth, have proportionately lower levels of income concentration. And the United Kingdom, which has relatively high income concentration, has a relatively lower wealth concentration.

The French experience thereby lies at the heart of Piketty's formula $r > g$, which states that the rate of return to capital tends to be greater than the growth rate. Put simply, even without a shift of income toward top earners, those with wealth tend to accumulate further wealth more quickly than those with lesser amounts. This is a natural function of economic growth and need not involve direct expropriation, changing tax regimes, and so forth. Here I don't want to be distracted by the criticisms of Piketty's arguments, which suggest a fixed economic logic relying on a neoclassical model.[4] For my purposes, it is the historical trends that are important. Piketty is one of a group of economists who have drawn attention to the astonishing rise

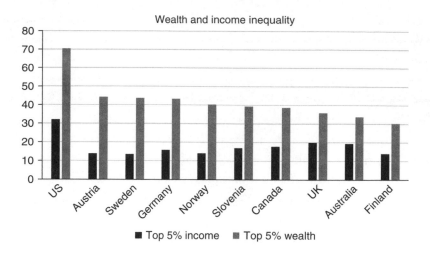

FIGURE 3.3: Wealth and income concentration in selected nations

Note: Percentage of total national income and wealth taken by the top 5%.
Data source: Fabian T. Pfeffer and Nora Waitkus, "The Wealth Inequality of Nations," The Inequality Lab Discussion Paper 2019-2.

of wealth stocks in recent decades. Davies et al. (2017) relate the staggering finding that the total amount of global wealth more than doubled between 2000 and 2014, from $117 trillion to $251 trillion. It is worth pondering this startling statistic. In a mere fourteen-year period, the total amount of wealth that had been accumulated over the course of many millennia of world history more than doubled. This emphasis on wealth also focuses attention on the distinctive profile of continental Europe, where the ratio of capital to income has increased systematically, even though they have not seen a marked rise in income inequality. The United States and United Kingdom are no longer outliers in these terms but very closely mirror the patterns of other developed nations. In fact, in 2010, the Germans and Italians had a higher capital-income ratio. Indeed, it is the older European nations where capital accumulation is more marked—a vital indicator of the fact that this historical legacy of the early capitalist modernizers, with their global empires, remains not only visible but also potent today.

Figure 3.4 shows that all the listed nations have seen a substantial rise of the capital income ratio since 1970. Germany has the lowest ratio, but even so, it increased from about 210 percent to 400 percent. Italy's spiraled from 230 percent to nearly 700 percent. Japan is unusual: After an exceptionally

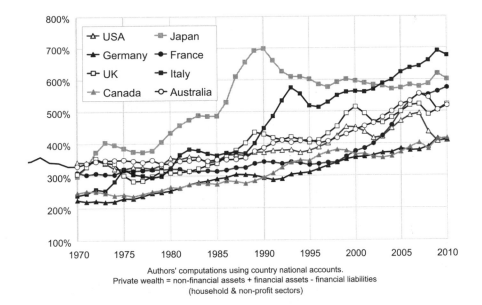

FIGURE 3.4: Trends in the capital-income ratio in selected nations, 1970–2010

Source: Reformatted from Thomas Piketty, *Capital in the Twenty-First Century* (Cambridge, MA: Harvard University Press, 2014), figure 5.3. Copyright © 2014 by the President and Fellows of Harvard College. Used by permission.

rapid increase until the late 1990s, it has stagnated but is still very high. The trends are less extreme but clearly evident, in other rich countries, though they are possibly more extreme in some developing nations, such as South Africa (Pabon et al. 2021).

So we have established that inequality, seen as the hold of the past over the present, can grow as a by-product of capital accumulation, even without the kind of relational field contestation that Bourdieu's field analysis or the analysis of shifting income shares brings to the table. This broadening out of our understanding of inequality brings inheritance fully into the equation. Using long-term French data, Piketty shows that the proportion of French people who can expect to inherit very large sums—the equivalent of the lifetime earnings of the bottom 50 percent of earners—has risen starkly.[5] In the nineteenth century, around 10 percent of French people could expect this sum of money, but as the French economy grew in the twentieth century, the proportion fell substantially. Only 2 percent of French people born between 1900 and 1920 could expect this kind of "step up." However, as households have become wealthier in recent decades, a remarkable 15 percent of French people are now expected to become major inheritors—of the order of 750,000 euros or more. This trend has opened up a major rift between a significant minority of French people who can expect to inherit substantial sums and the majority who will not. I need to underscore again that this has happened in a nation which has not seen the spiraling rise of income inequality like that seen in the United States. Indeed, it has happened even though inheritance tax rates actually increased in France during this period (see Piketty 2013: figure 14.2)—from 15 percent in the later 1960s to 45 percent by 2010. France is not unusual here. Estimates now suggest that in most developed nations, a staggering proportion of over half of aggregate wealth is now inherited, a marked rise from only fifty years ago, and this trend is common across all wealthy nations.

Similarly, bringing capital accumulation into view also means that we have a better handle for understanding the significance of debt—both public and private—in this analysis, too. Total debt has been rising fast and has a fundamental role in shaping economic policy (as seen most evidently in the recent eurozone conflicts but also around the globe; for instance, see Bear [2015] on the Indian case). The ratio of total debt (including loans and fixed-term securities of households, corporations, financial institutions, and governments) to the gross domestic product (GDP) has increased across a major group of developed economies over the past twenty years up to 2011. In the extreme British case, the ratio has gone from being 220 percent of GDP in 1990 to about 550 percent by 2011, but even for Canada, which has seen the lowest rise, the proportion has risen from 200 percent to 250 percent. Low interest rates have prevented the potential cost of debt to be manifest to many debtors, but this situation could change, in which case, the power of past transactions to drive current economic relations will become dramatic.

With this intellectual move, we have established our beachhead for recognizing the "weight of the past." Wealth inequality implicates the historical dimension more powerfully than looking at trends in income distributions.[6] To be sure, income levels have a history, too, and the wages we command are dependent on our prior skills, experiences, and opportunities, and in the context of historically constructed and unequal labor markets. Nonetheless, income is paid on a discrete and relatively short temporal basis—normally by the hour, week, month, or on a piece rate. Labor economists have demonstrated that especially in the middle levels of the income distribution, there is considerable scope to move up and down the income ladder, and there are prospects—even though constrained—for significant income mobility (see, for example, Jenkins 2011 on the United Kingdom). Wealth inequality is altogether more viscous. It is generally accumulated over a much longer period, not only over one's own life cycle but also often is being inherited from one generation to the next.[7] But there is also mundane accumulation. Very high earners are normally in high-profile jobs of one kind or another, whether they are sports players, chief executives, or expert professionals. But the build-up of wealth takes a more opaque form. This is partly captured through the "Matthew effect," whereby "those who have, shall be given more." Piketty's account of the differential return on capital investments between US universities is a nice vignette here. The truly old and distinguished institutions with massive endowments—Harvard, Yale, and Princeton—net a 10.2 percent annual rate of return compared to 8.8 percent for other universities with endowments of over $1 billion; 7.8 percent for those with endowments between $500 million and $1 billion; 7.1 percent for those with $100 to 499 million, and 6.2 percent for those with less than $100 million in endowments (Piketty 2013: 448). These distinctions are not warranted by the fame or intellectual prowess of the universities concerned: They are an effect of the size of the existing endowment, which is itself generated over long periods of time.[8]

I want to press home the significance of mundane wealth accumulation. Extreme wealth concentration is highly visible. In 2018, Oxfam argued that eight people owned as much wealth as the nearly four billion people who comprise the bottom half of the world's wealth distribution. This is a startling (even though contested) statistic; however, it focuses attention on a very small elite group. In fact, an important feature of the wealth distribution is the way that it percolates down to a larger chunk of affluent people. In most nations, trends in the concentration of wealth have been less marked than those of income concentration, and they have not returned to levels of the 1920s. There has been a significant extension of asset accumulation not just at the very top but also among the wider reaches of affluent population, perhaps comprising 15–20 percent of households, possibly even more. This demands a more nuanced analysis than can be provided by a simple analysis of top earners.

Piketty's shifting attention to wealth has not escaped criticism. Indeed, for Godechot (2015), in the American case, "the emergence of the Working Rich is a more radical transformation than the resurgence of capital." However, there is no real tension between these two perspectives; indeed, the two can reinforce each other. High earners generally invest their incomes in assets. But recognizing the significance of capital accumulation is vital to bring out the duration over which inequality builds. It takes attention away from market-based inequalities, which focus on distributional conflicts at a given moment in time. Whereas income levels are sensitive to labor market dynamics, wealth (or debt) are stocks that can accumulate without active market transactions (though admittedly they are valued on current market conditions and are especially liable to shifts in inflation rates, which over recent decades tend to have been low but in previous periods have been much higher). Because wealth is a force from the past, it detaches the economics of inequality from labor economics, in which income can be attributed to marginal productivity, human capital, and so forth. Now, unearned income ("rent," as it is often called by economists) comes fully into view.

This shift challenges the conventional liberal defense of economic inequality as a meritocratic reward scheme for the superior talents, work rates, or expertise of higher-earning individuals. Since much wealth inequality derives from inheritance or other kinds of unearned income, this ideology become irrelevant to the justification of inequality. Even if we differentiate between asset accumulation based on saving, economic appreciation, and inheritance, where saving can be seen as "deserved" or moral accumulation (though even here the capacity to save is dependent on prior economic resources), Piketty's demonstration of the enhanced significance of inheritance and appreciation shows that this component is not very significant. Appreciation has boomed with the massive "deserved" rise in house prices since the 1990s, and the rise in asset prices generally due to quantitative easing and can hardly be plausibly deemed as "deserved."[9] The logic of a meritocracy has little purchase for systems of inequality driven by capital accumulation.

Alongside this, attention shifts from the employed individual toward the family and household, units where wealth is normally possessed and inherited. Piketty has been criticized for neglecting gender in his analyses, and to some extent correctly, but in placing family dynamics, wealth, and inheritance at the heart of his account, he leaves a very rich terrain for these issues to be given more central attention than when only income shares are being emphasized. This move is part of a wider social science trend of insisting that demographic trends have crucial dynamics and that it is problematic to rip individuals out of these contexts and treat their fortunes as the product of their own situation alone.

Focusing on wealth often magnifies inequality across numerous other axes. The racial wealth gap in the United States is staggering: Black households have a mere 15 percent of the net worth of white households, and this share has been falling in recent times (Shapiro 2017). In 2016, Black child households had just one cent for every dollar held by non-Hispanic white child households. When, in 2020, in the Minneapolis memorial service for George Floyd, Rev. Al Sharpton called for White America "to get your knee off our necks," the weight of this knee is heavy with accumulated wealth. In the United Kingdom, Black Africans and Bangladeshi households have only 10 percent of the average wealth of white British households (Khan 2020). This is not a gap—it is a chasm.

To summarize: wealth is not simply another variable to throw into a multidimensional mix, where it might sit alongside income inequality and / or race, gender, or class. It has much more profound implications in pressing us to move beyond spatializing and distributional understandings of inequality. It drives us toward a more fundamental historical perspective, in which inequality between the old and the young, and across generations plays the fundamental analytical role. Once we think in these terms, we can readily see instances of the growing weight of the past. It becomes clearer why the politics of Black Lives Matter is so concerned with history—in terms of recognizing the long-term effects of slavery. It helps explain why Black Lives Matter protesters in Bristol were inspired to topple the statue of a frankly obscure eighteenth-century slave owner, Edward Colston, as part of their protest against institutional racism in the early twenty-first century

But how do we do bring this historical style of analysis into the picture in a way that still allows us to build on the insights of the relational approaches to inequality which I have emphasized in Chapters 1 and 2? We need to settle our accounts with the field analysis examined in Chapter 2. This will provide the platform we need to bring out the weight of the past in later chapters of this book.

3.2: Rethinking Modernity

I have argued that the concept of capital—and the concomitant accumulation that it generates—is crucial not simply in terms of its status as an economic variable but also because it demonstrates the inescapably historical forces driving inequality. It is important to insist on this point, since it is often the transformative and dynamic elements of capitalism that are emphasized. Karl Marx, in the *Communist Manifesto,* which he wrote with Frederich Engels in 1848, is often seen to trumpet the dynamo of capitalism, its turbulence, vitality, and never-ending flux:

> Constant revolutionizing of production, uninterrupted disturbance of all social conditions, everlasting uncertainty and agitation distinguish the bourgeois epoch from all earlier ones. All fixed, fast-frozen relations, with their train of ancient and venerable prejudices and opinions, are swept away, all new-formed ones become antiquated before they can ossify. All that is solid melts into air, all that is holy is profaned, and man is at last compelled to face with sober senses his real conditions of life, and his relations with his kind. (Marx 1969: 98)

This futurism sounds familiar. It forms our common sense today as we countenance driverless cars, robots, and cyborgs; as we go on diets, decide to get fit, and change our job. It can be found in Bourdieu's conception of the field, with contestants eagerly battling for advantage, and hip avant-garde pushing themselves to the fore. Yet Piketty's evocation of Marx points in a radically different direction, toward recognizing the long accretion of capital accumulation, and the returning weight of history this entails. It is this theme that needs to inform our analysis of contemporary social change.

Marx, as usual, had profound insight here. Despite the frequent hailing of him as a modernist, he was actually very aware of the force of history, and his writing in the *Communist Manifesto* was somewhat out of character (Stedman-Jones 2016). It is less well remembered that he also said, "In bourgeois society, therefore, the past dominates the present" (Marx and Engels 1969: 115). His metaphor that "capital is dead labour which, vampire-like, lives only by sucking living labour, and lives the more, the more labour it sucks" (Marx 1970: 342) brilliantly conveys the force of the past to haunt the present. And yet, it is revealing that even when insisting on this power, Marx resorts to a gothic metaphor that still equates the past with death and the present with life. He cannot avoid resorting to the familiar separation of the inert past and the active present, even where he queries this dualism. This is part of a bigger conceptual lacuna in contemporary social science. In this section, I explicate how our conceptions of time and change need to be radically rethought by thinking through how capital—and the inequality it generates—bears this weight of the past.

It should be clear by now that I view the integration of both spatial and temporal dimensions as fundamental if we are to really understand why inequality matters. This move has profound importance, as the social sciences have largely prioritized one of these over the other—normally spatial perspectives over temporal ones. It is possible, however, to yoke conceptions of capital as accumulation with the compelling model of the field that I laid out in Chapter 2. Bourdieu used both these perspectives in his work but failed to integrate them.[10] Thus, as I showed in Chapter 2, he has no explanation of why the "dominated" should continue to be invested in a field when they are bound to be the losers. We can redress this by recognizing that there are also temporal relations bound up with passions of the field. There is the "now" of the stakes of the field, which allows them to possess the intensity and excitement that is necessary for the people to be vested in the field itself. This is entirely in keeping with the sporting metaphor. Every game demands a distinctive start and end time (and often interval times, too). Processes of field contestation thus depend on elaborating a period of time in which the specific time of the contest takes place. At the start of a day's cricket, the umpire says "play," and its close, they say "time." When a darts match commences, the referee says "game on!"

This can most readily be understood as a separation between a now-time—in which the field is in operation—a past time, which precedes the genesis of the field, and a future time, in which the tensions of the field itself are resolved and thereby concluded. The first of these is indeed a central feature of Bourdieu's account of the development of fields, which sees their emergence as a part of the elaboration of modernity during the nineteenth century. For Bourdieu, the later nineteenth century was the crucial phase when artistic and scientific fields emerged, as "symbolic revolutions," in which artists—Manet first and foremost in the French case—broke from the patronage and authority of the state to allow painters to act "as a group conscious of its singularity, and able to invent and gradually impose the rival institutions that are constitutive of an artistic field" (Bourdieu 2018: 393).

Bourdieu, however, has no parallel conception of the "end" of the field contest. Instead, the assumption is of an endlessly reproducing autonomous field, with each generation producing its own avant garde to renew the spark of the game. But the sports player or the military general desperately wants the game to end (with themselves as winners, of course). For a field to have the intensity that is necessary for it to operate to mobilize its participants, it can't be an ongoing, perpetual process. For the field to have passion, it needs to build up to some kind of climax and conclusion. In the early history of cricket, many test matches between nations were "timeless," being played to a conclusion, however long this might take. After a famously boring match between South Africa and England in 1939 petered out in a draw, because the English players had to catch their boat home after nine days' play (spread over twelve days), all cricket test matches between nations henceforth were given a very clear time limit, normally five days. In a more serious vein, it is exactly in this way that David Roberts (2011) has brilliantly shown in his study of the modernist aesthetic, that alongside the drive for avant-garde progress and cutting-edge innovation, there is also been an equally powerful drive for "the total work of art"—the synthesis and reconciliation that marks the unification of the field itself and hence its conclusion.[11] As Rundell (2019: 78), reflecting on Roberts, puts it, under "conditions of alienated, dirempted modernity an aesthetics of 'autonomy' offered only sentimentality in the present, or genuflection before the monuments and masterpieces of the past. . . . The total work of art offered much, much more— an *escape route* from the past and the present through a subjective experience that was not only profound but also authentic" (italics mine).

By contrast, Bourdieu sees fields changing only when they are interrupted from outside by heteronomous external (usually economic) forces. Left to their own devices, fields will endlessly reproduce themselves as one vanguard replaces another. It is in this vein that he criticizes neoliberal market forces since the 1980s, which he sees as subordinating fields to economic drivers (for example, Bourdieu and Wacquant 1999). However, his implication that fields should be left as autonomous spaces in which "field-specific" values are given free rein fails to recognize the historicity of fields themselves.[12] It takes the specific and heroic moment in which fields originally form as if these endure indefinitely—so presenting them as transhistorical and persistent. By contrast, it seems more plausible to argue that over time, as capital stocks associated with the dominant players in fields grow, so fields lose their intensity, and their stakes become more trammeled by game playing and instrumentalist logics. Hence fields decompose as the participants lose interest in the stakes of the contest: The losers because they lose, time and again, the winners because they are the perpetual winners. In these conditions, intervening in other fields becomes more engaging and exciting

Therefore, it is vital to realize that field dynamics also require a culmination, and *hence that they contain the seeds of their own dissolution.* Thinking through the long-term dynamics of fields thereby leads us to the inescapable conclusion that the creation of a successful, autonomous field requires the production of a temporal ontology distinguishing past, present, and future, but also that this undercuts itself as the players on the field seek to conclude their striving through producing a *result.*

This allows us to see how the temporal ontology of the fields overlaps closely with conceptions of modernity itself (see K. Kumar 1978; Koselleck 2004), which also demarcate present from the past and future. In Blumenberg's terms, cited by Roberts (2011: 18), "Modernity was the first and only age that understood itself as an epoch, and in so doing, simultaneously created other epochs." Such theories read the past as residual and passive—which are then juxtaposed against an active present. In this framing of modernity, actions conducted in the present are seen to generate a contingent future. The past is ontologically over and can only be presented as some kind of fixed or residual order. The past has no agency.

It has been remarkably difficult to challenge this way of construing time, which has come to constitute the power of the modern transcendental. Thus, dominant sociological theories of modernity continue to draw on the conception that modern dynamic societies break from an older, stable, and fixed society (see variously K. Kumar 1978; Giddens 1971). As Latour (2012: 10), puts it, the "adjective 'modern' designates a new regime, an acceleration, a rupture, a revolution in time. When the word 'modern,' 'modernization' or 'modernity' appears, we are defining, by contrast, an archaic and stable past."

Sociologists are in thrall to this framing, which largely reflects that their own disciplinary expertise depends on differentiating complex modern societies (which they research) compared to "traditional" ones (which historians, anthropologists, archaeologists and so forth can analyze). This explains the hold of Max Weber's distinction between societies based on tradition, and those based on some kind of rationalizing modernity. Weber defines modernity by the dominance of a rational cost-benefit structure that allows agents to act with reference to their future aims, not their past habits. The intrinsic potential for dynamism, associated with this separation of ends and means, is thus tied up with the holding apart of past conditions, present agency, and future outcomes. Durkheim's (1997) functionalist rendering of this theme gives more recognition to pre-modern societies as being organic, which renders past societies as animal-like, and ultimately as "natural," but it has similar implications.

For both Weber and Durkheim, the past is ultimately static, close to "nature," and lacks the capacity to change without some kind of external stimulus or trigger. Agency—for instance, that associated with the passions and striving of the "field"—happens when individuals act reflexively in the present. Weber's thinking is perceptive here, because he brings out the tragic instability of this kind of rationality. Insofar as it can produce unanticipated outcomes that cannot be derived from prior assumptions, we are locked into an ontology of lack, in which we can never be fulfilled because we can never know what lies in front of us. In his most famous essay, "Science as a vocation," Weber dwells on the impossibility of being able to know how to live one's life in modernity, because there is no way of knowing what the outcomes of our actions will be, and because future progress will ultimately surpass our actions in the present.

We can see the architecture of these conceptions of modernity (or what Latour [1993] defines as the "modern constitution") as entailing an ontological separation between an unstable and contingent present and some version of a stable past. In this respect, conceptions of modernity are themselves performative and depend on retrofitting what actually happened into its framework (Koselleck 2004). But these perspectives are also part of modern commonsense: Koselleck (2004: 31, 22) explains how "modernity" transforms older conceptions of time that did not see the future as necessarily different from the past. By contrast, modernity sees

> a temporalization of history, at the end of which there is a peculiar form
> of acceleration which characterises modernity. . . . The future con-

tained in this progress is characterized by two main features; first, the increasing speed with which it approaches us, and second its unknown quality.

This concept of acceleration thus becomes endemic to modernity itself. Koselleck (2004: 40) traces it as "initially perceived in terms of an apocalyptic expectation of temporal abbreviation heralding the last judgement, (which) transformed itself—also from the mid eighteenth century—into a concept of historical hope." This means that sensing the present as accelerating is to project an uncertain future and identify reactionary currents, which look to preserve and reinstate the past as a means of holding these uncertainties at bay. These reactionary, conservative, romantic, and nostalgic currents of modernity make the past a passive object that needs to be reclaimed, returned to, or reinstated.

It should be clear that this modernist temporal ontology is precisely that which is disrupted when we realize that intensified capital accumulation leads to the enhanced weight of the past. The build-up of capital repudiates that the past is ontologically passive compared to an active and transformative present. Active forces from the past are actually key forces into the present, in the way that Andrew Abbott (2016) registers through evoking "historicality."[13]

In fact, classic concepts of modernity, which contrasted the world of "tradition" with that of the "new" have been under strain for many years. The modernist temporal ontology had depended on a colonial, or "orientalist" (Said 1977) rendering of the "modern" West against the orientalist global south. Imperial and colonial relations not only reinforced but also instantiated the cultural boundaries between modernity and tradition (see generally Bhambra 2007). As levels of absolute global poverty declined rapidly from the second half of the twentieth century, so the brute experience of "getting by"—the world of tradition—is declining and cannot be held up as the contrast with Western modernity (S. Hall 1992). Decolonization and new forms of political independence in the global south, linked to (unstable) economic growth further disrupted the contrast between the modern dynamic West, and "traditional" society. A growing recognition that there were multiple modernities (for example, Eisenstadt 2000) was symptomatic of the loss of certainty about what modernity was meant to entail. The increasing power of postcolonial critique was crucial to the unhinging of the classic modern temporal ontology.

It is in this light that the rise of "epochalist" thinking (Savage 2009) in the later twentieth century needs to be understood—as the last effort to shore up a modernist temporal ontology at the very moment that it was breaking down. The first major epochalist thinker of this kind was the American sociologist Daniel Bell, who proclaimed the emergence of postindustrial society as early as 1954. His vision was saturated by the optimistic progressive belief that economic growth would mark a transition to a new kind of social order:

> We stand today on the verge of a second industrial revolution . . . the development of continuous flow has now eliminated the worker almost completely . . . in this second industrial revolution there arises a new concept of work, of man as creator and regulator of delicate and precise machines. (Bell 1973: 14)

Bell's thinking drew on the powerful motif that the rise of the postwar "affluent society" (Galbraith 1958) marked a fundamental threshold in human development.[14] In contrast to scarcity and austerity, which was held to characterize previous periods in history, affluence unlocked a new set of social arrangements that broke from the modernity that earlier generations of social scientists had dissected (Zweig 1961; Goldthorpe et al. 1968, 1968b, 1969). A line could be drawn between a world left behind and a new world organized around emerging principles of consumer power, leisure opportunities, automated working practices, the decline of class antagonisms, and new kinds of privatized and individualized social relations.

Once the anchor of this originating condition of "traditional society" was eclipsed as the central reference category from which modernity could be seen to break, then acceleration itself becomes unhinged, as one theory of change is rapidly replaced by another. This explains why, since the 1960s, emphases on the ubiquity of change have taken on an increasingly hectoring, strident, and ultimately vacuous tone. During the 1980s, the claim that the world was becoming "postmodern" became a mainstay of cultural debate as a means of highlighting the loss of certainty and the rise of a commercial culture of pastiche, parody, and signification.[15] These cultural changes were often linked to globalization, the decline of mass industrial production, and the rise of "flexible" forms of production. But this is only the entry point to the badgering insistence over the past three decades that "new times" are raining down upon us incessantly.[16] This kind of epochalist thinking increasingly takes the form of appealing to this year's fashion, so conjuring up superficial novelty followed by obsolescence. It ultimately speaks to the playing out, the exhaustion, of the modern temporal ontology itself. The intensities of modern fields are being exhausted.

My account here underpins the overarching claims of my book. I have argued against Piketty's analysis of income distributions that we need a more phenomenological approach to social relations. Bourdieu's concept of the field helps provide this, but he neglects the temporal and historical aspects of field processes in favor of an overly spatialized account. The concept of capital provides a way forward. It draws attention to the tendency for resources to accumulate over time. These forces ultimately unsettle fields themselves that then unravel, and as they do so this also undermines the separation of past, present, and future on which field dynamics depend.

The rising significance of inherited capital is therefore both symptom and driver of the breakdown of modern temporal ontology. Fields of all kinds become dominated by inheritors rather than those who win their spurs through their own field-specific qualities. This process should not simply be equated with the incursion of economic capital into cultural, social, and political domains. Instead, this is a process of entropy, in which those who succeed in any specific field tend to convert their advantages to an "objectified" form that can be stored, transmitted, sold, and passed on. This usually takes the form of conversion to some kind of economic asset, which is the quintessential and hegemonic way of objectifying value, and hence contributes to the growing power of economic capital.

History therefore ultimately trumps geography. The relational power of fields, which was most marked in the early decades of modernity, is now being eclipsed as fields are decomposing, driven by internal pressures toward entropy, associated with the growing weight of capital. With this insight in mind, we can now understand contemporary social change in a different, and more historically nuanced, light.

3.3: Epochalism and Social Change Revisited

It is the commonsense of our time to insist that we are undergoing intense, endemic change. In our personal lives, this takes the form of incessant projects to improve ourselves. Organizations whip themselves up into a perpetual state of performance enhancement. Society at a global level faces the climate crisis and unprecedented medical challenges as the coronavirus pandemic has revealed all too well. New technological gear promises untold potential to remake and enhance ourselves.

I dispute the shallow and accelerationist thinking that somehow sees the solution to these problems as lying in grasping the future, through some kind of innovation or "fix." Instead, we need to come to terms with the past, which weighs down on us all. It is the major insight of inequality researchers to bring to light how this weight of the past has become ever more salient in recent decades. The argument here has a direct parallel with that of climate change and environmental sustainability. Until the second half of the twentieth century, it was assumed by modernizers that there was no price that future generations would have to pay for the extraction and use of fossil fuels. One could slash and burn into the future with impunity. It has now become abundantly clear that the carbon deposits that this extraction entailed, combined with the build up of other environmental hazards in fact mean that there is a very heavy price to pay indeed. Past activity cannot simply be wiped clean. This is exactly comparable to the social costs of inequality, which pile up to the point that they threaten social sustainability in the future. The scars of inequality, built up over centuries, fester and burn.

With this in mind, we can contest the claims of epochalism. Beliefs in speed up, transformation, and acceleration are not objective accounts of social change but a late reiteration of a still-persistent modernist ontology— but with the major bolt-on that because the original contrast with a traditional past defined by scarcity and constraint is further and further away, these idioms become locked into a spiral of ever-accelerating (indeed, vertiginous) presents, which rapidly succeed one another. These sociological theories of change thus conjure up a dazzling world of contingency, reflexivity, and dynamism—which is actually completely at odds with the growing "weight of the past" that capital accumulation entails and fails to offer an adequate handle on present-day conditions.

The arguments of eminent German sociologist Ulrich Beck are highly pertinent in this light. During the 1980s, Beck's thinking attracted major interest, both in his native Germany and later around the globe. He emphasized that classic modernity diagnosed by canonical sociologists was giving way to more reflexive versions, with the rise of systemic risks that cannot be anticipated in advance. Beck's appeal rested largely on the unanticipated way that a number of global events and crises had suddenly come to the fore during the 1980s: the fall of the communist system; HIV-AIDS; the Chernobyl disaster; global warming; mad cow disease. Beck therefore conjured up a world of growing uncertainty, in which the best-laid plans of scientists, economists, and engineers could end up producing entirely unexpected and challenging outcomes. He emphasized how these trends generated intensified reflexivity, as individuals increasingly had to weigh up different risks on their own account, without being able to trust experts, or being sure what the best course of action was. The architecture of this argument undoubtedly caught the zeitgeist of the 1980s, but it now looks dated. Beck largely extends Weber's arguments about the dominance of means-end rationality in modernity by positing a past time (classic modernity) of fixed aggregate categories, a present time characterized by contingency and breaking from this classic modern period, and a future of uncertainty. Thus, his differentiation between classical and late modernity becomes analytically equivalent to the "traditional" and "modern" societies that preoccupied Weber and Durkheim. However, because his thinking was not based on a concept of traditional society anchored in the constraints of scarcity, it becomes largely repetitive and derivative.

In retrospect, we can now see that the kind of unanticipated risks that were so evident in the 1980s, and seemed to confirm Beck's diagnosis, have faded. We now see crises of anticipated long-term threats—most notably, the utterly predictable coronavirus pandemic in 2020 (which was nonetheless surprising to governments around the world outside Asia), as well as the declining power of antibiotics, the growing threat of climate change, the significance of artificial intelligence, the economic instability produced by deregulated capitalism, the accentuation of geopolitical tensions, and the like. Far from a world of contingency and dynamism where "everything that's solid melts into air," we in fact are driven by the predictability of long-term processes, many of which had been repressed or ignored in the giddy search for novelty. But, and this is my crucial point, epochalist thinking is singularly badly disposed to offer the tools needed to recognize this "weight of the past," as it is locked into projections of novelty and contingency.

Epochalist thinking therefore reworks and indeed accelerates the temporal ontology of modernity even as the ground is being cut away from the foundations of this thinking. So long as the past can only be rendered as passive, lost, and fixed, the only way of registering social change is by breaking from this past, with the result that an energized and active present needs to be reinvented on a regular basis.[17]

The end point of this current of thinking is revealed in the subtle restatement of this epochalist theory of acceleration, that developed by Hartmut Rosa. Rosa is very clear that he is working in the paradigm of modernity (for example, Rosa 2013: 24), which he seeks to extend by arguing that acceleration is becoming even more trenchant than it was even in the twentieth century, so that it is now more fundamental than other sociological processes, such as differentiation, rationalization, individualization, and domestication (Rosa 2013: 60–61).

Rosa draws extensively on Koselleck to note how theories of acceleration date back to the eighteenth century, but then extends his argument to claim (following Lubbe) that the "time horizon"—the boundary—of the present is contracting. He pursues this theme by insisting on the triplicate nature of acceleration driven by technological shifts, social change, and the pace of life. In reiterating the fundamental differentiation of the present from past, he identifies how "presents" are now replacing one another ever more rapidly. He traces these faster shifts from generational to intergenerational paces of change:[18]

> I argue then that acceleration of social change as a whole is most clearly legible in the state of intergenerational relations: from a premodern situation in which structural and cultural stock was simply passed down through many generations, it led to a modernity in which, as Ansgar Weyman observes, "generations (functioned) as innovative and structure building collective actors," which thus allowed one to read off transformations from the change of generations, and then finally to a late modernity in which social relations are subject to fundamental change within the timespan allotted to a single generation. (Rosa 2013: 113)

It is difficult to square this emphasis on the decline of intergenerational transmission with the actual reality of returning inheritance. It is difficult to know how Rosa reconciles these actual trends with his claims about acceleration, other than to assume he is taking people's superficial perceptions as if they were literally true.[19]

This leads me to question Rosa's emphasis that identity is mutable and transformable, a matter of contestation and the challenging of boundaries. For Rosa, "in a society where the past has lost its obligating power, where the future is conceived as unforeseeable and uncontrollable, 'situational' or present-oriented patterns of identity dominate" (Rosa 2013: 146). Here, the expansion of the "present" is a means of emphasizing the contingency and importance of identity.[20] Choosing an identity becomes part and parcel of being an effective agent.[21] In fact, if we recognize the power of the past, these claims about fleeting identities look less plausible.

We have now reached the key part of my argument, which largely restates the crucial emphases of the philosophers of time Bergson and Whitehead, as well as their more recent exponent Gilles Deleuze. We should remember again Bergson's vital criticisms of defining time in terms of spatialized conceptions, such as "boundaries," "horizons," periods, or epochs (see more generally McLure 2005). We should heed these philosophical reflections regarding the logical impossibility of breaking time into instants because of the significance of force and velocity. The "formal definition of velocity requires reference to more than a single instant. It requires reference to a neighbourhood of instants. . . . No instantaneous fact can have energy, etc., intrinsic to it" (Hammerschmidt 1949: 20; see also Massey 2005: 76f). Isabelle Stengers links this orientation to the pragmatist William James's critique of the "specious present" and his argument that "the practically cognized present is no knife-edge, with a certain breadth of its own on which we sit perched. . . . The unit of composition of our time is a duration, with a bow and a stern, as it were" (quoted in Stengers 2011: 59). It follows that attempts to place boundary posts around temporal periods are bound to misconceive the nature of duration itself, *as a force that presses onward*. Any attempt to carve out the "present" as differentiated from past and future, which is inherent in conceptions of modernity, is premised on an unsustainable temporal ontology.

Real duration is that duration which gnaws on things, and leaves on them the mark of its tooth. (Bergson 1998: 46)

This refocusing of time as duration explicates the impossibility of rendering time as discrete events and observations—such as measured in linear time periods, dates, or times. Trying to define time horizons, such as those captured in the idea of the "present," appears somewhat akin to finding the pot of gold at the end of the rainbow. The lure is very clear, but that spot can never be found.

3.4: Conclusion

Focusing on wealth accumulation does not simply mean bringing a relatively neglected dimension into the analysis of inequality—though it certainly means that too! It involves a deep-rooted concern to understand capital as the weight of history, which brings with it a much stronger awareness of the power of time and duration than is found in much of social science. Within this reorientation, the claim of Piketty and his associates—that we are returning to the past—resonates clearly. It convincingly critiques the kind of shallow yet ubiquitous epochalist reasoning that has become so predominant in recent decades. And it extends our thinking to understand more broadly how duration is a force whose weight lies ever more heavily on the present.

So, now that we have broadened Piketty's beachhead intervention into a fuller appreciation of the significance of time, history, and duration, we are better placed to recognize a striking feature of social life today. Notwithstanding all our excitement about new gadgets, robots, and devices, we are actually increasingly in the thrall of the past. Contemporary society is trammeled by previous rounds of accumulation that are fundamental to our now-time. In the early twenty-first century, history exercises a hold over the present that has not been seen for centuries. The bold revolutionary hopes—endemic to modernity—of breaking from the past and ushering in a brave new world have been dashed. The debris of the past—accumulated in capital, urban infrastructures, military power, venerable institutions of learning, privileged families, and blue chip companies—now dominates the social landscape. The deeply held hopes for modernity to quash the past in the call of a brave new future have indeed burned brightly, but their light is going out.

My argument about inequality and the weight of the past is now in place. Later chapters will use this platform to show how inequality is seeing the return of past historical forms and the active reassertion of the old. I will pay particular attention to the reviving significance of empire, racial divides, elites, and urbanism. As a counterpart, I will also show how the kinds of misleading "presentist" self-understandings generated by modernity need to be placed in a more historical perspective that will allow some of the misconceptions about the significance of inequality to be rectified.

PART TWO

Inequality, Empire, and the

Decline of Nations

4

The Ranking of Nations

In Part 1, I argued that inequality research matters because it addresses our current state of affairs—our now-time. It does this by reasserting the importance of *duration*. This involves resisting the blandishments of an epochalism that sees the past as "left behind." History is not a skating rink, around which we can swoop to pick up attractive bouquets of flowers hither and thither. Instead, history has a force and a direction that cannot be reversed. Understanding our now-time means that we have to go beyond modernity's mundane differentiation of time into linear and separable blocks of past, present, and future. Recognizing the logic of capital accumulation and the build up of wealth in recent decades impresses on us that the force of the past is increasing. Tracing through the logic of Pierre Bourdieu's conception of field analysis, I have argued that the weight of the past erodes the spatial dynamics of open contestation, competition, and "organized striving," which lie at the heart of field relationships. With this development, our sociological toolkit, developed to analyze a modernity that is now unravelling, itself needs to be recharged.

I can imagine that some readers may have read Part 1 quizzically, possibly even with some frustration. They may understandably be wondering what these abstract reflections actually entail for understanding the stuff of inequality: poverty, domination, exclusion, institutional racism, patriarchy, class exploitation, stigmatization, and marginalization; the systematic ways that many lives are stunted while a few enjoy bloated privilege. Actually, these abstractions have a lot of things to say about precisely these questions.

I start by tackling, head on, how attention to history changes our perspective by reflecting on *The Spirit Level* by Richard Wilkinson and Kate Pickett (2010). This is the most iconic study to address the "so what?" question of why inequality matters, through its demonstration that the world's most unequal nations are also those with the most glaring social problems. Their arguments are compelling, but I show how their analytical strategy of spatial comparison obscures the force of history. In fact, what they demonstrate is the elaboration of an utterly compelling politics of *ranking* that has come to hold huge sway over contemporary life. This process, which sociologist Marion Fourcade calls "ordinalization," itself generates inequality and is a feature of the entropy of fields discussed in Chapter 3. I will bring out how the ranking of nations testifies to tensions about the unit and scale of analysis that reveal the geopolitics of inequality. Here I introduce the argument that will thread through the remainder of this book: that the increasing weight of the past is also implicated in the resurgence of imperial forms of territorial governance.

Another narrative sparkline will set off on this journey.

4.1: The Spirit Level

When Richard Wilkinson and Kate Pickett's *The Spirit Level* was published in 2010, it caused a huge stir. It rapidly became the most influential British work of twenty-first century social science. Selling over a quarter of a million copies, its key argument, that more unequal societies proliferate social problems and hence that more equality is better for everyone, engaged policy as well as academic communities, even leading to the formation of a high-profile campaigning group, The Equality Trust, which "works to improve the quality of life in the UK by reducing economic inequality."[1] It was also controversial for making no bones about its radical mission, thus challenging the view that social science should stay out of political debate. There was a huge push-back from political right-wing commentators who objected to its insistence that inequality was a bad thing.[2]

The Spirit Level proved profoundly important, because it gave the crispest and most direct response to the "so what?" question—why inequality actually matters. The research discussed in Part 1 sees inequality as a bad thing,

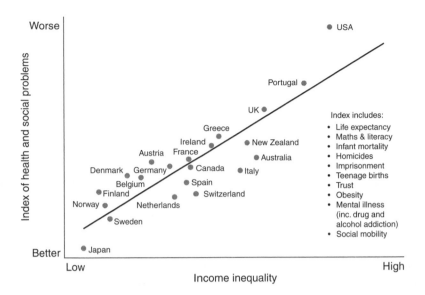

FIGURE 4.1: The correlation between high income inequality and health / social problems in selected nations

Source: Richard G. Wilkinson and Kate E. Pickett, *The Spirit Level: Why More Equal Societies Almost Always Do Better* (London: Allen Lane, 2010), figure 2.2. Copyright © 2009, 2010 by Richard Wilkinson and Kate Pickett. Reproduced by permission of Penguin Books Ltd. (The "Index includes" text was added by author.)

but the precise reasons for this assessment are assumed, left dangling. The income distribution trends highlighted by Piketty and Saez certainly show an upturn in income inequality in recent decades—but this was also a period when global absolute poverty fell to the lowest levels in recorded history. Pierre Bourdieu's study of French lifestyles reveals the systematic partitioning of cultural taste and leisure and its overlap with economic inequality, but perhaps this is just the segmentation of lifestyles, as market researchers would argue. Is his emphasis on these divides as driven by "domination" simply the typical projection of a left-bank Parisian intellectual?[3] And while there is no gainsaying the growth of wealth capital and inheritance, it is not clear that the "dis-inherited" feel they are thereby losing out. Jonathan Mijs (2019) has indeed shown that popular beliefs in meritocracy have, if anything, increased in many nations, at the same time that these capital stocks have risen dramatically.

It is for these reasons that Wilkinson and Pickett's research mattered so much, because they placed the political stakes front and center. By establishing correlations between higher levels of income inequality and poor outcomes across a range of issues that are utterly tangible for real people—how long you live; your health, well-being, experience of crime, and so on—they make a compelling case that inequality directly affect people's lives and well-being. Inequality is not just an abstract social scientific concern.

But the implications of the *Spirit Level* are actually not as simple as they initially appear. On one hand, the book brilliantly shows how inequality—and not just poverty or bad public welfare services—matters. It is also an exemplar in how interdisciplinary research could tackle the challenge of inequality in a more innovative way than when researchers in any of the social science disciplines (such as economics or sociology) construe it as a specialist subfield in their area of expertise.[4] However, these strengths came at a major analytical price. As I now show, the price was their dependence on a spatializing comparative method that—powerful though it undoubtedly is—fails to grasp the historicity of inequality.

Figure 4.1 is the iconic visualization that rammed home the message that inequality is damaging. It compares differing amounts of income inequality in numerous developed nations on the horizontal x-axis, with a range of health and social problems on the vertical y-axis. A line drawn through these observations demonstrates a strong association: Countries with higher income inequality also have worse problems—on multiple dimensions. On the face of it, this is a deeply disturbing analysis. And, just as in Piketty's research, the simple narrative sparkline does the core narrative work.[5] The story is compelling: those nations that are most unequal (notably, the United States) also have the worst social problems. Those nations that are least unequal (notably, Japan) score much better. There is a cluster of "good European" (mostly Scandinavian) nations that also report much better outcomes, and some "bad European" (especially Portugal and the United Kingdom) nations that are more akin to the United States. The United States turns out to be the worst-performing nation on a range of inequality metrics: rather than being a beacon of progress, it turns out to be dysfunctional, beset by systematic social problems. This is not an incidental or minor issue: Since its independence in 1776, the United States has been held up by many as the world's most iconic progressive nation, but it is now unraveling as a dystopian, fractured, inhumane nation. Most other nations fit somewhere between these two poles. There are no cases of relatively unequal nations that have relatively few social problems, or equal ones that have relatively more.

This analytical strategy is entirely consistent with Amartya Sen's (2009: 38) call for a comparative strategy that avoids transcendental claims about the value of equality, but focuses instead on tracing "realization-focused comparisons . . . interested in the removal of manifest injustice from the world that they saw." Wilkinson and Pickett (2010: 2) are very clear about their deliberate repeated, symphonic deployment of a core visual motif to make this basic point:

> Most of the graphs that we use in this book are charts linking income inequality to different health and social problems. . . . In all of these graphs we put income inequality along the horizontal line at the bottom (the x-axis), so societies with low levels of inequality are at the left, and societies with high levels of inequality are towards the right of the graph. . . . The different health and social outcomes are shown on the vertical line (the y-axis) on the left side of the graph.

This mode of visualization is deployed no less than thirty-eight times to examine the impact of inequality on no less than twenty-nine kinds of incredibly diverse outcomes, ranging from the number of patents (used as a measure of innovation) and mortality to imprisonment and teenage birth rates. A few bar charts and cartoons break up the presentation, but they are much fewer in number. Tellingly, no statistical tables appear in the body of the text. Therefore, although this is a work of considerable quantitative dexterity, it does not read as a typical detached social science report. It is a quintessential use of the visualized symphonic aesthetic to write a narrative of great moral power. As with Piketty's work, it is a classic exemplar of how simple visualization can be used to great effect to disrupt social science paradigms.

The Spirit Level uses a telling counterfactual to advance its narrative, to show that there is no connection between economic advance and well-being.[6] Some of the world's wealthiest nations have relatively poor life expectancy (for example, the United States), but others score well (for example, Norway). The nation with the best life expectancy (Japan) is about as wealthy overall as Canada, Belgium, the Netherlands, Ireland, or Denmark, which have much lower life expectancies. There is no narrative sparkline joining up these dots—just a largely random collection of observations. This adds to the critique of the modernizing story: Economic prosperity by itself does not produce social good. And this crisp message disputes the main policy mantra since the 1950s—that economic growth is the prime driver of human advance.

This visual repertoire has become a mainstay of those demonstrating that inequality matters. In 2012, the Canadian economist Miles Corak (2013) produced a similar graphic to that used in *The Spirit Level* to show that those nations with the largest Gini coefficients for income inequality also had higher "intergenerational earnings elasticities" (Figure 4.2). The relationship between parents' position in the income distribution and that of their children tended to be stronger in more unequal nations. This finding was taken up by Princeton economist Alan Krueger, the chair of the Council of Economic Advisors. The finding underpinned Barack Obama's argument that inequality was a growing threat to the American way of life.[7] The United States, which has long prided itself on being open and meritocratic, has actually turned out to be a relatively closed society with limited social mobility and numerous entrenched social problems.

What is important here is not only the scale and ambition of these comparative analyses, but the narrative style used to make the case. Although representative quantitative national surveys form the basis of the work, these are not presented in standard statistical formats. Quantitative analyses in a visualizing narrative strategy carries the argument. But this approach also gives cause for concern.

Some of the variables being analyzed don't actually vary that much. Most notably, in 2005, life expectancy only varied between 77 years in Ireland and 81.6 years in Japan. Variance is greater on attitude questions—notably on whether people are trusting—but this isn't directly a measure of well-being.[8] For some other variables with greater variance, especially that for teenage pregnancy, it is not straightforward to see high rates as indicative of low social well-being (Duncan 2007). More generally, however, this style of argument falls foul of the most standard of statistical objections that "correlation is not causation." Simply showing that the United States is unusually unequal, and that it also has much worse health and life chances than more equal countries does not actually demonstrate that inequality is causing the

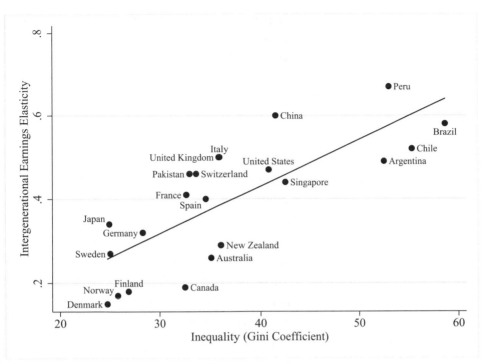

FIGURE 4.2: The "Great Gatsby Curve"

Note: Nations plotted by their Gini coefficient and extent of intergenerational earnings elasticity.
Source: Miles Corak, "Income Inequality, Equality of Opportunity, and Intergenerational Mobility," *Journal of Economic Perspectives* 27, no. 3 (2013): 79–102, figure 1. Supplemented by data provided by Miles Corak.

problem: there may be other factors at work. Or perhaps the United States is simply a strange outlier. This objection is the more telling because the small number of cases that are used to make the argument—twenty-two nations—is a long way short of being able to establish statistically significant associations.

This objection can be addressed by recognizing the use of repetition to make its point. I have already shown how Piketty deftly uses this with his repeated use of U-shaped visuals. Wilkinson and Pickett are similar. In this way, they do not rely on demonstrating causal relationships from one set of observations alone. The standard principles of statistical testing were elaborated as procedures to draw causal inferences from analyses of distinct, standalone data sets, usually survey based.[9] However, the repeated revelation of similar or consistent patterns across numerous comparable cases—such as those presented in *The Spirit Level*—seeks to establish causality through repetition. This form of explanation is commonplace in the humanities, notably in history. Historians extrapolate from a large battery of sources, drawing the most likely inferences from whatever sources are available, rather than establishing causality from the application of inferential statistical procedures on singular sources. This approach is consistent with large-scale, symphonic comparison, involving the narrative unpacking of patterns, often using visual motifs, which inequality researchers have championed.[10] It is also a method that unites sensitivities from the humanities and the social sciences.

That there is no fundamental difference between the social sciences, history, and geography is part of my critique of the modernist temporal ontology in Chapter 3. The view that the social sciences are fundamentally different from the humanities used to be commonly argued even in the last decade of the twentieth century but is now unsustainable. As late as 1991, the sociologist John Goldthorpe insisted that historians had a fundamentally different research orientation compared to social scientists, because they had no choice but to conduct research on the "relics"—the archival sources—left behind from the past, whereas sociologists (and by extension, other social scientists) had the capacity to conduct fresh fieldwork, using methods of their own design, to test hypotheses that they have theoretically established as pertinent.[11] He thus evokes the familiar modernist distinction between those in the humanities with no active agency to choose their sources (which lie in the dust of the past), compared to the heroic social scientists who can go forth and stride into the present to use cutting-edge research protocols unconstrained by precedent. This argument was contested even in 1991,[12] and it is obsolete today. In the wake of the dramatic expansion of social science data, nearly all quantitative social scientists conduct secondary analyses of surveys that have been collected in the past—and not only the recent past—and over which they have had little direct control in setting up.[13] Indeed, Piketty's crucial contribution lies very much in his mobilization of long-term historical data, designed by taxation authorities, as I showed in Chapter 1. Social scientists now rely on their relics, too. By contrast, humanities-oriented researchers (such as anthropologists, historians, and some sociologists) are more likely to do fresh fieldwork in the here and now—in the form of ethnography, oral history, qualitative interviews, and the like. The increasing weight of the past is also exerting its influence in the academy, too, and in this process undermining any useful distinction between history and social science.

Although the objection that correlation does not equate to causation can therefore be deflected, I need to turn to a more pressing issue regarding the inattention to time, history, and complex understandings of spatial dynamics. Extrapolating across cross-sectional surveys provides snapshots in time rather than a temporal series. Spatially, compared to Bourdieu's sophisticated field analysis (which lays out a complex national field though clustering multiple indicators of lifestyles and social positions), nations are reduced to a basket of indicators.[14] Figure 4.1 (and its many counterparts) thus turns out to be part of a bigger geopolitics about the use of national metrics that themselves entail the generation of inequality.

4.2: The Ordinal Comparison of Nations

Marion Fourcade (2016, see also Fourcade and Healey 2013) has emphasized how ordinalization—the rank ordering of observations—has become a major driver across broad swathes of life today. The principles of ranking have come to have a ubiquitous presence. The construction of league tables originated in sporting competition—harking back to the field relationships I discussed in Chapter 2. In the past, much sporting contest was organized around the one-off, head-to-head contest in which the drama of the clash between two players, only one of whom could win, lay at the crux. Medieval jousting is the clearest rendition of the brutality of this kind of head-to-head struggle. But over time, sports contests through ranked league competitions have steadily become more prominent compared to the knockout. As a boy growing up in England in the 1960s and 1970s, it seemed to me that that the sporting year was broken into epic head-to-head battles: the FA Cup Final, the Grand National horserace, cricket test matches, Wimbledon tennis, boxing, the Oxford-Cambridge boat race. These icons still glitter, but less brightly, and league principles now dominate. No soccer team would rather win the British FA Cup than the Premier League. Wimbledon victories are only one component of the jostling for global rankings. Does anyone even watch the Oxford-Cambridge boat race? Even the Olympic Games, the quintessential sporting head-to-head contest, is increasingly rendered in league table format by the preeminence given to national medals tables. The proliferation of league rankings means that one-off outlier results, in which an outsider pulls off a glorious surprise, are discounted by stacking them into a more predictable series of results, generating more stable and hence "reliable" and manageable set of rankings. (I am not a soccer fan, but since as a boy my local team was Wimbledon FC, even I was entranced by its astonishing FA Cup victory in 1988, having only been members of the Football League for eleven years. However, their success was not to be sustained.) To return to the analogy with Bourdieu's field analysis, rankings reduce the passion and intensity of any particular sporting contest and testify to the power of the "top dogs" to dominate. They mark precisely the entropy of field dynamics, as I laid out in Chapter 3.

Ranking has been extended outside sports to the evaluation of schools, hospitals, businesses, and universities. Indeed, any kind of entity can be, and is, ranked, simply by virtue of being an entity. Principles of ranking have increasingly been rolled out to measure effectiveness even in areas where metrics are intuitively difficult to establish—charities, philanthropic giving, cities, and so on. These ranking strategies have become an essential feature of market-led (neoliberal) policy making, which has played an increasingly prominent role as state-led intervention has been cut back (for example, in education; see Ball 2003). The ranking process is supposed to create incentives for entities to do better, encouraging them to reflect on how to improve their performance and so advance up the league tables. This process is also expected to be driven by informed consumers who wish to be treated by the best hospitals or to send their children to the finest schools, creating quasi-market pressures that reward those institutions whose metrics stack up most appealingly. This same imperative forces agents, people, and companies to enhance their market appeal by climbing the rankings ladder. As agents learn to play the game more effectively, this market-oriented logic is held to drive up overall quality.

An extensive literature on the construction and "performativity" of metrics insists that they cannot be an objective measure of what they claim to make transparent (see the classic work of Power 1997 and Strathern 2000). We can see this process in terms of the principles of field analysis. Organizations of all kinds are made to compete with one another in field-like spaces where rankings are used to determine winners and losers. But rankings impose a purely vertical logic onto the field, rather than permitting more complex differentiation according to a wider constellation of qualities. Fabien Accominotti and Daniel Tadmon (2020) have shown how using quantitative rather than qualitative measures generates more dispersion and hierarchy. When individuals are asked to evaluate the same colleagues using quantitative scores, rather than qualitative comments, this leads to those colleagues being more differentiated as a pecking order. The very act of ranking accentuates hierarchy. This is thus part of the steady march of the decomposition of fields and the rising power of the "volume of capital," as I have sketched out in Part 1. And so ranking is both a product and a driver of the breakdown of fields that are decomposing through the weight of capital operating within them.

Rankings only operate within parameters that define the population (of organizations, groups, individuals, or whatever) that is to be ranked. In the fields of business, commerce, and sport, global rankings have become more prominent, but nationally organized rankings predominate among public sector institutions, because they convey stakes and can drive funding and resources. In this ordering complex, there is an entropic principle by which rankers are themselves increasingly prone to be ranked. Nation-states rank operations within their territories. But nation-states are themselves increasingly being ranked. This is an area where inequality research has become strategically powerful. Since the 1930s, nation-states have conventionally been ranked by their levels of economic growth, as measured conventionally by gross domestic product.[15] These were often complemented by standard demographic measures (population size, life expectancy, and so forth), which have for many decades been available across most nations, even though in some cases the evidential basis for them remains shaky (especially in many poor nations with a weak public research infrastructure).[16] However, ranking has considerably extended national metrics based only on these indicators to include a far greater basket of social, cultural, and well-being indicators, and more specifically to *deploy inequality as a ranking metric*.

This obsession with national metrics seemed a strange endeavor twenty years ago, when the nation-state was thought to be giving way to forces of globalization. At that time, emphases on mobility, flows, and flux, empirically anchored since the early 1990s around theories of globalization, led to a widespread critique of "methodological nationalism" and a growing sense that nations were being eclipsed by diasporic formations (see memorably Appadurai 1996; Glick Schiller and Wimmer 2003; Urry 2000). Global flows of money, media images, people, commodities, and ideas (Appadurai 1996; Castells 1996, 1997) and the "eclipse of space by time" (Harvey 1989; Giddens 1990) had rendered the contemporary world as an increasingly cosmopolitan melee.

Since this heady moment of the 1990s, there has been a marked shift away from the view that nations have been eclipsed (see generally Calhoun 2007). Looking back now, the conjecture that globalization would carry all before it can be seen as fallout from the collapse of communism and the giddy currents that heralded it as the end of history (Fukuyama 1992). Now, the political appeal of nationalism across many parts of the globe points in a different direction: an enhanced politics of national securitization. In fact, the supposed revival of nationalism is not to be taken at face value. The ubiquity of ranking actually testifies to the subordination of national specificity to overarching global parameters. This process was memorably captured by John Meyer and his colleagues (Meyer et al. 1997: 145–146), who argued that nations have become preeminent only because a wider form of global culture sees them as the only possible building blocks of "world society":

> We are trying to account for a world whose societies, organized as nation-states, are structurally similar in many unexpected dimensions and change in unexpectedly similar ways. A hypothetical example may be useful to illustrate our arguments. . . . If an unknown society were "discovered" on a previously unknown island, it is clear that many changes would occur. A government would soon form, looking something like a modern state with many of the usual ministries and agencies. Official recognition by other states and admission to the United Nations would ensue. The society would be analyzed as an economy, with standard types of data, organizations, and policies for domestic and international transactions. Its people would be formally reorganized as citizens with many familiar rights, while certain categories of citizens—children, the elderly, the poor—would be granted special protection. Standard forms of discrimination, especially ethnic and

gender based, would be discovered and decried. The population would be counted and classified in ways specified by world census models. Modern educational, medical, scientific, and family law institutions would be developed.

Twenty-some years after it was proffered in 1997, this appears as both brilliantly astute but also wildly overoptimistic. Would we expect "standard forms of discrimination" (whatever they are) to be delineated and combatted in a new nation today? Would we expect the principles of citizenship rights to be so clearly laid out as a matter of course? I return to these points later in the chapter. Meyer's bigger claim, however, remains compelling. Nations are locked in an increasing battery of measures to evaluate and rank them, like it or not. There is no prospect for a nation to opt out of this process by claiming it is operating with principles that are incommensurable with such metrics—which will be applied, come what may. When the British government tried to opt out of a battery of national rankings that exposed their failure to effectively manage the coronavirus pandemic of 2020 by claiming that it was too soon to make comparative judgments, they were held up to ridicule. In fact, many metrics, notably the credit ratings of nations, come to have huge provenance for the economic fortunes of nations.

In the past twenty years, drivers associated with the Millennium Development Goals (later the Sustainable Development Goals) have driven this ranking complex. Chapter 1 discusses how these drove a renewed concern to measure absolute poverty rates, despite the doubts of social scientists who worried about whether it was meaningful to come up with a clear global poverty line. It is not incidental that these goals have encouraged metricization and have also used inequality variables as part of this repertoire. As Jeffrey Sachs (2012: 2206) put it:

> By packaging these priorities into an easily understandable set of eight goals, and by establishing measurable and timebound objectives, the MDGs [Millennium Development Goals] help to promote global awareness, political accountability, improved metrics, social feedback, and public pressures. As described by Bill Gates, the MDGs have become a type of global report card for the fight against poverty for the 15 years from 2000 to 2015. As with most report cards, they generate incentives

to improve performance, even if not quite enough incentives for both rich and poor countries to produce a global class of straight-A students.

Inequality research has thus come to play an important place in this expansion of metrics that evaluates "national performance" in an extended comparative frame. In this light, we can see better the importance of the project of elaborating Distributional National Accounts associated with Piketty and the team at the World Inequality Lab in Paris.[17] Their work is motivated by their political concern to extend the tradition of research originally inspired by Simon Kuznets, who elaborated national measures for both economic growth (in the form of Gross National Product) and inequality (distributional accounts). However, only the former was effectively consolidated and established into clearly institutionalized measures.[18] Piketty and his group see themselves as completing Kuznets's half-finished project to include inequality measures to round out measures of national accounts, which include inequality indicators. These interventions will assist with decentering economic growth as the only—or even main—criterion for assessing national performance. The fact that the world's wealthiest nation, the United States, or those with the highest growth rates, such as China, score very badly on inequality measures indicates how this research will be very significant in providing a more rounded comparative assessment of national economies.

4.3: Eurocentrism, Empire, and the Return of History

My querying about how ranking unsettles national autonomy and places nations into a competitive and hierarchical space leads me to turn to a theme that is central to the later parts of my book. I emphasized in Chapter 3 that we need to make Bourdieu's field analysis more historical. A fundamental feature of this requires it be to be "despatialized" by detaching it from its implicit association with "nation-spaces." This argument has already been made by those writing from a postcolonial perspective, in which the entropy of fields is linked to the resurgence of imperial formations.[19] Here I am indebted to recent scholarship in international relations and sociology, where there is an increasing current emphasizing how nations do not simply act as internal containers for their own fields of striving, but are arrayed on a global field of contestation and embody the striving for imperial power. Juilian Go (for example, 2011) has adapted Bourdieu's field analysis to emphasize the power of empires, and this recognition of the renewal of empire is an increasing refrain (see, for instance, K. Kumar 2010, 2019; Chatterjee 2012, 2017; Steinmetz 2005, 2013). This is a different perspective on empire to that which Hardt and Negri (2000) famously appeal. For them, empire is the product of globalized capitalism and reflects the erosion of national sovereignty. "The concept of empire is characterized by a lack of boundaries: Empire's rule has no limits" (Hardt and Negri 2000: xiv). By contrast, a field analysis of empires entails seeing them as competitive, territorial formations, akin to Parag Khana's (2008: 1) perspective when he notes that "these days it is not fashionable to speak of empires. Empires are aggressive, mercantilist relics supposedly consigned to the dustbin of history with Britain, France, and Portugal post-World War II retrenchment." Importantly, he goes onto argue that global relationships can only be understood today with respect to the tensions among three global empires: the United States, Europe, and China.

This theme, that imperial forces are returning in significance and intensity and are a crucial aspect of the return of history, may initially seem an odd jumping-off point to reflect on the proliferation of national ranking exercises. After all, the proliferation of ranking appears on the face of it to efface history, defaulting to a spatializing strategy rather than one that takes historicity more seriously. I therefore want to bring out how they actually register the revival of imperial modes of expertise.

I commence my arguments by reflecting on the expertise and authority that is entailed in index construction. Sally Merry (2016) has examined how the construction of composite indexes has become such a rife industry in the aftermath of Millennium Development Goals, and points to the political and intellectual compromises entailed by such well-intentioned work. Her study of the construction of composite indexes on gender violence, sex trafficking, and human rights reveals the tensions between statisticians drawn to commensurable measures versus advocates and campaigners attuned to the specific contexts of gender violence. These latter are attuned to the difficulties of summing across contexts in the way that transnational

measurements demand. Time and again, scholars close to the actual experiences of gender violence in diverse national settings and who insist on
their specificity rub up against statisticians who need to sum across such
particularities in order to create an index with global provenance. It follows
from the very nature of the ranking exercise that the statistical voice is the
one that generally wins out. And indeed, this ranking of nations using a
basket of indicators (however good and important these indicators are) represents a marked break from long traditions of scholarship that insist that
qualitative, rather than purely quantitative, comparisons are essential to
comprehend national specificity. I have already traced a similar battle with
respect to the delineation of poverty thresholds in Chapter 1. What is lost in
these rankings is the sensitivity, powerfully championed by disciplines such
as history or anthropology, which insists on the careful qualitative unraveling of national, local, and global processes.[20]

What is at stake here is contrasting the authority of text and language-based
expertise on the one hand, and quantification and scientific expertise on the
other. The hegemony of linguistic models of expertise has been a fundamental feature of previous imperial modes of governance, in which jurisdiction in an imperial terrain was stamped by a language of rule: Latin, English,
French, Spanish, and so on. This kind of linguistic expertise became locked
into a global assertion of supremacy. Pascale Casanova's (2008) study of how
global cultural relations have historically been defined according to the writ of
the French language is telling. Until the later twentieth century, French operated as the global meridian for the written word—the Greenwich Mean Time
of language. Casanova emphasizes that this writ cannot be rendered as simple
supplanting, in which the French language wiped out or subordinated its com-
petitors. Instead, it constituted the high ground of excellence, against which
other languages had to compete from more marginal positions. French was
thereby the central reference point in a global literary field that writers from
all other nations ultimately had to accept, even if through gritted teeth. It is
precisely this linguistic domination, underscored by the cultural values of the
metropolitan powers and their capacity to marginalize languages from other
parts of the globe as inferior and in need of "civilization," that defined the
global power of imperialism in the modern period.[21] It was in this register that
Frantz Fanon's memorably mused that "the more the black Antillean assimi-
lates the French language, the whiter he gets."[22]

This kind of dominance based on the hold of text and writing is however now waning. Plenty of evidence suggests that from the perspective of traditional, canonical forms of national cultural capital, that this is indeed the case. Nowhere is this more apparent than when we reflect on Bourdieu's (1979 [1984]) study, *Distinction,* introduced in Chapter 2, which reveals his own immersion in French—just as Casanova's (2008) "world republic of letters" indicates. There is no disputing, however, Bourdieu's profoundly antiimperialist politics. His active campaigning role during the Algerian wars of independence in the 1950s is well attested, though as Julian Go (2013) shows, Bourdieu was nonetheless unable to fully shake off a metropolitan French perspective, which his *Distinction* fully exemplifies. At the time of its publication in 1979, it was uncontroversial—"doxic," to use his terms—to assume this French frame of reference. He was steeped in the view that French culture was globally preeminent to the extent that its reference points had universal significance. And indeed, the global reception of Bourdieu's study indicates that the French example was taken to be symptomatic of broader, generalizable patterns (see Santoro et al. 2018). By drawing attention to the cultural distinction of the educated middle and upper classes, he implicitly draws out their affiliation to a Franco-European tradition. The detailed survey questions underpin Figure 2.1 inquire about taste for sixteen painters: seven French (Braque, Buffet, Renoir, Rousseau, Utrillo, Vlaminck, and Watteau), two Italian (Leonardo and Raphael), three Spanish (Dali, Goya, and Picasso), two Dutch / Flemish (Brueghel and Van Gogh), one Russian (Kandinsky), and one American (Warhol). The picture is slightly less Francocentric, but no less Eurocentric, when asking about music. Of the sixteen musical works he asks about, two are by Italians ("Four Seasons" by Vivaldi, "La Traviata" by Verdi), one Armenian ("Sabre Dance" by Khachaturian), one Hungarian ("Hungarian Rhapsodies" by Liszt), three German ("Well-Tempered Clavier" and "Art of Fugue" by Bach, "Twilight of the Gods" by Wagner), two Austrian ("Eine kleine Nachtmusik" by Mozart, "Blue Danube" by Strauss, Jr.), two Russian ("Firebird Suite" by Stravinsky and "Scheherazade" by Rimsky-Korsakov) and four French ("L'Arlésienne" by Bizet, "Le marteau sans maître" by Boulez, "Concerto for the left hand" and "L'enfant et les Sortileges" by Ravel). Remarkably, only one musical work was by an anglophone composer ("Rhapsody in Blue" by Gershwin). The dominance of French cultural references is most apparent in the questions asked about singers, who are all French, with the exceptions of the Spaniard Luis Mariano and Petula Clark.

These cultural references are therefore steeped in French icons with a few honorable additions from a wider European canon. Even so, cultural works from Britain, Scandinavia, and most of eastern and southern Europe are absent. Not a single English cultural figure (with the exception of Petula Clark who was actually more famous in France) is mentioned. The lack of American cultural producers (apart from Warhol and Gershwin) looks remarkable from an early twenty-first century perspective. The complete absence of figures from South America, Africa, Asia, and Australasia is a telling indicator of the Eurocentrism underpinning his study.

This kind of analysis is now impossible from the perspective of the twenty-first century. It represents the last blast from the very brief period of world history in which European hegemony held sway. In 1600, China and India dominated the global economy with two-thirds of the total world production. There is considerable debate about the timing of the relative decline of Asian economic power, with some historians pushing back the date to as late as the end of the eighteenth century (see Bayly 2004). Regardless of the exact timing, the nineteenth century saw first the European, then the United States, become the most significant forces in the world economy. This is the period when sociologists analyzed the rise of modernity, seeing this as almost coterminous with the rise of the European "West" itself. At the peak of empire in the later nineteenth century, several European imperial powers contested for global authority, with Britain, Germany, and Russia hard on the heels of the United States as the dominant economic force, and with China and India having lost their global lead. The scale of different European powers as imperial forces is revealed in Piketty's (2020) *Capital and Ideology*.

Figure 4.3 shows that the British empire remained paramount until 1914, and it is not incidental that as it declined later in the twentieth century, the United States assumed its global dominance. The "anglosphere" that straddled the Atlantic became a key global axis cutting across the European theater. By 1950, at the height of the cold war, US dominance reached its peak, with communist Russia a long way behind. By the twenty-first century, however, this American lead had diminished, with China (and to a lesser extent India) catching up economically. The European nations and Japan had all

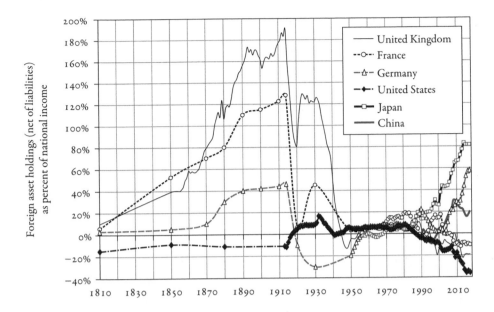

FIGURE 4.3: Foreign assets in historical perspective: The French-British colonial apex

Source: Thomas Piketty, *Capital and Ideology* (Cambridge, MA: Harvard University Press, 2020), figure 7.9. Copyright © 2020 by the President and Fellows of Harvard College. Used by permission.

fallen behind these three. The age of multiple powerful nations has given way to the economic dominance of two major global players—the United States and China, followed by a range of other large and powerful nations— India, Russia, Germany, France, and the United Kingdom. This is not a world of analytically symmetrical nations, susceptible to equivalent comparative analysis, but an unstable and unequal one, in which increased geopolitical tensions are coming to the fore.

These global shifts have disrupted the organization of cultural hierarchies, including the centrality of European norms. The Nobel Prize for Literature gives interesting clues on how the geography of cultural references might be changing. The list of Nobel Prize in Literature winners since 2000 includes two Asians (Gao, Mo Yan), a Trinidadian (Naipaul), two Eastern Europeans (Kertész, Müller), two Africans (Coetzee, Lessing), two Western Europeans (Jelinek, Pinter), a Turk (Pamuk), a South American (Vargas Llosa), and a Scandinavian (Tranströmer). The only French winner, Jean-Marie Gustave Le Clézio, now lives in Mauritius. But perhaps even more telling is that the authority of the Nobel Prize has itself been besmirched. The jury of the

Nobel Prize in Literature, organized by Sweden's literary elite, has been beset by sexual harassment scandals and stood down in 2017.

But it is the extent to which cultural hierarchies continued to be dominated from the global north that is most striking. Even while intense postcolonial critique of cultural Eurocentrism over recent decades (see, for example, Chakrabarty 2005) has exposed the whiteness of older highbrow cultural forms and valorized Black culture (notably that from Africa and parts of Asia), this has not seriously disrupted the cultural writ of the global north. But the center of Casanova's world republic of letters is no longer French but the English language. Even at the time Bourdieu was writing, anglophone cultural referents, especially American versions, were widespread in France, and his refusal to ask about any American icons (other than Gershwin) must be seen as a deliberately defiant act. By the early 2000s, "American movies and television are everywhere. . . . American music and books dominate less but are also present in all (European) societies" (Fligstein 2008: 250). The World Culture Report by UNESCO (2000) shows that a large share of cultural goods consumed in most EU countries is of American origin. In the Dutch cultural field, Dutch commercial television channels have a Hollywood-dominated orientation (Kuipers 2011). With respect to music, Schmutz (2009) shows that in the United States, France, the Netherlands, and Germany, newspapers reduced radically the amount of attention they give to (predominantly European) classical music and increased substantially their interest in popular music, which is more likely to be influenced by American models (see also Regev 1997).

The rising power of anglophone culture has numerous markers. Sapiro (2010) shows that the English language has become prominent in the relatively highbrow field of literature: The proportion of global translations from English to other languages rose from 45 percent to 59 percent between the 1980s and the 1990s. Admittedly, she also emphasizes the role of small-scale production in different nations, which continues to support an eclectic translation strategy, but from a more marginal position. In a similar vein, Savage et al. (2005a) and Savage and Gayo-Cal (2011) argue that in the United Kingdom, the younger, more highly educated middle-class individuals are increasingly attracted to off-beat American cultural forms, which they see as conveying distinction without appearing to be snobbish.

Of course, there are some contrary trends. A case can be made that South American literature, where literary magical realism in Spanish has achieved major renown, marks a significant exception. However, increasingly internationally recognized African literature has often been written in English (or some other European language). Gordon Li (2020) has shown that the economic development of China, the world's largest country, has led to (authorized) musical forms from around the world to gain more presence, but that these are disproportionately anglophone (and especially American).

In this light, we can see ordinalization, which abstracts from language and relies on quantitative indicators as further complicit with this anglophone dominance. This is for two reasons. First, their use is tied in with the global hegemony of the English language as the dominant scientific and business medium—and thereby plays into the power of a hegemonic anglosphere. The introduction of impact factors by Eugene Garfield, which allowed the systematic ranking of academic journals, has helped establish the global provenance of English, to the extent that academics across the Europe and the global south are expected to publish in English to demonstrate their prowess. Second and more importantly, any comparative project requiring quantification will be bound to be skewed toward historical centers of quantitative data and analytical expertise—that is to say, the old historical nations of the global north, with the legions of social scientists, research universities, and analytical and data capacity. The anglophone nations, with the United States leading the way, form the central axis of this complex.

The dominance of ranking procedures therefore needs to be placed in the light of this anglophone supremacy. However, there is a twist. On the face of it, ordinalization and the ranking of nations appears to treat nations as if they are analytically equivalent agents, each with the capacity to make a difference through their own policies and actions. Actually, I have argued that the reverse applies. Nations become arrayed as ciphers in global league tables, in which their own national frames of reference are decentered into competing globalizing frames. Lurking behind the apparent objectivity of numerical indicators is a powerful hierarchical politics.

Let us reflect on the oddity of ranking nations. How do we meaningfully render nations as analytically equivalent simply by virtue of their having national boundaries and some kind of (possibly minimal) national-state apparatus? The 200 or so nations in the world are highly asymmetrical in population and geopolitical significance.[23] They are deeply unequal. Clearly, no one compares the world's largest nation, China with its 1.3 billion people, with the world's smallest nation, by some definitions the Vatican City in Rome with its 700 citizens. Just seeing the Vatican City as a historical anomaly because of its historic role as the seat of the Catholic Church fails to recognize that this anomaly also has historical weight. In fact, around a third of the world's nations have less than a million inhabitants, meaning that they each are smaller than about 500 cities in the world (and well more than 100 cities of this size in China alone). A considerable number of these are tax havens, in which case, far from being historical residues, they serve powerful functions for contemporary capital accumulation (Zucman 2015). Perhaps some small nations are akin to "imperial city-states" (Halperin 2017).

Of all entities that we might want to compare, nation-states are therefore among the most asymmetrical. Nonetheless, the ordinalization of nations is legion. In practice, it is usual to exclude small nations which fail to have a sufficient "state capacity," including a research infrastructure to assemble national metrics (the Vatican City fails on this count). Most analysis focuses on relatively prosperous nations with sufficient population to allow the formation of a public research infrastructure robust enough to gather and manage national statistics at a certain level of competence. The member nations of the Organisation for Economic Co-operation and Development (OECD), who cooperate on data sharing and comparative research, are the most powerful vehicle here. The OECD claims that "today, our 36 member countries span the globe, from North and South America to Europe and Asia-Pacific."[24] But they actually remain resolutely European.

We can infer from Table 4.1 that because many OECD nations are located in Europe, there will be an implicit Eurocentric bias in any national rankings that are based on them. We see this very clearly in Wilkinson and Pickett's analysis in *The Spirit Level,* which compares twenty to twenty-two developed and hence wealthier nations, no fewer than sixteen of which are European. Furthermore, such comparative rankings generate an even stronger bias because of Europe's large number of relatively small nations. The United States, with its population of 300 million is here analytically equivalent to Norway, with a population of 5 million. European nations contain 27 percent of the world's nations, even though they only

Table 4.1: Nations by year of joining the Organisation for Economic Co-operation and Development (OECD)

Year	Countries	% OECD that Are European
1961	Austria, Belgium, Canada, Demark, France, Germany, Greece, Iceland, Ireland, Luxemburg, Netherlands, Norway, Portugal, Spain, Sweden, Switzerland, Turkey, United Kingdom, United States	89
1962	Italy	90
1963	New Zealand	86
1964	Japan	82
1969	Finland	83
1971	Australia	79
1973	New Zealand	76
1994	Mexico	73
1995	Czech Republic	74
1996	Hungary, Korea, Poland	73
2000	Slovak Republic	74
2010	Chile, Estonia, Israel, Slovenia	71
2016	Latvia	74
2018	Lithuania	76

Source: www.oecd.org/about/members-and-partners/.

have 9 percent of the world's population. Africa also has a greater share of the world's nations than population, but their limited research infrastructures, which would permit the appropriate metrics to be constructed, mean that these rarely get sustained attention (Helman and Ratner 1992; Ghani and Lockhart 2009). By contrast, Asia has a remarkable 61 percent of the world's population but only 25 percent of its nations. Two of Asia's nations, China and India, each contain more than three times the population of the whole of Europe.

National rankings, even while based in the infrastructure of the anglosphere, can thereby be tilted back to a Eurocentric framing. This is compounded by the way that European nations can be presented as beacons for more cohesive and less unequal societies than their anglophone counterparts. An arresting vignette is the way that the charity Oxfam has refocused their campaigning work in recent years to address inequality rather than just poverty reduction. Despite their own good intentions, their campaigning zeal has led them to develop composite indexes that come to hold up European nations as the best in the world for campaigning against inequality. Their Commitment to Reducing Inequality Index, first developed in 2017, "uses a new database of indicators covering 152 countries, which measures government action on social spending, tax and labour rights."[25] These three components are then used to construct a composite index with differing nations arrayed in league-table format. This paradoxically leads to a highly Eurocentric geography, with the nations scoring the best being entirely from Europe.[26]

The project of national ranking therefore implicitly values and weights the world differentially. Without any explicit recognition of this point, and despite the good intentions of those working in this tradition, the world is weighted toward (a) viable and "responsible" nations, many of which are European, with strong "state capacity," good-quality data, and effective governmental and nongovernmental agencies; (b) a few outlier "bad" nations, notably the United States, which clearly deviate from the norms of the viable nations because of the poor scores that they typically exhibit in their rankings; (c) a few huge nations (China and India), which often lie outside the purview of these global rankings (sometimes because they keep their statistics hidden), but where they do figure in these international comparisons, they don't massively weight the indexes, because they are only singular entities; and (d) the rest of the world, which is largely invisible by failing to have the data and analytical infrastructure that allows meaningful comparison. In the past two decades, again in the wake of the Millennium Development Goals, considerable energy has been spent in nation-building projects, with most effect in South America, but also in Africa and Asia to lift nations from category (d) to category (a).

It is with respect to those nations in category (d) that the proliferation of discourses of "failed states" have come to be very powerful. This term was designed to expose those nations that are deemed unable to act in the way nations should (that is, according to Eurocentric models). It is not incidental that the mainstreaming of discourses of failed or fragile states has taken place at the same time that the ordinalization of nations has occurred. Originating in the 2002 National Security Strategy paper of George W. Bush's administration, which declared that "the United States today is threatened less by conquering states than by weak and failing ones" (Woodward 2017: 26), the original failed state was Afghanistan. But by 2005, the UK's Department for Foreign and International Development had identified no less than forty-six "fragile states."

The ranking of nations therefore turns out to generate inequalities of its own. Some nations—such as "failed states"—don't even make the analytical cut. It is those nations with long histories of state development, especially in Europe and the anglosphere, that come to command pride of place. The problems this leads to are clear in Wilkinson and Pickett's research, the arguments of which are indebted to the similarities between four small, relatively egalitarian Scandinavian nations that each count as separate units in their analysis and thereby tend to push the authors' narrative sparkline. In a converse manner, the United States stands out as a "bad" outlier time and again. Rather than the United States being a beacon of progress, it turns out to be dysfunctional and beset by systematic social problems. This is not an incidental or minor issue: The ordinalization of nations leads to the world's most iconic "progressive" nation falling foul of its own precepts that it exemplifies the promise of a better life.

It turns out that the ordinalization of nations is far from being a neutral or objective ranking exercise. It is also implicated in broader geopolitical tensions. I recall, at a recent conference of Chinese social scientists, hesitantly asking for their views about the Hong Kong situation. My colleagues were initially reticent about being drawn out, but they became more forthright when emphasizing that Hong Kong's high Gini coefficient meant that it was a territory beset with problems. The language of inequality metrics becomes a way of registering geopolitical tensions in an appropriately dispassionate way. These rankings thereby compete with linguistic and text-based authority, previously linked with the imperial hegemony of European languages.

Ordinalization therefore reworks global cultural hierarchies. Nineteenth-century European imperial dominance depended on its capacity to define the very terms in which global relations could be understood, with the writ of its languages marking out imperial jurisdictions. As Chakrabarty (2008) has argued, this meant that internal contestation among European powers was transmitted to the world stage, whereby different cultural values became universalized as abstract principles themselves. Thus the supposed clash between French "civilization," which lay at odds with German "culture" (Elias and Jephcott 1994), became generalized around the globe. These were not simply historical residues: David Parker (2011) has traced the powerful contrast between the French avant garde emphasis on differentiation and art for art's sake compared to the German interest in synthesis and the total work of art. In this light, we can see debates among social scientists as echoing these divisions, albeit in the dispassionate language of quantification. When Danish sociologist Gøsta Esping-Andersen (1990) thus contrasted social democratic northern European nations with free market capitalist nations of the anglosphere, and conservative models found in southern Europe, he used intra-European comparisons to map out a broader set of analytical contrasts. More recently, Peter Hall and David Soskice (2001) mapped out varieties of capitalism to draw similar contrasts. Internal differentiation between a small range of developed nations become abstracted in quintessential Eurocentric ways as universalizing principles of social organization themselves. Intra-European tensions were therefore exported around the globe and became the defining ground in which "difference" was understood.

Conclusion

This chapter has taken us on a long but necessary journey. On the face of it, Figure 4.1 is a powerful visualization that shows the ways in which unequal nations experience a greater range of social problems. It mobilizes the "so what?" question of inequality in politically powerful ways. But it is not just to be taken at face value: There is much more involved than initially meets the eye. Its compelling narrative sparkline articulates a new technocratic politics of national ranking—or ordinalization—that abstracts nations from broader global processes and leads to a fixation on national-level interventions at the same time that nations themselves are subject to intensifying geopolitical pressures. It thereby represents the destabilization of nation spaces.

This pervasive ranking of nations by inequality indicators forms part of our now-time. It is implicated in a pervasive geopolitical contestation that values different areas of the globe differentially. I have shown that there are two major components in this space of contestation. The first of these is weighted toward European nations, which are generally relatively unequal and which report fewer obvious social problems, according to the battery of metrics and indicators that have been assembled. The other component is a technocratic politics embodying the values of a white anglosphere, in which the English language dominates. This is a fractious and contested space. The United States emerges as a high-inequality outlier, a dystopian nation. Other nations of the anglosphere, notably the United Kingdom and South Africa, have similar trajectories. By contrast, the huge nations of China and India largely lie outside the purview of these metrics, and where they are measured, their significance is diminished by their only comprising one unit of observation. Other nations of the world are less visible in these metrics, which itself is associated with the proliferation of "failed-state" narratives. The project of ranked national comparison is therefore far from being a neutral or detached one, but lead us to recognize the role of enhanced geopolitical tensions as central to our now-time.

Here, one key finding is clear. National ranking exercises portray the United States as the deviant, bad-boy outlier, set against a larger number of viable, mostly European nations that generally score much better on numerous indicators. This is itself a major fault line. Perhaps, therefore, the older imperial tensions between European powers, represented in the clash between German "culture" and French "civilization," now has a counterpart in the politics of technocratic expertise.

The Return of Empire

INEQUALITY ON A GLOBAL SCALE

In Chapter 4, I reflected that both numbers and texts construct hierarchies and inequalities—though with different stakes. For this reason, symphonic, social science visualization, which offers a powerful way of reconciling the generalizing power of numerical arrays with the narrative sweep of the humanities, offers a vital vantage point. With this in mind, let us begin with another iconic inequality sparkline. Since its formulation by economist Branko Milanovic in 2015, this icon of inequality has become so famous that it bears its own name: the elephant graph. Here the narrative line traces the elephant's bulky back before dipping down past its face, but then, the elephant's trunk trumpets.

This curvy line indicates a subtle, but arresting, narrative. It reports global income trends with respondents placed on the horizontal x-axis according to their place in the global income distribution in 1988: the poorest are to the left and the richest to the right. The vertical y-axis records the percentage change in their incomes from 1988 to 2008. The upraised trunk at the extreme right (point C) tells a familiar story. The top 2 or 3 percent of the world's top earners have done very well, reiterating themes that are familiar from the American experience: Their incomes had risen by more than 50 percent in this period. However, the bigger surprise is that those who have gained proportionately more are those in the bottom middle (point A), where incomes had typically risen over 50 percent. This was true for anyone from

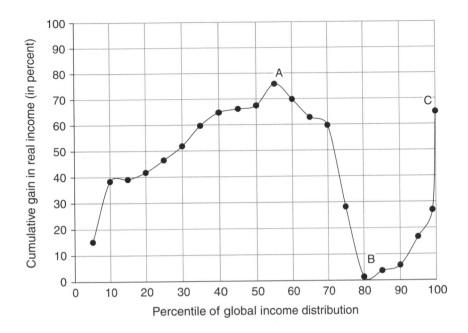

FIGURE 5.1: Change in real income according to position in global income distribution, 1988–2008

Source: Branko Milanovic, *Global Inequality* (Cambridge, MA: Harvard University Press, 2016), figure 1.1. Copyright © 2016 by the President and Fellows of Harvard College. Used by permission.

the bottom 10 percent as far as 60 percent in the global income distribution, over three billion people. The biggest proportionate winners of all are those exactly in the middle of the global income distribution in 1988, whose incomes rose by 75 percent.

By contrast, those ranging from seventieth to the high nineties percentile of the global income distribution (point B) fared much less well in relative terms. A small group at the 80 percent mark of the global income distribution in 1988 had actually seen their relative income falling. This is a group who had been among the world's most fortunate during the 1980s, but who then slipped behind those above and below them. Those in the bottom few percentiles of the income distribution have also done much less well than those at the top and in the middle.

What explains this storyline? Milanovic (2016) incorporates the dramatic economic rise of the emerging economies of Brazil, Russia, India, and China (often rendered by the acronym BRICs) into his global account of inequality.

Together, these four nations have more than 40 percent of the entire global population, and their staggering economic rise since the 1980s has transformed global inequality dynamics. People in previously poor nations have seen their incomes grow much faster than low- and even middle-income earners in the world's richer, developed nations. This entails the decline of "between nation" inequality, even though inequality has often been growing "within nations" (see also Anand and Segal 2015, 2017; Simson and Savage 2020).

On the face of it, Milanovic's work offers a powerful riposte to pessimists who fixate on the inexorable rise of the 1 percent as the overarching inequality story of our times. The situation of the billions of people living in Asia and parts of South America is more positive. Milanovic is also more sympathetic to Kuznets's arguments that economic growth leads to declining inequality and is more sanguine about long-term global trends. The United States may be an inequality outlier, but we should not fixate on its peculiarities and project its dystopia around the globe.

Milanovic's elephant graph has had remarkable take up, and in a few years, it has become a mini-orthodoxy. To a large extent it reworks familiar World Bank–inspired studies that had previously focused on global poverty thresholds, but by recasting these data sources and perspectives to address inequality, rather than poverty, it sidestepped many of the controversies and critiques that had dogged poverty research, as I considered in Chapter 1.[1]

In fact, even the pessimistic group of economists associated with the World Inequality Lab (who are responsible for maintaining the World Inequality Database, or WID) accept the gist of Milanovic's approach and argument, though with two crucial caveats. The first relates to Milanovic's use of survey sources to capture the incomes of very high earners, pooling a staggering 90 percent of the world's population into a composite database. This practice follows the World Bank model and is certainly a remarkable technical exercise. Comparable surveys are conducted across different nations and income comparisons drawn between nations using purchase price parity indexes allowing for like-to-like comparison of what income can buy in different nations (rather than the use of simple exchange rates, which do not control for the relative expenses of goods in different nations). Nonetheless, this impressive exercise does not address the problem that representative surveys tend to underreport top income. If this is corrected, it is possible that the elephant's trunk might run a lot higher than her body.

The World Inequality Lab economists therefore used their preferred taxation-based data to offer their corrective, so as to better register the incomes of the higher paid. By 2018, taxation-based studies only represent 60 percent of the world's population compared to Milanovic's 90 percent and are therefore not as comprehensive.[2] Nonetheless, assuming that the missing nations are not out of step, a comparable elephant graph using this more robust data (see Figure 5.2) can be set against Figure 5.1. The Lab's economists are also able to take the story up to 2016, considerably later than Milanovic's (2016) account, which runs as far as 2008.

On this basis, Figure 5.2 shows that the world's top earners were much more successful in improving their income levels between 1980 and 2016. The elephant's back is much smaller, while her trumpet rises well above her body. In fact, care is needed in making this inference.[3] Figure 5.2 telescopes out the top 1 percent to unravel very minute differences among fractions of the top 1 percent. Thus, while the top 0.0001 percent did best of all, with their incomes rising 250 percent, the top 1 percent overall did less well than those in the bottom 40 percent of the income distribution. Taking this into account, the story of Figure 5.2 is not greatly different from that of Figure 5.1: It is another version of the elephant graph.

Therefore, even using taxation data, Milanovic's interpretation of the rise of emerging countries and the prosperity of the global 1 percent is largely confirmed—even if downplayed. However, a second issue is more challenging. The elephant graph considers income increases relative to their 1988 levels. Therefore, because these top few percent started from such a higher position in 1988, their actual gains are much bigger than for those who were in the middle of the global income distribution (see Hickel 2017). Figure 5.2 thus reveals that even though the proportionate rise of the top 1 percent was not much greater than the bottom 50 percent, because the former started from a much higher base, they accumulated 27 percent of the entire gain in global national income, dwarfing the measly 12 percent captured by the bottom 50 percent. This point is developed by Nino-Zarazua et al. (2017: 673), who emphasize that "global inequality has increased, steadily and substantially, during 1975 to 2010 according to . . . absolute measures," which challenges narratives that rely on relative increments.[4] This is a perfect example of how relativizing inequality can limit our understanding of the power of historical forces. As I showed in Chapter 4, much inequality

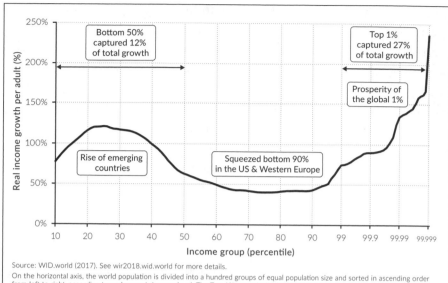

Source: WID.world (2017). See wir2018.wid.world for more details.

On the horizontal axis, the world population is divided into a hundred groups of equal population size and sorted in ascending order from left to right, according to each group's income level. The Top 1% group is divided into ten groups, the richest of these groups is also divided into ten groups, and the very top group is again divided into ten groups of equal population size. The vertical axis shows the total income growth of an average individual in each group between 1980 and 2016. For percentile group p99p99.1 (the poorest 10% among the world's richest 1%) growth was 74% between 1980 and 2016. The Top 1% captured 27% of total growth over this period. Income estimates account for differences in the cost of living between countries. Values are net of inflation.

FIGURE 5.2: Total income growth by percentile across all world regions, 1980–2016

Source: Facundo Alvaredo, Lucas Chancel, Thomas Piketty, Emmanuel Saez, and Gabriel Zucman, eds., *World Inequality Report 2018* (Cambridge, MA: Harvard University Press, 2018), figure 2.4. Copyright © 2018 by the World Inequality Lab. Used by permission.

research remains locked in a framework of comparing relativities within and between nations, as if nations were both autonomous as well as being analytically equivalent. Even though Milanovic's research, and the work influenced by it, allows a new path where national databases are spliced together, this construction of a globe-wide database raises a host of thorny issues.

We have already encountered some of these difficulties in my reflections in Chapter 1 about the challenges of defining a global poverty threshold. Constructing equivalence across different nations involves the use of purchase-price metrics, which are supposed to allow like-to-like price comparisons across nations. Reddy and Pogge (2010) and Ghosh (2018) have argued they actually tend to underestimate the effective weight of higher-income nations. European travelers to a poor nation benefit from the relatively cheap price of goods they can buy there, but an Indian will not be able to afford European prices. The project of creating the globe as an empty plane, or "empty homogeneous space" (to use the term that Benedict Anderson (1983) famously applied to modern nations) is an abstraction, akin to the ranking exercises discussed in Chapter 4, which can obscure messy territorial discrepancies. Simply flipping from nationally specific to a global level slides over a crucial middle level. I will concentrate on this territorial level, arguing that inequality trends are associated with elite formation among competing global powers, and that this is bound up with the resurgence of imperial projects. I break down trends at a continental level, starting with Asia (which dominates the world's population), before turning to the anglo-imperial nations (dominated by the United States) and then considering the distinctive patterns of continental European nations. Finally, I will discuss the more checkered experiences in South America and Africa.

Overall, these patterns are testimony to the rise of imperial inequality, as the world splits into contesting camps in which empowered elites drive aggrandizement across different territories. The revived power of empire speaks to my overarching theme of the increasing force of the past. What might be termed "viable" or "sustainable" nations, committed to projects of internal social cohesion, are fast being eclipsed by the renewal of imperial forms of domination and control. Far from being historical residues, empires are renewing their long-term traction.

5.2: The Historical Return of Asia

The trends in Figure 5.1 (Milanovic's elephant graph) are massively influenced by the changing economic fortunes of the Asian nations that dominate the world's population and whose remarkable growth—especially in China—has been central to the dynamics of global capitalism in recent decades (see also Milanovic 2019). The 50 percent of the global population who represent the elephant's body of rising income standards are mainly located in Asia, where 60 percent of the world's population live. It has long been the central puzzle of historical sociologists to explain why Asia, the historic center of human civilization from the birth of writing, was eclipsed by European dominance during the Enlightenment. Indeed, sociological theories of modernity—originally in its varied Weberian, Marxist, and Durkheimian forms, later by more critical and postcolonial variants—fixated specifically on this historical shift in the global balance of power. More recent historical scholarship has insisted on the role of colonial relations in securing European hegemony during this period, and this history still informs contemporary modalities (Pomeranz 2009; Parthasarathi 2011; Beckert 2015; Piketty 2020).

Until the later twentieth century, it was believed that the shift first to European global dominance and then to its settler outposts in the "new world" was irreversible and marked the defining feature of modernization itself: The task for Asia (as for Africa and South America) was somehow to "catch up." But it is now clear that we are witnessing a historical reversion, in which Asian societies are reclaiming their global historical primacy. From 1913 to 1950, Asian growth rates (0.2 percent) lagged behind America (1.4 percent a year), and Europe and Africa (0.9 percent). Then between 1950 and 1970, Asian growth rates leaped ahead and were almost on a par with those in Europe. By 1970, they were the fastest, and between 1990 and 2012, growth rates in Asia were twice anywhere else in the world. The twenty-first century is thus set to be the century when Asia reasserts its historical role as the center of global power.

Massively growing inequality in many Asian nations is somewhat obscured by the broad global patterns revealed in Figures 5.1 and 5.2. Even though economic growth in Asia has reduced inequality at the global level, it has increased inequality in much of Asia. Figure 5.3 lists trends for all large Asian nations with populations of more than 25 million people, using data from the World Wealth and Income database. Until the 1980s, inequality was very low in most Asian nations, in large part due to the high levels of poverty found across Asian society, as well as to the fact that Russia and China were communist regimes ostensibly committed to egalitarian principles.

Since the 1980s, this trend has changed substantially. The largest countries have seen a substantial rise in the national income taken by their top 10 percent. In the Chinese case, this trend has been very marked. In the 1980s, the top 10 percent of earners took about 28 percent of national income; shortly after 2000, they took over 40 percent—though this trend has stabilized since then. This proportionate increase took place in an economy that was growing exceptionally fast, so this was a stunning bonanza period for these top earners. Russia also saw a truly astonishing rise in inequality during

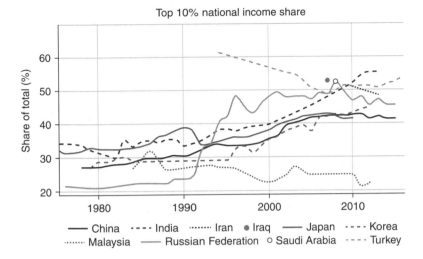

FIGURE 5.3: Share of national income going to the top 10 percent of earners in Asian nations
Source: World Inequality Database.

the 1990s as shock-policy market liberalization was introduced in the aftermath of communism being dismantled: The top 10 percent share of income doubled to nearly 50 percent—at the same time that the Russian economy crashed. Mareeva (2020) shows how the top 1 percent possibly have an even higher proportion of national income in Russia than in the United States. The Indian case also shows a clear upward trend in inequality levels that are now the highest of any Asian society—with the share of national income taken by the top 10 percent nearly doubling to almost 60 percent. The main outlier is Turkey, which had been exceptionally unequal in the 1990s and saw a slight trend toward declining inequality over this period, though this has recently been reversed. Malaysia also bucks this trend.

We can surmise that in most Asian nations, the greatest gains of economic growth went disproportionately to those who were already advantaged, thus accentuating inequalities in most Asian nations. The World Inequality Lab team have neatly bought together these trends in their comparison of the geographical make-up of people at different levels of the global income distribution in 1990 and 2016 (see Figures 5.4 and 5.5).

Figure 5.4 shows that in 1990, the bottom 50 percent of the global income distribution was overwhelmingly Asian (and to a lesser extent, African). By

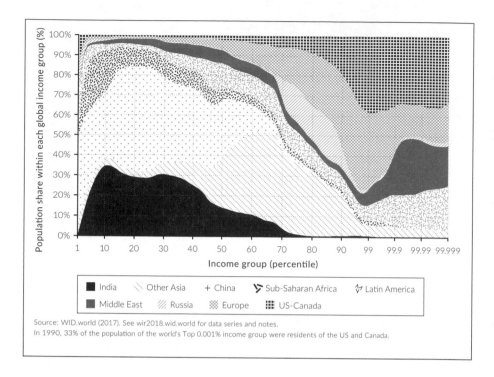

FIGURE 5.4: Geographic breakdown of global income groups in 1990

Source: Facundo Alvaredo, Lucas Chancel, Thomas Piketty, Emmanuel Saez, and Gabriel Zucman, eds., *World Inequality Report 2018* (Cambridge, MA: Harvard University Press, 2018), figure 2.5. Copyright © 2018 by the World Inequality Lab. Used by permission.

2016, the African population was much more directly concentrated on the poorer (left-hand) side of the global income distribution, whereas China has moved substantially to the center, and India has become more elongated, indicating increasing variation between rich and poor Indians. What is also striking is that "other Asia" (including Japan), which in 1990 was substantially more likely to be in the middle of the global distribution, has been stretched out, with substantially more of its population in the bottom 50 percent of the income distribution. This is also a marked trend for the Middle East, which in 1990 made up a sizable portion of the world's highest earners but by 2016 had fallen back substantially. Thus, the spectacular advance of China and India has been at the partial relative expense of other Asian nations, not only the developed nations in Europe and North America.

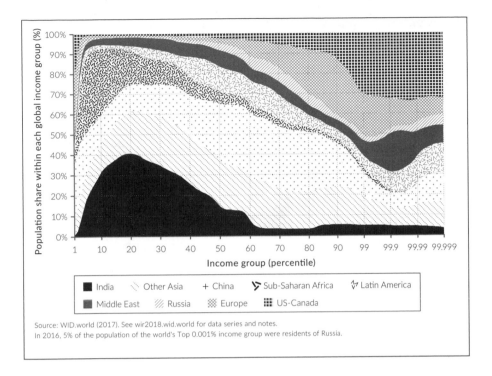

FIGURE 5.5: Geographic breakdown of global income groups in 2016

Source: Facundo Alvaredo, Lucas Chancel, Thomas Piketty, Emmanuel Saez, and Gabriel Zucman, eds., *World Inequality Report 2018* (Cambridge, MA: Harvard University Press, 2018), figure 2.6. Copyright © 2018 by the World Inequality Lab. Used by permission.

Focusing on the top 10 percent of global earners, the remarkable rise of Asia is powerfully revealed. In 1990, three-quarters of the global top 10 percent of earners were European and American. Specifically, there were 10 percent of Asians compared to about 25 percent of Americans. By 2016 (Figure 5.5) the proportion of European and American top 10 percent earners had shrunk to less than 50 percent of the global income distribution, and there were considerably more Asians than Americans. The Asian share of the global top 10 percent easily eclipsed the European share by 2016. Of course, proportionate to their populations, Asians are still far less likely to be in these top groups, but it is the absolute numbers that matter here—this is a shift of seismic proportions. For the first time since the seventeenth century, the majority of the world's affluent population lives outside Europe and

North America. This squeeze has largely been at European expense: the US and Canadian share of the global top 10 percent has declined much less.

To construe Asian processes simply in national terms—as if China or India were somehow "catching up" with France or Germany—is analytically unhelpful. To see China, population 1.4 billion, as analytically equivalent to France or Germany, let alone Sweden or Switzerland, is an anachronistic Eurocentric rendering. The distinctive role of China, Russia, and India is not only due to their massive population sizes, but also to their partial, hybrid adoption of a national model of governance. China and Russia moved from being huge and complex imperial states as late as the early twentieth century to being communist regimes, with nationalist forms largely being adopted (insofar as they were) as defensive devices against European and US powers. India was colonized by the British, and although it became the world's largest democratic nation from 1948, it retains a high degree of regional differentiation.

Analytically the rise of these three countries might be seen as taking a quasi-imperial rather than a national form. As with previous empires in history, they are authoritarian, have strong differentiation between metropolitan cores and provincial zones, have strongly militarized borders, comprise dominant and marginalized ethnic groups within their borders, and exhibit religious and imperial rather than purely nationalist zealotry. Hindu nationalism in India has its parallels with the role of Christianity in European imperial cultures. They are not predominantly territorially expansionist along the lines of nineteenth-century European empires. In this respect, they are closer to the American model of empire through indirect influence and holding economic sway. Seen in this light, the relative decline of smaller Asian and Middle Eastern nations can be linked to the growing hegemony of the three Asian empires in their spheres of influence. In this context, Turkey is an interesting and arresting limiting case. Alone of all nations in the world, it exemplifies a very powerful imperial legacy (the Ottoman Empire) with a very strong nationalist framing from the Kemalist period. It also straddles the European and Asian arenas. Under Recep Tayyip Erdogan's leadership, Turkey has yoked its nationalism to an imperial vision, which has also been accompanied by a reduction of inequality—albeit from very high levels.

5.3: The Geopolitics of American Global Dominance

Recognizing the growing significance of Asian inequality allows us to see trends in the anglophone nations of the United States, the United Kingdom, Australia, Canada, and Ireland from a different perspective, where high earners appear to be in retreat, in global terms. To be sure, as we have seen in Figure 5.5, these anglophone nations, and especially the United States, retain their centrality among the world's top earners. Milanovic identities seven nations where more than 5 percent of its population was in the global top 1 percent (that is, were at least five times overrepresented among the global top 1 percent). The United States easily led the way: 12 percent of its residents were in the global top 1 percent. Canada (7 percent) and the United Kingdom (5 percent) also figure. Three other nations in this group have very small populations: Singapore (5 million), Switzerland (8 million), and Luxemburg (0.5 million). This story of predominantly anglophone nations proportionately dominating the global "top end" is only complicated by the presence of Japan, where 6 percent of its residents are in the top 1 percent. Overall, Figure 5.5 shows that anglophone neoliberal nations, characterized by a strong financial sector, low taxation regimes, and liberal market economies, are key drivers of top-end inequality processes. The prosperous elites in these nations have seen a very marked relative improvement in (their already fortunate) economic positions.

The work of Anand and Segal (2017) reveals the singularity of American earners in the global top 1 percent. Linking national surveys with taxation data to provide an accurate account of top earners, these authors have produced the most comprehensive global account of the top 1 percent. Despite their growth in emerging economies, the global top 1 percent continues to be a massively disproportionate American phenomenon. This reveals the stark differences between the United States on the one hand, and China and India on the other. An astonishing 37 percent of the top 1 percent are American; in contrast, only a tiny proportion are Chinese and Indian. Many European nations are also overrepresented, but since they have relatively small populations, they are not very significant in the global 1 percent overall.

Historically, this resurgence of income inequality in anglophone nations is a relatively new phenomenon: during the 1970s, the United States, the United Kingdom, and Canada were among the more equal nations in the

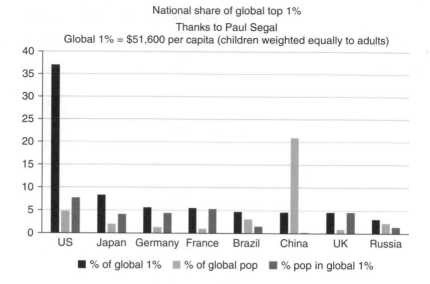

FIGURE 5.6: The national composition of the global top 1 percent

Data source: Sudhir Anand and Paul Segal, "Who Are the Global Top 1%?," King's College International Development Institute Working Paper 2016-02.

world, and the subsequent rise of inequality started from a relatively low base. Political initiatives involving tax cuts and changing employment law, often weakening trade unions, have been important here. These trends are also interesting to consider in view of Mann's (2005) claims that the United States exercises an informal imperial role in the world system. Its high earners have been involved in maintaining their dominance as global top earners even during massive economic growth in the emerging economies. This US dominance can be attributed to its military and corporate hegemony in a global geopolitical environment that hasn't questioned US authority since the 1980s. The United States, with 37 percent of the global top 1 percent of earners, also accounts for 36 percent of the global military budget. It is also home to ten of the world's largest twenty-five corporations.

The extent to which the super-high earners in the United States dominate the global inequality hierarchy indicates its singularity as a globally dominant nation. Its anglophone satellites, especially the United Kingdom and Canada, can be seen as part of its wider hinterland, which can provocatively (if not entirely facetiously) be identified as a renascent anglophone imperial

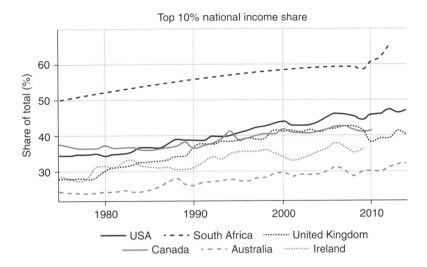

FIGURE 5.7: Share of national income going to the top 10 percent of earners in major anglophone former British colonies

Source: World Inequality Database.

formation. The marked rise of income inequality in these nations lies at the heart of a global model of neoliberal financialized growth that has a worldwide reach.

Trends toward increasing inequality in the anglophone nations have generally slowed since the 2008 crash (see Figure 5.7). The British case is especially noteworthy, as on the face of it, the share of national income going to the top 10 percent appears to have fallen in the United Kingdom and only increased moderately in the other anglophone nations, with the partial exception of Australia, which started from the lowest base. If the period from the 1980s to 2008 marked the boom period of the anglophone US-dominated imperial formation, the peak moment may appear to have passed. However, I return shortly to offer an alternative reading of these trends, after reflecting further on the European experience.

5.3: European Exceptionalism?

The situation of most European nations is different from that of the anglophone world. As Figure 5.5 reveals, the world's top earners are much less

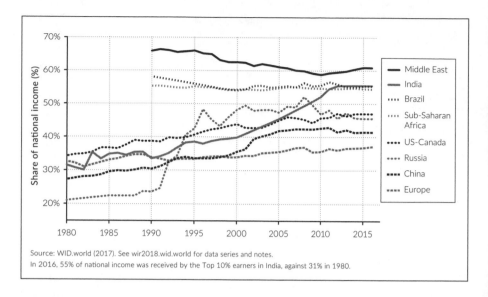

FIGURE 5.8: Share of national income going to the top 10 percent of earners comparing major global nations / continents

Source: Facundo Alvaredo, Lucas Chancel, Thomas Piketty, Emmanuel Saez, and Gabriel Zucman, eds., *World Inequality Report 2018* (Cambridge, MA: Harvard University Press, 2018), figure H.2b. Copyright © 2018 by the World Inequality Lab. Used by permission.

likely to be in European nations than they were even thirty years ago, and there are now more Asians than Europeans in the global top 10 percent of earners. The reason for this shift is not only economic growth and intensifying inequality in Asia, but also that many European nations have limited the growth of income inequality within their borders through their commitment to higher taxation and a redistributionist welfare state. The distinctiveness of Europe in the global inequality space is best revealed by Figure 5.8, which shows that Europe is now an outlier in a world that has seen convergence around a "high-inequality frontier." In 1980, Europe was considerably more unequal than Russia, China, and India and only slightly less unequal than the United States and Canada. By 2000, Europe had become the least unequal region in the world, and the gap with other regions has persisted since then. This is one of the main themes emerging from Piketty's collaborations with Atkinson and other European researchers from the early 2000s, which showed how trends in some European nations are countervailing exemplars to the dystopian American model (A. Atkinson and Piketty

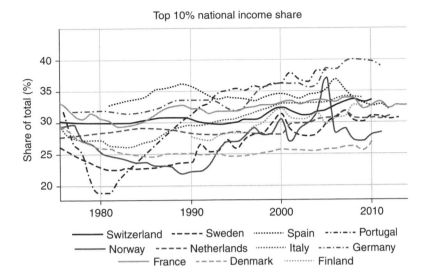

FIGURE 5.9: Share of national income going to the top 10 percent in select European nations with no history of communist rule

Source: World Inequality Database.

2007). Atkinson's thinking is strongly informed by the social democratic model and his emphasis on corporatist style arrangements to manage inequality (see Atkinson 2015). It turns out that the top seventeen most equal nations in the world, according to his measures, are all European.[5]

Figure 5.9 draws on data from continental European nations that had not been subject to communist rule. It shows that by 2010, Germany is distinctive compared to other European nations (apart from the United Kingdom; see Figure 5.7) in terms of its much higher inequality, with nearly 40 percent of its income going to the top 10 percent, much higher than the 27 percent in nearby Denmark. This coincides with the adoption of the euro in 2001, which some social scientists (Streeck 2014) see as bound up with increasing German hegemony in Europe.

In the United States, the top 1 percent took 22 percent of the national income in 2011, usually at least double, and sometimes three or even four times the level found in European nations. Even the United Kingdom, which is similar to the United States in its top pay trends, falls well behind. In Europe, Table 5.1 shows that Germany and the United Kingdom stand out from other nations in terms of the high income share of the 1 percent, with the

Table 5.1: Top 1 percent shares of national incomes, 1975–2015

Nation and share of national income taken by top 1 percent in most recent recorded year (percent)	Share of national income taken by top 1 percent in lowest recorded year 1975+ (percent)	Share of national income taken by top 1% in highest recorded year 1975+ (percent)	Increase 2000–2011 (percent)	Increase from the trough to peak year (and number of years between these) (percent)	Increase 1975–present (percent)
UK 12.9 (2011)	(1978) 5.7	(2009) −15.4	−0.4	+170.2 (31 years)	111.5
USA 22 (2015)	(1976) 8.3	(2007) −22.6	−8.8	+162.6 (31 years)	165
France 8.1 (2014)	(1982) 7.0	(2007) 9.3	+8.4	+32.9 (25 years)	−4.8
Germany 13.1 (2011)	(1995) 9.2	(2007) 14.0	+14.9	+52.2 (12 years)	25
Denmark 6.4 (2010)	(1995) 5.0	(1975) 6.8	+12.2	Peak precedes trough	−20.6
Spain 8.6 (2012)	(1981) 7.6	(2012) 12.7	−12.2	+67.1% (21 years)	(1981) 13.2
Sweden 8.7 (2012)	(1982) 4.1	(2000) 11.1	−19.1	+170.7 (18 years)	+61.1
Norway 7.8 (2011)	(1990) 4.3	(2005) 16.5	−25.2	+283.7 (15 years)	+42.6%
Netherlands 6.3 (2011)	(1998) 5.3	(2008) 7.6	+12.5	+43.4 (10 years)	+3.3%
Switzerland 10.6 (2010)	(1983) 8.4	(2008) 11.0	+1.9	+31.0 (25 years)	+20.5
Italy 9.4 (2009)	(1983) 6.3	(2007) 9.9	+0.3	+57.1 (24 years)	+32.4
Ireland 10.5 (2009)	(1976) 5.6	(2006) 12.5	+1.9	+123.2 (30 years)	+75
Portugal 9.8 (2005)	(1981) 4	(2006) 9.8	—	+145 (25 years)	+24.1

Data source: The World Inequality Database (WID.world).

most egalitarian nations being the Netherlands, Denmark, Norway, and France (in that order).

It should be recognized that in most European nations, there has been a specific period marked by a shift of income toward the top 1 percent at some point in the past forty years. Table 5.1 shows that nearly every European nation experienced a distinct "bonanza" period for the top 1 percent, in which their share of the national income rose greatly, sometimes precipitously. For five nations (Norway, Sweden, the United Kingdom, Portugal, and Ireland) this at least doubled the income share taken by the top 1 percent. The most extreme case is Norway: In a fifteen-year period from 1990 to 2005, the share of national income taken by the top 1 percent rose spectacularly from 4.3 percent to 16.5 percent.[6] By contrast, the nations that saw the lowest rise in income shares enjoyed by the top 1 percent were Denmark (which completely bucks the trend by seeing a declining income share of the top 1 percent from 1975 to 1995), France (where it rose only modestly from 7 percent in 1982 to 9.3 percent in 2007), and Switzerland (8.4 percent in 1983 to 11 percent in 2008). However, these are the exceptions. This economic shift is not necessarily part of a linear trend, but it does indicate how the balance of forces toward high-income earners has exerted a powerful hold, even in most nations that are relatively egalitarian.

In every European nation there has been a recent retreat from the peak income enjoyed by the top 1 percent in the aftermath of the 2008 financial crash. For most nations, the peak year for top incomes was around 2005–2008. In some cases, the shift away from the 1 percent since this period is very striking. In Norway, their share has halved. Only in Germany and Switzerland have top income shares held up. The distinctiveness of the United States compared to European nations is therefore even more marked now than in 2005–2008.

How do we understand these comparative findings? European exceptionalism might be attributed to the greater persistence of coherent national systems of governance. These tend to restrain market-based neoliberal drivers that lead to income inequality, instead favoring national social contract models that seek to rein in pressure from affluent groups to extract equivalent levels of income enjoyed in many anglophone nations. From this perspective, the European Union, far from overseeing the erosion of national models, has actually presided over the modernization of largely nation-based cultures. It is precisely in these terms that Perry Anderson (2009) sees the European project as a compromise, even a fudge, designed to shore up European national formations rather than undertake a more radical cosmopolitan endeavor.

Much of the recent sociological analysis of European societies has demonstrated the enduring power of national affiliations in Europe, even in the context of the European single market. Neil Fligstein (2009) has argued for the emergence of what he terms a "European field" in recent decades, which stands over and above constituent nations, but he emphasizes that it is largely well-educated managerial and professional workers who feel comfortable navigating at a European level. However, intensive qualitative research qualifies this argument. Favell's (2011) study of transnational European professionals working in London, Brussels, and Paris shows that most of these mobile Europeans do not feel entirely comfortable living outside the nations they were brought up in, and many of them harbor the desire to return "home." This is also the strong finding of Andreotti et al. (2015), who examined the values and attitudes of the upper middle class in Milan, Paris, and Barcelona and showed a very strong homing instinct among them. Although it was common to move to broaden career experience in other parts of Europe, these individuals mainly wanted to return to settle in the cities in which they had been brought up (see also Le Galès 2018).

The more muted trends toward growing economic inequality in many European nations can thereby be linked to the enduring power of specifically national attachments, which serve to limit the power of corporate and financial elites to defy national parameters, values, and frameworks. More specific comparisons in Europe support this argument. Denmark, of all European nations, has resisted the trend toward growing income inequality, and Grau Larsen and Ellersgaard (2015) have revealed an unusually cohesive corporatist and nationally specific power elite, with strong interlocks and internal cohesiveness. Along with the imprint of ongoing corporatist arrangements, this cohesiveness has prevented significant growth of inequality. We can hypothesize that this unusually cohesive Danish power elite acts to damp down pressures to marketize the top-level income that might be evident in other nations. It can also be seen as associated with the potential for relatively small nations (which would include other Scandinavian countries) to operate in a more cohesive way, with the capacity to form national social contracts, where public national elites help secure a form of national solidarity.[7]

The French case—where there has also been relatively little rise in income inequality—can be interpreted in similar ways. The state has not embarked on the large-scale deregulation of public services that has been seen elsewhere in Europe, and it continues to demand high rates of taxation on high earners. Comparative research has also shown how French professionals and managers continue to exemplify strong civic-oriented values, in which market rewards are not paramount; instead there is a stronger commitment to public values associated with a strong national culture. Power et al. (2013: 583) thus bring out the strikingly different orientations of elite graduates at Oxford and Sciences Po, in Paris. They relate that

> Our twenty Oxford graduates spoke enthusiastically of their futures and the opportunities that their elite education had made available to them. However, rather than looking to exchange their valuable qualifications for job security or a stable income . . . their narratives strongly confirm the trend towards the individualization of middleclass careers in which young graduates seek to pursue "life projects" which maximize the scope for self-development.

By contrast, elite graduates from Paris, even though they are from comparably privileged backgrounds, have very different orientations:

> While our Oxford respondents' futures are characterized by fluidity, our French respondents seek progression. The Oxford narratives are very thin on sentiments of social allegiance or public service. Our Parisian narratives emphasize obligations to state and nation. (Power et al. 2013: 587)

The irony here is that where national elites are most cohesive and solidaristic, they can most readily withstand the call of "market pressures," which allow top income shares to pull away. Katharina Hecht's (2018) study of top income earners in the city of London is very instructive as a counterfactual here. Exceptionally highly paid professionals and managers, mainly working in finance and law—often internationally recruited—saw their own high remuneration as due to a market logic, which they also enacted. They showed little concern for the public good or civic values. Furthermore, most of them had no conception of the British nation, seeing London as a space unto itself, a cosmopolitan financial center that needed to operate by its own global market logic and had no intrinsic link to the wider British nation. These very-high earners felt no compunction about earning vast salaries, sometimes in excess of £1 million per year, as a reward for their skill and talent in their market-oriented work. The fact that such salaries would be viewed as obscenely high by other Britons, especially those in the north, simply passed them by.

Germany is the continental European nation with the greatest income inequality. In keeping with my arguments here, its emergence as the dominant nation in Europe may be associated with a quasi-imperial trend affiliated to elite formation. Michael Hartmann's (2018) study of the transnationality of different corporate elites is revealing here (Table 5.2).

Hartman measures the extent to which CEOs based in different nations are transnational. Despite the rhetoric regarding globalization, all the major economic powers—China, India, the United States, Russia, and Germany—have seen little diminution of national recruitment. By contrast, the United Kingdom and Switzerland stand out with the highest proportion of foreigners among their corporate elite ranks. Other nations with strong inequality trends (for example, Ireland, Australia) also have relatively large numbers of foreign CEOs. Germany has relatively few, though not a negligible number of foreign CEOs (15.6 percent), but it has an unusually high proportion of CEOs who have foreign experience—indeed, it appears to be almost an expectation for them to have worked abroad. By contrast, only a small proportion of US CEOs have worked abroad. As Germany is becoming the imperial hegemon within a still nationally segmented Europe, this may be marked in the migratory careers of its business leaders, who are also better rewarded than in other European nations. It may be overstating this trend to see it as a counterpart to the Roman imperial practice of sending its military leaders to patrol the distant borderlands, or the way that British civil servants in India eventually returned to Britain, but it is an arresting parallel nonetheless.

This line of thought can be extended by drawing on sociological research on the transnational practices of Europeans, drawn from the EUCROSS

Table 5.2: Degrees of internationality and transnationality of CEOs of the world's biggest companies

	N of Table CEO	Foreigners (percent)	Foreigners coming from a different language area and cultural environment (percent)	Foreign experiences of national CEOs (percent)
USA	306	27 (8.8)	8 (2.6)	26 (9.3)
Japan	99	2 (2.0)	2 (2.0)	30 (30.9)
China	94	0 (0.0)	0 (0.0)	7 (7.4)
Great Britain	50	22 (44.0)	7 (14.0)	7 (25.0)
France	45	2 (4.4)	2 (4.4)	15 (34.9)
Germany	32	5 (15.6)	2 (6.3)	20 (74.1)
Canada	32	9 (28.1)	1 (3.1)	5 (21.7)
South Korea	27	0 (0.0)	0 (0.0)	8 (29.6)
Switzerland	25	18 (72.0)	11 (44.0)	2 (28.6)
India	25	0 (0.0)	0 (0.0)	6 (24.0)
Hong Kong	25	2 (8.0)	0 (0.0)	9 (39.1)
Australia	20	9 (45.0)	0 (0.0)	2 (18.1)
Netherlands	17	5 (29.4)	2 (11.8)	6 (50.0)
Spain	16	0 (0.0)	0 (0.0)	3 (18.8)
Taiwan	16	0 (0.0)	0 (0.0)	4 (25.0)
Sweden	15	2 (13.3)	1 (6.7)	6 (46.2)
Italy	14	0 (0.0)	0 (0.0)	8 (57.1)
Russia	12	0 (0.0)	0 (0.0)	2 (16.7)
Brazil	10	1 (10.0)	1 (10.0)	3 (33.3)
Ireland	10	6 (60.0)	2 (20.0)	0 (0.0)
Other countries	112	16 (14.3)	7 (6.3)	28 (29.2)
Total	1002	126 (12.6)	46 (4.6)	197 (22.5)

Source: Reformatted from Michael Hartmann, "The International Business Elite: Fact or Fiction?" in Olav Korsnes et al., eds., *New Directions in Elite Studies* (London: Routledge, 2018), 31–45: Table 2.1. Hartmann analyzes data for the top thousand of the Forbes Global 2000, an annual list of the world's largest public companies.

survey (see Recchi et al. 2019). Drawing on comprehensive surveys and qualitative interviews in six European nations, this reveals that in general, Europeans do not feel at home in other nations. There is a contrast between southern European nations (Spain, Romania, and Italy) where a majority of the sampled population do not identify any other nation with which they are familiar, and the northern European countries, where more people do report such a general familiarity. But even here only a minority is familiar with more than one other nation.

EUCROSS data also reveal the enduring historical affiliations driving contemporary transnational networks (see Savage et al. 2019). Denmark scores high among those familiar with Greenland, reflecting the strong historical and colonial ties between the two countries. Germany's pattern is more diverse. It is the only one of the six nations that has an overrepresentation of familiarity with other European nations—which speaks very much to Germany's Euclidian location at the very center of the European project as noted by Mau (2010). The relatively strong ties with the United States and Turkey speak to both Germany's past role as a source of immigrants for the New World and more recently as a long-established place of settlement for Turkish incomers.

The most revealing pattern is that for the United Kingdom, which overall displays the highest levels of close familiarity with locations far flung across the globe. These reveal the enduring significance of the British empire, since many of the areas with which Britons are familiar have been former British colonies: notably Australia, New Zealand, Canada, the United States, and South Africa. Conversely, lower levels of familiarity are shown toward South and Central America, and perhaps more tellingly, across the rest of Europe. This reveals how the United Kingdom is part of an anglosphere, dominated by the United States, in which British "cosmopolitanism" extolls a version of post-British imperial whiteness (Savage et al. 2005a, 2010).

The significance of cultural and colonial ties also emerges when assessing the patterns for Spanish residents, who demonstrate disproportionate familiarity with Central and South America. Otherwise, Spain has relatively high levels of social isolation from other nations outside Europe, patterns that are even more pronounced in Italy and Romania. The power of imperial migration diaspora therefore remains fundamental in every case to the movement of European people today. Transnationalism and globalization have

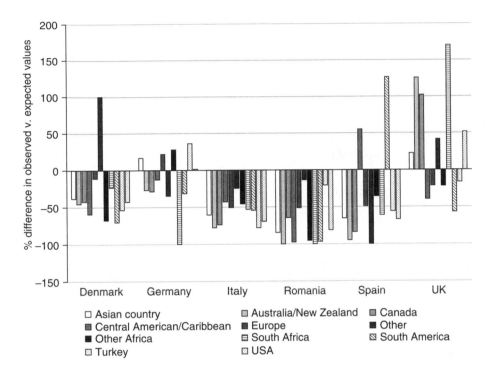

FIGURE 5.10: Global transnational familiarity of Europeans

Source: Reformatted from Mike Savage, Niall Cunningham, David Reimer, and Adrian Favell, "Cartographies of Social Transnationalism," in *Everyday Europe: Social Transnationalism in an Unsettled Continent*, ed. Ettore Recchi et al. (Bristol, UK: Bristol University Press, 2019), 35–60, figure 1.3.

not created a level playing field of global communication but has in fact allowed the proliferation of very specific historical geographies of contact, following routes and corridors laid down during imperial times.

In terms of global familiarity, the two most unequal nations in Europe, the United Kingdom and Germany, are characterized by unusually strong international affiliations. In Britain's case, these networks extend to its ex-imperial hinterland—both maritime European nations, and the old lands of the British empire. Germany's imperial ties can be construed somewhat differently, associated with its economic and geographical centrality in the European continent as a whole.

Figure 5.10 and 5.11 reveals the specific vectors of intra-European familiarity between European nations. As already indicated, Germany is at the center of European networks, and its residents report relatively high interaction rates

FIGURE 5.11: Internal European transnational familiarity of Danes, Germans, Britons, Spanish, Italians, and Romanians

Note: Percentage familiar with specified nation.
Source: Mike Savage, Niall Cunningham, David Reimer, and Adrian Favell, "Cartographies of Social Transnationalism," in *Everyday Europe: Social Transnationalism in an Unsettled Continent,* ed. Ettore Recchi et al. (Bristol, UK: Bristol University Press, 2019), 35–60, figure 1.4.

Danes' familiarity with other European countries

Germans' familiarity with other European countries

Britons' familiarity with other European countries

Spanish familiarity with other European countries

Italians' familiarity with other European countries

Romanian' familiarity with other European countries

with numerous European nations. Alongside its unusually close ties to Austria and Switzerland (based on linguistic ties), nearly 10 percent of its residents report close ties to France, Italy, and Spain. About 3–5 percent of its respondents report close connections with the Netherlands, the United Kingdom, Greece, Denmark, and Poland. These close connections demonstrate its central heartland role in Europe at large, though its apparent lack of reach into the Balkans and eastern Europe (except Poland) is noteworthy.

By contrast, the Danes' strong connections are to neighboring nations Norway, Sweden, Germany, Netherlands and the United Kingdom, along with Italy, France, Austria and Spain at the next remove. Clearly, the ties to Norway and Sweden represent Scandinavian ties (though the lack of connection found here to Finland is striking), which is of course underscored by the proximity of these nations to Denmark; a bridge and a joint airport link Denmark and Sweden. Taking out these Scandinavian connections would place Denmark as much less connected than the United Kingdom or Germany.

The United Kingdom is strikingly different due to the strength of its southern European ties (Spain, Italy, Greece, and Cyprus—see Figure 5.11). Indeed, note that all the nations where Britons report close connections are maritime countries (there is a striking absence of central and eastern European connections), thus underscoring again the imperial legacy with its historic naval routes.

This has been an extended but analytically vital detour to reflect on why European nations are now the global exceptions in being less unequal than other parts of the world. Distinctive national processes, affiliated with an older imperial heritage, remain powerful in Europe. They permit greater internal coherence and entail that national elites may be prepared to place their civic leadership roles ahead of pure market imperatives.

At this point, it is necessary to remember my argument from Chapter 3 that wealth ultimately trumps income inequality in importance. This allows us to place the relatively subdued shift toward greater income inequality in Europe in a different light. Many European nations have a relatively high amount of wealth inequality, and the continent as a whole continues to be a major center of global wealth accumulation, where its share has increased in line with global trends since 2000. Indeed, it continues to rival the United States and Asia on this score and has not lost significant ground since 2000. Europe's distinctive role in wealth accumulation goes back to its imperial

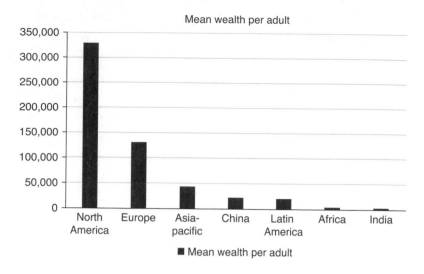

FIGURE 5.12: Mean wealth in different parts of the world

Data source: James B. Davies, Rodrigo Lluberas, and Anthony F. Shorrocks, "Estimating the Level and Distribution of Global Wealth, 2000–2014," *The Review of Income and Wealth* 63, no. 4 (2017), table 4.

history, and Gabriel Zucman (2015) has emphasized the role of European nations, led by Swiss banks, in driving recent offshore wealth accumulation. Europe's distinctive role in wealth accumulation is also evident when comparing the breakdown of large wealth holders, especially those with more than $100,000. Whereas millionaires are predominantly drawn from North America, Europe still outscores Asian millionaires.

From this perspective, Europe remains a global center of accumulated wealth. The singular nature of the British experience can best be understood in terms of its singular geopolitical location spanning Europe and the anglosphere. Advani and Summers (2000) have shown how the rise of top incomes in the United Kingdom over the past decade is associated with income derived from capital gains (and hence from wealth accumulation). Migrants are also strongly overrepresented among its top earners (Koenig et al. 2020), indicating its singular role as global entrepot for capital. In this light, the Brexit vote marks a distinctive repositioning of sections of its elite toward its older anglophone imperial heartland. Therefore, to represent Brexit as a nationalist reaction is not as accurate as seeing it as an attempt to revive an older imperial legacy (see Flemmen and Savage 2017; Bhambra 2017). European exceptionalism should be understood in terms of its residual affiliation to national coherence, in forms that are enduring but also under considerable strain.

5.5: The South American and African "Squeeze"

The South American and African situations share some similarities: unlike Asia, they were more completely colonized by European powers during early modernity. They were also subject to systematic structural adjustment policies from the 1980s (Hickel 2017). South American nations established their national independence from the early nineteenth century; African nations mainly decolonized in the middle and later twentieth century. Unlike in Asia, no dominant nations have been able to establish their supremacy, with the result that both continents are now fractured into numerous smaller nations: in this respect, rather akin to the European model. Having said this, in South America, Brazil dominates, being easily the largest South American nation: It was identified as one of the BRIC emerging economies.

It is difficult to generalize about inequality trends in South America and Africa. The WID data cover only a minority of nations here (see Figure 5.13), so we are mainly reliant on the kind of aggregate Gini coefficient measures that have been criticized by Piketty and others. Simson (2018, see also Simson and Savage 2020) helpfully draws together this comparative information into the most systematic form we have and points to significant variations in Africa and South America. However, she also shows that there is no general trend for inequality to rise as much as in the four "empires" I have sketched out. The main exception is South Africa.

We should be careful about drawing wider inferences. In the Brazilian case, where there is data from WID, the apparent decline of the Gini coefficient needs to be counterposed to the fact there has been a rise and or at least stability in the top income shares. The small number of African and South American nations with WID data is shown in Figure 5.13. Here, as in Europe, the trends are stable, even declining, with the stark exception of South Africa, where inequality has mushroomed and is now among the highest in the world.

Table 5.3 lists those nations that Simson identifies as definitely experiencing inequality decline in recent decades. With one exception, they are in South

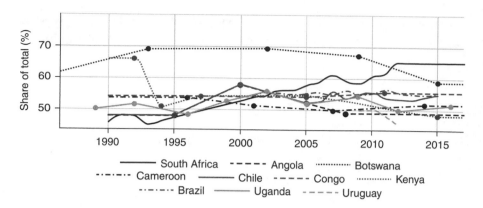

FIGURE 5.13: Share of national income going to the top 10 percent earners in select South American and African nations

Source: World Inequality Database.

America. Indeed, most nations on this continent have experienced some apparent decline—evidently bucking the trends in many other parts of the world. How should we interpret this? Partly it reflects that there have been historically high levels of inequality in these nations, so that these trends might be seen as a correction from a very high base. Exogenous economic factors are no doubt significant, but we can also reflect that there has been an unusual and historically important nation-building process occurring in South America, which does not have ready recent parallels elsewhere. The history of South America in recent decades is turbulent, in terms of shifts from democratic to authoritarian regimes and the persistence of armed conflict. Perhaps we can draw parallels to the significance of national formation that I elaborated in the European case. In South America, there have been major national rebuilding projects in nations such as Chile, Peru, Brazil, and Argentina, where this has been a process of recovery from fascist dictatorships and an attempt to reinstate liberal democracies. During the early twenty-first century in many of these nations, explicitly left-wing parties with social-democratic ambitions enjoyed electoral appeal, and their social spending was enabled by the commodity boom of the times. Such developments help underline the shift toward certain redistributionist policies, such as cash transfers, which are associated with some of the shift toward less inequality in South America. Just as European nation-building during the recovery from the world wars and decolonization during the middle decades

Table 5.3: Nations that have experienced definite inequality reduction, as measured by Gini coefficient

	Gini drop (points)	Population size (million)	End of dictatorship
Argentina	6.9 (1996–2012)	44	1983
Brazil	10.1 (1989–2011)	208	1985
Chile	5.2 (1987–2011)	18	1988
Columbia	3.9 (2002–2011)	49	
Dominican republic	4.8 (2003–2010)	11	
Ecuador	11.6 (1998–2011)	16	1979
Guatemala	6 (2000–2014)	17	1985
Mexico	6.8 (1996–2010)	128	
Nicaragua	10 (1993–2014)	6	1979
Panama	4.9 (1997–2011) (mainly since 2003)	4	1990 (US invasion)
Paraguay	7.2 (1995–2009)	7	1949
Peru	10.5 (1998–2011)	32	1980
Uruguay	6.6 (2002–2012)	3	1985
Venezuela	9.0 (2002–2010)	32	—
Thailand	7 (1990–2013)	69	2007

Data source: Rebecca Simson, "Mapping Recent Inequality Trends in Developing Countries," Working Paper 24, London School of Economics International Inequalities Institute, May 2018.

of the twentieth century was associated with a striking decline in inequality, perhaps we are seeing a parallel process in South America, which sets it apart from other regions of the world.

The African case might be explained in terms of the weakness of both imperial and national models. Between 1990 and 2016, the share of the world's lowest-paid 10 percent who were African rose substantially (from about 20 percent to over 30 percent). A continent ravaged by European imperialism and without the more powerful national models found in South America, Africa has not found the political forms to resist trends toward imperial global inequality. South Africa's unique position here is also a counterpart to its role as the dominant nation within sub-Saharan Africa—in this respect, it is the Germany of Africa.

Trends in inequality across Africa are remarkably varied as illustrated by Beegle et al. (2016: 125) and Odusola et al. (2017: viii). Outside of southern Africa, most African countries have a Gini coefficient below 0.5, and there is also variation in the trends in inequality. Simson and Savage (2020) identify Mali, Guinea, Burkina Faso, Niger, and Mauritania as experiencing declines in their Gini coefficients between the early 1990s and 2010. Yet the continent is home to areas of extremely high inequities. As measured by the Gini coefficient, ten of the nineteen most unequal countries in the world are from Sub-Saharan Africa (SSA) (Odusola et al. 2017). Thus, if these country coefficients are averaged, SSA sits alongside Latin America as the most unequal territory in the world. Indeed, five of the world's top ten most unequal countries, including South Africa, are from southern Africa (Pabon 2021).

5.6: The Return of Empire

I now draw my arguments together. Rising inequality is associated with the resurgence of imperial formations driven by aggrandizing elites. The dominant narrative of modern development, couched in terms of the rise of the nation-state (see, for example, Wimmer and Min 2006; Wimmer and Feinstein 2010), has run its course. Inequality challenges the coherence of national formations in multiple ways: by reducing internal solidarities in nation spaces; by producing wealthy elites with inordinate influence over national bodies; by reducing civic engagement; and by accentuating competitive pressures among major national powers, thus generating greater global instability.

My argument therefore suggests that the commonplace view that autonomous nations remain the key building blocks of social scientific analysis needs to be updated. Andreas Wimmer (2017) records that whereas in 1900, less than 40 percent of the world's area was governed as autonomous nation-states, by 2000, that figure was 95 percent. The globe, he reports,

> is divided into a series of sovereign states, each supposed to represent a nation bound together by shared history and common culture. To us, this political map seems as obvious as the shapes of continents and the rivers that run through them. With the exception of the Middle Eastern monarchies and some small European principalities, most of today's

states are ruled in the name of a nation of equal citizens, rather than dynasty or divine will. (Wimmer 2017: 606)

Even though technically this remains true, it fails to recognize how escalating inequality ruptures the coherence of nation-building projects and entails the aggrandizement of quasi-imperial elites pulling away from other citizens.

It is much more helpful to identify these trends with resurgent empire building than the banal idea of globalization—a term that is too loose. In fact, it is growing regionalization, whereby different areas of the world form discrete power blocs that is more significant here. Beckfield (2010: 1055), examining the role of international organizations, notes that "political ties among states and international organizations have become less dense and cohesive overall" and that there is "growing potential for substantial difference, centralization, fragmentation, and disintegration. The world (polity) is not flat."

Instead, recognizing the renewal of empire in a postcolonial world offers three major routes into inequality research. First, it sheds light on Piketty's point that we are returning to nineteenth-century patterns of inequality by acknowledging that this was also the period when imperial forms had their heyday. This point has been reiterated by Osterhammel (2014), who has criticized "modernist" theories of nationalism that project national projects into the eighteenth and nineteenth centuries. He has instead identified empire as the dominant territorial formation throughout the long nineteenth century. Perhaps, then, the return of imperial forms marks the end of the twentieth-century experience in which nation-states—briefly—interrupted the successive rise and fall of empires and also managed to establish lower levels of internal inequality.

Second, this imperial recognition builds on reflections on "state capture," the idea that national governments are operating hand-in-glove with increasingly prominent economic elites. This is precisely the theme that Joe Stiglitz (2011) pursued with his reflections on American policy being "of the 1%, by the 1%, for the 1%." It is also the theme that economic historian Walter Scheidel (2018) has drawn out as significant across history, where the meshing of economic elites with systems of rule is the norm. Wimmer's argument that most of today's states are ruled in the name of a nation of equal citizens, rather than by dynasty or divine will is increasingly under strain.

Third, by reflecting on national and imperial forms being in competition with each other, and as implicated by differing modes of inequality, we can generate a disturbing interpretation of global inequality trends and the geopolitics these entail. During the twentieth century and especially in the period between 1945 and 1970, the power of empires was radically curtailed as the nation-state became the most significant unit of political governance. This process of national formation was led by richer countries mostly from the global north. It entailed the construction of national-level social contracts, which bound differing groups to a common national project. Yet decolonization also went hand in hand with the consolidation of strong and entrenched inequalities between richer metropolitan and poorer (third-world) nations. Notwithstanding the persistence of inequalities within rich nations, the developed nations of the global north systematically benefitted from unequal relations with the former colonies and dependent territories of the global south. If you were fortunate enough to live in North America, much of western Europe, or Australasia, your generally affluent life chances were fundamentally depended on being part of the national project. This is what Branko Milanovic (2016) calls "citizenship rent."

In the decades since the 1980s, nations have steadily lost this overarching power to frame the economic and social fortunes of their citizens through some kind of social contract—or what, following my reading of Bourdieu, can be identified as nationally organized fields or "nation spaces." In many (even though not all) nations, there is increasing internal differentiation among citizens. As middle-income earners are squeezed, so one's shared national fate becomes less significant than whether one is at the top or bottom of the pile, thus enhancing competitive pressures within nations themselves. The wealthiest members of any nation become more intertwined in transnational networks and interactions, so their fortunes become less dependent on these national framings. However, those in the middle classes and more affluent working classes in the richer nations lose ground relatively, as they can no longer "hang on to the coattails" of their nation-state's aggregate prosperity. Migration systematically allows greater potential for people to move away from their nation of origin and so further intensifies the breakdown of these national orders.

These trends can be seen to mark the reassertion of the spirit of empire. Wimmer (2017: 113) historical definition of empires as "characterized by centralized bureaucratic forms of government, the domination of a core region over peripheries, an ethnically or culturally defined hierarchy between rulers and ruled, and claims to universal legitimacy" can usefully be applied to imperial resurgence today. It is certainly true that many of the most virulent forms of authoritarianism and nationalism—such as in Russia, Turkey, India, China, and the United Kingdom, are in nations with strong, and resurgent, universalist sentiments. Milanovic (2019) also brings out the success of state-led authoritarianism in Asia, testifying to the significance of bureaucratic governance. The problem for American imperial interest may well lie in the failings of its centralized bureaucratic rule.

Given that inequalities intensify hierarchies, and given the universalist economistic discourses that can underpin economic inequality, there is a mutually reinforcing cycle in which imperial forces intersect with growing elite power. This argument may appear to be counterintuitive, given the evident rise of nationalism in many areas of the world, but much of virulent nationalist sentiment can be better read as imperial aggrandizement—nowhere more evident than Donald Trump's invocation of "America first." This interpretation is consistent with key features of contemporary social change: the global hegemony of the American empire and its anglophone satellites; the loss of European global centrality; the rising significance of the Chinese, Indian, and Russian imperial fields; the significance of transnational religious blocs; the role of transnational corporations as corporate bodies extending above nations; and the power of metropolitan cities. In these cases, extended processes of accumulation have led to formations that transcend the boundaries of nation-states.

With these thoughts in mind, we can better reflect on the considerable historical significance of the large number of small nations for the global geopolitics of inequality. There are no fewer than thirty-eight nations with less than a million residents. Due to their size, they are little researched, and we know little about their social structure. However, many of these small nations are central to global capital flows and wealth accumulation. These include Luxemburg in Europe, the center of European banking interests; and the Bahamas, the Cayman Islands, and Bermuda, which are central locations for offshore wealth. For a brief period in the years before 2008, Iceland was also a major site of financial speculation (see Zucman 2015). These small nations are not obsolescent eccentricities left behind by the formation of modern nations (see Ogle 2017). Instead they are actually central players in the global economy as locations where offshore wealth can be parked to avoid tax liabilities imposed by larger nations. To leave out these nations from our analysis would therefore be profoundly mistaken: They act as trade entrepots mediating between major imperial forces. These city-state nations are also distinctive because of their high migrant populations.

Conclusion

In this chapter, I have sketched out a global interpretation of inequality trends that recognizes the variability of experiences in different parts of the world and explicates these experiences in terms of the renewal of empire. My point of departure has been to follow through on my insistence from Chapter 4 that we avoid comparing nations as if they were analytically equivalent units. Focusing on the relativities within national borders obscures the very different absolute sizes of nations. Similarly, simply extrapolating about global inequality trends—important though this is—obscures vital geopolitical considerations. This point is nowhere more evident than in the reassertion of Asian over European hegemony, which is taking place today, and which marks in the most direct way the cyclical return of history. The centrality of European national reference points in current social science debate and rhetoric is an artefact of the accretion of social science data and expertise in these lands.

In recent decades, those areas of the world that are experiencing greater inequality within their borders are predominantly the increasingly powerful imperial blocs—the United States and its anglophone satellites (the United Kingdom, Australia, and Canada), China, India, and Russia. Half of the global superrich now come from just these four nations (especially the United States). In these blocs, we are seeing particularly marked growth of income inequalities with accentuating and intensifying divisions between elites and popular groups. We witness more evidence of imperial formations, including militarism, authoritarianism, and xenophobia. By contrast, in those areas of the world where national forms remain more powerful—notably in parts of continental Europe and South America—recent trends toward escalating income inequality are much less marked.

The growth of inequality in many parts of the world (as well as wider economic and geopolitical shifts) can therefore be understood in terms of the reassertion of empire, in which there are now three major contending groups: the still globally dominant American hegemonic bloc, which competes with Russian and Chinese imperial blocs. These three imperial formations should not be understood as being symmetrical: whereas the Asian empires are territorial, the American bloc's power comes not so much from its territorial jurisdiction as much as its financial, military, and corporate global reach. Russia is smaller and weaker economically, but its history of military power and its sheer geographical size also define it as a major imperial presence. Behind these three major imperial players are several other quasi-imperial formations seeking their place at the table: India, the United Kingdom, and Turkey being the clearest examples. In every case there has been a substantial rise of inequality in these nations, as assertive elites become increasingly prominent among their ranks. They also have squeezed out higher earners elsewhere: in 1990, about 70 percent of the top 0.1 percent of the global income distribution (that is, the global superrich) came from outside the United States, Russia, China, and India. By 2016, this number had fallen to a little more than 50 percent. The world's superrich are increasingly being found in imperial heartlands. The squeeze at the top had mainly been applied to the Middle East, South America, and Europe. European nations and smaller Asian and Middle Eastern nations have thereby lost ground to these blocs, with Germany and Japan being partial outliers.

Inequality matters not simply because it reveals differential rewards among people, but also because it testifies to the return of history. Rising inequality within nations, allied to the patterns of global economic growth, testify to the waxing power of imperial blocs and the declining force of national entities that in the past have acted to damp down (to a lesser or greater extent) inequality within their borders.[8]

6

Insiders and Outsiders

RACE, GENDER, AND CLASS
IN LONG-TERM PERSPECTIVE

The *stuff* of inequality is all around us. But what is this stuff? Borrowing from network sociologist Harrison White (1992), the awareness of inequality ultimately derives from the contingency of recognizing that you are different from others. It is when we feel that a particular script does not, and cannot, apply to us, that difference slides into inequality. This stuff—this feeling—of inequality is historically tied up with the formation of social groups and identities. The systematic and pervasive power of race, gender, and class—along with numerous other divisions associated with hierarchical, exploitative, and unjust social relationships across time and place—is deeply felt around the globe and is amply attested by much scholarship, both academic and popular.

Yet, this "groupness," this *stuff,* which seems so immediate and direct, also turns out to be remarkably difficult to render analytically. Yes, it is associated with some kind of differential, exploitative, or unequal relationship between groups (or what social scientists formally refer to as *categories*), but beyond this, there is little consensus. I can attest to this, having spent many years in seemingly intractable debates about the definition of social class (for example, Savage et al. 1992, 2015; Savage 2000). Similarly for gender. Or is it actually sex? Or should we be concerned with gendering? And should we talk about racial or ethnic divisions? Should we put quotes around "race"? And what about other kinds of stuff? Age. Disability. Sexual orientation. Sexual reassignment. Location. Religion. And so on. In all these cases, the stuff of inequality seems so powerful, violent, and immediate, and yet it can lose focus as we approach it and try to grasp its essence, its distinctive qualities.

This chapter approaches these apparently intractable issues by reflecting on the significance of *duration*. Rather than treat the opacity of the stuff of inequality as a problem that needs to be rectified by a better theoretically, scientifically, or empirically validated set of measures, I instead treat this ambiguousness as itself the crucial issue to address. The very idea that inequality can be rendered through distinguishing between groups is itself historically strange and only became prominent at a specific historical period, that of imperial modernity. Defining groups—in which you are placed according to some kind of abstract set of characteristics, such as your occupation, sex, skin color, or any other feature—extracts us from the necessarily complex web of lineages, affiliations, social ties, and identities that surround us in our daily lives and often bring us into contact with a great variety of people.[1]

Chapters 6 and 7 tell a story of how the changing stuff of inequality matches the shifts in distributional inequality that economists have so powerfully brought out. It is common to separate out different axes of inequality, to prioritize some kinds over others, and to split them into different analytical registers—for instance, separating out inequalities of distribution, opportunity, and recognition. However, I resist this kind of siloing: The renewed force of history, in the form of intensified capital accumulation and the return of imperial elite power, weighs down on everything. I emphasize that there are links between distributional and categorical inequalities. Rather than the conventional wisdom of distinguishing the politics of redistribution from that of recognition, or setting economic inequality against identity politics, we need to realize how these dimensions are associated. Taking time and duration more seriously allows us to synthesize inequalities rather than fragment them into diverse and often competing lists, measures, and definitions.

I set the scene by reflecting on the different kinds of stakes involved in visualizing categorical inequalities, using as an example the changing definitions of "ethnic group" in the American census since 1790. This is instructive, because on the face of it, the trends seem to have little in common with the distributional curve of the economists, as revealed in Figure 1.1. There seems to be no obvious return to older patterns of inequality, no inverted Kuznets curve, in the manner that Piketty brought out. However, reviewing this example is a prelude to drawing profound links. Groups become historically salient during imperial modernity, which distinguished insiders from outsiders along numerous axes. In this respect, there is an affinity between the high-inequality regimes characteristic of the nineteenth century and the existence of very strong, hierarchically defined, social groups, especially with respect to race and gender. Categories organized groups into elite insiders set against outsiders, seen as not able fully to partake of the progressive liberal vision of civility, freedom, and enlightenment. This sets in train a long-term trend for the organization of these "classic categories" (as I will call them) to sieve out those "left behind" in the slipstream of capitalist modernity, leading to a politics of categorical redemption that might allow such excluded groups to enjoy the embrace of progress.

During the twentieth century, as economic inequality declines within nation spaces, groups become defined probabilistically—that is to say, less as natural, moral, or ontological categories and more in terms of the differential life chances, advantages, and disadvantages they experience. The very formation of nation spaces is bound up with mechanisms allowing the measurement of the differential life chances of its inhabitants, seen as located in its bounded territory. These construe field relations around national parameters. This was linked to a shift in the capitalist economy toward a more highly skilled workforce and maximizing stocks of human capital. All this depended on the rapid expansion of social science expertise and in particular, the application of probabilistic quantitative techniques. Thereby the analysis of categorical inequality was put on a supposedly more scientific footing by appearing to strip out the moralizing baggage of classic categories.

The weakening of nation spaces and the return of imperial inequality, which I have described in Chapter 5, has led to the declining significance of relative inequalities among much of the social body while elites have frequently pulled away. I will go on to argue in Chapter 7 that this weakening is bound up with the emergence of a visceral body politics in which categorical distinctions become increasingly marked on the body—and thereby return to older divides.

But this is leaping ahead.

6.1: Visualizing the Stuff of Inequality

Figure 1.1, with which I started this book, offers a crisp, clear narrative of the return of economic inequality. Let us bear this figure in mind when comparing it with Figure 6.1, which visualizes the changing labels used to define ethnicity in the US census from its inception in 1790 to 2010. It is immediately evident that Figure 6.1 lacks a clear narrative sparkline demonstrating clear trends over time (such as Figures 1.1, 3.1, and 5.1). Nor is there a neat regression line, such as that used by Wilkinson and Pickett (see Figure 4.1). There are no crisp lines, but at first glance a steady proliferation of ethnic labels, which might be taken to reveal growing sophistication and refined measurement of ethnicity. But, not so fast!

Censuses originated in most European nations in the later eighteenth or early nineteenth centuries and became fundamental to the formation of national polities throughout the world as they counted and classified their populations.[2] Indeed, from this period, the census became a central device for both imperial and later national formation—it was not possible to function as an imperial power or autonomous nation without some kind of census device to count your citizens. Thereby, although census categories only offer one way of rendering trends in how ethnicity is understood, it is very telling. State-sponsored classification is hugely revealing—they delineate the very terms through which categories are publicly measured and hence legitimated, and thereby provide a litmus test on how they are constructed, contested, and modified over time. This is amply indicated by the strident disputes about the measurement of sex and gender in the 2021 UK census, around which different kinds of feminists, social scientists, and trans-activists have come to blows.

With this in mind, let us consider what Figure 6.1 reveals. Here again, Figure 1.1, with its emphatic narrative of "inequality is back," is a useful foil. Figure 6.1 by contrast does not appear to show a return to the stark divides of the 1790s. Ethnic labels defy a linear format, and on the whole, they proliferate, appear, and sometimes disappear over time. The criteria being used to define them also shifts at different moments in history. In short, there is a much more tortuous and complex history than is revealed by distributional trends.

If we look carefully at Figure 6.1, some arresting features nonetheless swim into focus. First, there is an overarching racial divide, absolutely

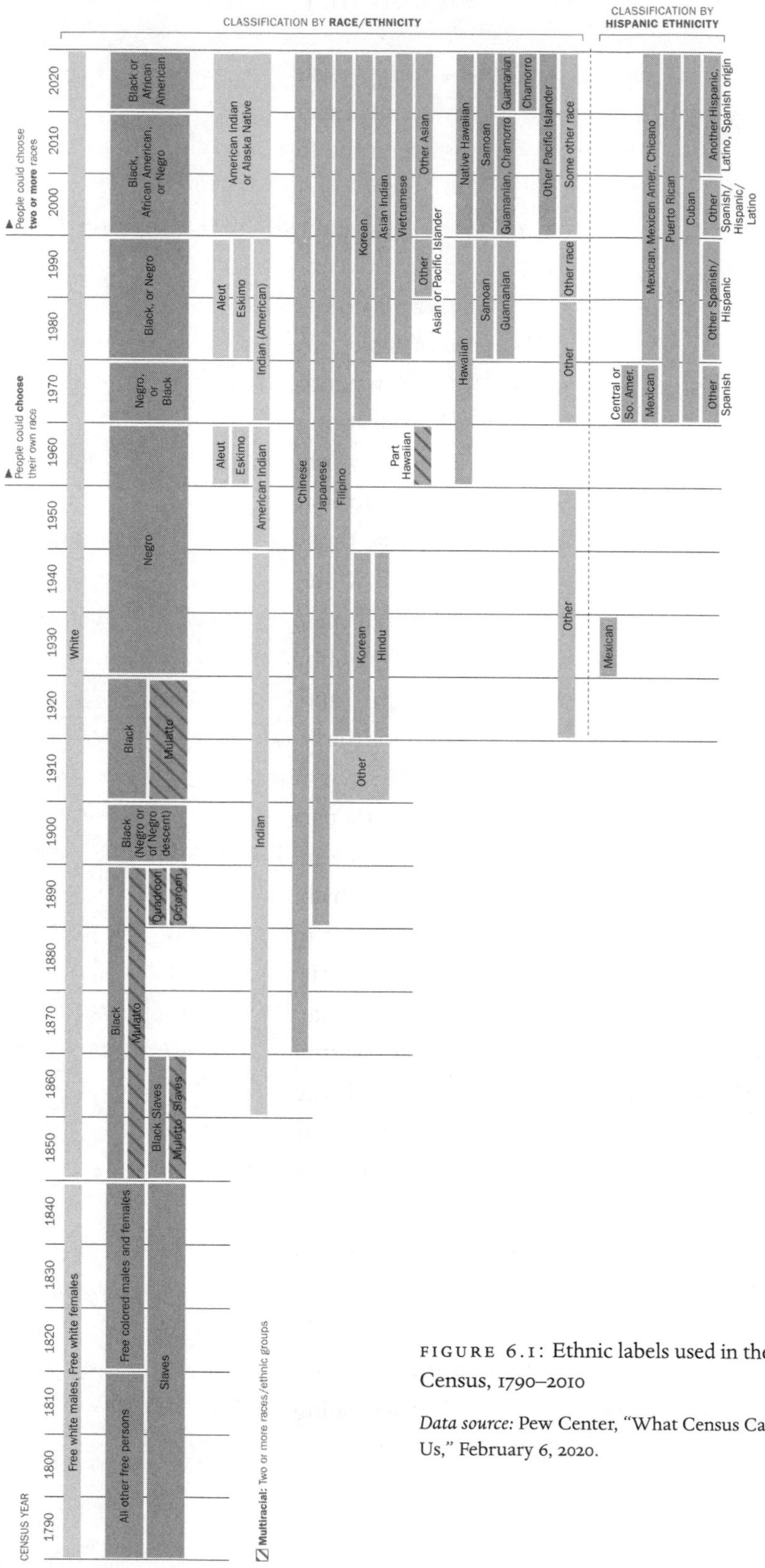

FIGURE 6.1: Ethnic labels used in the US Census, 1790–2010

Data source: Pew Center, "What Census Calls Us," February 6, 2020.

pivotal in the early decades, but which persists. At its inception in 1790, there were only three categories: free white males and females, slaves, and "all other free persons." This distinction between the free and enslaved was racialized and remains so.[3] The default that "white" people are free and thereby define citizenship itself, needing no further elaboration, remains constant until 2010. After 1860, the census differentiates between various kinds of South American and Asian populations, but there is no equivalent need to distinguish between types of whites. This is remarkable, given the differential immigration waves of whites from various European nations, which had a major effect on US history. From the US census classification point of view, German, Italian, English, Irish, Swedish, Jewish, and many other kinds of "whites" could presumably be assumed to be of the same free stock. By contrast, "blackness" is a much more minutely dissected term: thus the now largely arcane terms, such as mulatto (mixed-race black and white), octoroon (one-eighth black); quadroon (one-quarter black). These all speak to the cultural power of the "one drop" rule. We can also see anxiety about the labeling of blackness, revealed by shifts between "black," "negro," and "African American" labels over time. The term "Hindu" is deployed for thirty years beginning in 1920 to represent Asian Indians (who presumably may not actually have been Hindu). The terms used to label those who are not part of the free white default demonstrate the census makers' incessant uneasiness and anxiety about grasping and delineating the boundary of race, which has a founding, classic role in American history. As the Black Lives Matter movement has emphasized, and as I discuss further in Chapter 7, this core racial divide remains a fundamental feature of early twenty-first-century America.

We can also see a second principle, starting in 1860s, when American Indians are also counted. This is the period when there is redress for the most striking absentees from the initial census—the indigenous population, the oldest dwellers of North American, who are invisible in the early decades of the Census, despite the pedigree of their residence. Their numbers in Indian reservations were not counted until as late as 1890. Whereas Black slaves were outsiders who were nonetheless insiders in American society—by virtue of the forced labor they carried out for American capital—American Indians did not exist as meaningful and countable subjects until considerably later—in fact, after they stopped being a threat to the white settler way of life.[4]

From the later eighteenth century, the number of categories prolifer-ates as a tool to describe a much wider range of ethnicities with a much more refined measurement of different non-white populations. These do not eclipse the classic racialized divides but overlay them, offering a much greater palette of labels. This process reaches a peak at the end of the twentieth century, by which time there are nineteen ethnic categories. The time when categorical proliferation reaches a new height is when Asian and South American immigration takes over in numerical significance from European immigration. It is now the minute and highly specific na-ture of the differentiation which is striking. Samoans and native Hawaiians are distinguished, for instance. This process of proliferation is a precondi-tion for rendering categories as *probabilistic,* potentially identifying dif-ferent kinds of prospects and life chances across a complex, differentiated population.

In 1960, Americans were finally given the opportunity to choose their own ethnic category.[5] This ushers in an important moment, in which rather than expert professionals deciding what categories Americans had to use, the very act of categorization was deemed to be one that individ-uals themselves had the right to enact in their census returns. This has become increasingly powerful not only for ethnicity, but also for sexu-ality, gender, class, religion, and elsewhere. Rather than attesting to the declining significance of groups, it testifies to the increasing stakes at-tached to them, as discussed in Chapter 7.

Figure 6.1 therefore tells a story of continuity and change that does not appear to tally with the linear pattern of Figure 1.1. We see some enduring tropes: the racialized politics of white racism. Black and minority catego-ries are defined as "other" to white free default. Yet we also see a cascading process of categorical proliferation and enlistment, to the extent that these unsettle and disrupt the classic divide. From the later twentieth century, Americans themselves are enrolled in these measurements so changing the very stakes in which categories are defined. In fact, I will show that we can trace parallels between economic distribution and the ordering of the stuff of inequality. To make this argument, I need to set out—necessarily, given the vast range of the topic, in broad brush strokes—the historical genesis of classic group divides during imperial modernity.

6.2: Insiders and Outsiders: White Anxieties in the Genesis of Classic Categories

Categorical inequalities became prominent during the eighteenth and nineteenth centuries as a by-product of modernizing currents associated with early capitalist expansion through empire.[6] The Marxist concept of primitive accumulation alerts us to this: early capitalism depended on creating propertyless proletarians who had no alternative but to sell their labor. But the logic of dispossession should be extended beyond class alone to include the organization of gender and race at the very inception of capitalist development. Within this modernizing current, privileged white European elites saw themselves as exemplifying social progress and civility, which required differentiation from those who were seen to lack these qualities, but who could nonetheless be bent to serve this mission. It was in this spirit that imperial projects were pursued by the European powers, fully confident of their mission to educate and improve humanity around the globe.[7] Categorical distinctions crystallized out of these elite anxieties to differentiate themselves from those who could not be trusted to embody this progressive mission, but whose labor power, emotional labor, and acquiescence was necessary for their mission to be realized. The modern temporal ontology that I unpicked in Chapter 3 drove this engine, a central underpinning to the production and reproduction of core classic categories.

There has been a tendency to read the rise of modernity as driven by liberal, rather than imperial capitalist imperatives. Here, the familiar story is of the expansion of citizenship and democracy, respect for individual rights guaranteed by contract, and an emphasis on meritocracy and achievement as central to modernity. Such perspectives have even been underscored by those wishing to debunk the progressivity of the liberal project itself. Michel Foucault's (1976, 1977) arguments that the formation of "liberal governmentality" from the early nineteenth century elicited modes of individuality and subjectivity in the name of freedom have become very influential. However, notwithstanding the appeal of this critical riposte to normative liberal thinking, this approach misunderstands key historical dynamics. The early modern invocation to see individuals as possessing interior feelings and subjectivities did so by appealing to them as intrinsically belonging to distinctive social groups (Wahrman 2004).[8] Appeals that abstracted individuals from these characteristics only became dominant during the later twentieth century. Until this moment, modernizing capitalist societies were much more vested in creating classic categorical divisions, in which fundamental boundaries were set in place between "insiders" (those who were respectable and could be trusted to be bearers of the forward looking, modernizing, and civilizing project) and different kinds of outsiders who could not (and who somehow needed to kept safely outside, in their place, or brought up to speed).[9]

This complex typically generated an anxiety about the difficulties of outsider groups being fully able to participate in the newly emergent social and civilized "body" (on which, see Poovey 1995). Here, in diagnosing these boundaries of the civilized habitus, social science developed as a set of intellectual tools to diagnose and remedy the ills—the underbelly—of those living in imperial modernity but who could not be trusted to abide by its precepts. This was driven by research on the dynamics of poverty, crime, delinquency, insurrection, and deviance, both "at home" and in colonial territories. It was this rather unsavory complex that ultimately morphed into twentieth-century social science.[10] The history of categorical thinking cannot be detached from its roots in this elite modernizing anxiety concerned with differentiating those who could, and could not, be trusted.

Over the course of the nineteenth century, this elite anxiety came to systematize moral into "social" categories. In the early decades of imperial modernity, those not fully able to be a part of the liberal order were seen as morally deficient—work-shy, lazy, alcoholic, criminal, and so on. Within influential eugenics frameworks, these moral inadequacies were often seen to be rooted in biological characteristics associated with race and sex. There is a "progressive" story that over the course of the nineteenth century, these moralizing categories were challenged by social scientific research emphasizing that it was environmental forces, not innate capacities, which caused moral failings. But even here, the same intellectual architecture was at work. These environmental perspectives still saw fundamental moral differences between insiders and outsiders, even if they had a different kind of account as to why the distinctions came about.

This point modifies Foucault's influential thinking, which has had so much influence in our contemporary theorizations of liberal and neoliberal "governmentality." For Foucault, liberal governmentality is organized around rule through freedom, in which individuals come to know themselves by judging the extent to which their conduct is "normal," according to medical, legal, and governmental conventions. This framing has a certain power in the French context: In the aftermath of the French Revolution, the elaboration of republican principles entailed unusually powerful scientific tools (for instance, metricization), which could be used to establish abstract norms. However, in most places, deviance was categorized rather than individualized and "normalized." It was deemed to be possessed by specific outsider groups, located outside the civilizing process. Returning to the discussion in Chapter 1, the classic case is the definition of poverty itself. From the early nineteenth century, the view that relieving poverty was some kind of (often limited) communal obligation was increasingly challenged by utilitarians, who saw poverty as a moral failing that had to be dealt with by creating a cost-benefit environment that offered the least possible incentive to shirk the chance to earn money from employment. Enshrined in Britain in the 1834 New Poor Law, this differentiated "deserving" from "undeserving" poor, thereby drawing a categorical boundary between paupers and the social body. During the later nineteenth century, poverty was increasingly identified by reformist intellectuals as produced by insecure work and poor living conditions (Stedman Jones 1971). Those proclaiming this more "social" interpretation of poverty appeared at odds with those proclaiming it to be the result of moral failings, but in fact, these were two sides of the same coin—alternative ways of arguing why people fell onto different sides of fence. Socialist Fabian currents, including those associated with the early British Labour Party, shared with their liberal contemporaries the view that there were categorical boundaries between the poor outsider and civilized insider members of society, even when they disagreed about the reasons these boundaries existed.

In short, nineteenth-century capitalist imperial modernity engendered a systematic production of social categories, driven by elite anxiety about the boundaries around respectability and civility. This was a drawing of lines between the kinds of people who could be expected to be part of the progressive project, and those who were outside its bounds and had to be kept at bay, educated, or otherwise "managed." This process of categorical boundary became endemic across the globe and was bound up with imperialism: a famous instance being the way that Indian civil servants and British social scientists sought to define caste boundaries in India (Dirks 2001), replacing the more diffuse and fuzzy definitions that had existed previously (see also Bayly on "statistical liberalism" from the same period). This elaboration of classic social categories takes place along numerous axes, with race, gender, and class being particularly important.

6.2.1: Race

Race, interspersed with ethnic and religious affiliations, was the axial classic categorical divide for modernizing imperial capitalist societies. This is clearly evident in the American case, as illustrated in Figure 6.1. One crude but telling indication of this is the frequency of deliberate genocidal killings of groups based on racial / ethnic / religious lines that has systematically occurred throughout modernity—most tragically, of course, in the Nazi holocaust, but this is only one instance among many. Joseph-Achille Mbembe's (2003) term "necropolitics" captures well how racial categories are organized around death projects (he broadens this term to include the "living dead"). Although systematic projects of class-based genocide have occurred, they have largely been confined to communist nations, usually directed against "upper class" groups, such as kulaks in the Soviet Union, though this can be extended to include acquiescence in the death of swathes of poor peasants and laborers by famine, as in the Irish potato famine in the 1840s. Women have also been systematically and extensively violated, abused, and killed by men in nineteenth- and twentieth-century modern societies. These attacks can take on organized state-sponsored forms, for instance in the witchcraft persecutions or during wartime.[11] In addition, Sen (1990) has brought to light the systematic extent to which women in many Asian nations (in particular) are "missing" because of sex selective abortion, female infanticide, and poor female health care.

In all this terrible history of brutality, race is the paramount axis. Cedric Robertson used the concept of "racial capitalism" to emphasize that racial division has been a fundamental feature of capitalist development. "The tendency of European civilization through capitalism was thus not to homogenize but to differentiate—to exaggerate regional, subcultural, and dialectical differences into 'racial' ones" (Robinson 1983: 26). As critical race theorists have emphasized, racial boundaries were mobilized as part of the elaboration of modern imperial and nation-states.[12] There are several different threads here. The earliest pertains to the damage that imperial projects waged on indigenous populations, who became targets for subjugation as imperial projects moved into new lands. Subjugation could take genocidal forms, as with the white American treatment of American Indians or the British treatment of Australian Aboriginal people. Or it could take more indirect forms, as with the extensive mortality of indigenous populations in the Americas following the introduction of European diseases. In other cases, such as in India, indigenous populations were mobilized through the ordering of hierarchies. A famous case is the way that the British could better govern through incorporating and institutionalizing "native" caste divisions (Dirks 2001). Indigenous peoples were seen as fundamentally outside the modern project, not stakeholders within it, often being invisible (as revealed by Figure 6.1).

The situation was different with respect to Black populations, who were traded as slaves in the settler societies, mainly in the Americas. These individuals were of great economic significance in emerging imperial capitalist economies. In many parts of the "new world," the numbers were huge: 4.8 million Africans were sent as slaves to Brazil, and in the United States in 1800, 40 percent of the population (1 million) were slaves. In what was to become the United States, Piketty (2013: 159f) calculates that the value of slaves was equivalent to that of all the land in 1770, and in the southern states, over half of total capital was tied up in the value of slaves. Blackburn (1998, 2013) has recently renewed the spirit (if not the detail) of Eric Williams's (1950) and Walter Rodney's (1972) argument that the slave trade was essential for generating a capital surplus, allowing capitalist industrial development in eighteenth-century Britain. Sven Beckert (2015) has recently retold the history of the world's first modern industry—cotton textiles—not through the heroic entrepreneurship of English inventors, but in terms of the central role of slavery, as well as the British manipulation of the Indian economy. Slaves were inherently Black "others," and thereby marked the very frontiers of liberal rights as also bound up with racial divisions (see also Marable 1983).

The construction of categorical groups in imperial modernity was therefore centrally organized around these racial boundaries. Piketty (2020) has recently emphasized how the abolition of slavery in most nations during the nineteenth century was not a triumph of liberal values so much as the accentuation of property rights, as slave holders were economically compensated. There was also a further process of the categorical subordination of

Black populations in their nations as slavery was abolished, in which slaves were admitted to the modern order but on openly discriminatory terms. W. E. B. Du Bois's (1903) *The Souls of Black Folk,* written in the aftermath of the American Civil War and the consolidation of Jim Crow, was a foundational example. Du Bois insisted on the way that the American "negro" experience lay outside the terms of white liberal America, and how this exclusion produced a double consciousness, in which Black Americans were made to internalize their own inferiority. For Du Bois (1900: 47), "the problem of the twentieth century is the problem of the color line," which he insisted was "not simply as a national and personal question but rather in its larger world aspect in time and space" (see also Du Bois 1903).

This highlighting of categorical boundaries permitted in its wake the development of counter-projects of redemption from those excluded, exploited, and marginalized. The Haitian revolution thus placed the emancipation of slaves as central to its goals as early as 1792 (James 1938). Slave revolts were also endemic across the Americas (Blackburn 2013). It is not coincidental that Figure 6.1 shows that in the aftermath of the American Civil War in the 1860s, the anxieties over racial boundaries led to the definition of quadroons and octoroons as well as mulattoes, as part of this Jim Crow regime. Blacks thereby became defined as the "others" who were also inside emerging national spaces.

6.2.2: Gender

Gender formed the second classic divide in nineteenth-century imperial modernity. Numerous feminists have taken issue with the standard sociological view that women were subordinated in "traditional societies" and that the forces of modernity broke down such traditional gender divisions through a greater attention to individual rights (for example, Federici 2004, 2012; Mies 1998). Silvia Federici emphasizes that women's subordination was not a traditional feudal throwback but was itself generated in new and intense forms by the transition to modern capitalism. Adapting Marx's theory of primitive accumulation, Federici (2004) emphasized the systematic way that women were defined as care and reproductive workers and their exclusion from the labor market. Maria Mies (1998) pursued this argument by emphasizing the way that women were defined as subordinate, servile, and marginal workers as part of the transition to capitalist societies.[13]

This argument has a cultural as well as an economic inflection. Joan Wallach Scott (2019) saw the secularism associated with modernity as involving the powerful reinstatement of the universalism of gender divisions, seen to be based on fundamental biological, and hence, natural principles. Such projects undermined the significant presence of women in social and cultural life that they had previously enjoyed, especially in the religious sphere. Scott sees the liberal construction of the public sphere during the nineteenth century as directly associated with a renascent masculinist politics. Campaigns for the extension of the vote as a democratic principle were nearly entirely concerned with extending specifically male voting rights until the twentieth century. Alongside this construction of a public realm, there was also the sequestration of private, "family" relations, which were to be associated with women.[14] Indeed, seen in this light, the Enlightenment project and the extension of "rationality" can be seen as directly excluding women from the increasingly male public sphere of science and civic engagement.[15]

This gendered categorical division had its own distinctive features. Unlike the situation for indigenous people and slaves, some women were located partially inside the elite world of the progressive project, through their familial role as wives and mothers. Admittedly, this issue was fraught during the early Enlightenment, when some male writers claimed women lacked the intellectual capacity to be fully rational, intellectual beings, and hence able to educate the younger generation. However, as Offen (2000) shows, women's struggles from the eighteenth century largely successfully insisted on the strengths of women's cultural facilities, and by the nineteenth century, their capacity to be vehicles for cultured and humane learning was widely accepted. Even though women's formal education remained highly restricted until the middle of the twentieth century, their capacities as mothers, hosts, and cultural facilitators was seen to be crucial for the social progress of the "race" (as this issue was often thought about in eugenic terms).

The result was that women were seen as different kinds of categorical outsiders compared to Black racial groups, because they were subject to internal differentiation between "respectable" and "disreputable" women, the latter being targeted as the focus of intense moral panic, especially with respect to prostitution, criminality, and what was seen as inadequate mothering. Because some women were insiders in this highly segregated liberal project, feminist politics was slower to develop compared to conflict around race and class: It was not until the later nineteenth century that the term "feminism" was coined. Feminists had to articulate a new categorical label—gender—to contest liberal framings, which were oriented around "naturalist" repertories in which women were defined as inherently weaker—as ladies, mothers, and such like.

Gender categories became closely identified with nation-building projects— as mechanisms of articulating national communities. As democratic rights were extended during the nineteenth century so that all adult men were enfranchised, rather than just those who were property owners, so the stakes of women being excluded from these arenas rose, leading to the rise of feminist politics that insisted that women had equivalent rights to men. The declining significance of the private realm in which women had a place (albeit a subordinate one) for political and business affairs thus increased the stakes for women to formally have rights in the political sphere. Feminist politics therefore generally became more significant after the expansion of male suffrage. Gender categories became Janus-faced, with both an outsider and insider dimension.

6.2.3: Class

I have related how the primary organization of categorical inequalities arising out of the imperial frontier was bound up with race and gender. Class emerged at a later date and in a more restricted way. Class was an internal and defensive identity rather than an imperial one. When imperial powers were locked in struggles with each other, they were forced to confront the issue of how to engage "laboring men" (to use the term popularized by Eric Hobsbawm [1964]) who were located at home—and within their territories—and who were deemed to be outside its respectable and civilized core but whose efforts were needed to wage war effectively. In these circumstances, the delineation of class boundaries, organized around axes of respectability and moral rectitude, came into play. This mode of ordering could be used to order those "others at home," who needed to be enlisted to support the wider project of capitalist modernization and imperial aggrandizement. In some cases, notably settler societies with extensive slave or indigenous populations, racial boundaries became the main point of internal boundary drawing. This explains the relatively weak class mobilizations evident in the Americas and Australasia. However, in European nations where there were few resident

slaves or racialized indigenous peoples, class became a much more important boundary marker. Class boundaries differentiated between the upper
classes (in the anglophone context often construed as "gentlemen"), who
could be deemed respectable and hence were fully part of the progressive
project, compared to the lower class, who were outsiders and could not be
trusted, but whose labor and compliance were nonetheless essential. Around
this axial divide considerable energy was then directed toward delineating
where the fundamental boundaries lay—leading to internal debates about
who the middle classes were, whether there are "labor aristocrats," and so
on. The fact that these boundaries often overlapped with political rights and
freedoms (notably the right to vote, which was historically associated with
property ownership) also entrenched them.

The British case is iconic, because it demonstrates this association between
class formation and the defensive imperial complex. As Edward Thompson
(1963) famously argued, the first protean forms of working-class mobilization took place during the later eighteenth and early nineteenth centuries,
after Britain lost its American colonies and was engaged in bitter warfare
with France, so requiring more of its population to be mobilized than hitherto. After this moment of military insecurity passed, and as British imperial expansion resumed during the later nineteenth century, overt class politics declined in significance. Although workers' interest groups grew, notably
in the form of trade unions, they could be webbed into a politics of imperial expansion. It was only when empire building came under strain in the
later nineteenth century and the first major signs of resistance to metropolitan power emerged in the colonies that class tensions strengthened and
took on their modern, organized form. This was bound up with the consolidation of trade unions and the British Labour Party's development as a
major political force. This took its moral and political compass from identifying the terms on which the working class could claim to be national citizens, so wresting jurisdiction of these definitions from elite groups who had
previously driven the modernizing project. In these circumstances, the appeal of working class as representing the "ordinary" identities of skilled
workers became a very powerful refrain.

The association of class with nation building had an enduring legacy in
shaping subsequent debates about citizenship as it was to be forged in the
later twentieth century, in the wake of decolonization. This is evident in the

perspective of London School of Economics sociologist T. H. Marshall, whose thinking was inspirational to the remaking of conceptions of citizenship rights to include public welfare provision from the mid-twentieth century. He argued that the working classes would only be able to claim the full benefit of legal and political rights in nation-states if the meaning of citizenship was extended to include social welfare entitlements. Marshall reflected that if the working class was genuinely to be brought inside the emerging nation, the terms on which this needed to happen was by a broadening of the terms of citizenship to include social welfare, extending it from narrow definitions of legal and civil rights. This would allow the working class the means to become fully effective and engaged members of a national society, with a distinct set of stakes in a shared community.

Class therefore became a more significant divide in periods when imperial expansion was under strain, when nation-building projects came to the fore, and where racial and ethnic divisions were not internally strong enough to become the prime focus of elite boundary drawing.[16] This explains its centrality in the Scandinavian nations following the waning of the Danish and Swedish empires, and the way that class politics pulsed in European nations in the years after the First and Second World Wars as projects of nation rebuilding were central stage at the moment of imperial breakdown and turmoil.[17] One distinctive quirk of this national ferment in which class was forged was that every nation came to define their own histories and understandings of class.[18] This was different from the more imperially driven process of racial categorization, where eugenic framings were shared and elaborated by white elites across national boundaries.

I have covered a lot of ground highly schematically. My overarching point is that nineteenth-century imperial modernity was bound up with the systematic construction of boundaries between insiders and outsiders. The categories that were defined as part of this process were politically loaded, in that dominant elite groups, being older and more powerful groups, "held the cards" in projects of classification and control. The politics of categorization were driven by imperial projects, later modulated, especially around class politics through processes of nation building.

However, the partial and uneven construction of nations from imperial formations during the twentieth century led to a remaking of the very meaning of categorization itself. It was within emerging national fields—

what I have called "nation spaces"—that the meaning of categories was to be transformed into probabilistic forms. On top of the overarching principles distinguishing insiders and outsiders came a second process, which identified the differential terms of engagement that various groups had within national fields. This was the phase when categories were transformed into relational and relative entities.

6.3: Unequal Chances: The Relativization of Categorical Inequality, 1900–2000

As imperial capitalism expanded around the globe, its reliance on primitive accumulation involving the subordination of wage-earning or forced laborers was overlain by economic growth through productivity gains.[19] Profits could be made, and accumulation driven, not only (or even mainly) by the brute exploitation of slaves, penniless proletarians, female domestic labor but also by skilled expert workers, working on increasingly technologically advanced systems. This trend was massively amplified in the aftermath of the second and third industrial revolutions of the early and later twentieth century, respectively, which also underscored the economic advantages of the core metropolitan nations in Europe and North America (see in general terms Iverson and Soskice 2019). As productivity became central to capital accumulation, so classic categorical distinctions were overlain by probabilistic ones in which the differential capacities of various groups to be fully engaged in productive labor became central. In addition, the broader sphere of social reproduction in education, health, welfare, politics, and culture, which could facilitate these efforts, became more central. This was the moment when field dynamics were consolidated. And in this organization of relationships within bounded national spaces, the delineation of the relative chances of different groups took on a more pressing role.

During the twentieth century, the classic differentiation between the "civilized" and the "others"—those within and without—which predominated in imperial capitalism became overlain by differentiations specifying the "unequal chances" of various social groups in an increasingly codified and organized national space. In this process, the burgeoning expertise of social science played a key role. The Belgian statistician Adolphe Quetelet elaborated how the normal distribution allowed an elaboration of central tendency from which variation and thereby deviance could be measured. Through this means, normality could be established statistically and could also be associated with being "ordinary" and "typical" in a bounded national population (see generally Goldthorpe 2000).

As nation-states became institutionalized, they came to rely more heavily on social scientific expertise, which proliferated around the delineation, mapping, and codifying of various population groups (for example, see Dirks 2001; Mitchell 2002; Igo 2007; and Savage 2010). In his pioneering account Mitchell (2002) argued that social science expertise, notably that applied by the British in the Egyptian imperial context, elaborated concepts of the economy as some kind of autonomous sphere. This extraction of the sphere of the economy, akin to Karl Polanyi's (Polanyi and McIver 1944) celebrated argument about the disembedding of economic from wider social relations, allowed governments and businesses to position economic expertise at the heart of their governing apparatus. Especially strongly marked in the United States, but also extending to other national formations, the quantification of social scientific expertise changed the stakes of around which categories and social groups were understood. The very stuff of inequality was distanced from the gentlemanly, imperial, and evolutionary perspectives that had predominated in earlier periods. Old-style evolutionary historical social science on the model of Comte was treated as backward looking and largely became confined to the theoretical wings of sociology. In the empirical social sciences, expanding repertoires of census-based studies, later enhanced by the rise of national sample surveys from the mid-twentieth century, opened a new tool for the diagnosis of group differences (see Savage [2010] on the British case). Rather than appealing to broad metaphysical and naturalistic refrains associated with classic insider and outsider categories, more technocratic forces made it possible to delineate a range of groups that could then be used in multidimensional analysis. This social science could endeavor to reveal how such categories as class, gender, race, and ethnicity actually affected lifechances across numerous domains. This took the rendering of categorical divides away from looser cultural and moral inflections and placed them on a more measurable—and hence putatively more scientific—basis. Martin and Yeung (2003) relate how the variable of "race" became ubiquitous in American sociology by the end of the twentieth century, but also how this normally merely meant treating it as a control variable with little or no attention to race as a specific property. This mode of "variable-based" analysis became so mainstream in the later twentieth century and early twenty-first century quantitative social science that we need to remind ourselves that it is really a very odd way of construing the social world. This objection has been made most forcefully by Chicago sociologist Andrew Abbott (1992), who argues that the delineation of variables like this cannot help but slip into imparting agency—causal properties—to rarefied categories as if they have some kind of independent existence outside the specific measurement tools and context in which they are elaborated. Whereas classic categories ordered agency to different groups by distinguishing a forward-looking insider group against outsider groups mired somehow in the past, these new variable-centered and probabilistic categories denied agency to anyone. These categories were now defined as abstract variables able to produce effects—as could be revealed by skilled multivariate analysis.

These important developments affected the traditional ways that classic categories operated. Gender and racial inequalities had previously been strongly enmeshed in legal provision—such as around property ownership, marriage law, slavery, employment law, and civil rights. Although social class divisions were less strongly legally sanctioned, the right to vote, and employment provisions (for instance, regulating trade union activity) nonetheless also entailed formal provision. Classic categorical inequalities were thereby etched in the law. Before the twentieth century, it was not that women were less likely to vote—they were barred from doing so nearly everywhere.

The new mobilization of categorical differences in the twentieth century marked the relativization of these divides. During the later twentieth century, legal boundaries differentiating on the basis of race, class, and gender were reduced, even if not entirely eradicated, in most emerging nation spaces. Antidiscrimination laws became a major feature of national policy making around much of the globe from the later decades of the twentieth century. The end of apartheid in South Africa in 1994 appeared to be of major historical importance in marking the defeat of the last major bastion of racial boundaries to be enshrined directly in state law.

But these changes do not mean that the stuff of inequality was somehow removed. In fact, the changes underscored the elaboration of two new classic divides that were enshrined in law. One strenuously insisted on the boundary between independent adults and those not deemed capable of taking responsibility. This latter category included children as well as those seen as incapable for medical reasons or criminality. In the last decades of the twentieth century this radically enhanced investment in policing the boundaries between full adult and "dependent" status took on an almost hysterical quality, most notably around child protection. Public anxieties concerning pedophilia have largely eclipsed those around miscegeny, homosexuality, and extramarital sex. The new intense policing of the boundary between adult and child status reveals the hold of a nationally bounded frame of reference in which it became crucial to define those who were capable of being responsible citizens of the nation compared with some kind of infant and irresponsible "others." In these circumstances, the classic categories of race, gender, and class took a back seat.

The later twentieth century also saw increased obsession with differentiating between nationals and non-nationals. Until the early twentieth century, mobility across national and imperial borders was largely unregulated, with passports only being systematically introduced from the later nineteenth century. Significant levels of international migration took place within imperial rather than national borders and were indeed encouraged in the postwar period, such as when Black migrants were encouraged to migrate to Britain to take up menial employment (Gatrell 2019). This right to move within the British ex-imperial territories was in place until 1961. It was only during the decolonization of European empires in the middle and later twentieth century that the policing of national borders came to become a major security concern. In the postwar decades, those able to extract "citizenship rents" (Milanovic 2016) sheltered behind these borders. In this way, the categorical distinctions between immigrant and national became stronger at the same moment that the classic categories of class, gender, and race became more probabilistically defined.

The formation of nation spaces therefore involved an elaboration of a legal space in which all adult and responsible citizens were formally supposed to have equivalent rights. In this new political sphere, those in the previously subordinated classic categories mobilized so that they could finally redeem the freedoms held out as a central promise of modernization. In Martin Luther King's famous "I Have a Dream" speech delivered in 1963,

We have also come to this hallowed spot to remind America of the fierce urgency of Now. This is no time to engage in the luxury of cooling off or to take the tranquilizing drug of gradualism. Now is the time to make real the promises of democracy. Now is the time to rise from the dark and desolate valley of segregation to the sunlit path of racial justice. Now is the time to lift our nation from the quicksands of racial injustice to the solid rock of brotherhood. Now is the time to make justice a reality for all of God's children.

This kind of framing could readily deploy a progressive liberal reasoning, in which all national citizens were theoretically to be treated according to a common rule book, and then protesting when these principles were not, in fact, being applied. Demonstrating that there were substantial inequalities between groups, as revealed by probabilistic, multivariate analysis, proved to be a powerful lever indeed. The fact that women, or racial minorities, or the working classes were not actually treated as possessing intrinsically different properties (that is, as less cultivated, less respectable, or less able to become a full citizen) from anybody else—and yet still had systematically different life chances—became a ready tool for demanding redress. Documenting the relative inequalities between members of different categories was therefore part of the elaboration of coherent nation spaces.

This relativization of categories prospered at the very same time that the moral, temporal, and ontological status of classic group boundaries was being challenged. The case of social class is a fascinating case study. In most European nations, until the middle decades of the twentieth century, class boundaries were etched in law and employment practice. In the British case, there was a marked cultural divide between salaried white collar (or in Lockwood's 1958 parlance, "black coated") and wage-earning blue collar workers—enshrined in the differentiation between salary and wage, or "office" and "line" status.[20] However, during the later twentieth century, these markers were changed substantially. The British sociologist John Goldthorpe's redefinition of class analysis during the 1970s was a brilliant example of how class analysis was itself retooled as part of this probabilistic revolution. His early research on working-class culture and politics during the 1960s had been closely bound up with the classic framings concerning whether the "outsider" working class was being incorporated into the "insider" middle class as their wages rose in "affluent" sectors of employment (see Goldthorpe et al. 1968a, 1968b, 1969). But during the 1970s, Goldthorpe's approach to class analysis changed substantially as he embraced quantitative statistical methods. He subsumed his interest in whether the working classes were somehow becoming middle class into a survey-based analysis examining the ease of social mobility between different occupational classes. In taking up the topic of social mobility, Goldthorpe was seizing a new tool. The first major British study, led by David Glass, dates back to as recently as 1954 and pioneered a nationally representative survey to ascertain how class background determined the prospects of Britons to change their class positions compared to their parents. By detecting very significant differences in the prospects of children from different social classes, he was thus able to demonstrate the power of class in affecting one's relative life chances—regardless of the legal, moral, or cultural power of the class divide.

Goldthorpe took this interest in the relative mobility chances of men from different social classes to a more refined and sophisticated plane.[21] His work involved no ontological claims about the different kinds of people found in varying classes (indeed, he made it clear that he resisted this kind of "culturalist" baggage—see Goldthorpe [1981]). He insisted that he was not differentiating on moral or status grounds, but only on "objective" terms in which class was defined in terms of employment relations. He thereby contrasted a professional and managerial middle class—which he came to theorize as a "service class"—with a working class of wage laborers.[22] Although these ideas mapped onto the earlier classic class vocabulary that distinguished the working class from the middle class, he stripped these ideas of their moralistic origins. This move allowed him to distance himself from theories of class exploitation, which he saw as teleological in differentiating an emancipatory working class and a dominant bourgeois class. Instead, class inequalities were defined in more probabilistic and empirical ways—in terms of the different life chances that members of different classes might have (notably, Goldthorpe 2000; Bukodi et al. 2015).

This redefinition of categories was typical of how categorical terms could be reworked in probabilistic terms. Gender, race, and ethnicity were also subject to the same politics. Rather than being treated as ontological categories and deploying overtly moralistic idioms, categories became honed as variables, being stripped of these wider connotations. Analytical attention could

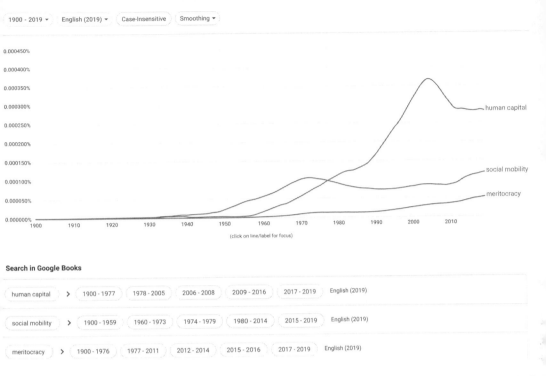

FIGURE 6.2: Google Ngram showing trends in the use of the terms "human capital," "social mobility," and "meritocracy"

Source: Google Ngram.

then be directed toward how different kinds of outcomes might be associated with them, and how these might be addressed in a nation space avowedly committed to treating all its citizens as equally deserving.

This relativistic shift explains why, across the developed world, the study of social mobility became such an obsessional concern beginning in the 1950s and gathering so much momentum in recent decades. In the era of classic categories, mobility across categories was simply not expected at all, barring exceptional situations. Indeed, this kind of mobility wasn't really welcomed. Classic categorical anxieties were so vested with distinguishing insiders from outsiders that the prospect of being able to change status was threatening indeed. However, as categories become probabilistic, so mobility between them became expected, with any deviation from equal opportunities becoming a cause for concern. The idea that a common nation space formally committed to treating citizens equivalently entailed that everyone had a chance, regardless of their starting point, and that some kind of meritocracy could be engineered to show that everyone, at least in principle, has a place at the national table.

This change is nicely illuminated by trends in English language use of the mobility terms "human capital," "social mobility," and "meritocracy." In 1900, the idea of social mobility hardly existed (see Mandler 2016, 2020; Goldthorpe 2013). This partly reflects the rarity of long-range mobility (Miles 1993), which was itself underscored by the dominant view that one was born into one's social position. Figure 6.2 shows that before 1920, the social science terms "human capital," "social mobility," and "meritocracy" were entirely absent from the English cultural lexicon. However, in the remarkable blast of social science energy that took place during the middle decades of the twentieth century, this all changed. Figure 6.2 shows the momentum being taken forward by two terms flowing in its wash: human capital and meritocracy, both of which expanded in their popular use. The term "human capital" was made famous by the economist Gary Becker in 1964 as a means of explaining how people who invested in their skills and education might expect to be rewarded for their efforts in terms of increased income and social position. As Mandler (2020) has shown, these currents began to inform UK government education policy beginning in the later 1950s. Exemplifying the cultural power of economics (rather than sociology) in commanding public debate, this term encouraged, and was also informed by, the educational expansion agenda during this period. By 2000, the term "human capital" was about three times more popular than "social mobility." It played into an economistic conception of mobility as bound up with strategic and instrumentalizing investment in one's assets—a conception that became strongly embedded in government educational policy, notably the focus on higher education in terms of its significance for employability.

Figure 6.3 presents the changing currency of lay terms that have been deployed to talk about life trajectories: the "calling," "career," and "vocation."[23] In the early nineteenth century, it was the concept of the calling that was utterly dominant. Borrowing from a powerful religious idiom rooted in Protestant culture, this had a very particular take on mobility, as "taking up" one's predestined position. This is precisely in keeping with Wahrman's (2004) arguments concerning the way that conceptions of the individual in this period

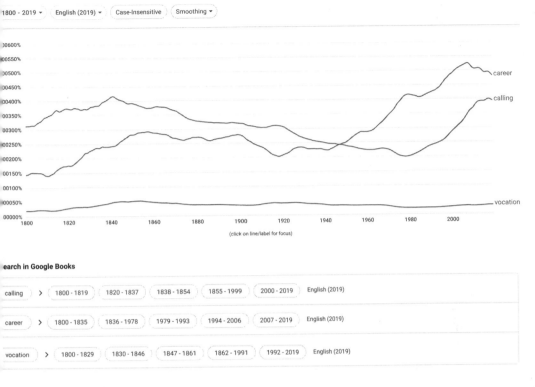

FIGURE 6.3: Google Ngram showing trends in relative English-language use of the terms "calling," "career," and "vocation"

Source: Google Ngram.

involved recognizing one's interior, subjective, identity as member of a particular group category. Following one's calling thus permitted the idea of mobility on a very clear pathway, as a means of achieving one's preordained destiny. The idea of the calling was increasingly secularized during this period, being taken up especially in professional cultures (such as medicine, law, and the military). It could also be adapted for wider familial roles, for instance with mothers being deemed have a calling to raise their children. It reaches a plateau during the mid-nineteenth century before a gentle slide until the 1980s, at which point, it increases its popularity again—which in the context of the arguments I will make here is of some interest.

It is the trajectory of the concept of "career" that is most striking. As Raymond Williams (1983) relates, the idea of career undergoes a powerful shift during the nineteenth century, away from its previous meaning of unpredicted movement (which still has a residue in the idea of a vehicle "careering out of control") toward its more recent formulation as a structured set of occupational moves, sometimes in terms of upward movement through structured promotion, but also as enjoying wider provenance. The "career" encompasses strategic conceptions of life trajectory in a form that the "calling" does not. This speaks to a shift toward a more relativistic and probabilistic concern with mobility between states. The situation was made more complex by interdisciplinary contestation within the social sciences. Sociology was especially important here. By elaborating its mission to critically champion those whose voices were neglected or otherwise unheard in the emergent national compact of "native adults," it gained increasing presence in the latter decades of the twentieth century—often in association with new social movements. This led sociology to strongly overlap with political movements—ranging from social democratic reformism to more socialist, Marxist, feminist, and antiracist affiliations (for example, MacAdam 2007 on the US case). It is for these reasons that major traditions of scholarship focusing on class, gender, and race inequalities found strong support from the discipline of sociology.

This relativization of categorical inequalities was part and parcel of the growing "methodological nationalism," in which the relative differences between categories could be delineated by being arrayed in autonomous national space with clear and definite geographical boundaries inside which life chances could be measured. This mode of thinking was largely absent during the nineteenth century, when societies were not seen as coterminous with national boundaries (which were anyway not always clearly defined), and where imperial, trading, and metropolitan alignments dominated. In these conditions, the idea of comparing the prospects of very differently constituted groups within a specific territorial location was utterly alien. At that time, the conception of a national space of individuals competing for resources and rewards was largely absent—these were imperially ordered societies with power and authority clearly vested in the chosen few.

Conclusion

In this chapter, I have traced how definitions of categorical inequality changed in a way that is largely consistent with changing parameters of economic inequality discussed in earlier chapters. The shift toward lower inequality regimes during the twentieth century is to be understood as tied up with the rise of nation spaces and the *probabilistic rendering of the stuff of inequality.* This reflects a world mired by the relativization of categorical groups seen as comprising differing national opportunity structures. Public services around the globe seek to identify and modulate (though not always with wholehearted commitment) these probabilistic inequalities. Corporations and employers of all kinds evaluate their members' categorical characteristics so as to manage equal opportunities—not always very successfully. This current has ushered in a way of thinking about inequality between groups not in terms of their intrinsic properties, but in terms of the relative advantages or disadvantages that they experience.

This idea that inequality is to be understood probabilistically is now utterly ubiquitous, almost to the extent that it is a truism. However, we should not see this framing as inevitable or necessary: Depending on the specific historical conditions that were obtained during the twentieth century, they were bound up with the formation of nation spaces out of the debris of empires shattered by global warfare. However, just as imperial forms are reviving in recent decades, so we are, in fact, now witnessing the erosion of probabilistic categories. These days, the stuff of inequality means something rather different. Actually, this new stuff turns out to mark the return of much older historical stuff of imperial modernity, as I will argue in Chapter 7.

Visceral Inequality in the Twenty-First Century

In 2015, a powerful storm of protest gathered across the University of Cape Town campus, demanding the removal of the offensive statue of British imperialist Cecil Rhodes (see Figure 7.1). Ramabina Mahapa, president of the university's Students' Representative Council, emphasized that this was not targeting a specific individual, but rather Rhodes as a symbol of institutional colonialism. Kros (2015: 152) commented that

> The scenes that played out around the statue, ending with it being hoisted by crane onto a flatbed truck surrounded by students cheering its banishment, are evocative of the scene in Sergei Eisenstein's quasi-documentary film "October: Ten Days that Shook the World" (1928), in which the statue of Tsar Alexander III is toppled by revolutionaries, marking the "proletariat's first victory on the road to socialism."

But it wasn't only in South Africa that statues of long-dead white male elites were gathering ire. In the United States, there were effective campaigns to remove statues of Confederate generals in former slave states. In the wake of a fight to remove the statue of Confederate General Lee in Charlottesville, Virginia, a group of white supremacists, defending its right to stand over the town, attacked antiracist protesters, leading to the death of a young woman protestor, Heather Heyer. President Donald Trump's refusal to take sides and unequivocally condemn the white supremacists, and his remarks

FIGURE 7.1: Rhodes Must Fall: Cape Town 2015

Source: Michael Hammond. Courtesy of University of Cape Town.

that it was "sad" that the "history and culture" of the United States is "being ripped apart" by the removal of Confederate statues, provoked outrage, which fueled antiracist protest that the Black Lives Matter movement had come to the fore in recent years.

These two vignettes demonstrate that history is back with a vengeance. Of course, history never went away. Nonetheless, the intense public attention directed toward old statues in the much-vaunted digital age of artificial intelligence is cause for us to ponder. These popular protests demonstrate the sort of passionate stakes that Bourdieu's field analysis emphasizes is part of the gestalt of social life. But these stakes take a very different form from those that he considers. Rather than a struggle to champion avant garde excellence in a "field of organized striving," it is the historical mementos of dead white male elites that are the target. This struggle over bodies shows how inequality has become visceral. This is a powerful and resonant thread across multiple domains. The outcry around endemic sexual harassment, which the #MeToo movement has brought to the fore since public revelations of Harvey Weinstein's abuse came out in 2016 is another telling example.

The prominence of antiracist initiatives associated with Black Lives Matter, sparked by police brutality toward African Americans, most visibly captured in the video of the police killing of George Floyd in May 2020, reveals very clearly the traction of visceral inequalities. The fraught debates within feminist politics regarding whether gender reassignment is a matter of personal choice or requires expert attestation (indeed, the status of biological sex itself) are all testimony to the profound centrality of bodies for the stuff of inequality today.

On the face of it, these forceful political movements don't appear to be directly addressing economic inequality. An influential current of thought has rendered them as "identity politics," bound up with seeking recognition, dignity, and respect for those who have been historically dominated and exploited. In this chapter, I show that this reading is superficial. Actually, these currents mark a profound reinscription of categorical inequality, which testifies to the exhaustion of nation spaces and the return of the classic divides that characterized imperial modernity. Not incidentally, then, that British imperialists (such as Cecil Rhodes) or Confederate, proslavery Americans (such as General Lee) are the focus of such intense agitation.

In this chapter, I show how this visceral politics arises from the exhaustion of the relativistic and probabilistic framing of categorical inequality that became powerful in the later twentieth century. By insisting on the physicality of inequality, this visceral turn reaffirms the ongoing traction of fundamental distinctions of gender and race that were characteristic of the onset of imperial modernity.

The first part of this chapter argues against the view that it is useful to characterize contemporary feminist and antiracist struggles as identity politics. This term depends on the kind of epochalist framing critiqued in Chapter 3, with its refrain that older material inequalities are giving way to a cultural politics reflecting the easing of necessity and the rise of expressive values. In the second part of the chapter, I explain how visceral inequality becomes more profound as relativities between aggregate social groups decline—as they have done with respect to class and gender—though not race. This may sound counterintuitive, as one might expect visceral inequalities to be more passionately attested to when there are more extreme economic divisions. But in fact, it is when these relative inequalities decline that the enduring power of visceral inequalities is more starkly felt.

In the third part of this chapter, I put a further twist on the narrative by returning to the figures of white elite men. This is the group whose wealth, power, and privilege have soared in recent decades. This is precisely the group that has come into view with the turning of the telescope, which I bookmarked in Chapter 1. It follows that the embodied, physical qualities of privileged elites—who turn out to be overwhelmingly male, often white or from a dominant ethnic group, and from advantaged families—becomes an increasing object of hostile attention. Since the general decline of relative inequalities encourages people to believe that there are no intrinsic reasons that certain kinds of people should ascriptively be in elite positions, this awareness truly grates. The pincer movement whereby large-scale relative inequalities decline at the same time that white male elites pull away, encourages a widespread visceral sense of being ill at ease and uncomfortable. This feeling seethes into anger.

7.1: From Identity Politics to Visceral Inequality

Chapter 6 traced how the terms by which trusted insiders were set apart from disreputable outsiders shifted from the nineteenth to the twentieth centuries. These group inequalities were increasingly seen not as ontological, natural divisions, but as probabilistic ones. They were thereby an aspect of the development of nation spaces where all citizens were (theoretically) recognized as having equivalent rights, and in which the relative positioning and life chances of different members of the national community became a matter of political mobilization and concern. This was the moment when we can trace efforts to establish national "social contracts" (for instance, the American New Deal, or the British post-1945 welfare state), which were intended to allow different constituencies to feel they had some kind of place at the national table. However, by the end of the century, the stakes around classification and categorization were changing. People themselves felt they had a stake in deciding who they were and what their interests and priorities should be. For the first time, in 1961, Americans were able to choose their own ethnic group when responding to the census. This vignette marks an important development—the wresting of authority about the adjudication of categorical membership away from officials toward vesting this power in the hands of people who directly claim the right to classify themselves.

Conventional interpretations of this changing politics of categorization interpret it as part of a "politics of recognition" (Fraser 1995), a shift toward "expressive" or "post-materialist" (Inglehart 1990) or "lifestyle" politics (Giddens 1991). For Nancy Fraser (1995: 68),

> The "struggle for recognition" is fast becoming the paradigmatic form of political conflict in the late twentieth century. Demands for "recognition of difference" fuel struggles of groups mobilized under the banners of nationality, ethnicity, "race," gender, and sexuality.

In her careful rendering of this current, Fraser articulated a set of binaries—the tension between the politics of recognition and redistribution, and between cultural and economic dimensions of inequality, which struck a chord. Although Fraser was careful not to reify these, seeing them as analytical rather than substantive differences, nonetheless, the implication was that the familiar world of redistributive economic politics was ceding ground to newer kinds of demands based on this search for recognition.

This route was similar to that taken by influential American political scientist Ronald Inglehart (1990), who on the basis of extensive comparative survey research on public attitudes over much of the globe claimed that there was a secular trend toward the rise of "post-materialist" values. This was also the thinking behind sociologist Anthony Giddens's view that new forms of "life politics," in which "the self becomes a *reflexive project*" were on the ascendant:

> Where things stayed more or less the same from generation to generation on the level of the collectivity, the changed identity was clearly staked out. . . . In the settings of modernity, by contrast, the altered self has to be explored and constructed as part of a reflexive process of connecting personal and social change. (Giddens 1991: 33)

On a first take, this view appears totally at odds with my emphasis on the returning imperatives of economic inequality and the renewed force of history. Indeed, Giddens was emphatic that "life politics" marks a new phase that broke from a material ("emancipatory") politics centered on life chances.[1] Fraser, Inglehart, and Giddens all underscored that this new politics is somehow orthogonal to an older politics of economic inequality and re-distribution. These kinds of experiential inequalities sit uneasily with the economic and political analysis of inequality and would not be wiped clean by changing pay differentials or shifting the wealth distribution (for example, Honneth 1996; Lamont 2019; Lamont et al. 2016). Indeed, this assertion of the significance of identity has led to a contrary reaction from those insisting on economic forces. In *Capital and Ideology,* Piketty (2020) confronts "the drift toward the dead-end politics of identity." The avowed liberal Mark Lilla (2017) is equally scornful of what he sees as the sectarianism of identity politics, which he critiques as unable to command the middle ground that is neces-sary to gain popular appeal. Once one appeals to one's own distinctive ex-perience, he asks, how can you command the center of political debate and appeal effectively to those who are different from you? Indeed, the argument that politics has fractured over conventional opposition between left and right, and that it has been overlain by a new cleavage, which sets apart lib-ertarians from authoritarians, has become part of accepted wisdom in much political science—as I will discuss in Chapter 10.

However, all this is a very unproductive framing. There is in fact a close association between escalating economic inequalities and what has conven-tionally been called "identity politics." It is not analytically helpful to distin-guish between a politics of redistribution and one of recognition. Indeed it only fragments what need to be seen as related concerns. Issues of respect, worth, dignity, and recognition can only be put in the wider context of the return of history and the rise of top-end economic inequality, which is also straining the power of nation spaces.

Most fundamentally, "life politics" is not really about choice, as Giddens claims, but is etched deeply on the body. The African American George Floyd did not chose to have a white police officer put his knee on his neck for more than nine minutes in May 2020, leading to his death by suffocation. To portray life politics as concerned with decisions or reflexivity evades the fact that feminist and antiracist politics are driven by anger at being physi-cally demeaned, abused, violated, and mistreated. In this spirit, British fem-inist sociologist Imogen Tyler (2020) has emphasized the role of stigma—literally, marks on the body—as fundamental to the contemporary production of abjection and inequality. Other sociologists have insisted on the need to recognize the power of "existential" (Therborn 2013) or "affective" (Bottero

2019) inequalities, which also attest to this fundamental corporeal component. Even for the analysis of social class, long treated as largely an economic
issue determined by one's place in the employment relations or income
distribution, the explosion of cultural class analysis in the wake of Pierre
Bourdieu's writing has emphasized the role of bodily appearance, clothing,
accent, deportment, and demeanor. The politics of worth and value, centering
on physical and sexual abuse, dignity, and respect as marked in everyday, often
one-on-one interaction, becomes a focus of the political agenda.

There is, however, a crucial historical question. Physical brutality is ubiquitous throughout history, and by many measures is much more subdued
than in the past. How can we account for this dimension becoming so contentious in recent decades? We get some clues to answering this question
by pondering the tone of two pioneering texts, both highly influential for
the development of feminist and antiracist politics from the later twentieth
century. These indicate the tenor of this visceral appeal. Simone de Beauvoir's *The Second Sex,* published in 1949, is generally identified as one of the
founding works of second-wave feminism.

> If I want to define myself, I first have to say, "I am a woman": all other
> assertions will arise from this basic truth. A man never begins by pos-
> iting himself as an individual of a certain sex: that he is a man is obvious.
> The categories "masculine" and "feminine" appear as symmetrical in a
> formal way . . . (but) the relation of the two sexes is not that of two elec-
> trical poles: the man represents both the positive and the neuter. . . .
> Woman is the negative, to such a point that any determination is im-
> puted to her as a limitation, without reciprocity. (Beauvoir 1953: 51)

Frantz Fanon's classic *Black Skin, White Masks* (1952: 7) proceeds in a similar way:

> All colonized people—in other words, people in whom an inferiority
> complex has taken root, whose local cultural originality has been com-
> mitted to the grave—position themselves in relation to the civilising
> language, i.e. metropolitan culture. The more the colonized has assim-
> ilated the cultural values of the metropolis, the more he will have es-

caped the bush. The more he rejects his blackness and the bush, the whiter he will become.

Both these accounts relate identity to a fundamental comparison in which the meaning of female can only be understood vis-à-vis male, and black compared to white. They thus depend precisely on the relativist, rather than naturalist, rendering of group inequality, which had come to the fore during the twentieth century. But they take this turn to its logical conclusion by insisting on the fundamental impossibility that awaits marginalized groups seeking their full and proper place at the top table *however hard they strive for it* and whatever crumbs of apparent recognition may be offered. The harder that women or racial minorities endeavor to belong, the more they confront the ultimate impossibility of succeeding. The terms on which belonging is constituted are not those which they have control over: They are condemned to skittle on the hamster wheel of history. Excluded categories are not "natural." Women and minorities can endeavor to behave like white men—but ultimately, they can never measure up. The body is simultaneously the marker and symbol of this impossibility, of this fundamental *lack,* which can never be overcome. In this light, much of what is construed as identity politics is not really expecting equal recognition—but is rather lamenting the ultimate impossibility of such recognition ever being possible.

It is therefore in recognizing the ultimate limits of probabilistic framings of inequality that the body has become pivotal. It also matters as the site of the "total work of art," speaking to an ultimate truth of bodily experience that trumps strategic game playing. It is not incidental that the body is the site and vehicle of so much successful contemporary artistic and cultural intervention, as evident in the appeal of writers such as Elena Ferrante or Bernardino Evaristo. Between 2006 and 2011, Norway was gripped by the writing of Karl Ove Knausgaard, whose long, six-volume set of novels on *My Struggle* became best sellers. His capacity to grip such a large reading public was spectacular when compared to the restricted, "high-brow" readership of the extended fictional works of modernist forbears, such as those by Proust or Joyce. The body lies at the heart of Knausgaard's writing, certainly his own tormented experience of shame, but also the bodies of others, most memorably that of his dead alcoholic father. Toril Moi captures the appeal of Knausgaard as "insisting on the importance of feeling without buying into affects." Deliberately breaking with the shallowness of postmodernist pastiche, where the clever artist shows that they know the rules of the game so as to be able to join the party, Knausgaard's long struggle is "to find a way of writing that doesn't shun feelings, that refuses to consider naturalism (the belief in the representation of reality) naïve, a way of writing that creates meaning and beauty" (Moi 2017).

Visceral inequality thereby articulates the fundamental impossibility of outsiders ever physically being at the "top table" in the present context of accentuating material inequalities. The irreducibly embodied dimensions of these inequalities are as inescapable as they are objectionable. Women can only be understood vis-à-vis men, Blacks vis-à-vis whites, in a manner that has been utterly routinized by social science from the mid-twentieth century. Appealing to your bodily experience disputes rhetorical blandishments about equality, transparency, and meritocracy in an age of escalating inequality. Recognizing the embodiment of inequality means that the historical slate can never be wiped clean by the glittering sheen of "modernity," because the enduring imprint of past experiences runs in and on the body. It is not incidental that feminist and antiracist politics is powerfully tied up with addressing historic wrongs, stretching back over decades and centuries. Even if relative inequalities in life chances are declining, this does not ultimately erase history but only goes to show how these scars fester even while economic relativities may have shifted.

Let us first consider social class. This is a revealing starting point because class more than any other division becomes the quintessential *relative inequality* in the later twentieth century. More pervasively than for gender and race, where biological markers remained a constant refrain, class was denaturalized by social scientists, and its significance was seen to lie in its power to differentiate life chances. The subsequent decline of class as a relative category is therefore symptomatic of wider trends.

7.2: The Decline of Probabilistic Inequality: Social Class

In chapter 6, I argued that social class became powerful at a later time, and more variably, than did gender and race, as imperial modernity was giving way to nation spaces. Class became mobilized as part of a defensive, nationally oriented rather than expansionary imperial frame of reference, and thereby largely became prominent only during the twentieth century as imperial power waned. By the later twentieth century, class was very largely seen in probabilistic terms, as a matter of delineating differential life chances among groups of national citizens. This was the period in which traces of overt class snobbery or elitism bound up with the sense that the upper classes were innately superior became more routinely sniffed out in the media as well as in public opinion. Even though such refrains continued to circulate, they were largely seen as out of keeping with the democratic tenor of liberal modernity (Savage 2010).

The close affiliation between the study of social class and social mobility research was in the vanguard of the probabilistic and relativistic reshaping of social science after 1945. Initially, this interest was led by a concern to empirically test how easy it was for different kinds of people to "get to the top"—a kind of hard-nosed assessment of the reality of the "American Dream." In the United States, Peter Blau and Otis Dudley Duncan (1967) led the way, with their sanguine, even optimistic account of social mobility. Their book appeared at a hopeful period of American history, with the civil rights movements making headway in challenging entrenched racism, second-wave feminist mobilization gathering pace, and an assertive counterculture powerfully challenging conservative values. In their clinical, technical, prose, Blau and Duncan articulated sociologically the spirit of this tempered optimism. On the one hand, they demonstrated the ongoing differential prospects of Americans from varying social backgrounds. There was no level playing field, whatever promises the American Dream might hold out. Nonetheless, it was still possible for many people, from all walks of life, to get on: There were no impermeable barriers to success in American society. Their "status attainment" model gave pride of place to the role of educational qualifications in permitting occupational success, even for those from disadvantaged backgrounds.

Blau and Duncan set out the parameters of a brave postwar liberal vision that echoed that of Kuznets in economics—as societies modernized and as educational provision expanded, ascribed inequality as measured by your social origin could be expected to recede. Even if the traces of old-fashioned class snobbery and elitism still surfaced from time to time, these were residual forces that could be expected to evaporate in the hot sun of affluence driven by economic growth. Technocratic and scientific advance in the context of post-industrialism could spell the end of entrenched traditional discrimination, to be replaced by merit and market reward. This view chimed with the sense of optimism strongly etched in American popular culture.

It was against this benign vision that British sociologists, led by John Goldthorpe, mobilized a gloomier view. It is not incidental that the 1970s marked the optimism of the 1960s giving way to a more pessimistic awareness of economic slowdown and stagflation, and notably so in the United Kingdom. In a pathbreaking study of social mobility in England and Wales, Goldthorpe et al. (1980) insisted that class structural divisions continued to systematically stunt social mobility prospects—and that there was no sign that this was changing.[2] A cornerstone of his case involved changing the terms of reference from *absolute* (measuring the actual frequency of movements between different classes) to *relative* (comparing the relative chances of mobility between different classes) chances. In terms of absolute mobility, Goldthorpe concurred with Blau and Duncan's optimism. For men, postwar Britain did indeed see significant upward social mobility: Your prospect in life was far from being determined by your class background. However, the situation was very different with respect to relative mobility—what Goldthorpe later called "social fluidity." Here, relative inequalities in social mobility could remain, even if there was significant absolute upward mobility from the working class.[3] Working-class boys could find opportunities to move into professional and managerial jobs in periods of economic growth as these jobs expanded. There was room at the top. However, at the same time, prospects for upper- and middle-class boys also improved—with very little prospect of them being downwardly mobile, most notably. Therefore, there was no "catching up."

Goldthorpe's argument was game changing in demonstrating that when group categories were seen in probabilistic terms, they turned out to be enduring and much more difficult to shift. This exemplar proved inspirational for social science research, much of which became devoted to exposing such relative inequalities—in all the nooks and crannies where they hid. By the early twenty-first century, this probabilistic framing has become the commonsense of our time. Indeed, Chapters 1, 2, and 4 in this book reveal the rich fruit that this harvest of bountiful relativities has reaped—whether in the form of Piketty's income shares, Bourdieu's field analysis, or Wilkinson and Pickett's *Spirit Level,* all of which are couched in these terms. Nonetheless, this move—while game changing in demonstrating the ongoing hold of categorical inequalities—had the utterly perverse effect of largely bracketing out actual historical change. This flattening of historical duration is endemic when relative measures are used, as it obscures both absolute changes in the frequency of differing states and also how entities themselves may change over time.

This problem is very clear when absolute social mobility—inevitably affected by structural economic and social change—is downgraded in significance compared to relative social mobility. It is absolute mobility that is likely to be salient to people as they navigate their way into and within the labor market and reflect on whether their careers have been facilitated or stunted—not some abstracted relativities of which they are unlikely to be aware.[4] It is therefore telling that the study of absolute mobility has largely receded from view, as the probabilistic and relativist social science tide has swept all before it.

There is, however, a further twist. Even construed as a relative state, it now appears that social class divisions—or at least, as defined by conventional class categories—have become weaker. Goldthorpe's emphasis that social fluidity has experienced only trendless fluctuation has not stood up in the face of more recent research. The most compendious volume to this effect is Breen's edited *Social Mobility in Europe* (2004), which pulled together trends across eleven European nations. Breen and his collaborators show that for men, social fluidity had been broadly stable in Germany (though it had fluctuated considerably there) and Great Britain, but had actually increased in France, Poland, Hungary, and the Netherlands. For women, there was also increasing fluidity, though Great Britain is the one case where this trend is less clear. Breen and Luijux conclude that "the results from our eleven countries then point to a fairly clear conclusion: there is a widespread tendency for social fluidity to increase, even though this might not be a statistically significant trend in every case" (Breen and Luijkx 2004b: 389). They go on to note that differences in social fluidity cannot readily be explained in terms of economic development or the levels of inequality found in different nations. In short, even when construed in the relative and probabilistic terms that became dominant from the later twentieth century, class inequalities are declining. Breen's findings have largely been underscored by further, more recent studies in other nations.[5]

Britain appears to be the outlier, the only nation where relative class mobility has been stable. These peculiarities of the British are increasingly well attested. Analyzing comparative differences in income mobility, the economists Raitano and Vona (2015) found that Britain has an unduly strong "glass ceiling," making upward mobility much more difficult than elsewhere. But even in the British case, relative social mobility may be increasing. Using the very large 1 percent sample from the British census (amounting to more than 500,000 respondents), Buscha and Sturgis (2018) detect a slight increase in relative social mobility. Goldthorpe's most recent work (for example, Bukodi et al. 2015) shows that even in the United Kingdom, social fluidity has increased for women and has possibly increased for men too, notably in the younger age groups. Older British men therefore appear to be one of the last groups, anywhere in the world, who have evaded the long-term trend for relative class mobility to increase.[6] But they are far from being typical.

It is not only with respect to comparative social mobility that relative inequalities have declined. Breen et al. (2009, 2010) show that across Germany, France, Italy, Ireland, Britain, Sweden, Poland, Hungary, and the Netherlands, class-based educational inequalities have also declined. The children of more disadvantaged families have caught up, to a greater or lesser extent, with more privileged children in terms of the qualifications they are likely to obtain. As the authors report:

> Social class disadvantages in children's educational careers have become less acute in the countries we studied, though this decline has been more pronounced in Sweden, the Netherlands, Britain, Germany, and France than in Italy, Ireland, and Poland. (Breen et al. 2009: 1513)

To conclude this discussion, concentrating on the relative mobility between social class categories was undoubtedly highly illuminating in its own terms. However, it also led us up a garden path and took us away from the historical analysis of social change and the experiential dimensions involved. It is both too esoteric (in using relative measures that are remote from people's own experiences) and too crude (in using a small number of "big class" categories). So, if we switch our attention to absolute shifts in social mobility, evidence of closure and declining mobility is becoming increasingly apparent—especially with respect to entry to topmost positions. In the United States, pathbreaking research led by Raj Chetty and his colleagues (2014) shows a spectacular decline in the proportion of Americans who can expect to earn more than their parents. Most Americans born in 1940 could expect to be better off than their parents, largely because the booming American economy was tending to increase prosperity across the board. This rising tide was lifting lots of American boats, including small ones. The only exception was actually among the children of very rich (in the top 5 percent of the income distribution)—as it's hard to keep up with very rich parents and there is much further to fall. However, for those born in 1980, the experience of upward income mobility substantially receded, reflecting stagnating income levels across the US economy as a whole. Only those born to parents in the bottom third of the income distribution were likely to earn more than their parents (see also Bukodi et al. [2015] for a related argument in the United Kingdom)

Chetty et al. (2014) make it clear that relative rates do not map onto these absolute patterns. Echoing Goldthorpe, they emphasize that it has not become more difficult to move between income ranks, compared to your parents: "children entering the labor market today have the same chances of moving up in the income distribution relative to their parents as children born in the 1970s" (Chetty et al. 2014: 10). There is a consistent advantage conferred on those born to parents in the top quintile themselves earning in the top quintile (just over 30 percent, though there is a slight dip for those born in the later 1970s). By contrast, the proportion of those born into the bottom quintile who radically enhance their income in relative terms so that they are in the top fifth of income earners is also stable at around 10 percent. There is a decline in the absolute but not relative prospects, because income levels in the United States are largely static or even falling across the economy as a whole.

The correct conclusion to draw from this research is that relative social mobility is of less substantive and historical significance than absolute mobility. Richard Breen, Goldthorpe's erstwhile ally and collaborator, puts this very crisply:

> although one would not want to say that fluidity can never make a
> difference (since we can easily construct examples in which extreme

patterns of fluidity will be highly consequential for the distribution of cases in a mobility table), within the advanced industrial and post-industrial societies, the range of fluidity that we observe is relatively inconsequential in determining variation in mobility flows and in the life chances of individuals and families as these are captured in mea-sures of class position. (Breen and Luijkx 2004b: 402)

It is therefore important to renew our focus on the experience of mobility and immobility, and how this is perceived and felt by different kinds of people. Here, there has been a considerable renewal of interest, partly in the con-text of the renewal of cultural class analysis inspired by Bourdieu, as well as feminist sociology such that as pioneered by Skeggs (1997), and research con-cerned with delineating the forces of institutional racism (Rollock et al. 2014; Meghji 2017, 2019). A major emphasis addresses the shaming of those who are restricted to insecure and precarious employment, and who are in-stitutionally vulnerable and marginalized (Bourdieu et al. 1999). In fact, the stigmatization of those in marginalized positions can be overstated. Many of those trapped in such positions feel personally proud of navigating the difficulties of their life (Koch 2018; Koch et al. 2020; Savage and Meersohn 2021), and value the fact that they are "ordinary" (Savage et al. 2001). Indeed, this pride is more evident, because they know that they have had to struggle against the grain, without the advantages that others have enjoyed. Those who are not upwardly mobile are frequently aware that the cards are stacked against them, though this feeling often takes a humorous, self-deprecating rather than openly political form (Mckenzie 2015; Savage et al. 2015).

The identities of the upwardly mobile are more complex than might be imagined. The standard view, derived from Goldthorpe et al.'s (1980) re-search, was that upwardly mobile men generally felt satisfied with their success, as a sign that they had indeed reaped the rewards of their own en-deavors. More recent research on the experiential aspects of social mobility has seriously qualified this view. Sociologists of mobility, such as Sam Friedman (2016), have explored the lived feelings of the socially mobile. They uncover a very striking finding. Even though such people have been suc-cessful in career terms, they don't feel fully at ease with themselves or their environment. It is true that Tak Wing Chan (2018: 200) contests the view that "upward mobility is in general a negative experience for those who have

achieved occupational success" and uses evidence from the British Household Panel Study to report that upwardly mobile respondents frequently report high well-being and life satisfaction. But it is perfectly possible to feel
proud of one's achievements while also being mindful of the slights and
snobbery that you might be subject to—indeed, one's own sense of achievement may be linked to a sense that you have overcome these (Savage and
Meersohn 2021). "Imposter syndrome" is not just a journalistic trope but is
marked on people's bodies. The visceral experience of mobility is fraught,
anxious, and tense: even though it may be possible to climb up the ladder,
this does not wipe clean how you feel.

This is a crucial point. Rendering inequalities in terms of relative chances
does not render people's lived experiences. Indeed, it is those who appear to
be have succeeded who can most acutely point to the distress they feel. The
erosion of relative inequalities can actually intensify the feelings of the upwardly mobile that they still cannot, ultimately, dine at the top table—even
though its bounties are close enough to smell. Enhancing social mobility
does not by itself alleviate personal distress, which may actually be more
manifest among those who succeed in being upwardly mobile.

7.3: De-gendering?

The trends for gender are even more clear cut than for class: There is no gainsaying the remarkable decline of relative as well as absolute gender differences in paid employment and in wage differentials around much of the
globe in recent decades. In most nations, the opening up of female employment has facilitated a major reduction in gender inequalities in the labor
market. On the face of it, the shift is historically unprecedented. Until the
1970s, women rarely were allowed to work in professional and managerial
employment, and a "marriage bar" that required women to retire after marriage was frequently in force.

In the later decades of the twentieth century, however, there was a rapid
increase in the number of women moving into higher education, and subsequently into more highly paid employment. The nature and pace of this
process has been uneven. The growing proportion of women in the middle
layers of the economic distribution is especially striking, especially in the

large swath of public professions. The sophisticated discussion in Kleven et al. (2019) of comparative gender wage differentials for full-time workers shows a convergence across the United States, the United Kingdom, Sweden, and Denmark. In 1980, men typically earned 35 percent more than women in the United States and the United Kingdom, but this had shrunk to less than 20 percent by 2013. The gender wage gap had always been much smaller in Denmark and Sweden, but it also fell slightly over the same period. The trends even in egalitarian Denmark point to a striking reduction of gender differentials: The average man earned 47 percent more than the average woman in 1980 (women were often part-time workers, so reducing their pay levels), but this had halved to a little more than 20 percent by 2013. In the United Kingdom, Brynin and Perales (2016: 162) identify what they call the "degendering of the occupational structure." Between 1993 and 2008, the gender wage gap halved.

The patterns are more ambiguous when examining women's mobility into professional and managerial posts, though there are some remarkable success stories. The proportion of female doctors has risen substantially, though there is considerable variation across nations. Nonetheless, Figure 7.2 shows there are several countries, especially in small nations in central or eastern Europe where around half, or even more, of doctors are now female. There are very clear differences between age cohorts, reflecting the speed of change: In most European and anglophone nations, the majority of younger doctors are female. Only in Japan and Korea are fewer than 50 percent of doctors under the age of 35 female. The elite medical profession, long identified as a seat of patriarchal professional control by elite men (for example, Witz 1992) has undergone a sea change.

But this is not a uniform process across all professional occupations. The most striking cases where women have penetrated previously male jobs are in public facing roles, often located in the public sector, but in managerial, financial, and corporate posts, including those in which income premiums are likely to be high, male dominance remains marked. Men are more likely to be managers in all countries, apart from Costa Rica (where the female-male difference is 0.3). Figure 7.3 also shows that in the more prosperous nations, where a larger proportion work as managers, there is a greater gender gap: only in the United States does the gap shrink to a few percentage points.

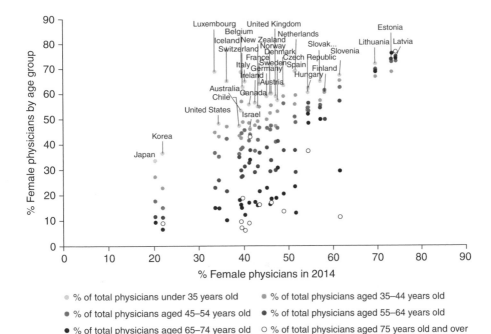

FIGURE 7.2: Share of female physicians as a percentage of overall physicians by age group

Data source: OECD, "Physicians by Age Group (Under 35, 35–44, 45–54, 55–64, 65–74, 75 and Over) and by Gender," *OECD Health Statistics 2020.* See its "Definitions, Sources and Methods" section for details on underlying data sources.

De-gendering is therefore far from being complete or comprehensive, especially in the most highly paid parts of the workforce. Kleven et al. (2017, 2019) note the obstinacy of a gender pay gap of around 20 percent that is difficult to reduce further, whatever policies seek to address it. They associate this with the continued tendency for women to leave the labor market to take on the bulk of childcare, with the implications this poses for their careers and earnings potential.

There has also been a considerable—though far from complete—narrowing of the gender gap in domestic labor, even though there continue to be ongoing gender inequalities in the organization of care work (Gershuny and Sullivan 2019). The most extreme shift was in France, where in 1961–1971, women spent five times as long carrying out adult and child care compared to men, a proportion that fell to twice as much by 2005–2009.[7] Similar but

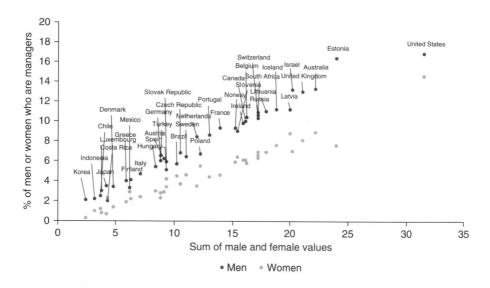

FIGURE 7.3: Percentage of employed who are managers, 2015

Data source: OECD.

less extreme trends were found more widely, though there were exceptions, such as Poland. However, Gershuny and Sullivan's findings suggest that once the ratio falls to about two to one, it remains obdurate thereafter, with it rarely falling significantly below this level: Denmark's ratio with women spending 1.8 times as much as men on adult and child care in 2000–2004 is the lowest rate that they find. There is a similar glass floor with respect to time spent shopping. In nearly every country, women spend at least 50 percent more time shopping than do men. But the amount of time that women and men spend on consumption and leisure is largely equal.

On the face of it, these trends are dramatic. In relative terms, the position of women vis-à-vis men has improved, indeed substantially. And this is precisely the point. Because it is less widely assumed that women and men *should* do different kinds of work, the continuation of systematic gender inequality becomes more contentious. The shrinking of gender differentials does not mean that women *feel* as if they are equals or could ever really be treated as such by men. Instead, it offers the lure and promise of equality for those women who are prepared to devote themselves to this cause, only to reveal the ultimate difficulties in their doing so. This helps clarify the power of Simone de Beauvior's heartfelt statement with which I opened this chapter: Closing the relative gap may make the remaining inequalities feel even more salient. Women remain in an inferior position—even despite the relative trends toward greater equality.

7.4: The Racial Divide

Race was the primary classic categorical divide at the onset of imperial modernity. This was most evidently marked by the inhuman institution of racialized slavery and the brutal treatment of indigenous populations. It continues to be the most obdurate categorical division. Racial inequalities have in some spheres become more prominent. This is therefore different from class and gender, where economic inequalities have become more attenuated. Whereas the relative gender pay gap has substantially reduced, the racial pay gap has changed little, if at all. In the United States, Mandel and Semyonov (2016) show how after a slight narrowing between 1980 and 2000, the pay gap actually increased between 2000 and 2010. Anthony Heath and Di Stasio's (2019) review of different field experiments in the United Kingdom between 1967 and 2019 in which fictitious job applications, whose names are used to signal different ethnic status, reveals persistent discrimination against black and ethnic minorities (including Black Caribbean, African, Indian, Pakistani, and Chinese) and no trend for this to improve over time. Unlike both gender (especially), and class, relative inequalities on race and ethnic grounds have proved much more difficult to shift.

Even so, as with class and gender, race has also changed its classic character, taking on more relativistic, mobile, and fluid form. In the United States, Larry Bobo (2011, 2017) has traced long-term shifts in American attitudes, showing that overt Jim Crow racism among white Americans has given way to more neoliberal forms. Here, although African Americans are not necessarily seen as intrinsically inferior, they are still not expected to be as capable, as skilled, or as expert as whites. Loury (2001) traces a similar kind of shift from when racial discrimination was primarily characterized by explicit differences in treatment by race to more indirect and covert forms (see also Pager and Pedulla 2015; Pedulla and Pager 2019).

In the British context, a similar argument was made by Stuart Hall (1996) regarding the emergence of "new ethnicities." Hall argued that during the post–Second World War decades, the Black experience represented a "critique of the way blacks were positioned as the unspoken and invisible 'other' of predominantly white aesthetic and cultural discourses" (Hall 1996: 442)—exactly as classic categorical divisions emerged from insider and out-sider oppositions during imperial modernity. Hall observes the replacement of the "essential black subject" by a "new politics of representation," in which the difficulties that Black populations face in establishing their equivalence lead to intensified contestation and disputes about how race itself is to be understood. Hall's emphasis on this fluidity of racial categorization has been taken up by numerous other antiracist scholars, so revealing how sensitivity to racial inequality may actually heighten when race is seen in more fluid terms (for example, Back 1996; Gilroy 2004).

With respect to race, however, there is a major difference compared to class or gender. I noted in Chapter 6 that as nation spaces formed during the twentieth century, the policing of "responsible adult status" and national citizenship has taken a more fundamental role in differentiating insiders and outsiders. This allows racial divisions to be reinscribed through the intensi-fication of a politics of racialized immigration status (see, for example, An-thias and Yuval-Davis 2005).[8] Following the abolition of slavery during the nineteenth century, and as nation spaces increasingly supplanted imperial states, the immigration of racial minorities, usually as poorly paid workers in metropolitan heartland nations, became commonplace. Gatrell (2019) has recently reasserted how economic growth in European nations since 1945 was dependent on the ubiquity of different migration flows, many of which involve Black populations from Asia, Africa, and the Caribbean.

Around the globe, racialization is inscribed by immigration, refracting race through a lens in which origin status retains a long shadow, even when immigrants are settled long-term in their destination country. The immigra-tion experience is extremely varied across groups, with the result that over-arching categories become decomposed into granular, highly variable pat-terns, nonetheless attesting to the efficacy of a powerful racial divides. Maskileyson and Semyonov (2017) bring out a striking vignette in their study of the incomes of immigrants from different ethnic and national back-grounds in the United States, compared to those of third-generation whites.

Figures 7.4 and 7.5 show that immigrants to the United States have very different economic fortunes according to their racial origins. White northern European migrants can expect to see income levels well above those of white

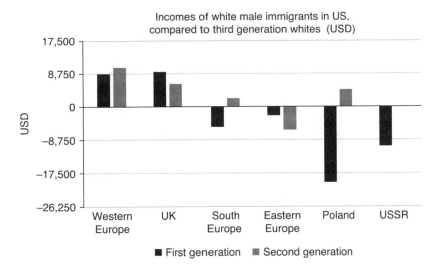

FIGURE 7.4: Incomes of white male immigrants in the United States compared to third-generation whites

Data source: Dina Maskileyson and Moshe Semyonov, "On Race, Ethnicity and on the Economic Cost of Immigration," *Research in Social Stratification and Mobility* 50 (2017): 19–28.

Americans: For them, the experience of immigration is likely to be of economic success and prosperity, very likely to be associated with class-specific recruitment routes via professional and managerial jobs, or through visas obtained to study in the United States.

By contrast, the experience of immigrants from southern and eastern Europe and also from Asia is much worse. With the exception of Indians, they can expect to earn considerably less than established white Americans. In some cases, this shortfall is very large indeed: The experience of these immigrants is likely to be one of economic hardship and marginality. Even more than this, for some Black and Asian immigrant groups, second-generation migrants continue to experience a major income penalty. Indeed, for those moving from the Caribbean, the second generation is even worse off than the first. However, white and Asian ethnic immigrant groups are more likely to see the second generation transforming their disadvantages into relative advantage. This is especially true of the Poles, the Chinese, and Indians. By contrast, the advantages of second-generation British immigrants slips back somewhat.

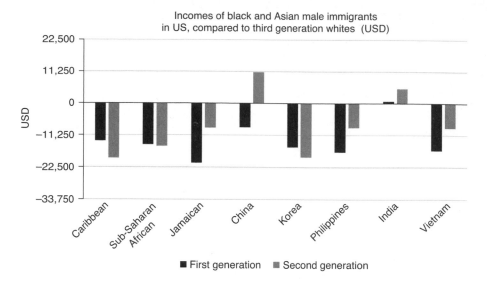

FIGURE 7.5: Incomes of Black and Asian immigrants in the United States compared to third-generation whites

Data source: Dina Maskileyson and Moshe Semyonov, "On Race, Ethnicity and on the Economic Cost of Immigration," *Research in Social Stratification and Mobility* 50 (2017): 19–28.

Racial inequalities therefore proliferate as old imperial divides are compounded by the racialization of immigration. In this light, we can better understand the power of Black Lives Matter and resurgent antiracist campaigns. These movements change the terms of debate about racism away from a set of abstract probabilities by insisting on the lived, bodily experience, including the historical and migration roots that cannot be effaced. The reassertion of the power of slavery as a defining feature of the ongoing Black experience plays a crucial role in the American and African context.

7.5: Visceral Inequalities and Economic Inequality

In Chapter 1, we examined the far-reaching shift that economists have staged in making inequality concrete through turning the telescope on wealthy elites, away from their long-standing attention to the poor. Whereas historically it has been the bodies of the poor that commanded attention—

disreputable, lower class, and racially excluded, as objects of pity and repulsion—it is increasingly the obscene bodies of bloated elites that have been brought into view. Piketty's deployment of income-share analysis, and its capacity to mine down in highly granular detail into very small percentiles at the top of the distribution captured the zeitgeist perfectly on its publication in 2013. Rather than hiding behind abstractions, such as the Gini coefficient, a top economist had made it scientifically acceptable—indeed cutting-edge—to zoom in minutely to real, excessively wealthy people.

This turns out to have huge implications. By portraying prominent elite figures, marked by their wealth, power, and privilege, people's relative lack can more readily be turned into anger and resentment. This is why the visceral inequalities experienced by women, racial minorities, and those from disadvantaged classes are not best understood as performative or identity based. They come to the fore when relative inequalities decline, so encouraging the sense that mobility should be possible—but also when the actual concentration of top-level inequalities leads in the other direction. The impossibility of ever winning the game, however hard you play—and even if you obtain a certain measure of success—becomes ever more apparent as the biggest victors forge further ahead. The overarching hold of those at the top who stand above you, judging you, and ultimately finding you wanting, becomes more grating. In this context, we can understand the anger expressed toward statues of Cecil Rhodes or General Lee not as purely symbolic struggles, or just as trying to set the historical record straight, but testify to the resurgent anger toward elites—in the form of powerful white men—who increasingly characterize the "stuff of inequality."

Visceral inequalities are linked to the changing dynamics of capital accumulation. The rise of relative categories was associated with economic growth based on productivity increases (or in Marx's terms, the shift from absolute to relative surplus value). As productivity growth in the expanding service sector is increasingly driven by worker's embodied qualities, where face-to-face and personal interaction plays a key role in making transactions, then physical appearance and deportment come to the fore. There is indeed an arresting feature of much visceral politics, which is that those who feel violated, abused, disrupted, and personally affronted include those who are in relatively—though not supremely—privileged positions. In this vein, McLaughlin, Uggen, and Blackstone's (2012) summary of research on sexual harassment shows that women in supervisory positions are more likely to report being subject to sexual harassment compared to lower-grade female employees. Rather than supervisory status giving insulation from harassment, it works the other way around. Friedman (2016) shows that it is often highly successful and upwardly mobile people in professional and managerial jobs who feel most personally unsettled and are able to point to personal slights and feelings of visceral unease with the way they have been treated. This literature extends to the now-extensive studies of upwardly mobile working class students feeling like "fish out of water" at elite institutions, such as Ivy League universities in the United States or Russell group universities in the United Kingdom (Reay 2001, 2018; Reay et al. 2010). This feature also surfaces in the strength of antiracist and decolonizing pedagogical movements in elite universities seeking to decolonize the curriculum. Visceral politics flourishes in elite institutional environments, and in situations where significant numbers of women, ethnic minorities, and people from disadvantaged class backgrounds have had some capacity to move into more senior posts, only to feel personally the ultimate impossibility of getting that seat at the top table.

The bodies of those who have been brought into view by the economists' income share analysis are very much those of white men. At the very top levels of the income distribution, among the top few percent who are the major beneficiaries of enhanced income and wealth, women have not moved proportionately into the highest pay brackets. This domain of the superrich remains very much a male, patriarchal world. Women remain highly underrepresented among top income earners in many advanced economies (Atkinson et al. 2018), being less than 20 percent of those in the top 1 percent of earners in most nations. They are even more underrepresented among the top 0.1 percent. It follows that the stretching out of income inequality as the top end "pull away" is a process that has benefited men in absolute terms far more than women. Women also continue to be substantially underrepresented among institutional elites (for example, Reis and Moore [2005]), and this is especially true in nations where inequality is higher. The relatively egalitarian Nordic states have a higher share of women among political and management elites than do corporatist Germany, Austria, and Italy.

In general, women are better represented in governance in smaller, less powerful nations rather than in the larger and more powerful imperial blocs,

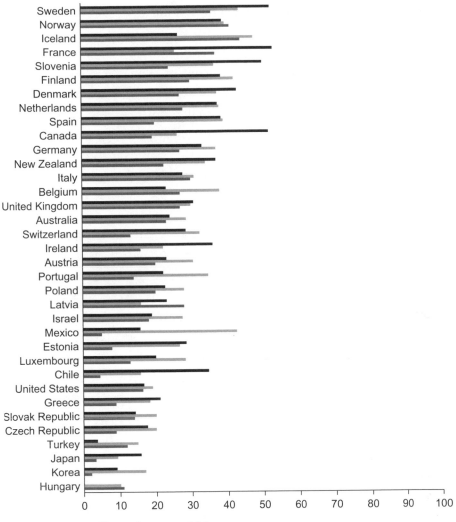

FIGURE 7.6: The share of women in governance "elites"

Data source: OECD.

the differences between which I have excavated in Chapters 4 and 5. Countries in the southern half of the African continent, in Central and South America, and in parts of Europe have the highest share of women in parliament.[9] These tend to be geopolitically weak nations.

This is the well-known Matthew principle of "For to everyone who has will more be given, and he will have abundance," but with the rider that Matthew is an embodied and corporeal presence and that "his" qualities, behavior, and activities will understandably be the subject of intense scrutiny, resentment, and anger from those without "his" rewards. It follows that when Stiglitz famously wrote that American policy was "Of the 1%, for the 1%, by the 1%," he might have added the rider, "and these are nearly entirely white men." When this male world does engage women, it does so on terms set by elite white men, as feminist ethnographers, such as Luna Glucksberg (2016) and Ashley Mears (2015), have shown. The world of superrich and wealthy men is deeply misogynistic. Mears's study of "VIP" clubs in New York reveals how the promoters of exclusive clubs recruit (unpaid) young women to bedeck the gatherings of rich older men, at the behest of mainly male intermediaries. Luna Glucksberg (2016) has explored the emotional travails of the wives of London plutocrats, who on the face of it live a life of opulence and yet are constrained to fulfill highly policed values regarding their appearance, and who need to devote themselves to bringing up the next generation as the inheritors of wealth. Even where women can gain entry to elite portals, as Lauren Rivera's (2016) study of recruitment to top American firms shows, they do so because they are seen as potentially good mates to hang out with for a beer after work.

As the circles of highly paid elites remain highly exclusive in gendered, racialized, and classed ways, so the feeling that however much you try, you will never succeed, becomes endemic. Thus, feelings of structural inferiority, discrimination, and oppression are rampant, especially among those who are within touching distance of this elite world, can see its operations first hand, and who experience their bodily exclusion from its inner court. The concept of intersectionality helps pin this down. The concept was famously elaborated by the Black feminist lawyer Kimberlé Crenshaw (1989) to make the fundamental point that different categories do not have additive effects, but instead interact to generate distinctive inequalities of their own. Intersectionality is embedded in the body. People's bodies are simultaneously gendered, raced, and classed (as well as being aged, having different capacities for mobility, and so forth).

Crenshaw's initial application focused on the intersectional discrimination directed at Black female workers at General Motors. But, if we change the telescope to look at the top, the mutually reinforcing intersectional advantages of elites becomes more manifest. In this spirit, growing interest in multidimensional analysis in social science research has allowed the simple proxy of privileged class backgrounds to be rethought in terms of the cumulative advantages of numerous intersecting processes. The Finnish sociologist Jani Erola argues that the parental resources that facilitate children's success cannot be reduced to a single variable, such as household finances. Parents influence the adult socioeconomic attainment of their children through two types of pathway: endowments and investments. Thus, there is a process of cumulative causality that comes together in household relations, not a single categorical position.[10]

In like manner, older, classic, "big" class categories, such as those distinguishing the middle from the working class, give little purchase on these intersectional elite dynamics. There is now general agreement about the splintering of broader middle or "professional and managerial" classes into smaller fractions. The trumpet was sounded by American sociologists Kim Weeden and David Grusky (2005, 2012), who were the first to take issue with the significance of what they termed "big classes." They stressed that granular micro-classes (that is, specific occupational groups) have their own distinctive properties that could not easily be bundled together into baggy classes like Goldthorpe's "service class" of professionals or managers. Bennett et al. (2009) and Le Roux et al. (2008) show that in terms of cultural participation and consumption, there is a clear differentiation between a distinctive elite professional-executive class composed of professionals and senior managers, separated from middle and lower managers. This is underscored by quantitative studies revealing how a smaller, senior, and more privileged professional and managerial class is increasingly distinct from the broader ranks of professionals and managers (see the discussion in Savage 2015). My study on the Great British Class Survey (Savage et al. 2013, 2015) brought out the distinctive advantages of a small elite class that not only was much better off than any other class but also had substantially more elite networks and cultural capital.[11] Similar arguments have been made by Jodhka,

Table 7.1: Average income of students' parents, by college-ranking tiers

University ranking placed in percentage bands	Average income of students' parents ($)	Share of graduates from top 1 percent households (percent)	Mean graduate income at age 34 ($)
Very top	277,500	26	123,600
Top 1 percent	200,400	19	81,200
5 percent	139,800	7.3	63,100
10 percent	116,100	3.8	52,600
25 percent	90,100	1.2	43,500
50 percent	64,500	<1	34,500
75 percent	45,900	<1	28,600
Bottom	15,600	<1	10,300

Data source: Raj Chetty, John Friedman, Emmanuel Saez, Nicholas Turner, and Danny Yagan, "Mobility Report Cards: The Role of Colleges in Intergenerational Mobility," Equality of Opportunity Project. An interactive tool to explore the data for hundreds of schools was created by the *New York Times*: https://www.nytimes.com/interactive/projects/college -mobility/city-college-of-new-york.

Rehbein, and Souza (2017) in their comparative studies of Germany, Brazil, and Laos that elites, though small in numerical terms, are utterly distinctive from all other social classes in terms of their propensity to pass on their advantages to their children.

This increasing availability of granular administrative data has brought home the intersectional distinctiveness of elites, and the operation of "power laws," in which their top-end advantages are accentuated across numerous dimensions. A fascinating example is revealed by Raj Chetty and his associates, who used tax data to extract information on the income and social mobility of graduates of all 2,395 American universities.[12]

Table 7.1 shows that there is a wide range in the incomes earned among American college graduates. The average household income of the parents of different college graduates ranges from a staggering $277,500 (at Colorado College), which is nearly twenty times that of the family households of graduates from the bottom-ranked college of $15,600 (United Talmudical Seminary). The proportion of graduates who were brought up in households in the top 1 percent of the income distribution reaches an astonishing 26 percent at Trinity College (Connecticut), but in most colleges, as we

Table 7.2: Proportion of UK senior professionals and managers who are socially mobile

	Share with parent in same job (%)	Share with parent from senior professional and managerial background (%)	Percentage premium earned by those from higher professional / managerial backgrounds compared to those from working class	Pay of those from working class backgrounds (GBP)
Doctors	17.2	53.3	39.4	43,160
Lawyers	8.1	40.9	48.0	38,168
Finance managers	4.6	30.3	44.9	41,808
Armed forces, police, emergency	8.2	24.2	41.6	40,612
IT professionals	1.9	23.9	30.9	43,264
Higher education	3.9	29.0	14.5	41,548
Scientists	2.2	29.0	1	34,684
Engineers	8.6	21.1	5.9	40,768
Accountants	4.6	25.6	11.7	42,276
Public sector managers	1.1	16.2	20.7	38,116

Data source: Daniel Laurison and Sam Friedman, "The Class Pay Gap in Higher Professional and Managerial Occupations," *American Sociological Review* 81, no. 4 (2016): 668–695.

would expect, soon falls off. Seventy-five percent of colleges have fewer than 1 percent of their students drawn from families whose incomes place them in the top 1 percent.

It is not the simple extent of variance that matters, but the fact that it occurs at the extreme top end. The mean income of graduates ranges from $123,600 at St. Louis College of Pharmacy to $10,300 at Paul Mitchell School. But the mean income earned at college on the top 5 percent boundary is $60,500, way below St. Louis College. The proportion of graduates who are from top 1 percent households falls dramatically from 26 percent for the highest ranked college, to 19 percent for the college that performs at the 1 percent threshold, and to 7.3 percent at the top 5 percent threshold.[13]

Sociologists Sam Friedman and Daniel Laurison examined the social mobility profiles of senior professional and managerial occupations in the United Kingdom in unparalleled detail (see Table 7.2). The first column of Table 7.2 reports the proportion of respondents in these specific elite occupations who had parents working in the same occupation. For doctors and lawyers, and to a lesser extent the workers in security services and engineers, there is marked self-recruitment, with children following parents into the same occupation—but this drops off rapidly for other occupations.

If the scope is broadened to consider what proportion of respondents in different elite occupations have parents who worked in any kind of highly advantaged senior managerial and professional work, these elite effects become more apparent. Whereas only a tenth of employees in the United Kingdom come from professional and managerial backgrounds, this number rises to over half for doctors and 40 percent for lawyers. Column 4 of Table 7.1 reveals what Laurison and Friedman call the "class ceiling": Those from more privileged backgrounds often earn more—sometimes substantially more—than those from working class backgrounds. This class ceiling is very evident in law, finance, the security services, and medicine, and then rapidly falls off elsewhere (though with information technology professionals also seeing a marked effect).

Conclusion

In the early twenty-first century, there is a collision of two worlds: a meritocratic belief that people should not have their lives dictated for them by their accident of birth, colliding with the actual reality that the accentuation of inequality is seeing the hardening of privilege in class, gender, and racial terms as the top pulls away from the rest. This conflict around sex, gender, and race is about worth and dignity set in the context of the accentuation of economic inequality and the hardening of processes of ascription and increasingly hereditary inheritance at the top. The bodily markers of these divides take on great importance, just as they did at the outset of imperial modernity.

There is therefore no contradiction between declining relative inequality along the lines of class and gender (though not of race) and at the same time greater antagonisms along these same axes. As top end, inequality becomes more marked, given uneven recruitment into it from different groups, an intensified recognition of the limited type of people who make it to the top. The American case is so revealing, because the United States is the nation that has seen an especially marked increase of income and wealth inequality in recent years, at the same time that its endorsement of meritocratic values has also endured. As accumulation builds up and "winner takes all" premiums expand, so multiple tensions arise. In a situation where it is deemed that everyone should, potentially, be able to live the good and affluent life (that is, that unlike the nineteenth century, the good life should not be confined to respectable and ascribed elites), but few people actually can, the build-up of resentment is entirely to be expected. Michele Lamont (2019: 662–663) identifies the resulting dilemma clearly:

> At a time when the lifestyle and the values of the upper-middle class are systematically being offered as the ideal to pursue by all—although *increasingly fewer have the means necessary to make it a reality*, . . . the middle class has seen its income significantly reduce post-2008 and the working class and low-income populations face growing insecurity. This tension feeds the increased 'wear-and-tear' or allostatic load associated with inequality, and a decline in collective well-being manifested in lower life expectancy, the ongoing opioid epidemic, and increase in suicide.

As economic inequality increases, and as accumulation of wealth grows, so it becomes more difficult for large numbers of Americans to obtain the material resources to live a comfortable life. In the circumstances, as Lamont identifies, it is harder for those excluded groups to feel they ever could belong, and marginalization, stigmatization, and discrimination intensify.

Therefore, in recent decades, the stuff of inequality is increasingly rendered as visceral, physical, and embodied, rather than abstracted into relative categories. This is a far-reaching process that generates tensions and conflicts that are increasingly virulent—and which can be expected to become more so. Visceral inequality recognizes the historically different mechanisms by which the stuff of inequality is rendered, or more exactly, categorical distinctions are produced. In the first phase of imperial modernity,

the insider-outsider dynamic locates certain groups as "outside the pale"—
because they are inherently the wrong, inferior, gender, race, or class. In the
second phase, competitive relations within twentieth-century nation spaces
render inequalities between groups in terms of their differing life chance
probabilities. These relativities typically become the arena for policy intervention and amelioration. We are now, however in a third phase, in which
categorical inequalities take on a visceral form as privileged elites pull away.
In this situation, nearly all people will be unable to enter these elites whose
gender, racial, and class privilege is increasingly exposed and visible. This
is part of a wider process involving the breakdown of nation spaces and a
growing sense from exploited groups that they can never fully belong to a
social order defined by a small and aloof elite.

These three phases are in keeping with the need to reinstate a fully temporal analysis into the inequality debate, more specifically Henri Bergson's
understanding of time as duration rather than as transition between linear
states. Thus, visceral inequalities are a response to the hardening of inequality, allowing rich insiders to be increasingly insulated from outsider
influence. Although this marks a return to the classic inequalities of imperial modernity, it does so in a different and transformed way. Precisely because
people have experienced probabilistic categories in nation space, so this relativistic framing challenges exclusions on the basis of categorical identity.

Visceral inequalities are therefore part of a pincer movement. One of the
pincers is the decline of relative inequalities, so allowing different groups to
compare one another in the recognition that they are not intrinsically different to anyone else. The other pincer is the concretization of inequality in
the physical, bodily, figures of elites, who are overwhelmingly white men.
Visceral inequality thus attests to the awareness that however hard you try,
there is no level playing field.

In this respect, visceral inequality marks the force of history in a very direct sense. Just as classic, insider-outsider categories that dominated during
imperial modernity were marked on bodies, with specific kinds of people
stamped, physically, as outsiders, so bodily inequality becomes an intensified marker again. It is therefore utterly explicable why race reemerges as
the quintessential divide.

Cities, Elites, and Accumulation

Two contrasting pictures front this chapter. Manet's *The Bar at the Folies-Bergère*, first exhibited in 1882, is one of the most famous impressionist paintings of all time. It was identified by the art historian T. J. Clark (1985) as the quintessential depiction of urban modernity. The painting is both highly detailed and realistic yet also ambiguous and opaque in the depiction of the encounter between the barmaid and her viewer / customer. According to some art historians, the oranges on the counter indicate that the barmaid was a sex worker. There is an extensive literature on the use of perspective entailed by the mirror behind the barmaid, including its distortions and omissions. Gordon Fyfe sees it as one of "three enigmatic paintings that always seem to stand on the threshold of a new order," the other two being Piero della Francesca's *Flagellation* (representing the fall of Constantinople) and Velazquez's *Las Meninas* (a new Enlightenment space).[1]

This painting thereby renders urban encounters in all their ambiguities. The fluidity and also the reinscription of gender entailed in the figure of the barmaid is associated with wider opacity about the relationship between customer and audience. There are few straight lines of the kind that I have used in previous chapters to explain the provenance of the inequality narrative. The opaque rendering of light, shade, and image dominates.

It is not incidental that *The Bar at the Folies-Bergère* portrays an urban encounter: The quintessential site of modernity from the later nineteenth century was the city. Artistic currents seized the city as the nexus of cultural modernism that embraced its transitory and fleeting qualities and hence its

FIGURE 8.1: Édouard Manet, *A Bar at the Folies-Bergère*
Source: Courtaud Gallery, London.

potential as milieu for artistic innovation (Bradbury and Macfarlane 1976; Clark 1985). Bourdieu identified the emergence of artistic fields in the work of Manet and Flaubert with Paris being "the capital of capital." As Accominotti (2021) traces, the rise of urban art dealers and galleries as brokers in making or breaking artists' careers was part of this mix. This set in train the city as base for a distinctive aesthetic, cultural, and social sensibility that proved influential throughout the twentieth century.

Figure 8.2, from the contemporary *Unequal Scenes* artwork of Johnny Miller, offers a very different kind of urban representation. It too takes advantage of twenty-first-century cutting-edge modes of visual representation, in this case from drones flying surreptitiously above the landscape. It reinscribes a highly realistic photographic tradition, a visual diagnostic akin to a medical scan, from which Miller unravels the line dividing slums and squatter settlements jostling against prosperous tracts of privileged urban

FIGURE 8.2: Johnny Miller, *Unequal Scenes*

Source: Johnny Miller.

housing. Here, sharp dividing lines on the urban landscape divide spatially as well as socially. Miller thus starkly reveals how twenty-first-century inequality is an intensified urban phenomenon.

Figures 7.1, 8.1, and 8.2 render three very different urban viewpoints. In Figure 8.1, the gaze is implicitly that of a male patron, directed at the female bar worker, and assumes his questioning poise. Is sex for sale, or not? In Figure 7.1 the telescope is turned, and the picture's line of sight centers on the dismantling of a statue of an imperial elite white man. The camera angle comes from below, among predominantly young Black protesters objecting to the statue on its dais. By contrast, Figure 8.2 represents the surveillance gaze made possible by the drone. This is the vertical perspective that geographer Stephen Graham (2016) has identified as fundamental to the contemporary urban imagination. This verticality evokes a new elite landscape akin to the spiraling corporate office blocks and penthouses of today's vertical global cities that identify elite power at its rawest—where, just as in medieval Italy, the control of height was a fundamental marker of power.

These are three urban pictures with inequality inscribed differentially into their angles of sight. Compared to the *Bar at the Folies-Bergère*, there is no ambiguity in *Unequal Scenes*. There is only utter clarity about the way that economic and social divides are etched in geographical space. Just like *Rhodes Must Fall* in Figure 7.1, this is not a modernist evocation of fluidity or contingency. It speaks to the hard reality of social division. It thereby marks the weakening hold of urban modernity itself. Just at the moment that the urban experience has become mainstream—with half of the world's population now living in cities—so urbanism is losing its modernist idiom and resuming an older historical identity. Cities have always been central sites for accumulation—as the legacy of urban cathedrals, temples, forts, palaces, and marketplaces across the world demonstrates very clearly. As liberal modernity burns out, and as nation spaces weaken, this historical role of cities as centers for accumulation is recharged. It is the steady accretion of accumulated capital—the historical residues of previous forms of economic, social, cultural, and political activity—that increasingly marks out the city in an era of massive and accentuating wealth inequality.

This argument immediately flies in the face of the persistence of a contrary-minded modernist mindset crystallized so powerfully in *The Bar at the Folies-Bergère*. Our preoccupation with the city as transitory, fleeting, and ephemeral, and our investment of urban life with hope and desire remain strong. Here, the metropolis seems to be forever the site of freedom, of contingent encounters and experiences, the harbinger of the future yet to come. It is the quintessential site of a modernity that is always changing, renewing, and extending itself, into late modernity, postmodernity, and beyond. A classic example is Marshall Berman's moving *All That Is Solid Melts into Air* (1983) with its profound elegy on the urban as fleeting, as only graspable by being ungraspable, as forever doomed to be tragic site for hopes and desires that are bound to fail. The remarkable resurgence of interest in the cultural theory of Walter Benjamin from the last decades of the twentieth century, whose thinking oozes with similar preoccupations about the nightmarish yet also redemptive qualities of urban experience, exemplifies the ongoing power of this vision. In a more social scientific framing, the appeal of Henri Lefebvre's emphasis on the social production of space cross-fertilized with Marxist political economy in the later decades of the twentieth century also promoted this conception of the city as mobile, dynamic, and transitory. Indeed, it is the persistence of this framing of the city well into the later twentieth century that is striking. Its later imprint can be found in David Harvey's work on the city as the site of capitalist investment as well as in Manuel Castells (1977) on its role as a site of collective consumption.

Although there is an extensive critique of the dominance of Western urban paradigms, and a growing insistence on the need to recognize the dynamic character of urbanization in the global south (see notably Simone 2004, 2009; Jenny Robinson 2006, 2011), as Jenny Robinson (2013b) has argued, this quintessential modernist sensitivity to urban dynamism remains largely intact (see, generally, Savage et al. 2003; Parker 2004). Urbanization in the global south is still often comprehended through this modernist lens, crisply captured by the great sociologist of African cities, AbdouMaliq Simone (2004: 9), who reiterates that cities are "the conjunction of seemingly endless possibilities of remaking."

It will be clear to readers who have read previous chapters that I dispute the pertinence of this modernist framing. There are ample reasons to suppose that this framing of the city as the quintessential site of capitalist energy and dynamism has run its course. It fails to recognize how the piling up of wealth and accumulation entails that cities can now better be understood through an older vision of them as the sedimentation of consolidated capital. This, of course, is the city of archaeologists and anthropologists, who have traced the emergence of cities several millennia ago in terms of their role as storage devices—in Anthony Giddens's (1985) formulation as "power containers." Cities today are sites for the location of stored and accumulated assets and resources, which thereby set them apart from their rural and provincial hinterlands. We do not get a handle on this through our now-dated modernist framing with its embrace of ambiguity and contingency. The build-up of historical processes of possession and dispossession need to be put center stage. This is the city of *Unequal Scenes,* clearly zoned and differentiated according to the resources and assets of different kinds of residents, which have been accumulated over time and which mark inequality trenchantly on the urban landscape. It is not incidental that psychogeographers, such as Ian Sinclair (for example, 2003), and others following in the footsteps of Walter Benjamin, now turn to the past to excavate the debris of urban contingency, to find the traces of cities that are "yet to be."

In this chapter, I first consider how large cities are not just products but also drivers of inequality. This is true with respect to income inequality and social mobility—where I draw on recent granular studies that allow us to dissect mobility on a local scale. I then go on to reflect on the power of cities as sites of wealth concentration. They are the paramount site for accumulation of economic capital, and hence for the wealthy elites who have emerged as the principal beneficiaries of capitalist economic trends. In the third part of this chapter, I return to the rise of visceral inequalities, examined in Chapter 7. This stuff of inequality has an affinity with urban living, tied in with the embodiment of emerging cultural capital.

8.1: Economic Inequality in the City

Johnny Miller's *Unequal Scenes* returns us to an old, historical view of cities. It evokes Frederick Engels's famous study of early nineteenth-century Manchester, *The Condition of the English Working Class*. However, this urban basis of inequality has not been adequately brought out in recent inequality research, which is fixated on measurement at the national level. There can be problems in getting adequate data on incomes and inequality measures at the urban level, and there are difficulties in knowing where to draw city boundaries in a way that does not lead to artefactual comparisons and that fails to recognize how urbanism spreads beyond city boundaries (see generally Brenner and Schmid 2014). Nonetheless, and with this caveat in mind, it is instructive to draw on data that has purported to rank the most unequal and most equal major cities in the world. In Tables 8.1 and 8.2, I link data from Euromonitor with information on national levels of inequality. These use the Palma ratio, which is defined as the share of income taken by the top 10 percent of urban residents compared to the bottom 40 percent and is thus more attuned to the income-share approach championed by Piketty than the more widely criticized Gini coefficient (which is still more commonly used elsewhere, for instance, by the UN World Cities Report [2016]).

Table 8.1: Twenty most unequal cities in the world, 2016

City	Palma ratio	Change 2005–2016 (%)	Country Palma	City Palma as percentage of national Palma
Johannesburg	13.4	—	South Africa 7.1	188
Lagos	12.3	—	Nigeria 3.0	410
Nairobi	11.7	+42	Kenya 2.8	433
Santo Domingo	10.7	−22	Dominican Rep 2.7	396
Cape Town	9.1	0	South Africa 7.1	128
Kuala Lumpur	8.5	+112	Malaysia 2.6	327
Rio de Janeiro	7.2	+17	Brazil 4.3	167
Guatemala City	6.4	−30	Guatemala 4.5	142
Sao Paulo	4.8	−18	Brazil 4.3	116
Miami	4.8	+14	US 1.9	252
Frankfurt	4.7	+105	Germany 1.0	470
Baku	4.5	+51	Azerbaijan 1.4	321
Salvador	4.4	−52	El Salvador 3.0	147
Bogota	4.4	−33	Columbia 4.5	98
San Jose	4.4	+36	US 1.9	232
Los Angeles	4.2	+4	US 1.9	221
Jerusalem	4.2	+55	Israel 1.8	233
New York	4.2	+4	US 1.9	221
Quito	3.8	−49	Ecuador 3.1	123

Data source: Euromonitor International, "Income Inequality Ranking of the World's Major Cities," 2016; World Bank, Global Monitoring Report 2014–2015.

Table 8.1 indicates that the nine most unequal major cities in the world are in the global south. Johannesburg, where the top 10 percent of earners earn a staggering 13.4 times more than the bottom 40 percent, is the most unequal on the planet, testifying to the dramatic juxtaposition of poor townships with exclusive elite neighborhoods, complete with their swimming pools and private security services.[2] It is noteworthy that these urban Palma ratios drop off fairly quickly: São Paulo, the world's ninth most unequal city, has a Palma ratio considerably less than half that of Johannesburg.

Table 8.1 shows that the Palma ratios of unequal cities can vary markedly from that of their host nation in surprising ways. Many of the iconic "unequal cities" turn out not to be so unequal in this light: for instance, Cape Town, Rio, São Paulo, and even Johannesburg are only slightly more unequal than their host nations. The most unequal city compared to its host nation turns out to be Frankfurt in Germany, with Nairobi (Kenya) and Lagos (Nigeria) close behind. Staggeringly, these cities report inequality levels four times as great as their surrounding nations.

There seems to be little global-regional patterning of which cities are excessively unequal compared to their nations. If we consider those cities that are twice as unequal as their nations, they would include cities from Africa (Nairobi and Lagos), the United States (Miami, San Jose, Los Angeles, and New York), Europe (Frankfurt), and the Middle East / Asia (Jerusalem, Baku).

Although cities tend to exhibit intensified levels of inequality compared to their host nations, this is not a universal trait. Even in Table 8.1 we can also find cases—such as Bogotá—whose high level of inequality mirrors that found in Columbia as a whole. Table 8.2, which reports the most equal cities in the world, also indicates this point clearly, though there is less variation at the bottom end, with no cities being a lot more equal than its host nation. But it is clear that we cannot conclude that cities are invariably more unequal than their surrounding nations.

These continental variations are revealing. The most unequal cities tend to be located in the Americas and in Africa. With a few exceptions, notably Frankfurt, there are no marked trends for European cities to be relatively equal or unequal—which perhaps reflects the fact that comparatively strong public service provision (Le Galès 2002) tends to flatten out inequalities between urban and rural areas.

In contrast, Figure 8.2 shows that large, growing Asian cities seem utterly distinctive in their subdued inequality, often in contrast to trends in their own countries, where inequality has risen substantially. Mumbai, Karachi, Wuhan, Guangzhou, Shenzben, Beijing, Tianjin, and Taipei all report among the lowest inequality levels of any cities in the world, sometimes reporting Palma ratios smaller than their host nations (India and China). Furthermore, intra-urban inequality appears to be falling.[3] The finding that Chinese cities are less unequal than rural areas and the nation as a whole is corroborated by

Table 8.2: Twenty least unequal cities in the world, 2016

	Palma ratio	Change 2005–2016 (%)	Country Palma	City Palma as percentage of country Palma
Mumbai	0.9	−7	India 1.4	64
Karachi	1.0	−66	Pakistan 1.2	83
Bratislava	1.0	−37	Slovakia 0.9	111
Wuhan	1.2	−35	China 2.1	57
Almaty	1.2	+6	Kazakhstan 1.1	109
Berlin	1.2	−4	Germany 1.0	120
Birmingham	1.3	−13	UK 1.6	81
Guangzhou	1.3	−67	China 2.1	62
Shenzhen	1.3	−67	China 2.1	62
Beijing	1.3	−53	China 2.1	62
Tianjin	1.3	−61	China 2.1	62
Leeds	1.4	+22	UK 1.6	88
Kiev	1.4	+3	Ukraine 0.9	155
Prague	1.4	−12	Czech Rep 0.9	155
Taipei	1.4	+11	China 2.1	67
Casablanca	1.5	−33	Morocco 2.0	75
Warsaw	1.5	−25	Poland 1.3	115
Riga	1.5	−20	Latvia 1.4	107
Tbilisi	1.5	−61	Georgia 2.1	71
Barcelona	1.5	+23	Spain 1.4	107

Data source: Euromonitor International, "Income Inequality Ranking of the World's Major Cities," 2016; World Bank, Global Monitoring Report 2014–2015.

other survey sources (Xie and Zhou 2014; Knight 2017).[4] The reason is that this relative equality in Chinese cities is due to a strong urban-rural divide, in which cities are much more prosperous than rural China (see Davis and Feng 2009). The very rapid growth of Chinese cities has attracted unusually large numbers of migrants, who are nonetheless constrained by having to live in specific urban areas, leading to an unusually strong divide between urban and rural populations, though there is some evidence that this might be declining since 2000.[5]

Therefore, the case of these relatively low inequality cities largely confirms the generalization that cities are engines of inequality: They either have unusually high levels of inequality in their own borders, especially in contexts of unconstrained high in-migration, or (as in the Chinese case) inequality is between generally richer cities compared to poorer surrounding rural areas. In many cases, both these processes might operate.

Cities therefore appear to be inequality hubs, though there is variability about whether this takes an intra-urban form, or through divisions between town and country. The plot thickens when we consider another important and revealing dimension of inequality: social mobility. Until the past few years, it has been very difficult to extract high-quality analyses on social mobility that allows the urban dimensions to be brought out compared to the more common national level of analysis. This is beginning to change with the use of "big data," which permits very granular and more detailed geographical analysis. This kind of research is currently restricted to a few nations, but the results are nonetheless revealing.

The most visible project examining the spatial contours of social mobility is by Raj Chetty and his associates in the United States, whose access to US tax data allows them to report mobility patterns at a highly disaggregated level.[6] Chetty et al. (2014) show considerable variation in the prospects of mobility according to where American children are brought up. In the 10 percent commuting zones with the best prospects, 52 percent of children moved up the income ladder. In the bottom 10 percent, only 37 percent do. This variation takes a regional form: "Upward mobility is lowest in the Southeast and highest in the Great Plains. The West Coast and Northeast also have high rates of upward mobility, though not as high as the Great Plains" (Chetty et al. 2014: 1593). But it is the urban dimensions that are important here. Those brought up in cities tend to enjoy less upward mobility than their rural counterparts (41.7 percent urban upward mobility from city children compared to 45.8 percent for those raised outside cities). However—and this is the crucial point—this difference does not stem from opportunities being worse in cities, indeed far from it, but because of the systematic migration of rural migrants to city areas: A staggering 44.6 percent of those brought up in rural areas had moved to cities as adults, and of those who were upwardly mobile, there were many who were likely to be urban migrants.

In short, those born in cities appear to do less well than incoming migrants from other parts of their nation (and from overseas). This can be seen as a "vortex" or "escalator" effect (see Hall and Savage 2015), which suggests that cities act as sites of mobility for those drawn into their orbit, but don't necessarily bestow these advantages to their own "locals," especially when these are from underprivileged positions. Indeed, this kind of effect has been found elsewhere, notably by Friedman and Laurison (2017: 495), who use an inflow analysis from the very-large-sample UK Labour Force Survey to show that whereas London is typically presented as the national "engine-room" of social mobility; in fact there are "distinctive patterns of elite closure in Inner London, with those from privileged backgrounds able to monopolize the Capital's highest earning jobs."

This process, testifying to accumulating urban polarization, is now a common finding.[7] In Germany, financial occupations in major urban centers have been shown to generate intensifying inequalities—which might help explain why Frankfurt and New York are among the world's most unequal cities.

Although detailed urban-level analyses of social mobility remain rare, these findings are consistent with a broader theme that has surfaced around the globe. Major global cities have become the preferred habitats for elite formation and reproduction. Whereas aristocracies were constituted as a landed class, contemporary elites depend on, mobilize in, and accumulate in cities where their presence is stamped indelibly in metropolitan centers. Thus, Maren Toft (2018) has demonstrated how the most affluent residents of Oslo are concentrated in its central western quarter and do not move extensively around the city in the way that less-affluent groups typically do. Toft insists that rather than poor groups being the most segregated, it is actually the elites who form the ghetto class:

> Although all types of residential trajectories are segregated, and increasingly so over time, trajectories in affluent environments are more isolated and particularly evident at high levels in adulthood. Individuals who are similar in their persistently affluent environments are thus in

close proximity to one another in the physical space, largely confined to the west-end of Oslo and its neighbouring municipality to the west, Bærum. (Toft 2018: 13)

Very similar points are made by Méndez-Layera and Gayo (2018) in their study of Chilean elites in Santiago. They draw attention to the way that certain zones of central Santiago have attracted a "systematic movement of the richest segments towards the barrio alto since the early 1990s. This has been followed by a more massive movement of the upper middle classes towards the same areas." Using a carefully constructed multiple correspondence analysis, they demonstrate how one specific area of Santiago is the apex of the entire Chilean class structure, acting both to perpetuate local privilege and also to draw in and interact with other elite sectors. Méndez-Layera and Gayo (2018: 50) note that the

> highest income groups at the top of Chilean society, are usually either established residents of Vitacura (two generations at least), or used to live in Providencia or elsewhere. . . . We see a consolidation not only in residential choice, but in intergenerational occupational terms. Parents and children are very often in higher professional or managerial positions. . . . In addition, their income comes from property rents as well as usually high salaries.

The situation in other parts of the globe seems similar. Burgeoning slum areas may allow migrants somewhat better prospects than in rural areas, but generally, there is little upward long-range social mobility in them. In South Africa,

> shack settlements appear therefore to offer a step up for former rural households, but conditions are clearly inferior to those in formal urban areas. It seems that a fair proportion of shack dwellers are able to access the opportunities available in urban labour markets. However, most are limited to lowerpaid, manual, casual and precarious jobs. The contrasting circumstances of shack dwellers and formal urban residents are likely to be among the reasons for community frustration and unrest. (Turok and Borel Saladin 2018)[8]

8.2: Cities as Sites of Accumulation

Cities often—but not necessarily—accentuate the economic inequalities of their national hinterlands. They do this not only because they are often the centers of highly paid employment but also because they are key sites for accumulation processes. Cities act as poles of accumulation within force fields that suck activity into them. They are not arenas in which all local residents benefit equally from the potential of agglomeration effects, or in which different kinds of residents actively compete against one other. It is those who already have advantages who are best placed to obtain the truly glittering prizes. Accumulation sediments historical advantage. Cities as "elite urban vortexes" (see Hall and Savage 2015) have become central to global geopolitics, as they increasingly challenge nation-states in their power and authority. Once again, we might see this as harking back to previous centuries, when such cities as Genoa, Venice, Constantinople, Baku, and Kabul dominated imperial trade routes, such as the Silk Road. Cities become central nodes in tying together the resurgence of imperial formations in the context of the weakening of nation spaces.

But history does not recur as a simple repetition of the past. Historical force operates as duration, modulating social change into new formations. There is no simple return to where we have been. And so it is that a very clear difference exists between cities as contemporary elite power bases, compared with pre-industrial (and even early industrial) times, when elites were a profoundly rural-based formation. The extraction of surpluses from systems of agrarian production operated through towns and cities as the sites from which trade was organized. Urban historians trace the rise of cities during medieval Europe to merchants and traders freeing themselves from the hold of rural noble elites by claiming forms of urban autonomy. The resulting struggles, which pitted urban against rural identities, were both complex and multifaceted. Agricultural elites sought their own urban power bases in these complexes, leading to aristocracies becoming a key force in many cities—in Europe, Asia, and Africa—into the twentieth century. Monarchical court and religious assemblages dominated capital cities, even though in many nations, monarchs moved these sites away from central urban locations in the early modern period (for instance, with royal courts moving out of Paris to Versailles; from central London to Hampton Court and Windsor; from Berlin to Potsdam; and so forth).

The terms of this encounter contrasted the city as "other" to a landed aristocracy based in rural locations, where the ownership of large agrarian estates was the fundament of accumulated capital. The urban social season, in which marriages were organized in a courtly swirl, thus took the aristocratic elite away from their rural seats into the circulation made possible within city locations, before the eventual return to country seats. In many nations, and notably in England and the United States, a profoundly antiurban current came to dominate during industrial expansion in the nineteenth and twentieth centuries, with successful industrialists purchasing estates in rural locations as a marker of their business success. The sustained appeal of garden city and utopian suburban movements articulated very directly the sentiment that, although the city may be a site for transacting business, social life, and cultural encounters, it was not itself the basis for accumulated and stored privilege, which continued to depend on a more rural and landed basis. This also explains why urban space became heralded for its radical and subversive potential from early modern times onward.

Today, however, the city has become a much more significant focus for the accumulation of capital—with investment in fixed urban infrastructure playing a vital role. This is David Harvey's (1975, 1982, 1985) theory of the "spatial fix," where capital is necessarily invested in a fixed built environment to resolve its tendencies for overaccumulation, leading to systemic boom and slump. Piketty (2013) offers a more recent elaboration of this theme. He shows that capital tied up in housing is an increasingly important part of capital assets as a whole. Since wealth is more concentrated than income, so urban areas become vital repositories of the accumulation of economic capital, as measured by their asset values (see Walks 2016). Piketty shows that in pre-industrial Britain in 1700, when national capital exceeded national income by a ratio of 7:1, agricultural land was the main source of this capital, with its share far exceeding housing and other domestic capital (such as in business). The share of national capital tied up in agricultural land declined precipitously: By the early twentieth century, it had become miniscule, and by 2010 almost nonexistent. By contrast, the share of capital tied up in privately owned (owner occupied) housing, which had remained steady from 1700 until about 1950, began to rise in recent decades. In 2010, the amount of capital tied up in housing exceeded the national income by a remarkable ratio of 3:1. No wonder that the mortgage market is such a key part of the economy and that it was travails in the American mortgage market that sparked off the 2008 financial crisis (Tooze 2018). Furthermore, capital tied up in housing generates investment in prime urban sites, where property values are highest. It is therefore central city locations—and not the countryside—that becomes the fundamental spatial locus for capital accumulation (a point that Harvey in particular has emphasized).

Piketty (2013) shows that this trend in housing has become a major part of capital accumulation in the United States, Canada, Germany, and France. Only in the United States is the capital tied up in housing less than half the total stock of capital in 2010, and even there, its proportionate share has risen considerably. It follows that seeing cities as centers of dynamic economic activity—important though this unquestionably is—should not detract attention from prime urban property sites as heartland for the accumulation of housing assets and other kinds of physical capital geared toward wealthy elites, who are attracted by top-end accumulation prospects found in prime location cities. The significance of owner-occupied housing assets in driving wealth accumulation is emphasized by Pfeffer and Waitkus (2019), who see housing as the key factor driving wealth inequality in the developed world. Lundberg and Waldenstrom (2018) draw attention to the fact that the global financial crisis of 2008 actually enhanced housing inequalities in Sweden.[9] Lisa Adkins and her colleagues (Adkins et al. 2019, 2020) see these urban assets as fundamental to contemporary class dynamics.

This growth of real estate value in metropolitan areas is evident across the world, generating what Wetzstein (2017) calls the "global affordability crisis," the "accelerating trend of housing-related household expenses rising faster than salary and wage increases in many urban centres around the world." In 2017, the most expensive cities in the world are listed in Table 8.3, using slightly different measures, but in general giving consistent listings. We once again see the significance of "top-end" outliers, with Monaco standing out in a class of its own, and the top four cities well ahead of the chasing pack. These cities do not strongly overlap with the world's most unequal in income terms (see Table 8.1). Thus Mumbai is one of the world's most equal cities, yet its property prices are in the global top ten. This anomaly reflects the fact that property ownership is a minority tenure in many nations and

Table 8.3: Most expensive cities in the world

City	Square meters of luxury property that can be brought with $1 million, 2017	City	Buying price (US$ per square meter)
Monaco	17	Monaco	60.114
Hong Kong	22	London	27,261
New York	25	Hong Kong	26,325
London	28	Paris	17,277
Singapore	39	New York	17,191
Geneva	41	Tel Aviv	17,149
Paris	46	Tokyo	16,322
Sydney	48	Moscow	16,021
Shanghai	54	Vienna	15,607
Los Angeles	58	Mumbai	15,525

Source: Knight Frank Research as reported in https://www.cnbc.com/2018/03/08/what-1-million-buys-in-real-estate-around-the-world.html; https://www.globalpropertyguide.com/most-expensive-cities.

can also be highly differentiated between the "prime" end and other parts of the housing market.

Many cities have seen their urban cores being redefined as top-end elite residential areas in recent decades, as older industrial and trading locations are moved out. Central urban markets have closed, and new elite business districts have opened, such as La Defense in Paris or the Docklands in London. The de-industrialization of central urban locations has been a long-term urban phenomenon, as has the counter-urbanization of populations toward rural and suburban locations. Such trends lead some writers to champion a distributed model of the city, which disputes the idea that central public space should remain at the heart of urban analysis (for example, Soja 1989; Amin 2007; Amin and Thrift 2002). But in fact, the accumulation of top-end property prices in central urban locations has led to a revival of urban cores, which have been subject to increased business as well as property investment (as in London, New York, and Mumbai). Indeed, one of the striking trends evident in London and other major cities is that central urban sites have reasserted themselves as central venues for elite residents and property owners, with the exodus of poor and middle-income populations to the urban peripheries (see Cunningham and Savage 2017 on the case of London).

This development is associated with the enhanced investment value of central urban sites, as well as with the redefinition of central urban locations as areas for an elite employment and consumer infrastructure, characterized by a select array of venues that cater for well-heeled residents, visitors, and tourists. These central urban spaces can only with difficulty be interpreted as the site of the ephemeral and unpredictable encounter, which urban modernism made familiar. The encounters are generally predictable and entirely choreographed around a limited range of consumerist motifs, usually concerned with top-end retail, tourist, or culinary "experiences." It is utterly predictable that the major design brands—Gucci, Prada, Yves Saint Laurent, and others—cluster in archetypal corporate style in such places. As Sharon Zukin (2010) has emphasized, urban "authenticity" is largely a manufactured phenomenon. Actually, the elite habitus is stamped onto central urban living, leading it to be predictable, ordered, lucrative—and also highly policed and surveilled. The much-lauded concept of the flaneur, designed to capture the promise, contingency, and desire of the fleeting urban experience, has little contemporary resonance these days other than as a marketing gimmick. The iconic urban street encounter has lost its unpredictability. Whereas Manet's *Bar at the Folies-Bergère* places women as sexualized objects for the male gaze within the commercial urban realm, Mears's (2015, 2020) and Glucksberg's (2016) studies shows how elite misogyny holds fort in private clubs and behind closed doors: It is not incidental that much of Harvey Weinstein's sexual abuse took place in his hotel rooms, or Jeffrey Epstein's in his private residence in fashionable New York.

8.3: A New Urban Cultural Capital

The forces of the past are reasserting themselves with respect to the cultural dimensions of urban life. Historically, cities have been the crucibles of cultural grandeur and display, of conspicuous consumption, from antiquity to early modern times. However, from the Industrial Revolution onward, this situation was modulated as national spaces emerged, which helped "flatten out" the nation by attempting generalized provision across national territories.

It is not incidental that as Franco Moretti (1999) has demonstrated, nineteenth-century novels frequently narrated their plots through movement of characters between metropolis and the provinces, perhaps most notably in the work of Charles Dickens. This process was driven by the consolidation of national cultural fields beginning in the later nineteenth century. This facilitated cultural capital becoming a more significant feature of the inheritance strategies of the privileged, as schooling and education became more significant for access to the most desirable forms of employment. In this context, the relationship between urban location and cultural capital remained distant, in accordance with the Kantian aesthetic, subjected to its own field-specific criteria of excellence. This thereby championed a vision of cultural excellence as keeping a certain distance from everyday necessity—so that it could define itself as universal and uncontaminated by pragmatic considerations. The medieval monastery was the quintessential exemplar of this cultural capital based in the Kantian aesthetic: set in secluded rural retreats so that there was no distraction from the pursuit of God. The rise of modern universities in many nations exemplified—with Oxford and Cambridge being paramount examples—this powerful vision of learning being dependent on withdrawal. In this framing, the urban experience was identified as polluting, plebeian, and disruptive, and increasingly so as cities increased in size and became home to a large urban proletariat. The kind of cultural capital that became enshrined in many national educational systems embraced the values of learning and cultivation, which hence shied away from the melee of everyday life that could increasingly be conflated with the urban experience. The result was to encourage a strong antiurban movement in many nations, which valued the rural retreat as a chance to contemplate abstract cultural good. Although strongly etched in the romantic reaction—as in the works of Wordsworth, Ruskin, and Hardy—this current was also strongly embedded in twentieth-century modernist art and culture. The composer Benjamin Britten's attachment to the small seaside town of Aldborough on the east coast of England was not an isolated instance.

Of course, it would be too simplistic to see the elaboration of cultural capital as inherently antiurban. In fact, one aesthetic modernist repertoire was to show an interest in the urban experience, as a means of extending the writ of cultural capital into new and "risky" territory, from which the artist would learn. Indeed, this concern was central to the modernist motif, which sought to distance itself from worldly economic privilege and hence found the plebeian world attractive as a potential site of artistic exploration. James Joyce's *Ulysses,* which narrates in the course of one day's movements across Dublin how the intellectual dilettante Stephen Dedalus ultimately seized the coarse, immigrant, and cuckolded mentorship of Leopold Bloom to be his midwife into maturity, exemplifies this theme. Nonetheless, cultural capital associated with modernism continued to have an ambivalent relationship with the unpredictable and dangerous world of the city. In some nations, such as Brazil, Turkey, India, and Australia, new capital cities were founded away from existing metropolitan centers. In Europe, it was more common for existing capitals to be uneasily adapted. This process involved the remaking of central urban spaces to render them more "ordered," and heavily investing in key cultural quarters—notably museums, art galleries, concert halls, and academies—in capital cities. The Parisian boulevards— driven by Georges-Eugène Haussmann through the popular quarters that had fed the revolutionaries of the Paris Commune—or Vienna's Ringstrasse were classic instances (Olsen 1988). Even though these spectacular examples were especially pronounced, capital cities routinely invested in cultural quarters that clearly demarcated them from the popular territories around them and hence continued to mark out cultural capital as consecrated and demarcated from their wider urban environs.

Nonetheless, if cultural capital was historically agonistic and ambivalent toward the city, recent trends, especially in the economically advanced cities of Europe and North America, have increasingly seen it flourish, in emerging forms, in central urban locations. This trend is part of the remaking of cultural hierarchies. Over recent decades, alongside the decomposition of fields, there is ample evidence that the classic highbrow aesthetic associated with the Kantian aesthetic is on the wane (see Bennett et al. 2009; Prieur and Savage 2013; Coulangeon and Duval 2014; Hanquinet et al. 2014; Savage et al. 2015). This does not mean that cultural hierarchy has become more pluralist or less unequal—educational attainment, and the ability to perform well in the highly competitive educational arena, are as important as ever—but rather that the stakes have changed. Cultural capital does not involve a fixed appreciation of the classic canon, but instead an ability to show sophistication by navigating between different genres and forms, to mobilize large stocks of information, and to display one's embodied competences of these multiple formats. The American ethnographer Shamus Khan (2011) identifies this ethos as being one of "ease," of knowing how quickly to "gut" sources of knowledge to be able to synthesize quickly. Irony, sophistication, and a distance from "old-fashioned" and "snobbish" culture are evident among younger, well-educated professionals.

As the Kantian aesthetic became less central, cultural capital takes on a more embodied and corporeal form. This shift has implications for the revaluing of "dirty" urban sites. Museum spaces move out of consecrated cultural quarters and take over old industrial infrastructures. The Musée d'Orsay, located in a disused station in Paris; the Tate Modern, built in an old power station in London; or the Guggenheim gallery, located in the center of the old docks in Bilbao, are all iconic examples of this reworking of urban space. Gentrification, originating in the global cities of New York and London, has now proliferated across the globe (Lees et al. 2015, 2016) in its re-consecration of poor urban life as a marker of cosmopolitan cultural capital. This involves a new mode of "cultured" urban living that is more fully at home within urban space. Zukin (2010) has identified this as the re-covery of interest in the urban "authentic," and Butler and Robson (2003) have emphasized how these new ethics of urban life are differentiated from what are seen to be more staid and respectable forms of middle-class culture found in high-class suburbs.

The older university model, linked to the monastic ideal, celebrated the scholastic retreat from everyday life, such as exemplified by Oxford, Cambridge, or the American "college town." However, this is increasingly put under pressure by the dominance of the metropolitan university. In some cases, as with Oxbridge in England, or Harvard and MIT in the United States, traditional universities can retain their elite position by virtue of their location in the hinterlands of large city regions (London and Boston, Massachusetts, respectively). Of the top ten world universities, as ranked by the influential QS, nine were part of major city regions, an hour or less away from central urban sites (MIT, Stanford, Harvard, Caltech, Oxford, ETH Zurich, Cambridge, Imperial College London, Chicago, and University College London).[10]

This therefore signals a return to central cities as consecrated sacred sites. As the autonomy of the cultural field breaks down (and therefore the privileged aesthetic no longer retreats from everyday life and immersion in a secluded environment) and as national space weakens, so cities reassert themselves as nodes of cultural exchange and conduits to global networks. This process is underscored by the significance of visceral inequalities—marked on the body—which I traced in Chapter 7. Previous historical experiences of marginalization and stigmatization generated a strong impulse for dissident groups to seek retreat in "safe spaces" away from the urban popular gaze. This endured until the 1960s counterculture, and the hippie quest for rural idyll. However, in recent decades, visceral inequalities have seen a wider re-engagement between countercultures and urban life. This is predominantly because the search for safe spaces (or more accurately, safer spaces) involves a search to live among people like yourself. In an age of enhanced communication, this typically involves shunning rural areas and small towns and self-sifting into specific urban districts, where you are more likely to "dwell amongst friends" (Fischer 1982).

In this context, urban space becomes powerfully trammeled by conflicting cultural values. Corporate and financial elites contest urban locations with stigmatized minorities, radicals, and social movements. As nation spaces fragment, urban spaces become the locus of political mobilization and contestation. The tendency of urban dwellers to articulate politically radical programs and social movements is attested to around the globe. Very few major cities are now establishment cities, even though elites depend on urban location. The result is that urban space becomes highly politically charged and is the site of sustained popular mobilization and protest.

Just as I argued in Chapter 7 that elite advantage takes an intersectional form, intensifying advantages of gender, race, and class, so there is an urban counterpart. Cities become the key arena in which different advantages reinforce one another in distinctive spatial environments. Regeneration work raises property prices and allows those with the cultural capital also to achieve economic rewards. This interplay between cultural and economic capital differs from earlier models, in which cultural distinction was more separated from economic wealth. The politics of urban location now make this differentiation much more blurred. A new bohemia (Lloyd 2004) reconfigures the relationships between economic and cultural capital, as the presence of artists and artistic dynamism in urban areas tends to give an added value for those who want to embody a specific urban cultural capital. Accumulated cultural capital increasingly depends on prime sites in urban locations: It is not possible to be hip and culturally elite in a remote rural location.

Conclusion

In the early twenty-first century, the ancient role of cities as elite centers of accumulation has resumed. Cities should not just be identified with sensory fleeting experience or sensation, important though this is to the urban experience. Cities are the site for those who have privileged stocks of capital, and more specifically, they are sites that allow convertibility between these different stocks. Cities have become the prized and defining sites for elite formation today. This is a fundamental facet of what has elsewhere been defined as the "urban vortex," as highly centralized, volatile, and discriminatory urban processes (Cunningham and Savage 2015; S. Hall and Savage 2015; Savage et al. 2015). Rather than elites being global transients (as argued by Castells [1996, 1997] or Bauman [2007]), they are increasingly bound up with location in privileged urban space. This link between cities and wealthy elites marks a return to older historical conditions, in which cities were the location of elite courts and arenas of display. It is not too farfetched to see parallel processes in contemporary cities, as they mark out central venues of grandeur, visibility, and manicured display.

This development is far reaching in its significance. In previous decades, economic capital was associated with agricultural holdings; cultural capital was distant from the city; and social capital might have been greater in small-town environments. But in the twenty-first century, there are good reasons for assuming that all three forms of capital, in their contemporary formats, now flourish in urban environments, so intensifying the association between cities and capital accumulation.

It is abundantly clear that the dramatic expansion of the super wealthy has fueled the growth of a quintessentially urban elite class, one that is defined by its presence and role in wealthy global cities. Here we see a fundamental shift from previous centuries, in which landed elites have been predominant. Urbanism today should not simply be understood as a process in which disparate and diverse populations mingle—it is also associated with the profound and far-reaching formation of an increasingly powerful elite whose footprint defines contemporary capitalism. Cities today are thus very ancient, in which old forces are most clearly manifested and come to have huge significance on the present and future. This will color the experiences and sensibilities of all kinds of urban residents and visitors.

9

The Force of Information and Technology

In this book, I have argued that we need to see growing inequality as part of a renewal of historical force, as a revisioning of imperial projects and the fracturing of nation spaces. Even sympathetic readers may be bewildered about the perversity of this line of argument. Surely, the dramatic technical advances of recent decades, notably in digital communication and information technology, point completely in another direction? We are surrounded by so much hype regarding technological innovation and the power of digital devices to remake society that it might seem entirely contrary to common sense to question this futurist vision. But this is precisely the aim of this chapter. Rather than the conventional modernist framing of technology as a driver of change, I instead stress how the purported "knowledge economy" actually intensifies the mobilization of past activity, through the hoovering up and manipulation of previously accumulated mountains of data. Thinking in these terms questions the dominant motif that technology is a driver that moves all before it. We instead end up with an argument that is the equivalent of Piketty's $r > g$ (as I discussed in Chapter 3): that the more information abounds, the greater the weight of historical force that can be mobilized through it. Knowledge and data do not blast us free of history; they more readily allow the past to be mobilized.

This view is counterintuitive, given the leitmotif that science and technology are profound drivers, the secular equivalent of divine will, most triumphantly captured by the economic historian David Landes's trumpet-blaring insistence that industrialization was the "unbound Promotheus":

It was the Industrial Revolution that initiated a cumulative, self-sustaining advance and technology whose repercussions would be felt in all areas of economic life. . . . Each innovation seems to have a life span of its own comprising periods of tentative youth, vigorous maturity and declining old age. . . . The climb has been spectacular. (Landes 1969: 3, 4)

Landes's words may be 50 years old, but his technological appeal remains compelling today. But this refrain is not to be taken at face value: It as an enduring legacy of the long-standing modernist sensibility that I have criticized in this book. Today, our current rendition of this long-held epochalist view fixates on how the rise of digital technology and robotification is pushing us willy-nilly into a new future, the shape of which we are only dimly aware. The imperative of innovation brooks no doubts. For Sebastian Pfotenhauer and Sheila Jasanoff (2017: 784):

Innovation has become a go-to answer, a panacea that carries the promise of curing socioeconomic ailments almost irrespective of what these ailments are or how they have arisen. Indeed, it has become virtually impossible to talk about economic development or social progress in terms that do not invoke, explicitly or implicitly, the need for innovation. Innovation is designated as the key to a better future, promising economic growth and competitiveness.

Such views are underpinned by the hyperbolic claim that we have moved to a knowledge, information, or postindustrial society marked by increasing reflexivity and the appliance of expert knowledge across swathes of economic, social, and political life. Given the highly visible infrastructure of extensive digital communication, big data, and the dramatic rise of "informational capitalism," this perspective can certainly seem utterly persuasive. And indeed, standing in the new spooky impersonal business zones of high-rise global cities, it might seem utterly perverse to resist the blandishment that we are not undergoing a profound techno-social transformation to some kind of new, glossy era unprecedented in human history.

Here it is vital to reassert my arguments about time and duration made in Chapter 3. We are not seeing a literal return of the past. This is not possible, given the way that duration is inexorable. Instead, the past returns as a force that carries increasing weight and is now eroding the nation spaces that were erected during the imperial breakdowns of the early and mid-twentieth centuries. These nation spaces had come to be seen as normal and permanent, but they now appear fragile. From this perspective, the power of information technology is a further historical force, a conduit that focuses the force of the past. Cathie O'Neil, one of the most perceptive critics of big-data hype, makes the pithy rebuke that "big data processes codify the past. They do not invent the future" (2016: 204). Marxists Michael Hardt and Antonio Negri (2019: 80) emphasize how data mining "provides a helpful lens for seeing how traditional extractive operations have migrated to social domains. Accumulation by means of social media-platforms . . . can involve not only gathering and processing data provided by users but creating algorithmic means to capitalise on the intelligence, knowledge and social relations they bring."

There are numerous examples of how digitalization allows the return of history, or to use Couldry and Mejias's (2019) valuable terms, evoke a new "data colonialism." Troy Duster (2003) emphasizes how new genetic technologies facilitate a "backdoor to eugenics" and the re-inscription of classic racial divides. The theme that big data is a mechanism for projecting future outcomes from the analysis of past traces is discussed by geographer Louise Amoore in her study of e-borders security systems:

> The specific modality of risk . . . acts not strictly to *prevent* the playing out of a particular course of events on the basis of past data tracked forward into possible futures but to *pre-empt* an unfolding and emergent event in relation to an array of possible projected futures. It seeks not to forestall the future via calculation but to incorporate the very knowability and profound uncertainty of the future into imminent decision. (Amoore 2013: 9)

The current hype regarding technological advance is therefore not to be taken as a literal account of contemporary social change. It is part of a long-term cultural repertoire that has its counterparts in the sense of speed up, intensification, and mobility, which has been endemic over the past two centuries. It is a contemporary renewal of the romantic disquiet about the dehumanizing effects of machinery, which has been a profound cultural force since the later eighteenth century. To this extent, the embrace of the technological imperative is a conservative cultural constant, and is associated with the shoring up of privilege.

An important undercurrent of this book is that social scientific expertise has itself been a driver of social change. I have traced this in numerous ways, especially emphasizing how the development of nation spaces depended on probabilistic modes of expertise that championed relational measures and concepts. My arguments—loosely affiliated to the "social life of methods" perspective (Savage 2010, 2013)—are indebted to legions of writers in science and technology studies who have pushed for an understanding of technology not as an exogenous force but as an intimate part of social relations themselves. Technology is complicit in the construction, mobilization, and deployment of power.[1] An important theme here is how technological forms are culturally embedded. Thus, David Nye (2013) has shown how the assembly line, which became an iconic device for twentieth-century Fordist mass production, was premised on American cultural norms and could only with difficulty be exported elsewhere.[2]

Yet I have argued in this book that we need to go further. The social construction of technology literature can still default to a modernist temporal ontology, with its embrace of contingency. In critiquing technological determinism, some advocates of science and technology studies have proposed the directly opposing argument that there is nothing at all inexorable about technological innovations, and that even familiar technologies could have taken very different forms.[3] However, there is also a historical force to technological developments that reassert the relationships between powerful institutions and the technological "bind" in ways that are fully complicit in the elaboration of inequality.

I elaborate this argument in three linked ways. First, I briefly reflect on the temporality of technology in order to pull out how its compelling form lies in its capacity to draw together pasts, presents, and futures. Second, in a more empirical vein, I reflect on the significance of "emerging cultural capital," and the way that this challenges the status of public and private knowledge. Third, I show how this relationship is closely associated with the shifting relationship between literary and visual cultures, in which the affordances of ordinary reading are giving way to a visual iconography that "black boxes" and hence sequesters expertise into powerful corporate hands. I also explore how the proliferation of visualization is associated with the revival of empire.

9.1: The Time of Technology

On the face of it, the technological embrace is fully complicit in the modernist vision, in which the contingency of the present shatters the hold of the past, so generating a new and unprecedented future. Indeed, technology is crucial to this modernist temporal ontology, since it has pride of place in shattering established social relationships, and it can remake the future—whether this takes the form of bold utopian visions regarding social progress or a dystopia of surveillance and control. This account was most famously associated with Karl Marx, who saw the rise of capitalism as intrinsically associated with the shift from hand-tools to fully mechanized processes.[4] It was by reversing these terms of reference that romanticism sees technology as encroaching on human experience, and thereby seeks to preserve traditional modes of community and sociality. The capacity of technological advance in transport and communication to erode the central role of face-to-face interactions as the fundament of social life thus became an enduring theme, from the work of Ferdinand Toennies through Georg Simmel (see Kumar 1978) and in more recent reflections regarding the decline of social capital and civic engagement (Putnam 2000).

However, the critique of technological determinism has become a unifying principle for scholars from science and technology studies. The most visible current, associated with Bruno Latour and "actor network theory" disputes the analytical distinction between technology and society. It insists that the social is always inextricably technological—and that the devices and apparatuses deployed in and across different social arenas are the very stuff of social relations. Latour thus adopts a spatializing sensitivity that is characteristic of relational thinking: The techno-social is understood as a web, a network, through which power traverses. This allows Latour to insist on the contingency by which specific technological devices are mobilized and contested. Latour's (1993) short polemical book, *We Have Never Been Modern,* uses actor network theory to offer a critical perspective on modernity, which stands on its head the humanism that the liberal project has traditionally invested in. Latour valuably argues that the "modern project" involves the holding apart of the technical and the social, so allowing technology to be treated as external to society, and thereby an exogenous force that can drive it. Ultimately, however, he falls back on modernist temporal ontology by insisting on the contingency of the relationship between technology and society. His famous quip that "technology is society made durable" vividly captures the way that he sees social relations as crystallized in and through technological forms, which harden and fix them, and thereby act to stabilize and solidify. But I have argued that the past does more than this: It is also an active force.

Here it is useful to draw out another theme from within science and technology studies, which argues that technology gains its cultural power not by making the social durable but by organizing duration, and in particular, projecting futures from the past. This argument has been made in several different registers. One well-established approach is framed under the "sociology of expectations," in which technology has the potential to mark future trajectories. A further perspective is the "sociotechnical imaginaries" perspective associated with Sheila Jasanoff, which sees "the growing recognition that the capacity to imagine futures is a crucial constitutive element in social and political life" (Pfotenhauer and Jasanoff 2017: 788).[5]

In pursuing this perspective on technology as the modulation of duration, it is necessary to distance ourselves from the centrality of the social study of finance toward one more oriented to engineering. The social study of finance has gained intense interest, because it speaks to the dramatic financialization of contemporary capitalism, which as the 2008 financial crash demonstrated all too powerfully, has major geopolitical significance. However, its focus on the rapid pace and short-term immediacy of financial trading also plays to familiar perspectives, emphasizing speed up and contingency, rather than being attentive to longer-term projects. Building on the foundational arguments of Michel Callon (1998) and Donald Mackenzie, scholars in this tradition have described the construction of financial markets based on financial algorithms, linked to the power of specific mathematical models, notably the Black-Scholes model, which became widely used on trading floors (Mackenzie 2005, 2008). Scholars traced the rapid, global transfers of financial products, notably through the hubs of the world's major

trading cities: London, New York, and Tokyo. This analysis of finance therefore lends itself to the kind of focus on instaneity and acceleration that I
have shown in Chapter 3 is a major—though flawed—trope to understand
contemporary change.

There is, however, an alternative sensitivity that is more attuned to engineering projects—in diverse fields ranging from infrastructure construction
through mechanical projects and transportation. Nichols and Savage (2017)
have examined the drawn-out temporalities of engineering in Formula One
racing, in which slow rhythms, elaborated over many years of design and
planning, are punctuated by bursts of intense action, and how these are only
possible in the context of long-term, accumulated processes of development.
Engineering can be seen to be a claim on the future that indicates the power
of the technical not to be an exogenous force for change but instead to be
bound up with the deployment, modulation, and organization of past forces.

Walter Benjamin (2002 [1931]: 104–105) famously reflected on the way that
modernity involved the stripping away of aura. He evocatively defines aura
as "a strange tissue of space and time: the unique apparition of a distance,
however near it may be. To follow with the eye—while resting on a summer
afternoon—a mountain range on the horizon or a branch that casts its
shadow on the beholder is to breathe the aura of those mountains, of that
branch." This uniqueness of aura is embedded in a specific tradition that ven-
erates it as a "cult." It is precisely this aura that Benjamin sees as eroded by
mass reproduction, of which digital reproduction is the ultimate endpoint.
However, if we see technology as bound up with the modulation of duration, it also has the power to constitute tradition and aura. This is amply evident around the cultic investment in devices, such as cars, phones, and
other digital gadgets whose appeal is far from resting on their instrumental
value alone, and extends to a more ritualistic steeping in cultic traditions of
engineering excellence, akin to the aura of relics and books held in medieval monasteries.

It is more persuasive, therefore, to see technology as a way of modulating
duration through reestablishing aura. David Nye (1996) has brought out in
the American context the power of the "technological sublime." He traces
the way that technology conveys the kind of wonder and awe that has historically been associated with "auratic" artifacts, tracing through the embrace of railroads, bridges, skyscrapers, factories, electricity, and on to the

atomic bomb and the Apollo Space missions. In these contexts, engineering interventions permit singular, unique spectacles. Nye sees this "technological sublime" as democratizing aura away from an elite experience: "in keeping with democratic American tradition, the American sublime was for all—women as well as men . . . whereas Kant had reasoned that the awe inspired by a sublime object made men aware of their moral worth, the American sublime transformed the individual's experience of immensity and awe into a belief in national greatness" (Nye 1996; 43).

This technological sublime welds the relationship between present and future together. It does this through imparting a potential future to a technological prototype that has a historic pedigree, can be mobilized in the present, and embeds future capacity. These prototypes can be more or less formed: They can exist as actual devices or simply imagined as blueprints. But in any case, they operate as "claims on the future." Demarcating a specific technological form is inextricably tied up with the claim that the future will follow the path that the device—and its surrounding infrastructure—permits. And it is precisely by this move that any technological form claims legitimacy.

Technological interventions thus permit the infusion of aura into everyday life. Objects ranging from cars, through mobile phones, cameras, and platforms, convey the design aura of their corporate makers, while also appealing to the democratic vista that Nye articulates. Thus, just as Marilyn Strathern (2000a) excavates the way that Hagen culture oscillates between insider activities and outward-facing performances visible to outsiders, so prized devices become bound up with this culture of insider secrecy, public launch, and consumer take up. Engineering is an inherently temporalizing practice involving the planning of futures through the mobilization of expertise, raw materials, and infrastructure into a powerful assemblage.

Twenty-first-century engineering therefore does not design revolutionary machines; instead it is bound up with the spectacular remaking of aura. The new is exciting and compelling because of the lineage linking it to the past. From this vantage point, examples of the way that the knowledge economy binds together past, present, and futures abound.

Consider the global power and significance of universities as central drivers of the knowledge economy. Despite their boosterism, universities with the highest prestige and standing actually tend to be old, venerable in-

Table 9.1: World's top twenty universities

Rank	Name	Date founded	Nation	Endowment
1	Massachusetts Institute of Technology	1861	US	$14.8 bill
2	Stanford	1891	US	$22.4 bill
3	Harvard	1636	US	$34.5 bill
4	California Institute of Technology	1891	US	$2.1 bill
5	Cambridge	1209	UK	£6.3 bill
6	Oxford	1096	UK	£5.07 bill
7	University College London		UK	£101 mill
8	Imperial College London	1907 (1823)	UK	£126.2 mill
9	Chicago	1890	US	$7.82b
10	ETH Zurich—Swiss Federal Institute of Technology	1855	Switzerland	?
11	Nanying Technological University, Singapore	1991 (oldest constituent 1950	Singapore	$2.3b
12	Ecole Polytechnique Federale de Lausanne	1853	Switzerland	?
13	Princeton	1746	US	$23.8b
14	Cornell	1865	US	$6.8b
15	National University of Singapore	1905	Singapore	$3.12b
16	Yale	1701	US	$27.2 bill
17	Johns Hopkins	1876	US	$3.4 bill
18	Columbia	1754	US	$10 bill
19	University of Pennsylvania	1740	US	$12.2 bill
20	Australian National University	1946	Australia	A$1.13 bill

As ranked by QS (Quacquarelli Symonds) World University Rankings in 2018.

stitutions. Table 9.1 shows that seventeen of the world's twenty top universities were founded before the twentieth century, and indeed, seven of them before the nineteenth century. Only two of them—Nanying Technological University and the Australian National University—were founded after the end of the Second World War. The digital age, which has seen the dramatic rise of new corporations that did not exist thirty years ago, has modulated rather than displaced the lure of the old Oxbridge quadrangles inspired by monastic ideals and venerable halls of learning, which still remain the heart-lands of global academic excellence.

The striking power of old universities is evident in their economic as much as their intellectual clout (see Table 9.1). Those institutions with the three largest endowments, Harvard, Yale, and Princeton, are all among the world's top twenty. Apart from Australian National University, the only universities in the top twenty that do not have large endowments exceeding $1 billion are based in entrepot trading nations with unusually strong financial cen-ters and off-shore wealth: in London (University College London and Impe-rial College London), Singapore (Nanying and National University of Sin-gapore), and Switzerland (ETH Zurich and Ecole Polytechnique Federale de Lausanne). The dynamics of global wealth accumulation straddle eco-nomic and cultural domains.

Knowledge and information are not epoch-shifting new forces that are somehow transforming the world around them. Instead, they direct and sharpen forces from the past, driving the accumulated expertise of numerous generations into the future. They are crucibles in which historically consti-tuted raw materials are melded together as part of the accumulation pro-cess. Through this mechanism, knowledge and information intensify in-equality rather than reduce it. This is an exact parallel to Piketty's emphasis on the historical force of capital accumulation.

One of the themes of my book has been to emphasize that the social sci-ences are themselves complicit in the social processes that generate in-equality. They initially elaborated imperial expertise and during the twentieth century and then became drivers of national projects. In both these times, they have been complicit in constructing categorical states—notably around class, gender, and race. The social sciences do not stand outside the world that they investigate. Nonetheless, the vision of knowledge as something that burrows down, reveals truths, underlying mechanisms, and exposes wrongs has become an overarching mantra. In these terms, education is not simply an instrumental good but is a powerful value in and of itself, with the power to transform lives. Formed in this enlightenment mold, we can feel the at-traction of "transparency" and "exposure," which critical and effective knowl-edge facilitates, and which can strip away unfairness and inequity and allow us to engender fairer societies.

From this perspective, the social sciences are fully implicated in what Charles Taylor (2004) identifies as the "modern social imaginary," the view that knowledge becomes public, transparent, and hence "ordinary" in modernity. It thus becomes identified with the democratization of knowledge, so permitting it to be a progressive force that allows agents to act knowingly and rationally, hence driving improvements forward. This underpinning conception is evident, for instance, in economic theories of markets, where price acts as a public signaling mechanism, as well as in numerous variants of sociological theory that see the possibility of dialogical communication as central to "the promise of modernity."[6] Thus, Jürgen Habermas's Marxist analysis of the emergence of the public sphere during the eighteenth century saw it as bringing with it the potential for dialogical communication. Liberal philosopher Charles Taylor (2004) further drew out this vision, where the "modern social imaginary" involves the democratization of experience as facilitating the concern with the "ordinary" and "authentic." He also shows how this experience is implicated in modernist conceptions of time. The eradication of the universal time of god means that "the new horizontal world in secular time allows for two opposite ways of imagining society. On one side, we become capable of imagining new free, horizontal modes of collective agency. . . . On the other we become capable of objectifying society as a system of norm-independent projects" (Taylor 2004: 164).

This modern social imaginary thereby appeals to knowledge as "transparent," and so permitting instrumental benefit and progress. It undergirds much critical thinking that sees transparency as a means of challenging inequality. For instance, the powerful campaigning group Transparency International thus emphasizes how low-corruption nations are thereby more likely to be equal. "Corruption and social inequality are indeed closely related and provide a source for popular discontent"[7] (see also Rothstein 2011 and Uslaner 2008, 2010). Recently, the open data movement, with its concern to make information legible and visible to anyone, is a contemporary manifestation of the ongoing power of this current.

This belief in the virtues of transparency is, however, naïve. This deep-rooted Western concern to "render relations" has been exposed by the anthropologist Marilyn Strathern, who sees this preoccupation as entailing a belief in visibility that fails to address: "what does visibility conceal?"

Strathern points to the way that in Papua New Guinea, visibility is bound up with demonstrating trustworthiness through putting on a show. She shows how visibility thus dances with temporal rhythms, of different processes in which inside and outside communication takes place. "Hageners engineer what they make visible and invisible, an alternation of social states that may also have oscillatory consequences. In the Hagen case not everything need be brought to the surface, but everything that is brought to the surface is then deliberately hidden inside again" (Strathern 2000b: 318). This is precisely the oscillation that can be detected through the role of deeply secretive and private social media companies, such as Facebook or Twitter, who nonetheless claim to be facilitating the sharing of information and hence to be agents of social advance.

The transparency motif is therefore a chimera, if not a smokescreen. The drive to make transparent depends on an enhanced infrastructure that generates its own forms of secrecy, closure, and exclusion. More specifically, it remakes cultural hierarchies through the capacity to harness, mobilize, and analyze information—the selfsame forces that crystallize intense inequalities. The erosion of older modes of "highbrow" cultural capital, dependent on the Kantian aesthetic and enshrined in notions of "Bildung"' (the German ethos of "self-cultivation") and the humanities, has edged toward more technical forms that are based on the capacity to process large amounts of information rapidly and with ease, and which can facilitate communication across specific domains of expertise and jurisdiction. This kind of emerging cultural capital breaks from a modernist temporal ontology toward a historically saturated one associated with the marketization and commodification of swathes of social activities. Emerging cultural capital is both novel, through its association with digital technical skills, and yet also reinscribes modes of elitism and advantage.

9.2: History in the Remaking of Cultural Capital

The idea that knowledge is bound up with the potential for enlightenment is most famously associated with Immanuel Kant. It has been an enduring theme in the prizing of education and critical reflection, which have been central to modernist sensibilities over the past two centuries. In his famous work, *Distinction*, which I discussed in Chapter 2, Bourdieu ([1979] 1984) took direct issue with Kant's belief in the disinterestedness and critical capacity of knowledge by insisting that in reality, cultural capital is a force allowing the reproduction of elites who were able to deploy their cultural resources to reproduce themselves.

Bourdieu made this analytical step by arguing that cultural capital involves the universalizing of cultural value through the institutional power of the "scholastic point of view." Knowledge was thus abstracted from specific local arenas—by being detached from ordinary daily life and being sequestered in ascetic seats of learning, such as universities, art galleries, and scientific laboratories—where it was attached to a historical canon that provided a platform for intellectual and critical advance. Bourdieu thereby took aim at the very heart of the principles of Enlightenment-based intellectual distinction by drawing attention to their narrowness rather than to the universalizing tropes they themselves deployed. Therefore, rather than seeing experts, academics and scientists acting as selfish cliques who contradicted their own universalizing principles, which therefore needed to be challenged by a more radical, comprehensive and authentic application of them, Bourdieu saw the problem as lying in the universalization of cultural excellence itself. Elite scientists performed distinction and thereby embedded inequality better not when they were acting as an "old boys club" (which they sometimes, indeed quite frequently, also do) but actually when they were true to their own self-proclaimed values of universality, transparency, and objectivity.

The implication is that rather than renewing the Enlightenment project itself, or just to permit subaltern figures who had been excluded from it to finally get their place in it, the very architecture of this thinking needs to be called into question. In taking up this cudgel, Bourdieu's own focus was on how cultural capital was embedded in the humanities, literature, art, and music, rather than scientific or technical modes of expertise. In Chapters 2 and 4 I noted that the account Bourdieu developed based on these classic forms of cultural capital has been increasingly called into question. There has also been a profound, reflexive critique from within leaders of cultural institutions themselves, which have been determined to "open up" and democratize cultural participation. When European researchers in the early twenty-first century explored patterns of leisure activity and engagement, they did not find a strong endorsement of highbrow or universalizing art and culture even among the highly educated middle classes. Indeed, there is considerable critical reaction to the elitism of the "old masters" and the classical canon. A dominant theme (for example, Bennett et al. 2009; Prieur and Savage 2011; 2013; Hanquinet et al. 2014; Friedman et al. 2015) was the gap between older age groups who were more attracted to canonical activities (such as veneration of classical music; highbrow theater; and the orthodox visual arts, including portraits and landscape painting), and younger well-educated groups, who appreciated more commercial and contemporary forms of culture (such as popular music, sport, information technology). These younger individuals were less drawn to the "hallowed halls of culture" as institutionalized in galleries and museums.

This new modality has been identified as "emerging cultural capital" (Prieur and Savage 2013; Savage et al. 2015; Friedman et al. 2015), which is more oriented toward technical expertise and knowhow, in which scientific and technical expertise plays a more important role than expertise in the humanities. This sensibility is at home with dabbling in social classifications and is keen to contest fixed definitions and identities. It is fully steeped in the politics of categorization and is suspicious (if not entirely hostile) to the classic categorical boundary drawing around divisions such as race, gender, and class.

The aesthetics of "ease" and assemblage has been detected in numerous works in cultural sociology—and seems especially marked among the highly educated elites. Shamus Khan (2011) argues that elite private schooling in the United States is not concerned with imbuing a Kantian aesthetic of learning and Bildung, but instead centers on juggling, getting by, game playing, and being strategic. For Khan, learning how to master these practices is central to the construction of cultures of ease that mark contemporary elite formation. This superficial deployment of ease depends on extensive performative work and the accumulation of historical reference points. This is exactly the kind of management of inside and outside performance that Marilyn Strathern emphasizes.

Rather than specific knowledge and skills seen to have universal resonance, it is this capacity to move effortlessly between cultural worlds that constitutes privilege today. This marks a rupture with the modernist model of cultural advance, which celebrated brilliance in one specific expert field. The forces of accumulation have valorized mediation between fields, rather than excellence in any one of them. Whereas older modes of distinction—notably through the model of the Kantian aesthetic—celebrate withdrawal, distance, and discernment, emerging cultural capital is more physical, externalized, and active, designed to practically achieve outcomes. It is an aesthetic of engagement, display, and activity rather than one of absorption and introspection. It has a strong association with physical activities, such as playing sport, going to the gym, using social media, and socializing with friends. As mentioned in Chapter 8, it is more oriented toward engagement and intensity in urban milieu rather than the ascetic rural retreat, and is thereby very much at home in city space (see generally Savage et al. 2018).

These observations complicate the very common argument in cultural sociology that privileged people are increasingly "omnivorous" in their orientation.[8] For some commentators, the trend for well-educated professionals to enjoy middle and lowbrow, as well as highbrow, culture is a sign of the democratization of culture itself. But more nuanced analyses have shown that in fact, the supposed pluralism of the well-educated has very clear limits, with some kinds of stigmatized activities still being very much off limits. As Alan Warde (2011) has shown, it is the capacity of the well-educated to demonstrate their cultural capital through the extensive display of the volume of cultural cues, which is important. In Prieur and Savage's (2011, 2013) review of numerous European studies, they show that it is precisely this "knowingness," and the ability to show when one is making links and associations, that is characteristic of cultural capital today.

Initially, the growing pertinence of emerging cultural capital might appear to mark the erosion of historical reference points and the further advance of a modernist sensibility of the "new, hip, and buzzy." A stuffy backward-looking older generation appears to give way to a new generation of dynamic professionals, testifying to the erosion of the power of history rather than to its renewal. But it is not quite as simple as this. The modernist temporal ontology that undergirded the development of national cultural fields depended on a cultural bifurcation between "old" and "new," so underscoring the separation between the canon and the avant garde. It was precisely this kind of opposition that Bourdieu imbibed as central to the generation of field dynamics and that drove the power of cultural modernism, as I brought out in Chapter 3. However, the concomitant erosion of fields that is tied up with the accumulation of capital also means that this tension between the forces of progress (the avant-garde), and reactionary conservatives (defenders of the canon) has now faded. In numerous artistic fields, postmodernist currents have flattened cultural hierarchies, thus stripping out "deep" cultural meaning behind endless pastiche and parody. Rather than this entailing the loss of historical reference points, it leads to the "massing" of all kinds of prior knowledge, which can then be extracted and assembled in bits and strategically deployed. History becomes a giant warehouse prone to being scanned and reassembled. This is the reason that apparently ignored, covered-up, and historical reference points become so pertinent. Rather than the canon being recognized as fixed, with avant-garde interventions therefore breaking from it, the canon itself becomes politicized and contested and available for remobilization in the present and future. We can see the politics of the restitution of plundered art works, the attack on slaveowner statues, and demands to remove sexist and racist works from public display as precisely revealing how the past is energized when the boundaries that differentiate a passive past and active present break down.

9.3: Cultural Capital, Visualization, and the Aesthetic Stakes of the Technological Sublime

Emerging cultural capital changes the relationship between visual and literary modes of communication. Text bound together the modernist aesthetic, yet it is the visual that has now become hegemonic. Within imperial modernity, it was attachment to a common linguistic medium—English, French, Spanish, German, and so on—that bound empires together as providing the tools of long-distance governance and administration. The power of these linguistic communities could, then, be seized by nationalist forces, and hence mobilized against imperial powers themselves. Benedict Anderson (1983) has highlighted how writing communicated the "imagined community" that was central to the power of nationalism. Narrative forms based on specific linguistic communities communicate national solidarities across "empty, homogeneous times." The form of the novel, in particular, contingently linked together strangers with no face-to-face links into an imagined sense of nationhood.

Emerging print culture disrupted the previous hold of visual representations and architectures to convey narratives, such as in the Western European traditions of biblically inspired paintings, which predominated until the seventeenth century. As reading became more widespread with the expansion of literacy, the popular appeal of visual icons receded. The idea that literacy was only expected of an elite intellectual class gave way to the belief that the capacity to read and write was necessary to be a modern national citizen tout court. Through this mechanism, literary fields became defined as national fields in which all had to participate, even though unevenly and with different stakes. This involved the expansion of "ordinary reading" whereby reading practices shifted away from expert storytellers toward an assumption of the need for an educated and literate population, in which the capacity to read and write became a fundamental feature of democratic citizenship. Accordingly, nation-building projects have always been vested in the development of mass literacy.

By contrast, visual culture was both transformed, and receded, in significance. As Alpers (1983) relates, visual motifs, memorably in seventeenth-century Dutch art, changed to a descriptive register that was a response to the growing hold of narrative in literary motifs. Moretti (2007) reflects on how this descriptive art—notably in Vermeer's painting—also tried to represent "ordinary actions" and was symptomatic of a wider invocation of narration that the novel took up from the eighteenth century. "Narration: but of the everyday. This is the secret of fillers. Narration, because these episodes always contain a certain dose of uncertainty" (Moretti 2007: 368). In this respect, textual narrative becomes part of the modernist temporal ontology that I unraveled in Chapter 3—whereas these narratives were difficult to convey using visual art—especially when biblical reference points, whereby viewers could be expected to understand by virtue of their Christian teaching, faded.

Throughout this period, visual registers were thereby on the defensive. They sought to compete with the narrative power of dominant forms of text, through emphasizing their sensuousness (as with impressionism), or their ability to extend their reach onto the everyday (as with early photography), before by the later nineteenth century embracing the kinds of field-specific qualities in the form of "painterly brilliance" itself that Bourdieu saw as central to Manet's revolution. From this moment, artistic excellence centered on the internal logics of artistic field—notably with the forces of abstraction and expressionism. Even so, as Christopher Neve (1990) brings out, some artistic currents, notably landscape art, remained concerned to bring out the immutability of time.

It was subordination of the visual to the textual field and the dominance of writing and literature that became crucial to the crystallization of twentieth-century nation spaces. Whereas reading became an ordinary practice, the appreciation of visual art—any kind of art—became socially exclusive, and hence driven by art enthusiasts as a badge of their cultural capital. It is therefore not surprising that "the denigration of the visual," as cultural critic Martin Jay (1993) called it, gathered pace during the twentieth century. However, this has changed dramatically in recent decades—driven in large part by the rise of film, television, and digital media. Their ascendance heralds the decline of national literary-based cultures. Probably the most tangible shift is the decline of national newspaper readership. In all nations during the twentieth century, a small number of titles came to exemplify the national public sphere. These characteristically differentiated titles were designed to appeal to varying political, social, and cultural milieux and constituted an effective newspaper system, which exerted strong influence on public decision making. In numerous nations, the state was directly involved in forms of public broadcasting.

Especially since the growth of the digital media, newspaper readership has plummeted across most nations. Research on the theory of "de-reading" (Griswold 2011) has suggested that increasing numbers of people are not reading significant amounts of text. Admittedly, wide-scale reading has never been a common phenomenon, leaving aside the special case of newspapers. Southerton et al. (2012) indicate sharply divergent trends. Some nations with subdued inequality, such as Norway and France, saw the amount of time spent reading actually grow between the 1970s and 1990s. In the highly unequal United States, there was a very marked decline in the amount of time spent reading, and the number of minutes each 16- to 61-year-old adult read per day—eight minutes—was by far the lowest among the nations studied. Strikingly, readership rates were substantially higher in smaller and more cohesive nations, such as the Netherlands and Norway.

Around the world, including in the global south, the smartphone has become the new way of accessing information (see Slater 2014). The phone detaches its users from specific locations and permits a highly flexible means of communication. Crucial to its success, as in the platforms it mobilizes, is the hybrid incorporation of brief text in a wider visual array, whereby design becomes central to slick communication. The deployment of icons, whether these be apps, memes, or messages, defines the medium of contemporary communication. Photographic images can readily lend themselves to this format. Such visual arrays can travel across cultural and linguistic divides and can mobilize immediacy in defining matters of concern. When a video recording of the killing of George Floyd in Minnesota in 2020 went viral, it had a catalytic effect, mobilizing the Black Lives Matter movements around the globe in a way unimaginable from a newspaper report alone. Visualizations now occupy a central role across professional, scientific, and medical fields, where scanning has come to have enormous force. This increasing capacity of visualizations to drive controversy is endemic in contemporary culture. Debates about pornography, sexuality, the representation of race, and more broadly the visual signifiers of performative categories are part and parcel of this current. It is precisely for these reasons that the use of visual motifs by inequality researchers has enabled social scientists themselves to turn this current to their own advantage, as I have brought out in this book. The visual repertoires used by social and political movements, whether these are the colorful displays of banners by the Occupy Wall Street movement and Greenpeace, or through terror attacks, such as those on the World Trade Center in New York in 2001, have become utterly central to their effectiveness.

The plethora of data rendered through these intensified forms of digital communication need to have narratives to possess power. Complex and aesthetically elaborate visuals drawn from big data arrays may look superficially attractive but fail to convey the kind of punchline that inequality researchers have used to such good effect.

In this politics of narrative visualization, three devices play a central role. The first of these devices is a simple ranking procedure, in which objects of interest are arrayed in an ordinal hierarchy according to some dimension chosen by the analyst. As I showed in Chapter 4, rankings are increasingly eclipsing broader group categorizations across numerous dimensions of social and political life—though there continue to be arenas in which the latter persist. A case in point is the classification of university degrees, where a UK model (which divides graduates into class categories) is losing ground globally to an American ranking model (based on a grade-point average). The generation of league tables of all kinds depends on a ranking process in which even minor differences between cases—including those that fall within the margin for error—are translated to places on a ranked list. This involves a telling shift of focus: Rather than examining whether a specific school (for instance) meets a certain category (in which the category, such as "grammar school," can thereby appear to have some kind of ontological status of sorts), attention is instead directed to how that specific school compares to other schools in the ranking hierarchy. Measurement is therefore much more granular, but it is also moralized and narrativized by placing objects in a clear pecking order in which one end (top or bottom, depending on what is being measured) is "better" than the other. It is hardly possible to rank anything that does not convey this kind of moral narrative. We have seen how debates on inequality are profoundly affected by this move, in which a higher Gini coefficient or a greater income share for the 1 percent are seen in and of itself to constitute a powerful narrative. The deployment of these ranking narratives depoliticizes fields of debate through arraying league tables in which those ranking poorly are told to catch up with those ahead of them.

The second and related device is the widespread use of maps, which have proliferated through the universalization of GPS devices. Interactive mapping has become utterly mundane due to its deployment on phones and in motor vehicles. There is also increasing skill in preparing narrative maps. Heat maps, in which analytical issues of interest are superimposed onto one another, offer a routine example, permitting observations on a great range of diverse places to be threaded together into a narrative of some kind. As the work of radical geographers, such as Danny Dorling and colleagues (2006), demonstrates, mapping of inequality variables has come to occupy a very powerful position in this repertoire. Showing how inequalities are spatialized—whether between nations, cities, or at some other scale—becomes tantamount to demonstrating that inequality matters. However, this mundane use of mapping can also undermine the potential for critical narratives, as it can flip into a spatial determinism.

It is for these reasons that I have highlighted the third and final device, the use of what the eminent social scientist of visualization, Edward Tufte, elaborates as sparklines. These are simple visualizations that avoid graphic flourishes and compress relevant information into one line, which performs the work of narrative. The curved line represents a trend or narrative about information from at least two dimensions, one of which is often a time axis. Tufte sees the popularization of sparklines as a key feature of contemporary graphical representation. Indicators, such as stock prices, inflation, and unemployment are routinely presented in these forms. One of the arguments of my book is that the most powerful repertoires have shown how the story of inequality itself can be rendered through the use of sparklines to devastating effect (see Halford and Savage 2017).[9]

These three devices have now become central devices for communicating narratives, in ways that disrupt the older dominance of text as the overarching mechanism stitching narratives together. And in the process, they have challenged the temporal ontology of plot-like contingency on which modernist framings rely. Visualizations act not as representations but instead capture a narrative in a highly stylized form that permits large-scale data gathering and processing to be harvested to a preferred storyline. Whereas literary texts are profoundly individualistic in their production (through the writing of a lone author) and often through their readership, visualizations are collectively produced, generated, and consumed: They thus return to a culture of cultic production and communication. They depend on rendering historical data relics—many of which can stretch back many years. They are profoundly historical constructions.

In these terms, the "knowledge society" marks the renewal of older, medieval kinds of communication. These are produced by skilled corporate insider communities for a wider nonexpert public that picks up on the narrative embedded in simple visualizations, using a set of widely understood techniques and refrains. The power of these visualizations, allied to the global dominance of English as the technical and scientific language, marks the erosion of older national literary cultures, which were the crucial mode of communication during the period when national fields predominated.

At the end of the Introduction, I noted that in this book I would "walk the inequality line." And so, with these reflections on the pervasive forces of visualization, we have come to the end of our long journey. We can now revisit Piketty and Saez's sparkline of income distribution trends (Figure 1.1), as well as any of the other visuals that I have used in this book, with a surer understanding of why these visuals have been so successful at revealing why inequality matters.

Conclusion

Knowledge and information have long been held out to be the driving force of change, shifting from the hidebound world of tradition and habit toward the possibility of reflexivity, strategy, and progress. It is in this spirit that prophets of the "information society" or the "knowledge economy" have emphasized how the expansion of knowledge permits a new kind of postindustrial capitalist society that breaks from the traditional frameworks of liberal capitalism (see the broader discussion in Webster 2014). In this chapter, however, I have argued that the information society, such as it is, challenges the separation of past, present, and future and thereby reasserts the force of history. My argument here is a riposte to Scott Lash's (2002) view that the "information age" marks the end of critique. He mobilizes a familiar argument regarding the flattening of knowledge so that all kinds of data become "equivalent." This is tantamount to the erosion of a distinction between canonical knowledge (which is identified as part of a tradition) and cutting-edge knowledge (which is seen as state of the art and reflects the potential of the present to break from the past).

By contrast, I have argued that information allows the embedding of history through the modulation of duration. Any and all kinds of data can be meshed into assemblages, allowing them to be built up in huge accumulations, so that extensive historical precedents can be used to make inferences. These accumulations of information and knowledge rendered in visual forms (which array them into narratives) can then be deployed by strategically powerful agents to gain relative advantages over those without the resources to access and analyze such information.

The overarching mantra of transparency, which lies at the heart of contemporary cultural dynamics, is therefore a chimera. The opening up of data has gone hand in hand with the accentuation of inequality for the reasons I have laid out. Transparency is itself a conceit: As sociologist Harold Garfinkel (1967) pointed out many years ago, once information becomes subject to outside scrutiny, it changes its form, and some things are left implicit or unsaid. Transparent information that can be rendered as data can most effectively be harvested and mobilized by powerful corporate agents with the resources to analyze, interpret, and deploy its messages. Hence, insofar as information is made portable and transparent, it becomes a resource for powerful agents to deploy. It becomes part of the process of accumulation itself.

PART THREE

The Politics of Inequality in the Twenty-First Century

Reinstating the Time of Politics

In the decade since the challenge of inequality surged to the fore, there has been a renewed drive to recharge the policy toolkit. The last major book written by the guru of the economics of inequality, Anthony Atkinson (2015), elaborated fifteen areas of policy intervention, some—such as setting up a national pay policy—harking back to social democratic principles, others—such as providing a universal endowment for all youngsters when they turn eighteen—opening up new vistas. There has been a revived interest in increasing progressive taxation, not only for those with high incomes, but also on wealth and corporate profits (notably Saez and Zucman 2019; also Piketty 2013, 2020). Campaigns for universal basic income in which everyone is paid a certain guaranteed sum, so providing a basic safety net and allowing people more control and autonomy in deciding how they want to balance work and other uses of their time (Standing 2017) have gained traction around the globe.

This renewal of policy to redress inequality offers real hope. However, it also begs a major question. What is the capacity of policy to make a difference in a world of escalating inequality and weighted by the forces of history? More specifically, what potential is there in the arena of democratic electoral politics (which since the Second World War has been held out as the principal domain for deliberation and enactment of policy prescriptions) to be responsive to the inequality agenda? Most if not all of Atkinson's (2015) fifteen (impressive) proposals to tackle inequality in the British context default to assumptions about policy making through democratic deliberation and enactment.

It is of course entirely desirable to promote public policies designed to redress inequality, but this chapter reflects on the very capacity of national democratic politics itself. For, we don't need a very long historical scan to recognize the sheer oddity of nation-states, and more particularly those with a fully democratic political apparatus. Only a little more than a century ago, in 1914, European empires controlled 60 percent of the land mass around the globe, and their influence showed no signs of shrinking. Early nationalism was a by-product of the imperial order. Partha Chatterjee (2012) has illuminatingly reflected on how the early forbears of nationalism in North and South America in the late eighteenth and nineteenth centuries were not markers of a bold new principle of governance. Instead, they emerged out of an imperial context in which white settlers insisted on the equivalent constitutional rights that they would have enjoyed in their imperial European homelands.[1] It was, in fact, only following the traumatic shock generated by the First World War, provoking in its wake chronic economic and political instability that formed the ground on which fascism came to the fore, that these imperial behemoths fought one another to a standstill. Principles of autonomous nationalism only became fully institutionalized in the wreckage of the post–Second World War period. Only in the mid-twentieth century did decolonization extend principles of nationalism away from white settler regimes (mostly in the Americas and Australasia) and into the world's most populous areas of Africa and Asia. Even so, communist regimes kept national self-determination at bay in Asia until the very last decades of the twentieth century. It was only with the collapse of Soviet Russia in the later 1980s that principles of national autonomy were enacted in Eastern Europe and Central Asia.

The universalization of the nation-state came very late in the day. Only from the 1980s did the nation become the utterly expected modus vivendi for the modern polity. Even then, China continued to articulate its own alternative vision of the national project, one that embraced an authoritarian state-led path to development (see generally, Milanovic 2019). The historically unprecedented state of affairs at the end of the twentieth century cannot be overstated. Monarchical rule, which until the end of the nineteenth century had dominated throughout human history, had been eclipsed around the globe. Imperial models, which as late as the mid-twentieth century could be held up by feted historian Arnold Toynbee as the universal principle of governance, seemed to have collapsed as decolonization swept across the global south. Religious influences had waned: The extra-territorial jurisdiction of the globe's dominant religion, Christianity, had been almost eliminated, with secular national government trumping its authority nearly entirely. Judaism, which in the build-up to the Holocaust had been increasingly pilloried as the religion that had no national "home," gained statehood in 1948 with the creation of Israel, so affirming the conception that all powerful religions needed some kind of national base. It is therefore utterly understandable why Francis Fukuyama (1992) saw the collapse of the communist model and this embrace of nationhood, mostly organized on liberal democratic principles, as marking the "end of history." The long historical record of endemic feuding and contestation between elites, clans, corporations, and religious blocs seemed to have finally been eroded by a world of rationally organized, institutionalized politics, within clear national boundaries, organized around largely accepted rules of the game, both within and between nations.

There is, however, an alternative to the teleology in which all historical roads ultimately lead to the nation-state. Extensive postcolonial scholarship emphasizing the ongoing significance of empire insists that the legacy of empire continued to loom over the present. From this vantage point, it is, in fact, the fragility and short timespan of nation spaces that is striking. Far from being fundamental to modernity, they came to the party late and are now failing. The revival of political Islam in the aftermath of George W. Bush's "war on terror" and the associated "clash of civilizations" rhetoric has been one visible way in which imperial currents have reasserted themselves. But this is only one instance. If we look at the nation-state from an imperial perspective, we are also struck by how resilient imperial formations have been—even when they have adorned themselves in national trappings. The United Kingdom, most notably, has never mapped onto a national identity, being composed of at least four nations within its borders. Britishness came to the fore as a fundamentally imperial identity (Colley 2005), and its failure to host an effective nation-state has played out over centuries. The persistence and revival of Irish, Scottish, Welsh, and English nationalism has become so powerful that it forced Britain's exit from the European Union, despite that the UK state apparatus wished to remain a member (see Nairn 1977; Bhambra 2017). The world's dominant power during the twentieth century, the United States, also embraced imperial characteristics (see in general M. Mann 2012), and it is possible to see structural adjustment and global economic policy from the 1980s as also embedding an imperial economic mission (Hickel 2017).

If we extend this more historical approach, the nation-state can be better seen as a contingent response to the imperial meltdown in the total wars of the early twentieth century. Rather than marking a stable and enduring mode of government, perhaps it only represents a short-lived phase before the resumption of "imperial business as usual." This accords with my argument that the weight of history has returned with a vengeance—not as some kind of residual imprint but with force. This argument may seem initially outlandish. Much of our intellectual infrastructure is premised the primacy of the nation, which has indeed seeped into the framing and methodologies of everyday social science (in the scholastic equivalent of what Billig (1995) famously identified as "banal nationalism"). It is not incidental that the extensive literature on the rise of nationalism does not question the inevitability of the rise of the nation to global dominance, but only focuses on the when and the how, where those emphasizing the ancient primordial roots of national identity battle against those seeing it as driven by the rise of print culture and education during eighteenth- and nineteenth-century modernity.[2]

We need to disentangle this association between nationalism and modernity. As Chatterjee (2012) has emphasized, the seventeenth-century Westphalian principles that established territories as bound in geographical space were part of an imperial—not national—moment. As he puts it, "the cartographic representation of national boundaries that is now the foundation of the geographic knowledge of schoolchildren everywhere in the world was universally established by the global spread of modern empires" (Chatterjee 2012: 89).[3] In a similar vein, many of the currents that were articulated by early sociologists as principles of modernity emerged before the nation-state moved center stage.[4] Osterhammel's ringing words that the "nineteenth century was an age of empires, and it culminated in a world war in which empires fought each other" (Osterhammel 2014: 466) forces this point home. Indeed, even further into the mid-twentieth century, Hitler, Churchill, Stalin, and Hirohito, and even Roosevelt, were fighting an imperial war.[5]

The argument I pursue in this chapter is that the late rise and recent erosion of the nation-state formation is directly bound up with the changing dynamics of inequality sketched out in earlier chapters. The clash of insider, establishment forces against outsider groups that underpinned classic categorical divides also generated passions that crystallized into national fields of organized contestation. During a certain formative period, these energies could be harnessed into the making of institutionalized national-state forms. These might appear to be stable and enduring. However, as inequalities have in recent decades become entrenched, and as manageable relative inequalities have transmuted into more visceral forms, so these energizing forces have dissipated. As capital accumulation builds, nation-states reach their breaking points. As this national political infrastructure fractures, so the hold of instrumental, rational action perspectives—which came to the fore when there were clear "rules of the game" and which underpin national policy initiatives—has also weakened. Groups who feel they have no voice become increasingly strident in disrupting the "rules of the game" and so the political field itself is further weakened.

In this chapter, I begin by tracing how the emergence of nation spaces arose from formative passions. This is often neglected because analyses of national polities became spatialized and insufficiently attentive to the temporal trajectories of nationhood. Second, I trace how the national political field—the "nation space—that had become taken for granted in the last two decades of the twentieth century is now under major structural pressure and is breaking down. The procedures that became institutionalized since the Second World War to stabilize the political arena around accepted rules of the game are buckling under the weight of history. Markers of this lie all around: popular disengagement, wealthy business elites marauding into political life and tearing up the rule book as they do so, the rise of populism, growing political volatility, and the sense that intermediaries are no longer able to operate effectively to manage the political process. As the stability of the political field breaks down, a visceral politics of anger, frustration, and resentment becomes increasingly prominent from those who feel excluded from the political process. In the final part of this chapter, I lay out the full gravity and significance of this moment.

10.1: Restating the Time of National Politics

If we put to one side our commonsense belief that nation-states are the necessary and inevitable form of modern governance, how can we explain their rise during the twentieth century? The crises associated with imperial state breakdown during the two world wars were certainly crucial sites. It is these kinds of wartime contingencies that have been emphasized by Scheidel (2018) and Piketty (2013, 2020) in challenging of inequality in the early twentieth century. However, this only takes us so far. It does not account for the vitality and passion of nationalism, the roots of which had previously been germinating in imperial modernity. The global dominance of late-twentieth-century liberal democratic nation-states did not come about just by political tinkering in the aftermath of imperial state breakdown, they were also fiercely desired as the "imagined communities" by vast numbers of people, as Benedict Anderson's (1983) iconic text put it.

Desmond King and Patrick Le Galès (2017) draw on Italian sociologist Giafranco Poggi's reflections about the "unifying energies" behind state building. Focusing on the American and Europe experience, they emphasize that

> state and nation making were long-term processes articulated in and forged through war, trade, industrialization, colonization, revolutions including cultural processes, conflict-solving mechanisms, bureaucratic rationalization and national standardization. A dynamic project, the nation-state comprised the making of a political community within defined frontiers, the delineation of enemies, the assimilation of migrants, and the regulation of capitalism. (King and Le Galès 2017: S13)

Reflecting on the emergence of political "logjams" associated with contemporary governance, of which Brexit in the United Kingdom is a particularly prominent example, they argue that the flames associated with these unifying energies have been flickering and are now going out.[6] The energies that burned so powerfully and led millions, indeed billions, to invest their emotional feelings in the national project are not historically inevitable. Instead, these passions were dependent on the "unifying energies" associated with the institutionalization of the social cleavages between insider and outsider groups that I introduced in Chapter 6. However, these are now giving way.

The historical aspect of my argument is neither contentious nor original. It has a familiar pedigree in political science from the Norwegian, Stein

Rokkan. Strongly influenced by the modernization theory of sociologist Talcott Parsons, he saw the differentiation of social relations, abstracted from local face-to-face communities, as driving the development of modern political cleavages that underpinned the nation-state. Rokkan was fascinated by the way that competitive party alignments became utterly central to the operation of modern liberal democratic nations. They did this through articulating and institutionalizing insider-outsider tensions that originated in imperial states, forming enduring cleavages that generated identities and stakes, around which national identity itself could form. Rokkan thus emphasized how nation-building elites pitted against subjected populations and also against traditional forces, such as the church. State building intersected with the economic cleavages caused by industrialization, thereby setting rural and landed interests against commercial ones, as well as a property-owning bourgeois classes against tenants and workers.

Rokkan was particularly interested in the role of social class in institutionalizing party cleavages (see famously Lipset and Rokkan 1967). He saw this class divide establishing the primacy of the differentiation between the political left and right, which was to become an utterly routine part of the political landscape around the globe. O. Heath (2016: 2–3) summarized this opposition as the "working class tend to prefer redistributive policies, and so they vote for parties on the left, whereas the middle class try to resist these claims and so vote for parties on the right." Although Rokkan carefully recognized the variability of political cleavages between nations, in practice, his approach underpinned the consensus among political scientists that class trumped everything else. In the words of Oskarson (2005: 87), class was "the most universal cleavage that could be found in most industrial democracies."

Rokkan's style of scholarship was abstract and formal, and it is easy to neglect that passion, struggle, and energy drive the motor of his account. However, this is redressed by the influential arguments of one of the world's most foremost Marxist historians, Edward Thompson. He was scornful of the abstract categories used by social scientists, but his classic work, *The Making of the English Working Class,* can easily be read as a case study of Rokkan's analytical argument. Thompson insisted that class came to matter in British politics by being emotionally charged, and that this passion informed not only political debate but also the very meaning of Englishness itself. Thompson took aim at the established myth of progressivist British history, which traced a democratic lineage back to the signing of the Magna Carta in 1215, when the monarchy first accepted constraints on its rule. Thompson insisted that that the slow and tortured expansion of democratic rights in England during the nineteenth and into the twentieth century was not the product of benevolence handed down from on high, but was only achieved because the working classes actively fought for a place at the democratic table, in which they "nourished, for fifty years, and with incomparable fortitude, the liberty tree" (Thompson 1963: 832). The aristocratic and moneyed elites who profited from monarchical rule did not willingly extend the franchise to subaltern groups: This right had to be wrested from them. These are exactly the kind of intense cleavages that Rokkan saw as lying behind the origin of party politics in liberal democracies across the world.

Thompson's arguments attracted global interest, because the British case was iconic in the canon of modernity: the world's most powerful empire in the nineteenth century, also the first site of industrial capitalism, and all the while brandishing its self-proclaimed beacon of "liberty." His insistence on the conflict that lay in the underbelly of British history spawned a massive, often critical literature. Some of this took issue with his emphasis on early nineteenth-century radicalism as a working-class movement. This was variously interpreted as misconstruing radicalism that was actually driven by traditional artisans rather than factory workers (for example, Calhoun 1982), and by failing to recognize that radicals had no elaborated conception of class (Stedman Jones 1984). However, these objections only underscore Rokkan's point: Social divisions become salient as part of the wider institutionalization of political oppositions themselves, where cleavages solidify across political, economic, and social domains. Thompson very clearly articulated how national identities are hammered out from these very conflicts: His own work was a passionate defense of a popular nonconformist Englishness, which he associated with democratic socialists and plebeian artists, such as William Morris and William Blake.

The architecture of Thompson's thinking spawned a critical literature pointing to the sexist and racist biases of his work. This could take a feminist form (as in Sheila Rowbotham's (1973) *Hidden from History*, which was to inspire much subsequent feminist scholarship) and an antiracist and antiimperial form from within the "subaltern studies" tradition (for example,

Chakrabarty 2000, 2008; Chatterjee 2012). All these families of critiques could be harnessed to a wider awareness of how national projects got their emotional force from a multiple politics of outsider mobilization, in which those originally outside governing elites demanded their place at the table. This style of thinking also enjoyed widespread resonance in comparative analysis. Barrington Moore's *Social Origins of Dictatorship and Democracy* (1966), written just a few years after Thompson's classic work, demonstrated the adaptability of this perspective. Like Thompson, Moore argued against the view that there was a natural evolutionary trajectory leading to the liberal nation-state, in which economic growth could be expected to extend democracy through some kind of political equivalent of the "trickle-down" effect. Following in Thompson's footsteps, he argued that those nations that during the twentieth century had become beacons of democracy—Britain, France, the United States—also had their own history of exploitation and violence. There was no comfortable escalator peacefully leading from pre-industrial society to mature democracy. He drew a contrast with political trajectories leading to communism (Russia and China); fascism (Germany and Japan), and liberal democracy (Britain, France, and the United States) not in terms of differing degrees of violence but the different modalities it took. In the "bourgeois revolutions" of France, Britain, and the United States, feudal aristocracies were eroded by commercializing pressures, which thereby made these elites more aware of how they could remake themselves as commercial capitalist forces. They thus embraced a project of capitalist modernization. Where aristocracies sought to shore up their feudal powers, as in Germany, the potential for reactionary politics was enhanced as they defended their traditional privileges, leading to opposition from capitalist interests and to fascism. Where peasants were strong and independent, as in China and Russia, their resistance to autocracy facilitated their mobilization behind revolutionary insurgency, ultimately leading to communist regimes during the twentieth century. Moore therefore insisted on the brutality and internal struggle lying at the heart of any kind of nation building. As his later work was to show, Moore invested strongly in a humanistic vision concerned to expose injustice in all its forms, thus once again insisting on the emotional drivers of stage formation.

Rokkan, Thompson, and Moore wrote their influential books more than fifty years ago. Taken together, they illuminate how nation building emerged out of contentious and intense struggles between unequal social groups. In the aftermath of major wars, these passions could be turned into projects of nation-state building and reconstruction, in which warring parties could also find common cause to build a national footing from the shell of collapsed imperial regimes.

But from the perspective of the early twenty-first century, the major limitations of their work have also become more apparent. The problems cluster around their weak conception of temporality and duration. They tend to reify and fossilize national political formations, seeing them as enduring and persistent. Rokkan was very clear about this. He was emphatic that those cleavages which became institutionalized during the state-formation process tended to endure: they became "frozen" at the time when democratic systems became established, and would then stay in place, even though they might be modified and adapted. Rokkan thus showed his indebtedness to a modernization theory assuming that all (noncommunist) roads led to postwar liberal democracies. Once put in place, these could be expected to endure for all time. Moore saw took the historical trajectories of his chosen nations during the inter-war years (liberal democracy vs. fascism vs. communism) as his object of comparison. Although this is a telling comparative analysis, from the early twenty-first century it offers little handle on contemporary dynamics since the politics of these nations had changed substantially. Germany and (to a lesser extent) Japan are now mature liberal democracies—indeed more so than Britain or the United States, which Moore took to exemplify this path. The communist route has also fractured between the Russian and Chinese paths.[7]

For Thompson, this lack of sensitivity to duration takes a different form again. Oddly, given his enthusiasm on blowing the trumpet of historical analysis and objecting to the abstractions of social science, his thinking tends toward a universalization of a radical tradition, which can be found across time and indeed reanimated in the future. Thus, his rather tenuous account of the artist William Blake as part of a radical tradition going back to the Levellers in the English Civil War (Thompson 1989) feeding all the way up to his advocacy for late Victorian socialist William Morris (Thompson 1956) and his own leadership of the Campaign for Nuclear Disarmament in the 1980s.

The problem in all this work—important though it is—is assuming that a certain kind of temporal trajectory is normal and expected, and that deviations from it need to be understood as failed or deviant projects, which then require some kind of remedial or corrective action. The implication is that the normal cases are held up as not needing the kind of equivalent explanation as the "deviant" ones. The French case—with its revolutionary tradition and its republican heritage—exerted particular resonance to those on the political left. Thompson's most vociferous Marxist critic, Perry Anderson (1964), saw him as ultimately too indebted to his plebian English patriotism, and instead lambasted the British failure to follow the revolutionary French model, and to fully modernize.[8] Anderson thus argued that there needed to be a further rallying of subaltern forces to finally push through on the delayed and thwarted British modernization. This emphasis remained redolent in British politics, versions of it being evident both in Margaret Thatcher's Conservative administration in the 1980s and Tony Blair's rallying of "New Labour" during the 1990s. Anderson's perspective, allied to the thrall for French theory that animated his editorship of the *New Left Review*, might be seen as an academic version of Casanova's (2008) diagnosis of the global hold of the French language. Ultimately, he too relied on an implicit modernist temporal ontology. The assumption that Britain was wedded to tradition, and therefore requires "speeding up" through some kind of remedial modernization, spoke to 1960s countercultural currents but failed to recognize the active agency of history. The modern does not operate akin to a newborn baby—sometimes needing a smack on its back to bring it properly into life. Currents in postcolonial scholarship have also held up the French experience as the norm from which the global south experience, India in particular, differs (for example, Chibber 2014). However, as Piketty (2020) has recently underscored, this holding up of the French experience as being the progressive norm to which other nations should aspire hardly stands up to scrutiny in the context of its brutal imperial record and its commitment to defending private property rights.

The lack of a theory of duration goes together with an undue weight attached to national boundaries. This comes out especially clearly in Moore's account, which compares nations as if they were independent of one another, thus treating them as separate units of observation, each to be dissected separately. However, as subsequent literature in comparative and historical sociology emphasized, this obscured that borders are porous and that relationships between and across nations were central to the revolutionary processes that concerned Moore. Theda Skocpol (1979) famously took up this insight in her comparative study of revolutions in Russia, America, and France. Although she began her studies working in Moore's footprints, she ended up arguing that revolutions depended on the international dynamics leading to the breakdown of powerful states, and hence the possibility of revolution. She thereby queried the possibility of seeing national processes as existing autonomously from one another.[9] This perspective has been massively amplified in recent decades through the emergence of "global history" and "connected sociology" (for example, Bayly 2004; Bhambra 2007; Osterhammel 2014).

The obsessional concentration on national comparison over historical sensitivity is evident in the work of Rokkan's followers, and notably in the way it spawned the field of comparative politics. Stephan Bartolini's (2000) discussion of the changing nature of class cleavage and the political left in Europe exemplifies the limits of this comparative strategy. Strongly influenced by Rokkan, Bartolini's ostensible aim was to understand the trajectory and future prospects of the political left in European nations. However, he was deflected from this historical question, because he recognized that the left was no longer on the ascendant in Europe. Indeed, his take was ruminative. "The passing away of working-class politics, and of class politics as such, leaves open the question of how many of its aims have actually been achieved" (Bartolini 2007: 1).

As his book proceeded, this concern with the possible future of left politics transmutes into a comparative strategy comparing the different fortunes of the left across European nations. Here, he was struck by the similarity of "party landscapes" and the extent to which variations in the popularity of left parties were longstanding. Taking his analysis up to 1985, Bartolini noted the general stability of the left vote in Europe, as during "the entire post–World War II period the European left does not evidence any clear secular trend" (Bartolini 2007; 90). Devoid of an obvious historical story, he thereby switched his attention to an alternative question: Why did the left vote vary so much across Europe?

Bartolini's analysis of these variations is systematic and convincing in its own terms, but it reveals how easy it is for burning questions about the "time" of politics to become displaced onto spatial coordinates. Since the

1980s, this vein of comparative analysis has become hegemonic in social science, as time increasingly becomes something that is "controlled for" in the search for what are seen as more telling spatial variations. Gøsta Esping-Andersen's (1990) influential *Three Worlds of Welfare Capitalism* launched an entire research program in this vein, mapping welfare regimes onto different types of national formations. He helped consolidate the emerging trend for the small and exceptional Scandinavian nations to command undue analytical interest because of their highly effective and relatively egalitarian social-democratic public welfare systems. I have already reflected in Chapter 4 on the implicit Eurocentrism of this kind of work. The sheer idiosyncrasy of this strategy of fixating on small number of national comparison should be underscored, even though there are important exceptions (for example, Abbott 2001; Pierson 2004).

As the lauding of the Scandinavian model indicates, national comparisons have come to normalize and moralize differing national forms. This is rarely deliberate or intended, but it becomes inevitable.

10.2: The Political Field and the Rules of the Game

National political fields are not preordained as the necessary product of modernity, rationality, or economic complexity. They cannot be taken as the given parameters of political life. Rather than the emergence of nation-states marking a new stage of history from which we will never return, they are products of a particular historical conjuncture that came to a head in the early and mid-twentieth century. They are now unstable and creaking badly at the seams.

Analytically, it is useful to conceive nation spaces along the lines of Bourdieu's field dynamics. As I showed in Chapter 2, projects of organized striving between participants mold fields of contestation into place. Political fields thereby emerge by drawing on the energies between insider and outsider groups, and institutionalizing these passions into more organized and regularized forms, in which certain "rules of the game" could be more clearly identified and established. During the later twentieth century, across numerous regimes, democratic mechanisms became central to these games, through the choreography of electoral cycles, the formation and dissolution

of governments, and the institutionalization of the executive functions themselves. However, just as I emphasized in Chapter 3 how field dynamic are
not eternal but subject to decomposition from within as the victors pull away,
so it follows that national political fields are prone to stress and break down.
I make this argument in five steps.

10.2.1: *The Push to the Center and the Formalization of the Political Field*

I have followed Rokkan, Thompson, and Moore in seeing the genesis of national fields arising from intense contestation of cleavages between insider
and outsider groups that then become institutionalized. However, over time,
these cleavages are subjected to a systematic push to the center, in which
the middle ground of the political field becomes the magnet. This perspective was very clearly articulated early on by Anthony Downs, in his influential paper "An Economic Theory of Political Action in a Democracy" (1957).
He emphasized how political parties were akin to private companies, competing for market share from a choice-oriented electorate. Downs pursued
this thinking through highlighting the "median voter," the winning over of
whom was vital to electoral success. The model is akin to that which economists have used to understand how competitive firms will seek to maximize
their markets. Atkinson's (2015: 117) anecdote nicely illuminates this point:

> As the American economist Harold Hotelling showed in the 1920s, there
> is no reason to suppose that market forces produce the right location
> of sellers. Imagine that there are two ice cream vendors on a beach
> (each selling the same ice cream). If there is a uniform density of po-
> tential buyers along the beach, then profit-maximising sellers would lo-
> cate next to each other in the middle of the beach. Both in effect offer
> the same product. But to minimise the total distance walked by buyers,
> we want them to spread out. It would be better if each seller located a
> quarter of the way along the beach, but that outcome would not be
> sustainable as a market solution, since each would gain customers,
> given the position of the other seller, by moving towards the centre.

Hotelling's vignette underpins the behavior of rational political parties,
seeking to maximize their vote share and chances of being elected. Rather

than needing to appeal to their core loyalist voters, who could be expected to side with them anyway, parties should pitch toward the "sensitive" voter, sometimes identified as the "floating" voter, whose votes were strategically more important to win elections. This implication is that over time, the traditional cleavages identified by Rokkan, or the passion invoked by Thompson, winds down, as politics becomes recast as an exercise in strategic marketing pitched to the center ground.

The quest to win over the median voter became a leitmotif of those who sought to define the rules of political engagement as the franchise became universalized (Hotelling 1929; Downs 1957; Page and Shapiro 1983; Erikson et al. 2002). This generated extended research on the political alignments of "floating" voters, who were not seen as constrained by traditional cleavages and whose ability to act as rational consumers testified to the vitality of the political field itself. Thus, as Corwin Smidt (2017: 365) relates: "Scholars emphasize that floating voters provide valuable elements of flexibility and pragmatism within the electorate" (see also Berelson et al. 1954; Zaller 2004). This economic perspective underscored the formalization of rules of the game and the firming up of national boundaries as the container in which politics would be contested. It was only within these bounded territories, akin to a playing field or Hotelling's beach, that the rules of the political game could operate. Organized party politics could then become the central conduit of political mobilization in an era of mass democracy (Harmel and Svåsand 1993, 1997).

This institutional turn encouraged research on how comparative differences in the organization of electoral systems and state organizations could themselves impact the political process. First-past-the-post electoral systems, such as found in the United States or the United Kingdom, did not exhibit so much of the pull to the center that was evident when proportional representation permitted parties with relatively small vote shares to win a proportionate share of seats. In Britain, it remained possible for political parties to win enough seats to form governments with considerably less than half the vote, hence creating less incentive to appeal to the middle ground. In 2005 the Labour Party, under Tony Blair's tired and discredited leadership, won a third term of government with a comfortable majority while only winning 35 percent of the vote. Along these lines, Iverson and Soskice (2006, 2019) showed that regimes with majoritarian electoral systems tend less toward a redistributionist politics than those with proportional representation, where parties in the center are more likely to form coalitions with parties on the left. This kind of institutional analysis became the bread and butter of a political science oriented toward the operation of political institutions themselves, so distancing the study of politics from the hurly burly of social life itself.

The formalization of the rules of the game also involved an expanded role for the media. Opinion polling began in the 1930s, permitting increasingly sophisticated ways of eliciting "public opinion" (Osborne and Rose 1999; Savage 2010), though initially there was skepticism about its accuracy and effectiveness. After the Second World War, even though polling became more established, it remained common for political leaders to "take the temperature" by using their own networks down to the 1960s. Only from the 1970s did pollsters come to operate with such clout. This was part of a wider constellation of political intermediaries—lobbyists, think tanks, brokers—whose role was both to sell political interventions to various stakeholders as well as to win over uncertain players.

During the later decades of the twentieth century, the power of political game-playing rose to its apogee. A notorious—though highly effective—example was Tony Blair's rebranding of the British Labour Party as "New Labour" in the mid-1990s, which helped propel it to an electoral landslide in 1997. Blair absorbed and implemented all the key lessons of economistic perspectives. He listened to voter opinion using not only standard surveys but also bespoke focus groups, carefully worked with media stakeholders to win their support, sought to define a new political brand through a carefully marketed relaunch, and surrounded himself with professional advisors. This was a very skillful and effective repositioning of political party to win over the median voter, akin to a business seeking new customers in a competitive environment.

Yet this formalization of the political field contains the seeds of its own demise. It engenders the increasing monopolization of political office by professional career politicians and growing credentialism of office holding. The proportion of elected representatives who were university graduates rose dramatically in the decades after 1945. In the American House of Representatives, the proportion of members with postgraduate as well as undergraduate degrees rose (from an already high base) to 72 percent of the

House members in 2019.[10] In the United Kingdom, the proportion of members of Parliament from manual working-class backgrounds has declined substantially: O. Heath (2016) estimates that it has fallen from about one-third of Labour members of Parliament in the 1960s to around 10 percent by the 2000s. As the rules of electoral politics become formalized, mobilization that lies orthogonal to these insider concerns and lies outside these rules of the game led to the hiving off of social movements that played by different rules and lobbied from the outside. Thus, the growing power of feminism, environmentalism, and other forms of direct action was held at arm's length from the dynamics of electoral politics itself.

In sum, this push to the center, which was part and parcel of the formalization of political fields, allowed institutional forces to shape political agendas, but in this process, they sapped the passions bound up with the founding energies of nation spaces. The process enhanced the significance of field-specific "political capital," encouraging new breeds of political insiders, thus distancing themselves from the vast majority of the electorate, who felt they had less direct stakes in politics themselves. The intellectual shift of political science toward embracing institutional state-centered perspectives was itself part of this trend toward the accumulation of political capital. From this base the political field itself began to unravel, as those without political capital felt increasingly disenchanted about their lack of voice in the system, which they came to find alienating. This is precisely the tendency to entropy and breakdown, endemic in field relations, which I traced in Chapter 3.

10.2.2: The Decline of the "Left"

It is not incidental that the rise of the organized socialist and communist parties was fundamental to the rise of national political fields. Rokkan, Thompson, and Moore, in their different styles, all fixated on the prospects and potential of the political left. Underpinning this was the belief that the organized left was on the historic rise, with conservative forces on the defensive. It is difficult now to remember how pervasive the view was that ultimately the left would triumph: One of my early political memories is my father (a Liberal supporter) proclaiming pompously to my mother following the US defeat in Vietnam in 1973: "Everywhere, the world is moving left." (My mother was a Labour supporter and did not appear unduly distressed by this prospect.) But in the early twenty-first century, a very different climate prevails.

This sense that "The Forward March of Labour" was being halted, to use the phrase made famous by Eric Hobsbawm (1981) came to the fore during the early 1980s as conservative parties increasingly went on the offensive. As a lifelong communist, Hobsbawm's (1981) harrowing diagnosis of the decline of the British Labour movement commanded great attention, if only by throwing dirt on his home team. His pessimism was soon matched by that of other left-leaning social scientists. Adam Przeworski's (1986) adaption of median voter theory was especially influential, not least also because of his own affiliation to Marxism. Przeworski argued that left socialist parties had little choice but to move to the middle ground, in order to win over centrist voters as the industrial working class declined in significance. His analysis brilliantly addressed the dilemmas of socialist parties, which were increasingly finding it harder to win support and therefore had to adapt a centrist political stance (see also Kitschelt 1994; Piketty 2020).

This initial awareness of the problems facing the left has recently given way to a much more comprehensive sense of an era coming to an end. Figure 10.1, elaborated by Simon Hix and his colleagues (Benedetto et al. 2020), offers the clearest narrative sparkline of the changing fortunes of the "left" vote in Europe over the past century. The proportion of left voters is different, naturally, if this is taken as a share of the total electorate, including those who do not vote (dashed line), or actual voters (solid line). Regardless, the trends are similar in all cases.

Figure 10.1 suggests—against Rokkan—that historical party alignments are becoming unfrozen as the left weakens. More than this, the decline of the energies of the left changes the stakes of the political field itself. The left became prominent in Europe in the years between the First and Second World Wars, as forces representing outsider interests also able to lead projects of national reconstruction. Figure 10.1 shows that they never commanded a majority of voters during this period, indeed, rarely obtaining more than a third of the vote, and a quarter of the electorate, across European nations. The left vote plateaus at about 32 percent in the years after the Second World War. It then begins to oscillate, diving in the early 1970s, rallying in the 1980s, before falling further during the 1990s, with this slump continuing largely unabated into the twenty-first century. This decline has taken place earlier

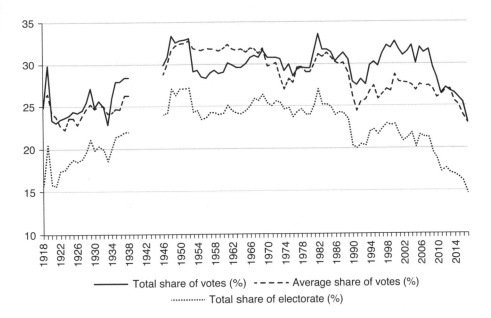

FIGURE 10.1: The rise and fall of the left vote

Source: Reformatted from Giacomo Bendetto, Simon Hix, and Nicola Mastrorocco, "The Rise and Fall of Social Democracy, 1918–2017," *American Political Science Review* 114, no. 3 (2020): 928–939, figure 1. Used by permission of Cambridge University Press.

in the mature democracies of Western Europe and later in the newly democratized eastern European nations. This is compounded by the decline of electoral turnout, which became a further general trend from the 1980s: The proportion of the total electorate who voted left fell by a third, from 27 percent in 1981 to 18 percent in 2017. By this point in time, the socialist left had become a rump that could hardly drive the political agenda in the way that it had done for much of the twentieth century. Free market libertarian conservatism, nationalism, issue-based campaigning, and the politics of resentment took the political driving seat.

Figure 10.1 is Eurocentric. But trends in other parts of the globe don't offer a very different picture. Whereas communist and socialist politics made major advances across Asia, Africa, and South America during the middle decades of the twentieth century, these largely came to a halt by the 1980s and indeed largely went into reverse. Even those parts of the world where (a version of) communist politics remained dominant, especially in China, have done so by yoking overt socialist ideals to authoritarian state-led capitalist development models. The weakening of the organized socialist left, based in European heartlands, to act as central conduit for "progressive" political currents entails that social movements no longer orient themselves within its "gravitational field." We have, in an eerie sense, returned to the political parameters of the nineteenth century, when party politics in largely restricted democratic franchises was not organized on a left-right axis but organized along intra-elite axes, often organized around religious or geographical divides.

It is utterly obvious that Figure 10.1 offers a striking parallel to the inequality trends of economists, which formed the entry point to my book in Chapter 1. Just as Figure 1.1 showed how income inequality fell during the middle decades of the twentieth century, so the left vote rises, and as inequality increases from the 1980s, so the left vote fell. This may appear counterintuitive, as we might expect the growth of inequality to muster popular support for redistributionist left politics. In fact, the relationship operates the other way around. Perhaps declining income inequality was caused by the enhanced power of the political left in the years after the Second World War, and the weakening of the labor movement in many nations from the 1980 was the precondition to the growth of inequality?

There is more to this issue than just the decline of the left vote. There is also the erosion of class voting itself, in which support for the left was predominantly drawn from a working-class base, pitted against middle-class voters who were more likely to vote for the right. The view that this relationship between class and voting was breaking down originated in the later 1970s, led by political scientist Ivor Crewe's research on the class dealignment of British politics. During the 1980s, these arguments were temporarily held at bay by sociologist Anthony Heath and his colleagues (1985), who showed that in probabilistic terms, there had only been "trendless fluctuation" in the relationship between class and vote. Even though the Labour Party had lost support from the working class between the 1960s and 1980s, this reflected the general decline in the popularity of Labour across the board, rather than a specific falling off among working-class voters. This approach was elaborated comparatively by Geoffrey Evans (1999) and other political sociologists to emphasize the persistence of class voting in many democracies. However, it has become increasingly clear that even in relativistic terms, class voting is declining in the twenty first century.

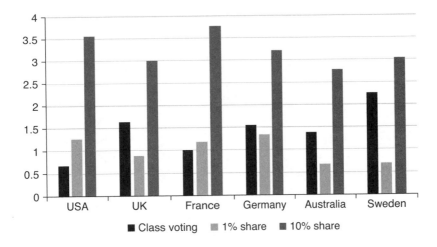

FIGURE 10.2: Class voting and inequality, 1960

Note: The measure of class voting uses the Thomsen index, which provides log odds ratios. To be able to visually compare with class voting, measures of income shares have been deflated by 10.
Data source: Paul Nieuwbeerta and Nan Dirk De Graaf, "Traditional Class Voting in 20 Postwar Societies," in The End of Class Politics, ed. Geoffrey Evans (Oxford: Oxford University Press, 1999), 23–56; World Inequality Lab.

Nieuwbeerta and de Graff's (1999) study is instructive in showing the scale and significance of these shifts. Figure 10.2 visualizes the relationship between occupational class and voting at the time when class voting is usually seen to be at its strongest, 1960. I have also superimposed this with measures of income inequality. A score of zero indicates no relationship between class and vote whatsoever, and the stronger the score, the higher the probability that the working class will vote for the left, and the middle class for the right: A score greater than 1 indicates marked levels of voting. Behind the black bars are the percentages of income earned by the top 1 percent (light gray) and top 10 percent (dark gray).[11]

Figure 10.2 shows that in 1960, each of these nations exhibited some dimension of class voting: even the American case, long seen as exceptional for the weakness of its socialist politics still sees a marked tendency for the manual working class to vote Democrat rather than Republican. It is the inverse relationship between class voting and levels of inequality that stands out. More unequal nations (the United States and France) have lower levels of class voting than more equal ones (Sweden and the United Kingdom). This relationship is only partly explicable in terms of the fact that those

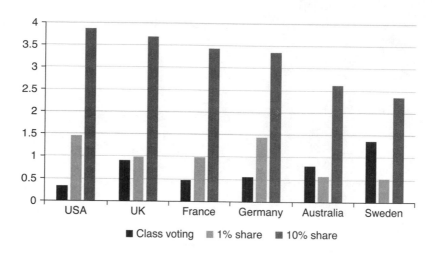

FIGURE 10.3: Class voting and inequality, 1990

Note: The measure of class voting uses the Thomsen index, which provides log odds ratios. To be able to visually compare with class voting, measures of income shares have been deflated by 10.
Data source: Data from Paul Nieuwbeerta and Nan Dirk De Graaf, "Traditional Class Voting in 20 Postwar Societies," in *The End of Class Politics,* ed. Geoffrey Evans (Oxford: Oxford University Press, 1999), 23–56; World Inequality Lab.

nations with strong social democratic parties had done more to reduce inequality through progressive taxation—for as Piketty (2013: 499) shows, progressive taxation in the United States was far more marked than in Germany and France by the 1950s.

Figure 10.3 shows how this picture had changed very considerably even by 1990. In all six nations, class voting had declined: whereas in 1960, only the United States had log odds ratio of less than 1, by 1990, only Sweden had log odds over this threshold. The inverse relationship between higher levels of inequality and lower left vote has also faded: Britain sees the second-highest rate of class voting as well as the second-highest levels of inequality. In short, the period between 1960 and 1990 largely sees the eclipse of class voting, even in relative terms.

Rokkan's belief that party cleavages were frozen at the time party alignments originated has not stood the test of recent time. Left politics was strongest in the founding decades of electoral democracy, as a means of staking and establishing outsider claims. However, as an energizing force, it is no longer in the driving seat, and with this shift, the political field itself loses the organizing force that originally generated it.

These trends are specific to Europe, but similar processes can be found elsewhere. In those many parts of the world in which nation building took place after a process of decolonization, party cleavages typically took the form of pitting insider groups who led struggles for national independence against different kinds of outsider groups. The role of the Congress Party in India, or more recently the African National Congress in South Africa, is symptomatic of this cleavage structure.[12] Typically, after a period when the party of national independence enjoyed high levels of electoral support to the extent that it could be identified as the "natural" governing party, democratic rule can be interrupted by one-party state regimes, which may then also generate outsider parties responding to perceived clientism and cronyism. Even where regimes collapsed due to revolutions or war, there were still older party organizations that could mobilize afresh. It was only in these conditions that class divisions were likely to come to the fore as a modality of dealing with these divisions. In the African context, the major debate has been on the centrality of ethnicity for party formation (Brambor et al. 2006; Mozifar et al. 2003). Comparative analyses of party identification across different continents do not find class to be a strong force. For Lijphart (1979: 452), "religion turns out to be victorious, language is a strong runner-up, and class finishes as a distant third."

10.2.3: The Decline of Political Engagement

During the initiation of mass democratic regimes with universal franchise political enthusiasm runs strong. Electoral turnout was typically high, as most people felt vested in newly established electoral practices that gave them a say in choosing governments. However, across numerous democracies, as intensely charged cleavages decline, and as political insiders with political capital increasingly control political agendas, those with fewer stakes in the game of politics feel excluded and see less interest in participating. The competitive model of the political field, based on the organized striving among interest groups, is breaking down.

Concern about the health and viability of the political arena and anxieties about lack of popular engagement in politics have a long history, but from the later 1990s, they became a major cause for concern through the trailblazing work of political scientist Robert Putnam, who claimed that "social capital" was declining in the United States. Putnam took inspiration from de Tocqueville's view that effective democratic politics was dependent on a rich infrastructure of participation in voluntary associations, where public interaction and civic responsibilities could be facilitated. Drawing on extensive evidence of membership trends across numerous arenas of life, Putnam showed that from a high point of voluntary activity in the 1960s, participation in all kinds of clubs and voluntary associations was falling in the United States. Inferences from his previous studies of political culture in Italy, where he contrasted the rich democratic traditions of the north where there was an extensive network of voluntary associations with the clientalist and familial politics of the Italian south, led him to argue that this fall in social capital would have deleterious effects on democratic engagement and reduce the vitality of civil society more broadly.

Putnam's work inspired a major comparative research program exploring trends in social capital across numerous nations. This work qualified Putnam's arguments in three significant ways. First, trends in social capital in many nations did not match the American pattern. Adam's (2008) analysis showed that in European nations, between 1980 and 1999, participation in voluntary associations increased. Subsequent research has also shown that trends even in the United States were not unambiguously downward (Braer and Grabb 2001; Dekker and van den Broek 2005). This issue is compounded by the fact that in many parts of the world, the culture of public voluntary associations on the American model is weak, even nonexistent, but this does not entail that forms of solidarity and cooperation were absent; indeed in many cases, they are very strong. Putnam's view about falling social capital turned out to be a narrow Americo-centric one.

Two more challenging points did emerge from this social capital debate. Peter Hall (1999) established that even though there was no trend for declining participation in the United Kingdom, there was an increasing stratification of engagement by social class, with the working class being more likely to drop out of public organizations. This argument has been extensively confirmed, both in the United Kingdom (for example, Li et al. 2002, 2003) and internationally. Studies of cultural participation undertaken across Europe have underscored this divide. Well-educated professional and managerial groups tend to be actively involved in public life—including not only through membership in voluntary associations but also partaking in public cultural activities, such as attending art galleries, museums, theaters, and organized sport (Bennett et al. 2009; Prieur and Savage 2011, 2013). Disadvantaged people seemed much more disengaged from these activities. Insofar as it is possible to examine trends over time, this division has grown, in large part because of the decline of popular associations, such as trade unions, clubs, and churches, which had previously been supported by less-advantaged groups.

Growing inequalities in political engagement have been identified in numerous nations. The British case is exemplary. Evans and Tilley (2016) agree with the consensus that class is less strong in predicting electoral choice than in the past, but they emphasize that it has become increasingly significant in shaping differential levels of political engagement. Thus in 2015, only 44 percent of the working class voted for one of the three main parties (with 35 percent not voting at all), compared to 72 percent of the "old middle class" (Evans and Tilley 2016: figure 7.1). This theme is rammed home in their important concluding chapter, which shows that the class gap in nonvoting has risen precipitously since 1987 (their table 8.3).[13]

This finding suggests a self-reinforcing dynamic, in which the culturally engaged and affluent middle classes feel at home in the public realm and are keenly politically involved, whereas those relatively disadvantaged increasingly feel excluded from it. Rather than the political field being contested by competing groups in which all can expect to be heard (even if differentially), considerable numbers of people have largely dropped out of the game of organized politics altogether. This is exactly what happens when capital accumulates within a field and thereby its passions dissipate, as outsiders feel less vested in the game itself.

The other substantial point to follow from the social capital debate is that the informal aspects of social capital, oriented toward different kinds of social networking, was more important for mobilizing, rather than participation in formal organizations. This body of research also came to recognize the cliquish dimensions of schmoozing and especially the way that more privileged social groups are especially skilled in deploying their networks to their own advantage. Ronald Burt (2009), for instance, showed that those business people whose networks spanned "structural holes"—cliques that would otherwise not interact with each other—were more likely to enjoy advantages of salary and status. The principle of homophily, in which "birds of a feather flock together" underpins much social network analysis.[14] However, this informal social networking able to benefit from this homophily is geared toward those who are already privileged.

In conclusion, although the social capital debate inspired by Putnam failed to demonstrate a generalized decline of engagement, it did point to a powerful fault line differentiating an engaged and voracious middle and upper class from an isolated, marginalized and increasingly excluded group of outsiders. This changes the dynamics of the political field through encouraging a return to the insider-outsider dynamic, which existed during the origins of national political systems.

These tendencies toward the dissolution of the political field become self-reinforcing. Political parties become increasingly strategic in orientation, using targeted campaigns to segment voters, so that they can appeal especially to those they think might be won over. Rather than generalized public debates, this is likely to produce echo chambers among groups who share similar views, which are not challenged from other political parties who are focused on winning over their own specific segments of the electoral market. The accentuation of political gaming is especially powerful in nations with first past the post electoral systems.

10.2.4: The Rise of New Cleavages

Over recent decades, new cleavages that cannot be mapped onto the axial left-right divides have been identified as increasingly significant in the political landscape of advanced democracies. This transformation is often associated with a younger generation's embrace of a postmaterialist, expressive, or lifestyle politics (Inglehart 1990; Giddens 1990). This leads to political cleavages organized along two dimensions rather than just one. Redistributionist politics pitting left against right is orthogonal to a secondary opposition between liberals and authoritarians.

A key contributor was Hanspieter Kriesi, who in his 1997 Rokkan lecture took issue with those who emphasized a generalized shift toward postmaterialist values. By contrast, Kriesi (1998) argued that there was an evident structural split in the middle class between those in managerial and business occupations whose loyalty was to their organization, and professionals and cultural experts whose loyalty was to their professional community. This led managers toward conservative business-oriented parties, whereas professionals were more attracted to liberal, socialist politics more attuned to public health, welfare, and education. Kriesi emphatically revealed the strength of this opposition in Switzerland, and evidence from numerous other democracies backed up his claims (see variously A. Heath and Savage [1995] on the United Kingdom, Brooks and Manza [1997] on the United States, and Oesch and Rennwald [2018]).

With this important intervention, Kriesi skillfully adapted Rokkan's framework by demonstrating how different wings of the privileged middle classes drive party cleavages. Thereby, new divisions articulate internal oppositions among those with stakes in the political field, creating oppositions and passions among insiders, while leaving those with weaker investment in the political field with less of a foothold into organized politics.

The structure of this argument is close to that of Bourdieu's model of the field, which I reviewed in Chapter 2. Indeed, numerous Bourdieu-inspired sociologists have adapted versions of it, especially in Scandinavian research (Harrits et al. 2009; Flemmen 2014). A similar kind of argument has also been developed by Piketty (2020), who differentiates what he terms the "Brahmin left" from the "Merchant right." Synthesizing evidence from France, the United States, the United Kingdom, and India, he shows that the trend from left parties to win support from the well-educated, and for the right to be supported by business groups is pervasive across electorates and now eclipses older economic class divides. Symbolically, the British case is striking because of its iconic reputation as a bastion of class voting. Although Anthony Heath (Heath et al. 1985) convincingly demonstrated the ongoing power of class and voting as late as the 1980s, by the early twenty-first century, it was clear that Tony Blair's New Labour project increasingly recast Labour as a party oriented toward a middle-class electorate. More surprisingly, this gentrification was actually enhanced as the Labour Party moved to the left after it lost government in 2010. For the first time since 1918, more working-class voters chose the Conservative Party rather than the Labour Party in Britain in the 2019 election.

These important developments testify to the erosion of field dynamics that take place when capital accumulates. From this perspective, the differentiation between Brahmin left and the Merchant right represents an internal dispute within the more privileged sections of the electorate, so further marking the erosion of the political field as encompassing national citizenry as a whole. In my study of the rise of racist and nationalist sentiment in the

British electorate (Flemmen and Savage 2017) we showed an internal divide among professionals and managers between those with a strong commitment to multi-culturalism contesting with those more attracted to older imperial, potentially racist identities. The latter were often more likely to be in private-sector and corporate employment. The deep cultural values embedded in this opposition suggests that Piketty's model—which reduces this divide to the instrumental calculations of a Brahmin left of upwardly mobile graduates committed to social mobility through higher education contrasted to a "merchant right" electorate that prospers on the basis of its wealth and high incomes—is too economistic and reductive.

A more plausible explanation is that as nation spaces fracture, so the very conception of what a cohesive national project should be becomes more bitterly contested among the more privileged and elite electoral rump still strongly vested in organized politics. The Brahmin-left constituency seeks to re-energize a civic project seeking to defend the public sphere and a commitment to social cohesion, while the merchant-right subordinates public interests to the operation of business principles, including positioning the nation to compete internationally against its rivals. It was around this opposition that the politics of austerity was waged in the 2010s and came to a head in the United Kingdom during the Brexit referendum.

This interpretation also sheds light on the intensifying racialization of political debate, especially as immigration and national security are "weaponized" by the merchant-right political constituency. As white disadvantaged voters become increasingly disenchanted with the idea that the national political system can deliver for them, so the idea that excluding immigrants and shoring up, even restoring, nationally based citizenship rents appears attractive—given the extent to which this message is so powerfully politically authorized by the merchant-right wing of the elite. By contrast, ethnic minorities and immigrants themselves, alongside large numbers of white disadvantaged voters, become key bases of support for social democratic parties wishing to renew coherent inclusive national projects.

The rise of new cleavages therefore is not to be seen as simply the product of a bold and exciting new political agenda, as epochalist theory such as that of Inglehart might imply. In fact, the reverse is true. The flickering "organizing energies" that Poggi elaborates leads to enhanced infighting among politically engaged, generally advantaged voters committed to radically competing visions of what a national project might entail, while large numbers of disadvantaged voters feel increasingly frustrated at their lack of voice. The very idea of the nation itself fragments into different projects with competing values. Different players no longer think they are operating by the same rules, or that the aims of the game are agreed on between them. And this paves the way for the coup de grâce: the return of the political "big men."

10.2.5: *The Politics of Elite Capture*

One of the most striking features of democratic politics in the past twenty years has been the return of plutocrats to the political table. These wealthy elites typically have little or no political capital in the form of experience of office, and their rise to power is frequently associated with either forming a new political party—such as Berlusconi's Forza Italia in Italy, or in winning the support of a party initially opposed to them, as with Donald Trump's co-option of the Republican Party on his way to becoming president of the United States. With the election of Jair Bolsonaro as president of Brazil, or Pinera of Chile, it is now clear that the return of the "big men" is not an aberration. It is becoming an utterly familiar feature of modern democratic politics around the globe. The success of such figures is to be understood as part of a wider process of electoral kickback against political insiders. The Italian Five Star movement led by comedian Beppo Grillo announced its arrival in 2007 with "Fuck Off Day" and attracted more votes than any other party in 2013.

This phenomenon would have been unimaginable fifty years ago, when the logic of the political field demanded that its leading officers were all familiar with its rules of the game and had accrued the requisite amounts of political capital. When Ronald Reagan was elected president of the United States in 1980, this raised eyebrows, because his initial fame and reputation arose from being a film star rather than a political operator; but even so, he had a long political track record and had earned his spurs as governor of California.

In the 1970s, Marxist political sociologist Nikos Poulantzas (1969, 1978) had insisted that capitalism structurally required autonomy between political and economic elites, to ensure that the state was not caught up in internal elite faction fighting and could thereby act more effectively to protect the interests of capital in general. His devastating critique of Ralph Miliband's (1969) careful analysis of the intersections between the British political and business elites carried the day. Today, Polulantzas's claims seem utterly quaint, as economic elites strut up and down the political stage. Wealthy and authoritarian leaders use democratic vehicles for their own purposes, and to enhance their business opportunities. Michael Miller (2013, 2017) refers to this as "electoral authoritaranism" and points out that since 1945, it has become "the dominant form of dictatorship," with examples including Russia, Venezuela, Jordan, and Malaysia. Miller sees the rise of electoral authoritarianism as linked to the desire of autocratic regimes to win international respectability, associated with the strategic view from these elites that they can expect to win over "a large mass of poor voters who can be co-opted through clientelism and state assistance" (Miller 2017: 1). Plutocratic elites are political leaders across all types of regime: democratic, authoritarian, and hereditary. The fact that the world's two major military powers, Russia and the United States, have both been led by such figures tells its own story. The success of these plutocrats in winning democratic elections is only possible because of the fracturing of the political field. Those who for many years have felt they have no stakes in the political system are attracted to vote for those "big men," who make no bones about the fact that they are outside the political field and are keen to fix the system.

An important feature of the success of the "big men" is their appeal to feelings and emotions rather than the narrow instrumental concerns which economic theories of political mobilization made central (see generally Davies 2015). This appeal proved redolent in allowing those who felt excluded by the political field in identifying with plutocrats who claimed to be likewise excluded by political establishments (see, for example, Hochschild 2018).

It is not only premiers who are "big men." The saturation of wealth and political office is also evident more widely. The American case is especially well documented. In the United States, half of the members of Congress are millionaires (Gilens 2015). Political representatives also appear to be influenced by the wealthy (Bartels 2008; Rigby and Wright 2013; Gilens 2015). Gilens argues that it is especially on policies where affluent and nonaffluent voters disagree that the views of the affluent are taken more seriously (see also Gilens 2012). This sets in train a vicious circle, whereby those with the most political capital intersect with those with more wealth, leading to an increasing tie-in between the values of these groups. Daniel Laurison (2015) shows in the British case that the propertied elite are more likely to contact public officials and feel politically effective than even moderately affluent professionals. And indeed, the very wealthy appear to have considerable political coherence. Persson and Martinsson (2016), examining the Swedish case, show that when the size, as well as the existence, of assets is taken into account, it is those with great wealth who are especially predisposed toward right-wing parties.

In these conditions, internal feuding between elites takes on increased significance. Such disputes were very apparent in the UK Brexit referendum, when a minority of business elites who wanted Britain to leave the European Union played a powerful role in resourcing the Leave campaign. Contests among elites on the "field of power" are thereby ramped up and in the process, generate a politics of elite theater. The implications of this theme have been pursued most powerfully by Hacker and Pierson (2010), who coin the phrase "winner-take-all politics" to dispute the tenets of median voter theory. They emphasize that

> the sharp upward skew of income since the 1970s is exceedingly hard to explain with models that revolve around the strength or limits of median-voter influence. Instead, it calls for an alternative perspective— which we call "politics as organized combat"—that emphasizes the role of organized interests in shaping large-scale public policies that mediate distributional outcomes. (Hacker and Pierson 2010: 154)

The rise of wealthy political operators indicates how simply having political capital is no longer sufficient. Hacker and Pierson bring out the fact that when inequality increases, the median voter is less representative of the electorate, as the "top end" pulls away. Floating voters, so beloved of median-voter theories, are themselves declining. Smidt (2017) argues that fewer Americans change their vote between elections, with the proportion of floating voters falling from 14 percent in the 1970s to 4 percent by 2015. By contrast, the proportion of "standpatters," who are decided in their preferences, rose from around 45 percent to nearly 60 percent in the same period. Smidt sees this process as associated with increasing separation and differentiation of political party platforms, which ultimately underscores the rise of elite politics.

It is therefore completely explicable why xenophobia becomes the most potent issue in this new plutocratic politics, often manifested by the mobilization of antiimmigrant sentiment. This xenophobic politics invests new energies through the targeting of groups located outside the nation. In this respect, it recharges cleavage politics along insider-outsider axes through playing on a racialized axis. This alliance between Brahmin right elites and white disadvantaged voter seeks to shore up national citizenship rent. Across many nations, race and ethnicity now has a far more direct impact on voting preferences than does social class alone (for example, on the United Kingdom, see Khan and Sveinsson 2015).[15]

Political economists Wolfgaang Streeck and Colin Crouch have drawn out the wider significance of political elites. Crouch (2005, 2011) goes so far as to claim that there has been a corporate takeover of the neoliberal state, which has increasingly blurred the boundaries between the political field and the corporate business world. Numerous examples of this blurring can be found, including privatization policies, regulatory policy, the subcontracting of large parts of the state to the private sector, and antitrust policy. Streeck focuses on the overloading of demands on the contemporary state and what he calls "plutocratic plunder" and "oligarchic redistribution and the trend towards plutonomy" (Streeck 2014: 75). He also sees an increasing stress between capitalism and democracy.

Elite capture is thereby much more complex than a simple conspiratorial takeover of the state by a wealthy power elite. It can only be comprehended within a wider understanding of how the fabric of the nation space itself— centered on the democratic political field—is fraying.

Conclusion

This chapter has argued that if we are to forge policy to address inequality, we need to recognize how the unmaking of nation spaces will make this a difficult terrain on which to build. The rise of national democratic politics, which was trumpeted in the decades after the Second World War as the universal principle of governance, and which appeared to become utterly hegemonic in the aftermath of the collapse of the Soviet model, is now under unprecedented stress. The attraction of political science to a modernizing paradigm that assumes the normality of liberal democratic regimes and adopts a predominantly institutional perspective is itself part and parcel of this crisis. Its investment in comparative and spatializing methods have neglected the trajectories and duration of liberal democracy itself. We should not assume that liberal democratic regimes, once formed, will operate in steady state, driven by their own feedback mechanisms (such as those associated with the median voter) and will only be overthrown by some kind of exogenous shock. Thus, even the sensitive accounts of Steven Levitsky and Daniel Ziblatt (2018), who argue that democracies "die" when there is political mismanagement by its insiders entailing the breakdown of "mutual toleration" and "institutional forbearance" among political intermediaries and representatives themselves, lack this sense of the dynamism of deeper historical processes. Their diagnosis appeals to effective skilled management by political insiders to do better, when in fact this kind of political management is part of the problem itself.

My fuller historical account is that democratic national projects begin in the aftermath of imperial breakup, with high levels of involvement and engagement because of the energies that founding insider-outsider cleavages impart. The political field matured during the later decades of the twentieth century as a form of political settlement in which internal competing forces could learn to work around institutionalized "rules of the game." This permitted internal distributional struggles to be stabilized around a national consensus, often emphasizing progressive taxation and strong public support for services. However, as the political field stabilizes and becomes routinized, political capital accumulates, and insiders seek to manage the political process through effectively applying the rules of the game. Those without this political capital increasingly come to feel like outsiders on the political stage and become less energized and engaged. Those who remain vested in the political field fragment between "Brahmin left" and "merchant right," to use Piketty's (2020) terms, but can fail to recognize that they are not engaging large swathes of a disenchanted electorate. Over time, they feel alienated and unrepresented. This weakens the political field so that it becomes easier for those without political capital to enter the field of politics with a view to challenging the status quo.

This liberal democratic political field, which became dominant beginning in the 1980s, is breaking down as a result of the increasing weight of history associated with rising inequality. There is a clear parallel to the process I traced in Chapters 6 and 7 regarding how classic categorical identities arose as part of incessant boundary drawing bound up with imperial capitalist projects that was evident around the globe during the nineteenth century. These thresholds distinguished trusted insiders from disreputable outsiders, leading to axial divides around race, gender, and class that endured. Such conflicts were exclusionary, but they also generated energies that drove the formation of political fields, as outsiders struggled to gain access to citizenship rights and to be fully accepted members of their nation. The resulting negotiations around the terms of this access mobilized the energies of participants and ultimately made it possible for these tensions to be productive and even unifying. However, this was only for a certain period of time: they stabilized into organized political and institutional forms that began to unravel the stakes of the field.

I have shown how the question of time and duration is therefore central. The modernist temporal ontology pitched a forward-looking and progressive "left" against a defensive, traditional, and conservative "right." In thus rendering a passive, defensive past pitched against a "future yet to come," the political dominance of the left-right cleavage in democratic nations also evoked an understanding of time itself in which agency is equated with the act of casting one's ballot. Indeed, election day became consecrated as the specific conjuncture in which contingent results could be levered out of the lure of past and future. Through this mechanism, the institution of liberal democracy embedded the modernist temporal ontology with its rupture between past (conservatism), future (socialism), and present (election day). However, as the force of history returns, this axial temporal split breaks down, and with this, notions of progress, future planning, and strategy are called into question.

What Is to Be Done?

In this book, I have argued that the challenge of inequality lies in the accumulating force of the weight of history. In recent decades, inequities have been viewed complacently from a present-day perspective as being historical residues that will be eliminated by modernization, more effective policy, and transparent and rational governance. However, this has not come to pass. We have instead witnessed the restoration of inequality. The very conceptual and methodological tools that have been used in a modernizing framework are themselves part of the inequality process. We need to rethink our entire intellectual apparatus, including the way that social science disciplines themselves operate. Inequality is not simply a discrete topic for inquiry but also requires a paradigm shift in the way we conduct social science more broadly.

My last chapter reflected on the scope for policy reform by placing this within a broader discussion of the historical limits of national political fields. The implication of my argument is clear: We should not assume that policy intervention by itself will be enough to respond to the gravity of the challenges involved. This is not to dispute that policies to tackle inequality are vital—they surely are. However, the changing character of the political field and the capacity for these agendas to be bend policy interventions to other agendas need to be understood. A deeper and more comprehensive political agenda is needed.

It is for this reason that my closing chapter ruminates on how we can now respond to Lenin's (1902) famous call to arms—what is to be done? This reference point is deliberate because it articulates the most common alternative to pragmatic policy-based movements, through a call for revolutionary action. It will be clear to those who have read earlier chapters that I regard such an "accelerationist" call as utterly unpersuasive. We cannot abolish history and reset the clock at year zero, however much we might like to do this. Revolutionary "calls to arms" are a manifestation of the endemic mantra that "innovation will solve our ills," which I criticized in Chapter 9.

The task that I therefore lay out in this chapter is to excavate a politics that seeks a more profound political transformation than is countenanced by a politics of reformist policy intervention and yet that avoids a futile and self-defeating accelerationism. My starting point is therefore, necessarily, the huge disconnect between the analytical power of the broad Marxist vision, which I have underscored and endorsed in much of what I have said, and the fundamental flaws of the Leninist political project, which for much of the twentieth century dominated the socialist political landscape. Most fundamentally, Marx's emphasis on the centrality of capital accumulation was narrowed into a primordial and obsessive focus on economic class as the central category, as both the product of the exploitative forces engendered by capitalism and its redeeming force. This is clear enough in Lenin's tract, which proceeds by pitching bourgeois against working-class interests as a necessary precondition to his polarizing political program, in which the revolutionary party leads the working classes to the promised land of socialism. In fact, Lenin's actual evocation of the working class turns out to be largely gestural, as it transpires that they need leadership in order to realize their mission. They form a categorical group, but actually not enough of a group to be able to recognize their own interests.

I have argued in this book that a full and proper appreciation of capital accumulation goes a long way beyond a class-centric interpretation of economic inequality. There is no analytical warrant for forcing a marriage between theories of capitalism and an exclusively class-based model of politics. Drawing on Piketty and other economists, I have repeatedly emphasized that income and wealth inequality cannot usefully be collapsed into categorical divisions, especially at the top end, which has been driving the inequality charge in recent decades. And, even though classic class categories undoubtedly had huge import in the early phases of capitalism, when primitive accumulation involved brutal dispossession, they always competed with (and indeed were surpassed in importance by) other categories, especially race and gender, as theories of racial capitalism and feminist theories of patriarchy have insisted over many years.

I have also followed the sociological refrain, most famously but not exclusively championed by Pierre Bourdieu, in extending our understanding of capital away from the economic domain alone to include cultural and social capital. A sustained focus on capital accumulation across domains entails a multidimensional and multiperspective approach, not a reductive class-centered framework. If we follow this logic, capital, above all, represents the weight of the past over the present and future, and it is the inequality between generations—of the dead over the living and the living over those who are yet to be born—that is the most fundamental inequality of all. It is for these reasons that inequality needs to be positioned in a wider ecological politics that places the question of economic and social sustainability alongside (and integrally linked to) a wider environmental politics. The politics of sustainability itself needs to be broadened out to take on the economic, social, and cultural issues that researchers in the inequality paradigm have brought to the fore.

The need to link inequality to environmental sustainability is now gaining increasing recognition (Chancel 2020; Piketty 2020; Hickel 2020). I have pushed this argument to its necessary conclusion by insisting that we need to have a better understanding of temporality and duration. Gareth Stedman Jones (2017) argues that whereas Marx's thinking is largely couched in a classical historical tradition, in the hands of Frederick Engels, it was molded into a modernist evolutionary framing that then led it in to a "vanguardist" strategy. Lenin's thinking became the ultimate representation of this current. He strangely blended the modernist temporal ontology with Marx's historically oriented thinking. As a fervent revolutionary, Lenin was in no doubt that the capitalist order needed to be shattered so that the clock of world history could somehow be restarted. Under the careful stewardship of an enlightened communist party leadership, an egalitarian and rational social order could be put in place that would bring about much higher levels of well-being, prosperity, and genuine freedom than had been possible before.

Yet rereading his pamphlet "What Is to Be Done?" today, we cannot but be struck by the way that he wrestles so uncertainly with time—even while speaking about it so confidently. On one hand, he states that capitalism has an unerring temporal logic that imparts a definite causal direction to history. But on the other hand, even though socialism is historically inevitable, it turns out that this historical necessity will only come about when the moment is seized by those who understand its inevitability—the revolutionary party.

Ultimately, even the most ardent advocate of historical inevitability needs to recognize the contingent moment of "freedom," in which the course of history can be turned. And if the course of the past can be steered by reformists into an opportunistic direction, so it also follows that under the right political leadership, which truly understands the course of history, it can become an opportunity to allow historical necessity to be realized. In this way, the present is made more dramatic because of the power of history bearing down on it, so intensifying the responsibility of those whose task it is to actually redeem the past through their heroic and decisive action in the present:

> We are marching in a compact group along a precipitous and difficult path, firmly holding each other by the hand. We are surrounded on all sides by enemies, and we have to advance almost constantly under their fire. (Lenin 1902: 3)

In short, the oppositions in this Manifesto between past, present, and future generate unstable and irreconcilable oscillations—between inevitability and freedom; structure and action; revolution and opportunist reform. The problems of this perspective come fully into focus when we recognize the severe limits of this conception of temporality. Nonetheless, it is precisely this Leninist repertoire that has been endemic to political repertoires of all kinds during the twentieth century. The Russian Bolshevik revolution of 1917, which proved the platform for further communist advances during the middle decades of the twentieth century, was not aberrant compared to other models that prevailed in Western Europe and North America. They all shared a similar template of acting in the present to remedy the ills of the past and create a more advanced social order. As Bauman (1989) has emphasized in the case of the Nazi holocaust, even the fascist route invoked a similar separation of ends and means. Built into this very architecture of thinking is an engrained rationalism that is made possible by an underlying modernist temporal ontology.

In the early twenty-first century, a very different political climate now faces us. The comprehensive forward-looking political projects of the early twentieth century that grew out of imperial modernity—whether these take the form of fascist movements for racial purity, communist egalitarianism, or even aspects of liberal democracy—look utterly tainted. The future looks both uncertain but also more of a management project, in which achieving a welter of incremental targets dominate the horizons of governments, corporations, and individuals alike. In this scenario, inequality can surely take its place as another problem that needs to be addressed with the appropriate metrics and set of experts to monitor them—a nascent "inequality industry." My book argues that we need a much more radical approach. We are living in a world in which older imperial forms—and the racial hierarchies, elites, oligarchs, lineages, and urban power bases that they entail—are no longer simply puddles that will eventually evaporate in the scorching light of the modern sun. The heroic barriers put in place to sequester the modern progressive world from that "left behind"—between public and private; past and present; rational and affective; society and nature—were never watertight but are becoming increasingly leaky. In this context, the accumulation and secretion of capital, in all its often-mundane forms, has entailed the return of older historical forces—not just as passive traces, ghosts, or legacies but as active forces pressing down on the present.

When returning to our overarching question of "what is to be done," we therefore need to avoid the tempting accelerationist seduction of a brand new policy, or scientific device. Attempts to rustle up some further bold future are flaying a very tired horse indeed—and one where the idea of a technical fix has then generated longer-term problems. We need to come to terms with the detritus of the past, to modulate these historical forces so that they become productive and enabling for future generations. Recognizing the weight of history requires us to go beyond the conventional political repertoires of recent decades centered just on reducing relative inequalities between groups. Simply tackling relativities—important though this is—does not tackle the absolute shifts in the size and significance of wealth accumulation. By fixating on relativities, the absolute growth of wealth and accumulation is hidden from view. To use the obvious ecological parallel, we need to place the question of sustainability at the center of our social analysis. Just as reducing relative gaps between nations with high and low carbon emissions will not tackle the climate crisis unless absolute levels are controlled, so the challenge of inequality requires addressing absolute shifts in the mass of wealth. In what follows, I lay out modest proposals to encourage this debate.

11.1: The Revival of Radicalism

Chapter 10 notes that during the twentieth century, the modernist temporal ontology was institutionalized in the difference between the progressive left and conservative right. This axial divide organized a series of related dichotomies between past and future, tradition and progress, religion and secularism, old and young, and traditional economic forces (agriculture and extractive industry) and modernizing ones (technically advanced and consumer-oriented production). This bifurcation still has an enduring hold on us.

By the end of the twentieth century, this organizing temporal principle was already fraying. The "progressive" forces of the political left found themselves increasingly on the defensive, locked into a politics of defending older modalities of public provision. It was the forces of the right that now embraced an "accelerationist" agenda of speeding up innovation and capital accumulation by cutting regulation, stripping away tradition, and embracing a bold neoliberal world. This inversion of left and right allows a critical space for social movements to come to the fore. Antiracist, feminist, and antidiscriminatory campaigns have had considerable success in driving legal change and provoking institutional reforms in numerous parts of the world. They are also part of a wider historical renewal of radical politics.

As I discussed in Chapter 7, many explanations for the power of these campaigns takes the epochalist form of emphasizing the significance of new "expressive," "identity," or "lifestyle" politics, which are seen to be eclipsing materialist concerns. I have a different take. Identity politics is not a helpful way of labeling these movements. Instead, they reflect the historical force of long-standing inequalities that take an increasingly visceral form in the context of a more unequal economic environment, in which more visible, increasingly hereditary, and exclusive (on gender, racial, and other lines) elites operate with increasing power and abandon.

In critiquing these elites, we can learn from the self-proclaimed radical politics that had its heyday in world politics from the end of the eighteenth century to the middle decades of the nineteenth century. Here, radicalism involved confronting the weight of history as it was experienced in these times: the accumulated forces of elite privilege, entrenched corruption, and cronyism. In Britain, William Cobbett railed against "The thing."[1] This radical tradition inspired anti-imperial revolutions, notably the American war of independence, and democratic political reform movements across the world. Analytically, the main intellectual planks for this radical tradition were the concepts of value and rent. The differentiation between productive and unproductive labor was taken up by Ricardo and Marx, to draw attention to the unfair rewards going to rentiers, derived from some form of monopoly control (or "opportunity hoarding," to use the term from Tilly 1999). The differentiation authorized modes of political populism to criticize the power and influence of "place holders." This kind of refrain has become increasingly powerful in the political repertoire today, just as it was in the eighteenth and early nineteenth centuries.

The early movement of radical politics in Britain in the 1830s and 1840s came to a head with the six planks of the British Chartist movement (Chase 2007; Stedman Jones 1982), which today mostly appears as an uncontroversial liberal manifesto.[2] Most of the Chartist demands now look utterly routine (paying members of parliament, having a secret vote, ensuring constituencies were of equal size). However, rather than treating the Charter solely as a demand for absolute universal liberal rights, it can be better understood as a strategic device to constrain elite power. All six points sought to pry influence away from vested interests by constraining the autonomy and discretion of governing elites. It is this strategic capacity of radicalism to challenge the accumulated resources of elite power by refusing the separation of past from present and future that has much to teach us today.

From the middle decades of the nineteenth century, radicalism became fragmented between liberal and socialist renderings, and it lost its overarching political identity. This needs to be rectified. Radicalism challenges the sequestering of space and time that underlies the modernist project. Thus, I have taken issue with avant-garde conceptions of social and cultural fields that underpin Bourdieu's account of social space and pursue inward-looking "progressive" projects to advance the supposed principles of the field itself.

Radicals, by contrast, contest the very rules of the game. They do this via a politics that refuses binaries of continuity and change. Radicalism urges fundamental reform and change but only as part of a renewal of what is best from the past. As the very term radicalism indicates, the focus is on the renewal of past truths as a critique of those using the banner of progress to promote projects to accumulate advantage. This explains the conservative and romantic aspects of radical thought. Radicalism cannot therefore be encapsulated in the standard differentiation between "left" and "right" that has organized political discourse since the early nineteenth century and permits modernist binaries of all kinds to follow in its footsteps. This is a strength that we need to recover in the twenty-first century. We need to reenergize this vision today, to seize its mantle of resisting depredation, privilege, and cronyism while also championing the best historical forces. Let me now spell out in more concrete ways what kind of politics this approach engenders.

11.2: The End of Growth Models

This proposal is not controversial: It has been scoped out extensively by heterodox economists, social scientists, and environmentalists. Nonetheless, it needs to be reiterated. The idea that economic growth is a political panacea lies at the heart of the modernizing paradigm. It performs several roles. First, it creates a secular version of the millenarian belief that future progress compensates for past and present problems. It recognizes that scarcity fundamentally limits human capacities and sees modernization as a force that brings multiple wider benefits. Economic growth has thereby been a crucial feature of both left- and right-wing political platforms around the globe. This appeal to the "new" and the power of "change" as an article of faith is not only a major political platform but is also embedded in routine organizational practices. However, when the invocation for change is not simply nebulous, it has become obstructive.

Second, appealing to growth sidesteps structural issues of inequality, because all parties can be seen to gain. It therefore evades a redistributionist agenda that debates whether the division of the economic pie is just. Thus, economic growth will lower poverty rates even without touching the fortunes of the very wealthy. The most hackneyed phrase used to express this view is that "a rising tide lifts all boats."[3] Through this means, questions of justice and fairness can forever be kept on the sidelines, a kind of skillful disappearing trick. However, the problem of inequality doesn't actually go away. Indeed, it festers.

Third, the growth discourse appeals to a technocratic politics of political management, in which effective governance can be exercised to allow an aggregate expansion of the economy. This scientistic logic, which underpins the legitimacy of growth models, relies on the production and refinement of economic measures dependent on remarkable intellectual and organizational work. The successful development of economic indexes dates to the first half of the twentieth century and are most notably encapsulated in estimates of GDP (or GNP). Once put in place, these measures come to have a power of their own, permitting legions of experts to attend to their growth. As numerous critics have shown, these metrics are at best partial (for instance, they omit domestic work), at worst misleading, but nonetheless as I have discussed in earlier chapters, they prove difficult to disrupt, and they cannot simply be made to "disappear." Thus, the efforts by economists such as Alvaredo, Piketty, and Zucman to develop inequality measures that thus disrupt the centrality of ones based on growth alone has major significance. Ordinalization has a driving momentum of its own.[4]

Appealing to growth involves enlightened rule by experts who are able to monitor trends and exercise the right kind of stewardship, sometimes bestowing the rewards of growth on different sections of the population to modulate inequality in its relative forms. It facilitates alliances between national experts and international bodies, in arenas where economists enjoy great influence. Successive waves of influential policy models, from structural adjustment to the Washington consensus, have been driven by this axis.

But the hegemony of this growth model is now under increasing attack because of the crisis of sustainability brought to light by the growing environmental crisis. Recent decades have seen unparalleled stresses on the global ecosystem. Notwithstanding the usual appeal to technological innovation to "solve all ills," further aggregate growth will only provoke additional environmental concerns. Kate Raworth (2017: 45) has expressed this as the need for a "doughnut economics" that "points towards a future that can provide for every person's needs while safeguarding the living world on which we all depend."

The question of social sustainability has been put on the agenda through Thomas Piketty's neat formula that the rate of return to capital tends to be greater than the growth rate. Sidestepping the extensive critical arguments about whether this generalization can be claimed to be a fundamental law, empirically, the benefits of economic growth have indeed been concentrated among those with the greatest resources—and this is unlikely to be a historical aberration. As accumulation of capital piles up at the top, market mechanisms are increasingly driven by excessive top-end demand by those who are better able to mobilize and make themselves heard than can those from other groups. Increasingly wealthy elites act in ways that are divorced from wider social needs.

This politics of social sustainability feeds into my most general criticism of growth models. The pursuit of growth endorses the classic separation of ends and means that lies at the heart of modernity. This poses fundamental challenges to living the "good life." Modernist thinking classically places the question of the good life as a private individual concern that can best be pursued when individuals have the resources to pursue their private passions. However, we are now recognizing the problems that this separation has permitted. Critical theorists have emphasized how economic growth impoverishes the "life world" forms of rich human experience.

In recent years, there has been an important development of a "no-growth" politics (for example, Hickel 2020). This does not simply reverse the terms of debate so that "not growing" becomes a counter-panacea. These writers are emphatic that in some contexts, notably in poor parts of the world, economic growth is valuable and desirable. In Raworth's (2017) formulation, we should be agnostic about growth rather than anti-growth. The important point is to decenter the overarching importance of growth as a good thing in and of itself. Instead, we can stage a more balanced and rounded debate about what we value and how far, if at all, growth might allow us to achieve this.

11.3: From a Politics of Scarcity to Holding Capital to Account

My third proposal to address "what is to be done" follows closely from my embrace of a recharged radicalism. This radical vision need not entail some kind of abstract theory of liberal rights (which, as economist Amartya Sen points out, leads to an apparatus to enforce it, which will be bound to spawn its own baggage, in precisely the way that the proliferation of metrics designed to measure and permit the alleviation of social problems, ends up by generating inequalities in and of themselves). Instead, this vision can exhibit a fundamental awareness of how those with privilege operate and how they deploy their historically acquired advantages for their own purposes. This a way of recasting socialism away from a doctrinal redistributionism and toward a politics directed at scrutinizing, criticizing, and holding to account those with undue resources, power, and authority. This approach thereby moves away from a personalized criticism of specific individuals (though at times it can certainly be this) to a wider critique of the structural arrangements that allow elite power to flourish.

This radical reworking of socialist ideals thereby reverses the telescope by redirecting the gaze away just from those deemed to lack sufficient resources. This emphasis, endemic to growth models, sees the problem as lying in "deficit." Such a politics readily slips into a wider normative framing that marginalizes and stigmatizes those who are somehow seen to be lacking. Although there is no doubt that this politics of lack has been associated in the past with a humane concern to alleviate suffering, it sidesteps the rich and powerful. The politics of poverty reduction has, of course, historically been profoundly important in raising living standards and capacities, but it is ultimately inadequate to the contemporary challenges of inequality. In its relativist conceptions, it buys into a politics of growth. The problem of poverty and exclusion becomes necessarily intractable, a dog chasing its own tail. Furthermore, this kind of approach de-politicizes the aggregate social mainstream by not recognizing entrenched inequalities in the social body. It thus lacks analytical traction in recognizing and seeking redress for the pulling away of the top, which has been a crucial part of recent developments.

To rectify this, a radical politics should address the politics of abundance, through "holding capital to account." This is the reversal of the telescope with which I started this book. This does not mean ignoring issues of poverty and welfare, but it does mean changing the way we orient to them. The easiest way of holding capital to account might be by the expropriation of high-level assets. I strongly support redistribution, but this needs to be done more subtly than targeting specific groups as such. I have in this book criticized the centrality of "categorical" politics, which came to hold sway in imperial modernity that systematically stigmatized certain categories of people, fundamentally treating them as less than moral subjects. Categorical politics has mainly been directed to those in subordinate, marginalized positions—for example, ethnic and racial minorities, women, and sexual minorities—though on occasion, most notably under communist regimes, it has been applied to various kinds of elite and advantaged positions. Regardless, this categorical politics in any of its forms has been the most debasing and vile in human history. It has permitted acts of violence—both physical and symbolic—and wanton destruction inflicted on many billions of people.

Categorical politics depends on mobilizing boundaries, which become moralizing and ordering devices. There is no doubt, as I argued in Chapters 6 and 7, that such categorical analysis has exposed fundamental inequalities, and in their relativist guise played a crucial part in the reduction of inequality in numerous spheres as nation spaces were forged during the twentieth century. But categorical politics comes at a significant cost. It imparts morality not to specific people, as they face their difficulties and dilemmas, but to the aggregates that they lump together. However categorical lines are drawn, they act as devices to partition. This mechanism permits the systematic moral distancing that Bauman (1989), following the philosopher Emmanuel Levinas, identifies as central to genocidal projects. Furthermore, it is problematic in and of itself, given the ultimate arbitrariness of categorical boundaries. How can they distinguish wealthy elites from the wider population? Is it the top 0.1 percent, 1 percent, or 10 percent of income earners? Those with particular amounts of wealth? Do we look at individuals or households? Whichever line is chosen is ultimately arbitrary in that two virtually identical people could be placed on either side of it. The same anxiety over boundary drawing has been endemic, for instance in the obsession with lines of descent that is central to racist politics. It thus illuminates all too clearly the sheer impossibility of pursuing projects of categorical "purity" of any kind.

We need a different kind of politics, in which capital is held to account and involves an enhanced role for public stewardship. The fundamental driver leading to high-level rewards has been the isolation of reward mechanisms from wider considerations of social value due to the sequestration of systems of reward to private, economistic, or instrumental criteria. Mazzucato (2018: 55) has explored how concepts of rent have moved from their classical pedigree in which rent arises from "redistributing value and not from creating it" toward the marginalist conception in which rent is only derived from situations of market imperfection. As Mazzucato (2018: 74) puts it, "if value derives from price, as neo-classical theory holds, income from rent must be productive. Today the concept of unearned income has therefore disappeared."

Rather than accepting the logic of shareholder value as the overriding value by which to assess merit for economic reward, wider social considerations can and should be included in an evaluation. This requires much wider assessments of which human and social values to include. Of course, we cannot expect any final or definitive ruling of what is or is not "valuable," but this issue can be treated as subject to deliberation rather than reduced to an economistic calculation. This can intensify the stakes involved in public discussion and will enhance democratic debate.

The problem of a politics of growth as a means of redressing scarcity is that it assumes that positive projects, passions, and desires are fundamentally private affairs and that the role of public intervention is to ensure private individuals and households have enough resources (even if only at a threshold level) to pursue these. This reinforces identities of disadvantage, which can be profoundly stigmatizing and disempowering. As Foucault famously brought out, this process of normalization is endemic, and even where stigmatizing labels are contested and subverted, this focus on them only reinforces their hold. A particularly striking trend is the proliferation of mental health issues, which now abound in economically prosperous nations and are ways of identifying means by which people cannot compete with those who are "truly successful."

11.4: Rounded Conceptions of Well-Being

My fourth proposal addresses the limits of instrumental and strategic conceptions of human agency that lie at the heart of modernizing agendas. This is not to say that such perspectives are not valuable. They have proved to be a powerful means of drawing attention to the way profound inequalities structure the differential capacity of people to achieve their goals. As in Bourdieu's field analysis, they have led to a conception of inequality that is bound up with the competing interests of those with different stakes. However, I have also endeavored to bring out the limits of this perspective, especially in Bourdieu's vacillation between phenomenological and strategic conceptions of social life.

Increasingly, we are surrounded by terms trying to register a richer concept of human well-being than that within a rationalist liberal tradition. The appeal of terms such as "resilience" point—albeit vaguely—to the value of a richer concept of human life. Amartya Sen's concept of "capabilities" has enjoyed particular traction in pinpointing the decisive virtues of this approach. Sen deliberately uses this term to capture the way that individuals should be supported to achieve forms of human flourishing according to their own values and priorities, and not judged by some external criteria. He thus continues to work within a means / ends distinction but democratizes it so that the ends are those in which all humans are able to judge their own values and priorities. "The main reason why the capability approach holds that it is better to focus on the ends rather than the means, is that people differ in their ability to convert means into valuable opportunities (capabilities) or outcomes (functionings)" (Sen 1992: 26–28).

Sen's approach has been profoundly significant for extending analyses of poverty away from purely economistic considerations to recognize wider social and cultural capabilities. However, ultimately his endorsement of the means / ends distinction entails that individuals at the top end, fully able to pursue their capabilities with almost unlimited resources at their disposal, cannot themselves be held to account or made responsible. Ultimately, therefore, this approach fails the radical test that I have set. For similar reasons, the concept of capabilities can lend itself to universalist renderings, as with Martha Nussbaum's (2001) attempt to distil its ten core features.[5]

One way to resolve this problem is to focus not on capabilities but on "the search" at the heart of the human condition. This harks back to immanentist modes of thinking associated with Spinoza and more recently reinvigorated by Deleuze and Guattari (1988). This approach seeks a humanism that does not specify a specific state that is to be normalized as preferable to any other, but recognizes and endorses human life as an ongoing questing endeavor. The quest is a fundamentally social process: it involves being able to deploy the economic, social, and cultural resources necessary to journey through "the good life." It thereby offers a conception of time as processual rather than as divided up into linear states. This perspective can also lend itself to a critique of top-end "rent" as unearned privilege rather than associated with questing actions. It follows that those who can draw on unusually large or favorable resources which are deployed simply to extract additional advantages are not able to justify this behavior in terms of their quests. Thus, whereas providing resources to allow leading ballet dancers, musicians, or entrepreneurs to achieve more of their potential would indeed be worthwhile, those seeking to extract rent would not.

This offers a way of addressing the visceral inequalities that I have identified as a defining feature of the current politics of inequality, notably through the resurgence of racism and sexism. I have emphasized that focusing on relative inequalities between groups, attributing them to bland epoch descriptions (such as "identity politics") or simply identifying them as some kind of historical residue that has not yet been tackled by the right kind of policy, fails to grasp the urgency of these issues. In recent decades, there have been very important initiatives to extend the liberal discourse of rights away from purely abstract principles (such as liberty, property, and contract) to include human rights and discrimination. Vital though these initiatives are, they have failed to address the entrenched nature of racism, sexism, and other inequalities, such as those concerning disability, sexual orientation, and sexual assignment.

Placing the human "search" at the heart of analysis may appear to be illiberal. It challenges the mantra that individuals have the primordial liberty to pursue their private passions, whatever these might be. It thus also challenges the alliance between markets and consumption, in which economic activity is geared toward the satisfaction of private consumer demand as akin to a primordial imperative. Rather than liberal conceptions of rights, the fundamental recognition of the human "search" can provide a platform for a radical politics that addresses inequality. The human "search" is plural insofar as it can only be defined and followed by people according to their own values and priorities, which themselves are subject to change. It is a search, because it need not be specifically goal oriented, with the implication that it involves a split between a now-time (in which a specified goal is set out) and a future time (in which the goal can be achieved). The concept of goal orientation, with its separation of ends and means, deploys a disabling temporal ontology. If goals are actually achieved, they can become meaningless and disappointing. As Terence Kilmartin (1985) wryly noted, Proust's fundamental vision was that life is disappointing, not because our dreams are not realized, but because they are. This concern with the search instead involves a fluid temporal ontology that links pasts, presents, and futures. It challenges the stigmatizing language of stasis and stability, in which those who are "stuck" can be seen as somehow deficient, and it also challenges the view that those who are somehow reflexive and strategic are superior. It recovers the mobile and processual nature of human being as lying at the heart of a politics of inequality.

This reference to the "search" may sound abstract, but it chimes in with numerous currents. I have already mentioned Sen's concept of capabilities, which recognizes the fluid nature of human striving. This kind of thinking has also been championed by Mariana Mazzucato, who has emphasized the power of "mission-oriented" thinking. Taking aim at the centrality of metrics that governs much managerial intervention in the name of cost-benefit analysis, she insists on the power of broader missions to give overarching purpose for advancing value. One of the attractive features of mission-oriented thinking is that it has affinities with the emphasis on the "search" that lies at the heart of immanentist thought and bestows a wonder and uncertainty on the definition and promotion of the mission itself, which can be profoundly empowering. Missions thus mark a break from scientistic and objectivist thinking, which views progress and evolution as historical givens, and thus defines human endeavor as a subsidiary working out of this teleological logic. By contrast, mission-oriented thinking recognizes the human embeddedness of endeavor. This thinking marks a return to older conceptions, often wedded to religious world views, which insist on the broader cosmological importance of human quest.

11.5: Sustainable Nationalism

My fifth proposal regards the renewal of the national project. In this book I have emphasized the fragility, rather than endurance, of national spaces.

Over recent decades, many nation-states have become enhanced projects of imperial aggrandizement, bound up with the empowerment of elites. This has generated a populist response from less-advantaged populations, such as those who have lost relative economic ground in their countries and seek to revive national projects as a means of restoring their own fortunes. Their ire can be directed against those who are more committed to cosmopolitan ideals, which are viewed as transcending national boundaries.

This cleavage between versions of nationalism and cosmopolitanism has become the central political fault line across much of the world, and it lends itself to extensive moral calling out of those who are seen to fall into the other camp. The cosmopolitan position commands the liberal high ground, often berating what is seen as the xenophobia and blinkered visions of those attracted to national visions. But this a priori valuation of the cosmopolitan position is problematic. As Craig Calhoun (2002) has emphasized, despite the positive aspirations that lie behind it, cosmopolitanism largely operates as an elite discourse, privileging those with the resources and capacities to be readily mobile across national boundaries. These are not displaced by "ordinary cosmopolitan" practices, which are often conducted from marginalized and stigmatized positions. We need to distance ourselves from the Kantian universalism associated with cosmopolitanism, toward a recognition of the imperial norms of many actual transnational practices. It is those with extensive transnational trading, corporate, security, and financial ties who occupy the most privileged elite positions—in a manner that has parallels with the ruling lineages of eighteenth-century absolutist states. The cosmopolitanism associated with finance, corporate power, and other institutions of economic regulation are inextricably bound up with the regime that has facilitated the rise of global inequality. The same is true of the cosmopolitanism of elite professionals, academics, and intellectuals, whose own cultural capital is underscored by their ability to traverse national boundaries.

In this context, sustainable nationalism can be a reasonable, indeed radical, way of defining communities that share some kind of collective commitment to act responsibly together through commitments to all their members. These forms of nationalism are best able to modulate the mission-oriented thinking discussed in section 11.4 above, so that it is detached from imperial and elite-driven values and is not simply anchored in the wishes of wealthy individuals (as, for instance, the desire of elites to fly to Mars seems to be). This recovers a model of the nation-state that sees the commitment to dialogical exchange and communication as central to its practices and self-identity. Sustainable nationalism invokes working with other nations on a shared basis, with no assumed supremacy for any specific nation or group of nations. In Chapter 5, I showed that where sustainable nationalism is most in evidence, the spiraling growth of income inequality has been most effectively held in check in recent decades. The example of the European Union also demonstrates that the most effective forms of supranational collaboration take place when there are also strong, sustainable national cultures within it. This does not make the European Union free of corporate elitism, but it does underscore that the effectiveness of actual transnational governance depends not on the dissolution of constituent national entities but on their effective coordination.

Sustainable nationalism is under threat in the global arena. In the period since the collapse of the communist regimes in the later 1980s, a resurgent imperial nationalism has been in the ascendant. Here, nation-building projects are also tied to claims for regional and global supremacy. The American case speaks for itself, though there are many others where such politics abounds: in the United Kingdom, China, Russia, Turkey, and India. Claims to national superiority are associated in these contexts with racism and religious bigotry. In such situations, inequality surges, as it seen as vital to empower "the best" people as part of the aggrandizement of imperial elites. Simply holding out for the need for democratic rights is unlikely to be an effective critique of such imperial nations. More telling and effective would be the radical exposure of regimes of corruption, cronyism, and elite lineages that are endemic in imperial nations and that generate popular unrest, which can be harnessed in a powerful way.

I am not querying here the moral value of cosmopolitanism: far from it. I am instead emphasizing that cosmopolitan projects necessarily empower those in elite positions with the capacity and resources to work across contexts. The distinction between sustainable and imperial nationalism is not hard and fast. However, this does not call into question the value of trying to recover forms of nationalism that are committed to recreating the ordinary communities that were imagined in the early decades of modernity. Although the American model, which has been the central torch bearer of visions of liberal modernity, has now lost its capacity to command such a progressive mantle, we can still return to laud those American radicals who were determined to fight oppressive British power in the later eighteenth century. It is by recovering this energy that we can most effectively meet the challenge of inequality.

Conclusion

I have scoped out how the challenge of inequality can be broadened into a radical manifesto, returning to themes that enjoyed great resonance at the birth of modernity and that championed conceptions of popular power. Aspects of this radical tradition are found both within liberalism and socialism, but they can usefully be intertwined. Here I close by bringing out how this radical critique can elaborate a mindful politics that avoids both liberal rights-based discourses (which have largely been co-opted into elite modes of power) or a socialist form of state control (which veer into authoritarianism).

A politics addressing the meaning of relative richness and privilege is fundamental. There have been extensive discussions about the meaning of relative poverty and how the poor need to be seen in relationship to wider social norms and expectations. However, there has been no parallel discussion of the definition of affluence, and in particular what kinds of income or wealth may be excessive. In the absence of this kind of discussion, focus is directed toward ad hoc individuals whose lifestyles seem particularly extravagant. But there is a serious discussion to be had about whether it is reasonable to have more than one home, more than one car per household (or individual), luxury consumption items, and such like. It would also be reasonable to extend this discussion to whether being able to afford private education, health care, and such like can be justified. This kind of public debate, when informed by social research, is a serious opportunity to reflect on what levels of top-end privilege for particular nations are allowable in the context of facilitating the human search, which is central to well-being.

It should be entirely possible to lead this discussion in such a way that it avoids a politics of envy and is directed toward serious reflections about prosperity and well-being. Of course the ability to do this will depend on the quality of civil society and the infrastructure of sustainable nationalism, for only if there is a commitment to dialogical principles is it likely for such debates to be reasonably conducted. This approach might also permit progressive politics without invoking categorical divides. Thus, rather than abolishing private schooling of all kinds, there might be a case for endorsing certain kinds of private schooling that support important values, or for children with special needs or talents. Similarly, this kind of dialogical thinking, allied to my arguments about the centrality of the "search," could lead to a democratic politics that acknowledges that it is unfair to ban any specific activity if it is central to the goals and values of any particular person. But that activity could reasonably be taxed at a rate acknowledging that it conveys privileges that should be compensated for.

I am under no illusion that these kinds of proposals would be readily accepted by privileged groups in society. The liberal discourse of rights, infused with market principles, has instilled very powerfully an ethic of "I should have the right to spend my money on whatever I want." But if it is clear that any changed policies are not categorical or simply driven by envy, and that they fully respect the humanity of the affluent in conducting their own search like everyone else, there is more prospect that it will be accepted.

A strengthened progressive taxation policy needs to be at the heart of an empowered politics of inequality. It is indeed the strong consensus that high levels of personal taxation are associated with lower levels of inequality, notably in postwar developed nations. It is a contemporary political mantra that the electorate is hostile to high taxation, and few political parties have been prepared to countenance going to the polls to argue for higher taxes. However, this is integrally associated with the way that parties have adopted an economistic mode of politics that emphasizes the power of cost-benefit calculations. In those situations where solidarity is highly valued, then there is no reason why different priorities cannot be brought to bear.

There is no doubt that it is the taxation of wealth and inheritance that must be central to a politics of equality. This issue has been emphasized by Piketty (2013) in his call for a 1 percent annual taxation on wealth and has also led to discussions about property taxation in particular. Currently, policies on inheritance tax vary greatly in different nations and are largely unimaginative in form. Furthermore, corporate vehicles are often used to limit inheritance taxation. In many parts of the world, there is little popular enthusiasm for inheritance tax, because these are seen as insensitive and possibly damaging to "ordinary" households understandably wanting to pass on resources to their children. There are examples of imaginative proposals for taxing inheritance that do recognize this understandable reaction and yet focus on excessive inheritance. Here again, there is scope for social research to better explore what is seen to be reasonable.

This focus on tax may appear to emphasize redistribution rather than "pre-distribution," or in other words, seeks to redistribute what is unequally generated rather than a more fundamental rebalancing of unequal incomes. This objection somewhat misses the point, since there is no zero-sum tension between re- and pre-distributive strategies. A commitment to high levels of progressive redistributive taxation in no way detracts from a politics addressing pre-distributionist inequality. In fact, the contrast between these approaches is overblown, since those nations with higher taxation also tend to have lower pre-tax income inequality. (Indeed, the distinction draws on the unhelpful liberal temporal ontology—hence the "pre-" and "re-"). But there is no question that pre-tax income inequality has risen in many parts of the world, and that this is linked to the dominance of financial and trading circuits, which allow those working in such sectors to cream off high levels of "rent" in the name of building shareholder and trader value. Challenging the dominance of financial markets is crucial to reducing inequality, and focusing instead on "engineering value," incorporating manufacturing, design, and service skills for long-term and sustainable benefit.

As these reflections make clear, the challenge of inequality requires systematic and broad thinking across multiple research domains—as I have conducted in this book. A historical perspective attuned to the role of duration requires us to place inequality as part of a wider politics of environmental and social sustainability. The challenge of inequality is bound up with the accumulation of capital, wealth, and resources, which is seeing the reassertion of older historical forms. Only then will we be able to develop the framework to harness these historical forces most effectively as we search for a viable and sustainable future.

Glossary

Although the chapters of this book can be read independently, several recurring themes thread though the book. To assist readers in drawing narrative threads between chapters, a brief guide to each of the main concepts is included here, where I also refer to the specific chapters in which they are discussed in more detail. These definitions are offered as sensitizing devices, to familiarize readers with the stakes involved in invoking them, rather than as formal and abstract devices. This glossary thus focuses on the reasons for invoking these concepts as much as on their formal definitions.

Capitalism

Following Marx, I see capitalism as inherently driven by the dynamics of accumulation (see Chapter 3). I thereby downplay theories of capitalism that reduce it to some kind system or see it as defined by overarching laws. I thus emphasize how the accumulation process is central to the *immanentization* of social life (that is, the capacity for the emergence of new and unstable processes).

Theories of capitalism thereby are based on the significance of *capitals* seen as processes that have the potential to augment themselves. In keeping with my emphasis on immanentization and the need not to reduce capitalism to one specific system, I follow Pierre Bourdieu in recognizing that capitals can take several different forms and are not confined to the economic arena.

Concepts of cultural and social capital are vital heuristics that recognize how forms of accumulation are not confined to a narrow economic realm.

Similarly, capitalism does not only instantiate economic class inequalities. As discussed in Chapters 6 and 7, theorists of racial capitalism have argued that it also generates inequalities of race. Marxist feminists have emphasized the co-constitutive role of gender divisions in capitalism. Accumulation processes are also bound up with the generation of categories (see below).

Categories

Categories, which I examine in detail in Chapters 6 and 7, can be understood as the "stuff" of inequality. Class, gender, and race / ethnicity are most commonly referred to, but this readily can be expanded (for instance, to include age groups, groups defined by sexual identity, and religion). Categories also overlap with "states" (such as groups in a state of poverty, as discussed in Chapter 1) and "cleavages" (as discussed in Chapter 10).

More exactly, categories are to be understood as groups whose membership is defined vis-à-vis some other kind of abstract category. Clans, tribes, and families form social groups, and they are distinguished from other clans, tribes, families, and so forth, but not according to abstract criteria that the term "categories" invokes. I argue that abstract categories, which are central to modernity, can broadly be distinguished into three major forms listed here.

Classic categories

As discussed in Chapter 6, these distinguish "insider" groups, whose members are privy to some kind of (self-defined) civilizing mission associated with imperial projects, from "outsider" groups, whose members are seen as needing to be kept outside, controlled, or educated into this overarching mission. Classic categories were fundamental to the spread of imperial modernity from the sixteenth to the twentieth centuries.

Relative categories

As discussed in Chapter 6 and 7, these distinguish abstract groups on the basis of the probabilities of differing life chances, or likelihoods of fully becoming national citizens. They thus make no overt ontological claims about inherent differences between groups, or to any absolute differences between people in different categories. Relative inequalities are frequently mobilized most powerfully in *nation spaces,* in which assessing and alleviating relative inequalities becomes central to governance. Relative categories are often deployed alongside distributional accounts, such as those examining the shape of the income distribution (see Chapter 1). When relative categories give way to ordinal rankings (see Chapter 4) this can be a sign that they are losing their influence.

Visceral categories

As discussed in Chapter 7, these are categorical inequalities that are experienced in some kind of bodily form. This may be through the operation of stigmatizing processes, such as systematic abuse and denigration. They may also involve bodily projects such as seeking to change categorical states by redefining one's body.

Visceral categories often overlap with classic or relative categories, but they are not entailed by them. It is possible for "outsider" groups to feel fully equal at a bodily level to "insider" groups. It is also possible for relative inequalities to persist even without people in these categories sensing this physically or even being aware of it.

Modernity

Modernity, discussed directly in Chapter 3 and throughout the book, is a classic sociological concept that explores the decline of "traditional" social relations, seen as relatively fixed, habitual, and oriented toward stability and persistence, and the rise of more dynamic, fluid, and goal-oriented relationships. Theories of modernity can thereby encompass structural changes (such as urbanization, industrialization, and the rise of capitalism) alongside social and cultural changes (such as the elaboration of instrumental rationality, and the power of contract and exchange).

I fundamentally see modernity as bound up with a distinctive *temporal ontology,* which distinguishes past, present, and future (and thereby, in Bergson's terms, spatializes time) and ontologies of *abstract space* (whereby space is bundled and parcelized). I contest the view that these ontologies are inevitable in wealthy societies and emphasize the historical contingency—and fragility—that underpins them.

Epochalism is a by-product of the modernist temporal ontology that bundles historical periods together through the use of an overarching term, which is then used to give that specific period a coherence. Initially associated with the discipline of history (for example, Erwin Panofsky's discussion of the "gothic"), in recent decades, this is a widely used perspective in social science, especially sociology (see Savage 2009).

Imperial modernity

I invoke the concept of imperial modernity to contest the view that modernity is necessarily associated with the rise of the nation-state, individualism, and liberal democracy. Rather, the term "imperial modernity" recognizes that this shift took place from the seventeenth to the mid-twentieth century during the expansion of imperialism, and it emphasizes that many of the classic themes that concepts of modernity point to are thereby better understood as imperial constructs. Chapter 5 considers the significance of renewed imperial modernity for contemporary inequality trends.

Nation space

I invoke this term—rather than nation-state, or nation—in situations where national projects are organized around a field of organized striving (on which, see Chapter 2) to secure a "national social contract," that is to say, a set of arrangements in which all national citizens are identified as having citizenship rights and are—at least in principle—empowered to participate. My aim in invoking this term is to recognize that nation spaces historically emerge later than national projects—which are more likely to be historically associated with imperial formations—and to emphasize the fragile stakes in maintaining these contracts over time. I therefore contest the assumption that nation spaces are normal and secure, and argue that they only became widespread after 1945, and have become increasingly under stress.

I explain this fragility through my account of Pierre Bourdieu's field analysis (which is explained in Chapter 2) to recognize that over time, the contested nature of nation spaces fades as those with most resources and power come to command national infrastructures, thus leading to disengagement from those who feel excluded (see Chapter 3). *Cultural modernism* is associated with the formation of nation spaces. It sets out stakes that distinguish "pure" artistic qualities and hence sets up relationships that consolidate national fields.

I argue that we should not prioritize the national scale of analysis, as it is only in specific, contingent situations that it takes on overarching significance. In Chapter 4, I consider the implication of national ranking procedures, in Chapter 5, I consider global and continental scale of analysis, and in Chapter 8, I examine the urban scale of inequality.

Liberal modernity

I see liberal modernity as the modulation of modernity that occurs in nation spaces. This definition recognizes that modernity historically originated as an imperial, rather than nation based, project, and that liberal modernity is fragile and contingent. Rather than liberal modernity being largely synonymous with the "modern" more generally, it is in fact only a fleeting part of it. I discuss the fate of liberal modernity with respect to projects of national democracy especially in Chapter 10 and Chapter 11.

Figures

Tables

Notes

Preface

1. This event became part of the defining folklore of British socialist history. Samuel (2016) includes papers from this event and later reflections on it.

2. I have written a full account of the trajectory of British class analysis in Savage (2016). Goldthorpe (2016) is his most emphatic statement about his vision for class analysis.

3. For those wishing to review this debate, see especially Savage et al. (2013, 2015). Critical responses include Mills (2014), Bradley (2014), Rollock (2014), and an entire issue of *Sociological Review* (September 2014).

4. I use "now-time" rather than "present day" or "contemporary" for reasons I lay out in Chapter 3. This distinction between focusing on the "stuff" and "now-time" of inequality is loosely indebted to the philosopher Gilles Deleuze's distinction between the real and the virtual, between striated and smooth space, and to his concern with recovering immanence. I am not a Deleuze scholar and can at best claim only a loose affiliation, but it may be helpful to indicate this debt here, in case readers think that I simply plucked these terms out of the blue.

Introduction

1. The case of the Bolsa Familia in Brazil, introduced during the presidency of Luiz Inácio Lula da Silva (known as "Lula"), has been iconic, but there are numerous examples around the globe.

2. See Hirschmann's (2016) discussion of the work of Krugman (2004) and Piketty and Saez (2003), who explore the formation of these stylized facts.

3. A powerful testament to these growing fractures in American society is Putnam's *Our Kids* (2016).

4. Gitlin (2013), Calhoun (2013).

5. The definition and debate around the significance of the Gini coefficient is discussed in Chapter 1.

6. "By the early 2000s almost 45% of American economics Ph.D.s worked outside of education, with up to one-third of these employed by the federal government" (Reay 2012: 48). Furthermore, American-trained or American-style economists were numerous and prominent members of the staffs of major transnational organizations, such as the World Bank and the International Monetary Fund (IMF), and were increasingly to be found in national education systems and governments outside the United States (Fourcade-Gourinchas 2001; M. Reay 2012: 48).

7. The arguments in the next three paragraphs draw on my previous studies of the history and organization of contemporary social science, notably in Savage (2008, 2010).

8. In sociology, this was characterized by the term "methodeinstreit."

9. On economics, the key reference is Timothy Mitchell's *Rule of Experts* (2002). See also Fourcade (2009), Fourcade et al. (2015), Hirschman and Berman (2014), and Reay (2007, 2012). More generally, on the cultural power of the social sciences in the postwar years, see Mandler (2013). I have discussed the specific features of sociological knowledge on British society in *Identities and Social Change in Britain since 1940* (Savage 2010).

10. This divide has been extensively discussed by Gibbins et al. (1994) as involving the differentiation between "type 1" and "type 2" knowledge.

11. This argument is made in more detail in Halford and Savage (2017).

12. Here I use the term "economic inequality," as the broader term "inequality" is dominated by journals in mathematics and the natural sciences, where it has different connotations.

13. I specifically examine the take-up of categorical inequalities around gender, race, and class in Chapters 6 and 7.

14. The four types are urban governance, global or regional governance, national governance, and climate change mitigation and adaption.

15. In this respect, my argument recognizes the theoretical critiques of "Enlightenment" principles that have proliferated over recent decades, such as in proponents of postmodernism, deconstruction, postcolonialism, and so forth. However, I will show that these arguments fail to push the logic of their critique far enough, and they largely remain in thrall to the master "Enlightenment" concepts that they so powerfully critique.

16. He also shows how philosophically, this can best be understood not through some appeal to abstract principles of the "original position" but by drawing on Adam

Smith's appeal to the "impartial observer," who can detect unfairness not abstractly but by comparing the outcomes in different situations to reflect on what kind of arrangements appear to lead to the better or worse outcomes.

17. For exemplary cases, see Harvey (1989), Beck (1992), Giddens, (1990, 1991), Castells (1996, 1997), and Bauman (1989, 2000, 2007).

CHAPTER 1. TURNING THE TELESCOPE

1. Figure 1.1 is the version that is used in Piketty (2013), which updates Piketty and Saez's original figure to include later observations.

2. For more on the relevance of this work for historical analysis, see Guldi and Armitage (2014). Economic history, which in the early twentieth century had been seen as a major part of social science, and which underscored the development of the influential French Annales School, had become an increasingly specialist discipline. Piketty's work (2013, 2020) marks a powerful reassertion of the value of economic history.

3. National sample surveys became established only in the years after 1945, and it would not be possible to construct time series going back to 1910 without the use of taxation or some other kind of administrative data.

4. See Walter Benjamin (2008 [1935]). It is not necessary for my purposes here to go into the extensive debate this work has generated, though I have explored the relevance of Benjamin's thinking for social science more generally in Savage (2000).

5. His book uses twenty-six kinds of U-shaped visualizations that copy the core motif of Figure 1.1. He is very clear about his strategic use of these icons: "To cut straight to the heart of the matter: Figures I.1 an I.2 show two basic patterns" (Piketty 2013: 23).

6. Keeping the same focus on time periods on the x-axis, he introduces the inverted-U shape in chapter 1 (a nice mirror to the U shape). Then in figure 1.3, he shows how the U shape and the inverted-U shape might relate to each other (the world share of income taken by Europe-America rises until 1990 but then falls (the inverted U), whereas the African and Asian share takes the U shape of rising and falling). Here this analysis of the world share of income going to different parts of the world is of a fundamentally different nature than income inequality in the United States, which Piketty begins with. Nonetheless, using brilliant symphonic techniques, he finds a way to render this diversity on a common visual template. His key device here is to standardize measures by expressing them as relative proportions to a national or global average (Savage 2014), rather than in absolute terms. The latter would tend to produce both more diverse visualizations and also ones that tend toward the kind of growth models that Piketty is critical of. Interestingly, Piketty's recent *Capital and Ideology* fails

to deploy one overarching image among its extensive figures—which is perhaps a reason why its overarching narrative has enjoyed less resonance than *Capital in the Twenty-First Century.*

7. There is now a growing debate about Piketty's use of visualizations (for example, Wright 2015), but this largely adopts a narrow social scientific concern about assessing the realistic accuracy of his graphs. It is certainly true, as is evident from Figure 1.1 that Piketty crops his *y*-axis, which thereby might appear to exaggerate the fall and then rise of inequality. But in his defense, by labeling his axes, this is entirely evident and is not a sleight of hand.

8. They do not cite this $1.90 metric, but note that their calculations are based on World Bank metrics, originally set at $1.01 per day in the 1990s, then increased to $1.25 per day by Ravaillion et al. (2009), and most recently revised upward by Ferreira et al. (2016) to $1.90 to take account of economic fluctuations and different currency conversion rates between nations. These changed dollar figures therefore do not indicate any loosening of the amount of income needed to be out of poverty, but reflect currency and other economic fluctuations, notably those of "purchase price parity" ratios, which are discussed further in Chapter 5.

9. Agamben (1998) and Rancière (2006) see the ambiguity of the relationship between the poor and the political body as central to constructing conceptions of democracy and society itself. More generally, see Brown (2015).

10. This is not the place to review the extensive discussion about the nature of liberal governmentality. See Rose (1999) and Joyce (2003, 2013).

11. Linked to this trend lay a concern to establish whether it was up to poor people themselves to decide what constituted social necessities, or whether more detached criteria could be used. See the classic debate between Townsend (1979), Piachaud (1987), Mack and Lansley (1985), and Sen (1983, 1985). See also Ravaillon (2012).

12. See the entry at https://eur-lex.europa.eu/legal-content/EN/TXT/?uri=CELEX:31985D0008.

13. The initial jumping off point was research in the 1970s that examined what proportion of people would be in poverty globally if the Indian poverty line (46 percent of the Indian per capita national income, $1.12 per day) was projected globally. It was later triangulated by examining data from twenty-five different nations.

14. See Hickel (2017, chapter 1) on the various ways that this goal was adjusted and finessed to make it appear achievable. On the problematic way that poverty reduction strategies have become an imperative with their own baggage, see Ghosh (2011).

15. Francisco Ferreira (personal communication, 2020) notes that this issue has been addressed in recent surveys that carefully seek to take into account how subsistence agriculture affects income estimates, but it is not clear that such allowances have been made for projections going back to the nineteenth century.

16. On Quetelet, see Goldthorpe (2016) and Desrosières (1998).

17. There have been attempts to develop more hybrid measures that deploy an income-shares approach with a singular ratio. For instance, the Palma ratio, comparing the income of the top 10 percent with the bottom 40 percent, is used to measure inequality.

18. In recent years, there has been intense debate about the relative merit of survey and administrative data in the social sciences (see Savage and Burrows 2007, 2009; Goldthorpe 2016). The way that Piketty and Saez succeeded in using taxation data for analyzing income inequality is one of the best examples of the power of mobilizing new data sources rather than relying on surveys alone.

19. See, for instance, the key handbook by Atkinson and Bourguignon (2000, 2015), which emphasizes the need to go beyond income inequality and includes discussions of multidimensional inequality, the income-equivalent approach, measuring inequality by subjective satisfaction, capabilities, and inequality of opportunities (Atkinson and Bourguignon 2015, xxvii–xxxi). And see also the central focus of income inequality in Bourguignon (2015) and Milanovic (2015). The exception, which I discuss fully in Chapter 3, is the interest in wealth inequality, which is taken up by Piketty (2013).

20. Piketty has been considerably criticized for these omissions, especially concerning gender (for example, Perrons 2014). I take up these issues later, especially in Chapters 6 and 7.

21. As an interval variable, income does take the form of a continuous distribution, but even in this case, the shape of this distribution can differ substantially in ways that might not be captured by comparisons of percentile distributions. But the main point here is that many categories (for example, gender, race) are not continuously distributed.

CHAPTER 2. SOCIETY AS A SPORTS FIELD

1. The literature is too vast to provide a comprehensive bibliography, but useful starting points are Coulangeon and Duval (2014) and Hanquinet and Savage (2015). The British study, of which I was a coauthor, has been influential—Bennett et al. (2009).

2. See especially Bourdieu's very early *The Bachelor's Ball* (2008), with its brilliant use of photographs, and more generally, Back (2009). This was a recursive relationship as Bourdieu was fascinated by how visualization was used in routine social practices. See Bourdieu and Whiteside (1996) and Bourdieu and Bourdieu (2004).

3. The classic reflection on Bourdieu's field theory here is Martin (2003).

4. Methodologically, Bourdieu used multiple correspondence analysis, on which, see Le Roux and Rouanet (2010) and Hjellbrekke (2018). Multiple Correspondence

Analysis (MCA) indicates how many axes or dimensions are significant in structuring the oppositions found in survey responses, and Bourdieu shows that in the French case, there is also a third dimension. Visualizations on a flat surface can only readily display two axes (x and y), which leads Bourdieu to present the third axis separately. The social space is therefore not simply a flat space of two dimensions. For further discussion of the principles of MCA, see Bennett et al. (2009) and Hjellbrekke (2018).

5. See Majima (2008) on the relationship between market research and Pierre Bourdieu's sociology. On the contemporary power of geodemographics, see Burrows and Webber (2018).

6. There are numerous methods for dealing with the way that the number of axes exceed two dimensions. See Healy and Moody (2014).

7. The restaurant was downgraded from three stars to one in 1996. Its specialty was pressed duck, raised from its own farm. Diners were awarded a certificate if they chose to eat it. Its 450,000-bottle wine cellar had an estimated value of 25 million euros in 2009.

8. It is undoubtedly the case that sociologists have neglected this economic dimension of Bourdieu's analysis and have been more effective in exploring the cultural dimension. This partly reflects the unfortunate division between economists and sociologists, which this book is seeking to redress.

9. Of course, Bourdieu is still using Cartesian coordinates to map these responses onto the fixed space of Figure 2.1, so there is still a latent Euclidian framing in his work. Nonetheless, there is a grounded inductive procedure in operation here. Rather than assuming that artistic taste is more stratified (and hence spread out) than newspaper preferences, for instance, this becomes evident from inspecting the visual array.

10. There is an extensive literature in anthropology on boundaries and ethnicity, inspired by the work of Fredrick Barth (for example, 1998). There is also considerable discussion in sociology—see Lamont and Molnár (2002). This issue is discussed further in Chapters 6 and 7.

11. See the valuable synthesis in Dieter Vanderbroek (2018). Much of my previous research has been oriented in this approach: See the overview in Savage and Silva (2013), and for a more applied study, see Savage and Gayo-Cal (2011).

12. There is a huge literature on these traditions; see Schütz (1965) and Berger and Luckmann (1967).

13. This includes in the sociology of consumption, which had previously been dominated by Bourdieu's perspectives. See Warde (2005), Hennion (2007), Boltanski (2011), and Bottero (2019).

14. See, for instance, the somewhat different take up of field theory by DiMaggio and Powell (1983), Fligstein and McAdam (2012), and Go and Krause (2016).

15. This critique of variable-based social science follows on the crucial contributions of Andrew Abbott (1992, 2000).

16. My account differs from the more formal and systems-oriented perspective given to it by many social scientists, such as Fligstein (2001) and Fligstein and McAdam (2012). For further reading, see Savage (2010) and Savage and Gayo-Cal (2011).

17. This argument is made more fully by Hanquinet et al. (2014) and is also developed in Chapter 3.

18. In fact, despite the self-proclaimed autonomy of artistic excellence from those promoting art for art's sake, many modernist artists (such as James Joyce) depended either on wealthy patrons or had independent fortunes (such as Marcel Proust). I return to push the implications of this point later in this chapter.

19. Bourdieu's indebtedness to a modernist frame is clear in his emphasis on the artist Manet as leading the "symbolic revolution" that was quintessential to the development of modern fields (Bourdieu 2018).

20. The best introductions to this sociological canon are Giddens (1971) and more recently, Joas and Knöbl (2009).

21. The following section summarizes an extensive body of recent research. Key contributions include Bennett et al. (2009) and Prieur and Savage (2011).

22. It is perhaps telling that neither of these items might appear to constitute popular culture in the early twenty-first century: I return to the nature of change later in the chapter.

23. The debate on cultural omnivorousness is extensive—see Warde et al. (2007) and the recent overviews in Karademir and Warde (2016) and Gayo-Cal (2016).

24. I use the phrase "appear to have withdrawn" advisedly. It is specific listed cultural activities that appear to be less frequented by those with little capital: this is not the same thing as saying that they have withdrawn more widely; indeed, they appear to be closely associated with activities involving kinship and neighbors. See the discussion in Savage et al. (2010).

25. This model "attributes a weighting and a price to various standardized characteristics of the work, typically including dependent variables such as signature, size, medium, condition, provenance, date, subject-matter, as well as independent variables: artist's birthdate, sales date, the city where the sale took or is due to take place, the weekday of the sale, auction theme, etc." and so arrives at a composite value for any art work by summing these various factors. See Upton-Hansen (2018: 19).

26. This argument has been contested, and in some studies where it is possible to ask highly specific questions concerned with particular tastes, something of the older capital composition axis might still be found. The strongest proponent claiming that the capital composition is still at work is Will Atkinson (2017), who has reanalyzed the British 2003 Cultural Capital and Social Exclusion study, which Bennett et al. (2009) had originally claimed to show that the capital composition axis had declined and had been replaced by an age axis. Atkinson's analysis of the "space of lifestyles" claims to show a second axis akin to Bourdieu's. However, the variables he used to construct this space

of lifestyles exclude many of the areas that Bourdieu himself used: most notably any questions on musical taste, literature, holidays, and eating. And the differentiation on the second axis, which he claims to be that of capital composition, is largely driven by questions on sport alone (nine of the seventeen modalities with above-average contributions to the second axis pertain to sport), which as he also shows are influenced by age and gender rather than capital composition. Furthermore, this second axis constitutes only 18 percent of the variance, compared to 56 percent for the first axis. The subsequent debate between W. Atkinson and Deeming (2016) and Flemmen and Hjellbrekke (2016) regarding the structure of British eating practices further suggests that Atkinson is looking to reproduce Bourdieu's original findings in ways that stretch the evidence.

27. This argument is also made by Savage et al. (2015) in their study of the Great British Class Survey, where they argue that differences in economic capital are more powerful than those of cultural and social capital in structuring contemporary class relations.

28. "It is not entirely clear whether in the strictest sense there is any need for capital as a distinct theoretic term, if one also has field position" (Martin and Gregg 2015: 53).

CHAPTER 3. RENEWING MARX

1. Economists have pointed out, however, that Piketty says remarkably little about the Cambridge value controversy, which animated the discipline in the 1960s and 1970s. He thus largely avoids explicating the theoretical status of capital (Soskice 2014).

2. There is a lively and important argument about the timing of the development of a distinctive youth culture, with several historians pushing this timing back to the early twentieth century and downplaying the 1960s. In fact, this timing would fit the curve of Figure 3.1 even better than those who emphasize the moment of the 1960s counterculture.

3. Piketty's recent *Capital and Ideology* makes his determination to bring the negative aspects of French experience to light even more apparent. Much of this book emphasizes that the French Revolution in 1789 actually facilitated the consolidation of property and accumulation during in the decades afterward.

4. It is true that Piketty's calculations are premised on findings from a specific time period—mainly 1975 to 2008—when rising asset prices, especially in owner-occupied housing, allowed the historically unusual accumulation of wealth assets (Offer 2017). These findings are reflected in Piketty's market-based conception of wealth as tradable assets, rather than a more theorized conception of capital (see notably Soskice 2014; Boushey et al. 2017). See more generally Mazzucato (2018), who explores how modern economics—by implication including the thinking of Piketty—fails to distinguish

value from price and hence defaults to a framing that cannot conceive capital in terms other than the price it can realize in market exchange.

5. In 2010, this figure was 750,000 euros, which has been deflated appropriately for previous periods.

6. Here, Piketty follows closely in the footsteps of other economists who have concentrated on capital, for instance Joan Robinson (1952: v), who famously argued for the significance of dynamic analysis that "cannot explain how an economy behaves in given conditions, without reference to past history," whereas "static analysis purports to describe a situation of equilibrium."

7. Admittedly, these stocks of capital are defined at today's "market" prices. It does therefore follow that current market transactions do matter a lot, even if you yourself don't sell. Thus, changes in market conditions can have a dramatic impact on the value of your wealth, even if you don't make any transactions: housing is especially important here (see generally Soskice 2014).

8. According to the QS World University Rankings 2019, Harvard places third, Princeton thirteenth, and Yale fifteenth.

9. Note that A. Atkinson and Harrison (1978) analyzed the savings side properly, whereas Piketty did not (to Atkinson's disappointment). See my review of Piketty (Savage 2014) for a brief comment on this point.

10. It is symptomatic of Bourdieu's remarkable analytical gifts that he invokes both a historical / temporal and spatial sensitivity in his writings. However, these are not effectively synthesized, and it is notable that his appreciation of capital from the mid-1960s precedes his interest in field analysis, which takes over from the 1970s and which largely leads him away from sustained concerns with temporality thereafter.

11. Seen in this light, modernist literature can readily by seen as evoking this redemptive project. Although clearly concerned with an avant-garde literature of "writing for writing's sake," a central theme of Marcel Proust's work—indebted to his Bergsonian concern with duration and "time recovered"—was artistic synthesis and reconciliation. As Roberts (2011: 202) notes, this synthesis involved challenging temporal differentiation: "Proust's own artistic dream to construct his magnum opus like a church or a cathedral." The same redemptive currents are central to James Joyce's iconic *Ulysses*, not least in its climactic last sentence proffered by Molly Bloom: "then he asked me would I yes to say yes my mountain flower and first I put my arms around him yes and drew him down to me so he could feel my breasts all perfume yes and his heart was going like mad and yes I said yes I will Yes."

12. Bourdieu's account of the effectiveness of autonomous field processes for producing value is best elaborated in his account of scientific knowledge (see Bourdieu 2004), but as Tony Bennett (2005) shows, it underpins all his extensive work on cultural fields.

13. Abbott's (2016: 52) definition of historicality is "the sum of those processes by which events contrive to leave relatively permanent traces of themselves in the ongoing present." Although theoretical critiques of standard linear conceptions of time are commonplace, with a frequent insistence on the comingling of time, history, and social science (for example, Abrams 1981; Adam 1990; 1998; Giddens 1992; Abbott 2001, 2016; Pierson 2004), these frequently do not draw out the wider implications of pursuing a deeper attention to history, as I propose here. A partial exception is the work of Andrew Abbott (2001, 2016), whose *system of professions* offers an exemplary account of long-term processes of social change that can be developed by using an elaborated conception of time. Social scientific research generally defaults to these linear conceptions of time as a matter of course even though theoretical reflections on temporality lead in other directions.

14. To be sure, earlier precedents can be found, perhaps the most interesting of which was Antonio Gramsci's discussion of the rise of "Americanism and Fordism" during the interwar years, but his conception was not itself taken up until much later.

15. The classic discussions are Jameson (1993) and Harvey (1989). See also Featherstone (2007).

16. Terms that have been used by sociologists to characterize these shifts include the emergence of "disorganized capitalism" (Lash and Urry 1987), "post Fordism"' (S. Amin 1990), "individualization" (Giddens 1990; Beck and Beck-Gersheim 2001), "reflexive (or late) modernity" (Beck 1992; Beck et al. 1994), the "risk society" (Beck 1992), "globalization" (Albrow 1996; Robertson 1992), "neoliberalism" (Rose 1999), and the "network society" (Castells 1996).

17. This temporal ontology is locked into key analytical moves in sociology, such as the distinction between structure and agency, which is premised on this ontological temporal difference between past, enduring structures, and a contemporary, contingent agency that breaks from them. This debate was central to Anthony Giddens's structuration theory, which proved to be highly influential in the 1980s and beyond, as well as in the long-term distinctions between macro- and microsociology.

18. The reliance on concepts of "generation" here is itself problematic, as Abbott (2016: especially chapter 1) demonstrates, because it places arbitrary boundaries around fluid sets of lives and trajectories.

19. To be fair, Rosa's work is not an empirical study so much as a sophisticated theoretical reworking and updating of how conceptions of modernity involve an ontological focus on the "present." Nonetheless, Rosa's understanding of the significance of the past is necessarily limited—as is bound to be the case for anyone working in the paradigm of modernity. For instance, his categories of inertia serve as a "brake" on "acceleration" (two highly revealing terms), which renders inertia not as a systematic force in the sense of mainstream science (that of gravity, for instance), but as ad hoc exceptions to his general claims about the ubiquity of acceleration. He admits that

there are natural limits to speed, "islands of deceleration" (he cites the Amish community), dysfunctional side effects (for example, the traffic jam), ideologies of deceleration (such as "slow towns"), slowdowns as time out (for example, retreats), and finally "structural and cultural rigidity." These points hardly amount to systematic inertia, but they are at best the backwash of the acceleration processes he privileges. It is something of a shock to realize that these are his main admissions to the significance of the past in contemporary social life.

20. This conceptualization, however, is odd. Philosophically, this use of the "present" extends away from an existential moment of awareness (as discussed in the phenomenological tradition, see, for example, Merlau-Ponty 1989; Munn 1992; Hodges 2008) into a longer process defined by a distinctive time horizon. So, we might construe the present as also existing in five years (or five weeks) time, according to this logic, if the same time horizon is in operation.

21. Ultimately, Rosa resorts to a problematic argument that "the present, then, is the time-span for which (to use an idea developed by Reinhart Koselleck) the horizons of experience and expectation coincide" (Rosa 2003: 7), which thus abstracts experience from longer-term historical process and assumes that boundaries can be placed around it as some kind of time horizon. Consider Bergson's (2002: 159) brilliant critique of this mode of reasoning: "What you are considering is the concrete present such as it is actually lived by consciousness we may say that the present consists, in large measure, in the immediate past. In the fraction of a second which covers the briefest possible perception of light, billions of vibrations have taken place of which the first is separated from the last by an interval which is enormously divided. Your perception, however instantaneous consists then in an incalculable multitude of remembered elements; in truth every perception is already memory. *Practically, we perceive only the past.*"

CHAPTER 4. THE RANKING OF NATIONS

1. See https://www.equalitytrust.org.uk/.

2. The critical literature on *The Spirit Level* is considerable, including Goldthorpe (2009), Saunders (2010), and Delhey and Dragolov (2013).

3. Bourdieu's sociology is littered with conceptual terms that read such tastes as deeply embedded in power and domination—but the extent to which they are necessarily organized in such terms is more uncertain and contested. It is for these reasons that Bourdieu-inspired sociology can be seen to impart a more antagonistic view of social relationships to its analysis than might be warranted by people's own reported views. See Warde (2011), Irwin (2015) and Bottero (2019). For a stronger and more agonistic view, see W. Atkinson (2010).

4. The powerful interdisciplinary perspective has become even more evident in Wilkinson and Pickett's follow-up, *The Inner Level* (2019).

5. There is no evidence of mutual influence between the work of economists such as Piketty, who champion income-shares approaches, and Wilkinson and Pickett. The fact that they both nonetheless adopted a similar visual strategy is itself telling.

6. There is now an extensive literature on the "economics of happiness," triggered by Anthony Easterlin's (1974) paper "Does Economic Growth Improve the Human Lot? Some Empirical Evidence," which backs up the Wilkinson and Pickett core argument that once a certain threshold of material prosperity is achieved, further economic growth does not enhance aggregate levels of "happiness."

7. See https://www.pbs.org/newshour/politics/obama-set-to-speak-on-income-gap-between-rich-and-poor.

8. The variance on trust goes from a low score of 10 in Portugal, to a high of 66.5 in Denmark.

9. To be sure, principles of statistical inference are increasingly used in comparative research, especially for establishing whether variation among cases may be due to chance or error. These approaches are indeed consistent with the large-scale comparative research championed in the inequality paradigm. But my main point here is that statistics has no monopoly on establishing causality, and there are ways of elaborating causation using narrative-oriented methods that are more strongly embedded in the humanities.

10. Bourdieu's *Distinction* is a partial exception to this point, as his work is more consistent with the literary monograph approach, with visuals used as singular illustrations. As I have shown in Chapter 2, this is because Bourdieu himself was writing before the recent take-off of the inequality paradigm.

11. "Historians, we may then say, are concerned with finding their evidence from among a stock of relics. In contrast—and this is the difference I want to stress—sociologists have open to them a possibility that is largely denied to historians. While sociologists can, and often do, draw on relics as evidence, in just the same way as historians, they can, in addition generate evidence. This is of course what they are doing when they engage in 'fieldwork.' They are producing, as a basis for inferences, materials that did not exist before. And it is, I would argue, such generated evidence, rather than evidence in the form of relics—in other words, evidence that is 'invented' rather than evidence that is discovered—that constitutes the main empirical foundations of modern sociology" (Goldthorpe 1991: 213–214).

12. In fact, Goldthorpe's article was also widely disputed at the time, and might now be read as the last blast of a "modernist" social science manifesto—see Bryant (1994) and M. Mann (1992).

13. Goldthorpe's own recent advocacy that sociology model itself on demography, the social science discipline above all others that relies on long-term historical records

often derived from registration records (such as birth, marriage, and death certificates), demonstrates how far he has moved from his 1991 position.

14. Wilkinson and Pickett do conduct some spatial comparisons within nations (notably between American states)—but this does not alter their fundamental reliance on a small-*N* comparison between geographically defined cases.

15. Mazzucato (2018) draws attention to the historical compromises in constructing these measures and the sometimes arbitrary reclassification of what counts as "national income." But for the purposes of my argument here, it is the success of such measures in gaining legitimacy that matters.

16. On the problem of deriving adequate measures in Africa, see Jerven (2013).

17. Notably, Piketty et al. (2017). The principles are laid out Alvaredo et al. (2016).

18. See Mazzucato (2018), who explores how these measures are also skewed toward assets that can be sold and are hence misleading in their own terms.

19. This argument has been eloquently made by Julian Go (2008: 207), who argues that "we can think of a *global field* or 'global political' field as a worldwide arena in which states or other actors (corporations, nongovernmental organizations, international organizations) compete with each other over species of capital." See also Go and Krause (2016), and Krause (2015).

20. It is remarkable that only twenty years ago, major advances were made by scholars developing strategies for qualitative comparative analysis, which emphasized that national characteristics could not be reduced to a basket of indicators and that progress in comparative analysis required an understanding of the constellation of processes involved (for example, Skocpol and Somers 1980; Ragin and Becker 1992; Mahoney and Rueschemeyer 2003; Ragin 2014). The idea that nations could be reduced to basket of metrics would have had very little purchase from within this framing.

21. The literature on imperialism is vast. Edward Said's (1977) classic *Orientalism* articulates the centrality of colonial relationships to the elaboration of European highbrow culture.

22. Fanon (1952: 6).

23. It is telling that there are different ways of enumerating "nations" and hence no definitive agreement about how many there are.

24. http://www.oecd.org/about/members-and-partners/, accessed July 7, 2019.

25. See https://www.oxfam.org/en/research/commitment-reducing-inequality -index.

26. The top ten performers are Sweden, Belgium, Denmark, Norway, Germany, Finland, Austria, France, Netherlands, and Luxembourg. See https://oi-files-d8-prod .s3.eu-west-2.amazonaws.com/s3fs-public/file_attachments/rr-commitment-reduce -inequality-index-170717-en.pdf (p. 8).

CHAPTER 5. THE RETURN OF EMPIRE

1. See the discussion of this tradition of poverty research in Chapter 1.

2. Effectively this means including China, India, and Brazil, and large numbers of Middle Eastern nations in their analyses. However the World Inequality Database (WID) coverage of many smaller nations in South America, Africa, and Asia is very patchy. See Simson (2018) and Simson and Savage (2020) for the fullest discussion of the global trends.

3. Figure 5.2 defies Tufte's (1990, 2001) principles of social science visualization, because its x-axis does not use a linear scale. A quick glance at Figure 5.2 could lead to a biased understanding of global inequality trends.

4. They also note that "there has been a paucity of empirical studies within Economics that have employed absolute or centrist measures, despite the fact that there is no economic theory that favours relative over absolute notions of inequality" (Nino-Zarazua et al. 2017: 663), which is exactly the point underscoring my emphasis on the need to understand the weight of history.

5. In A. Atkinson (2015), figure 1 measures inequality in selected world countries by comparing the Gini coefficient in twenty-four European nations, seven Asian nations, seven North and South American nations, one African nation, and Australia.

6. The reason Norway experienced its record year in 2005 has to do with changes in tax legislation, which came into effect in 2006. Stock owners prepared for this and took out more fiscal income than usual that particular year.

7. The comparative differences within European elites are explored by Korsnes et al. (2017); see notably the paper by Hartmann (2017).

8. These processes would also explain the decline of inequality during the twentieth century, which lie at the heart of Piketty's (2013) critique of the Kuznets curve. Piketty's argument, echoed by Scheidel (2018), is that these declines reflect the break-up of capital as a result of war and revolution. While this is undoubtedly true, these decades were also the years when European nation-building projects were fully in train as their empires were lost. This process of nation-state building led to a concern to establish a national consensus in a way that had not been so significant during their imperial formations. The significance of the Beveridge report in Britain after the Second World War exemplifies this argument perfectly, but it has its counterparts in many other nations. We can thus distinguish between national formations that are better placed to address inequality and imperial formations that generate inequality through their elaboration of powerful elite corps that become central to imperial leadership. This line of reasoning suggests that the success of the European Union was precisely as a means of allowing European nations to collaborate while retaining large swathes of their political, social, and cultural autonomy. Brexiteers wrongly see the European Union as undermining national autonomy, when in fact it has allowed national models to adapt to

globalized and financialized capitalism with relative (even if creaking) effectiveness. It is likely that by seeking to evoke the British imperial model in a situation where British power is massively diminished, Brexit will leave the United Kingdom in an unfortunate "no person's land."

CHAPTER 6. INSIDERS AND OUTSIDERS

1. It should be clear from the framing of this paragraph that I see the organization of categorical inequalities as historical and not as natural constructs. As legions of writers have emphasized, the way that these inequalities are deemed as natural is often—though not always, as I go on to discuss—central to their organization and I do not impart any analytical significance to this "naturalization." For theoretical discussions about categorical inequality in general, see Tilly (1999) and Douglas (2007).

2. The literature is now vast. See Porter (1995), Desrosières (2002), and Ruppert (2011).

3. Emigh et al. (2015) note that formally, the categories of slave and free do not entail racial divisions, but they go on to show that these legal statuses are racialized and gendered. They conclude: "In sum, around 1850, race, not class, had become the most important determinant of legal rights in the United States (especially in contrast to Europe). . . . Rights were highly racialized: blacks, even if free, were assumed to be biologically inferior to whites, and slavery was restricted to blacks" (p. 496).

4. Evelyn Ruppert (2009) has shown how the initial foray by the Canadian government to conduct a census of indigenous peoples in 1911 involved military-style interventions.

5. In very interesting work, Evelyn Ruppert has traced the "double identification" produced by the Canadian Census, whereby not only was the state counting people, but also people were themselves learning to become subjects of the state.

6. On the cultural power of liberalism, see, most famously, Michel Foucault (1976, 1977) and his admirers, such as Rose (2001), Joyce (2003, 2013), and Bennett (2003).

7. The most powerful accounts of this current are from postcolonial scholars (for example, Chakrabarty 2003).

8. For Wahrman (2004: 277), talking of the "making of the modern self" in later eighteenth-century England, "in practice we often find the emphases on individuality and on essentialized identity categories seamlessly braided together."

9. My point here pushes on a well-known argument that it is only in the neoliberal period of the later twentieth century that the elicitation of individuality becomes central to governmental strategies. Foucault's own focus on the boundary of 1800 as marking the rise of modern regimes, for instance those associated with the panopticon, appears to misjudge the timing of these developments.

10. The very strong association between eugenics and the development of social science methodology is now well established; for example, see MacKenzie (1981) and C. Renwick (2012) on the British case.

11. On witchcraft, see Brian Easlea (1980) and Silvia Federici (2004). In wartime, the Japanese state organization of about 200,000 "comfort women" as sexual slaves to Japanese soldiers during the Second World War is a notorious case. (It is noteworthy here that the women involved were also ethnic outsiders, mainly being Korean and Chinese.) The mass collective rape and abuse of women by men in warfare contexts would be another instance of state-sponsored violence.

12. On critical race theory, see the accounts of Gillborn (2005). An excellent account of concepts of "racial capitalism," which are consistent with this argument, is Gargi Bhattacharyya (2018).

13. For Mies (1998: 38), "capitalism cannot function without patriarchy, that the goal of this system, namely the never-ending process of capital accumulation, cannot be achieved unless patriarchal man-woman relations are maintained or newly created."

14. The designation of family law as a "separate realm did not leave 'tradition' intact; rather it involved transformation through processes of codification and standardization. What had once been an integrated set of social behaviours (family and property, for instance, were inseparable) . . . were now separated and subjected to different but formally defined legal jurisdictions" (J. Scott 2019: 44).

15. The campaigns against witchcraft, which were especially powerful from the later sixteenth century to the eighteenth century, are an iconic case in point.

16. This relationship has been most emphatically studied by Michael Mann (2012), to whom the arguments of this section are indebted.

17. Andreski's (1963) military participation ratio encapsulates one aspect of this trend.

18. The British case is again iconic here—see the discussions in Szreter (2002) and Savage (2010).

19. Forms of primitive accumulation do continue until the present day, especially in situations involving the opening up of new markets. See, for instance, Elyachar (2005) and J. Chan (2014). In recent decades, the commercialization and expansion of care work has been a major driver of this shift. See Bridget Anderson (2000) and Chang (2000). The return of modern slavery is also striking testimony to this point.

20. The literature is extensive. See McKibbin (1998), Todd (2014), and Savage (2015).

21. Goldthorpe's focus on men was controversial and led to a strong feminist critique (Stanworth 1984; Britten and Heath 1982). Although he defended his position strenuously (Goldthorpe 1983), his later work has invariably included women along with men.

22. The concept of service class can be confusing, as it is often conflated with "service workers," who might be conducting routine work, such as customer assistance. For

Goldthorpe, following Austro-Marxist Karl Renner, the term connotes those who "serve" their employer by offering special skills or by possessing delegated managerial authority. This distinguishes them from laborers who conduct discrete productive tasks. See the extensive debate about the service class concept in Goldthorpe (1982), Savage et al. (1992), Butler and Savage (1995), Evans and Mills (1998), and Goldthorpe (2000).

23. But note that any of these terms (especially "calling" and "vocation") could be used in contexts that have no bearing on issues of mobility.

Chapter 7. Visceral Inequality in the Twenty-First Century

1. "Life politics *presumes* (a certain level of) emancipation. . . . While emancipatory politics is a politics of life chances, life politics is a politics of lifestyle" (Giddens 1991: 214).

2. The most important statement of Goldthorpe's "class structural" perspective remains *Social Mobility and the Class Structure in Britain* (Goldthorpe et al. 1980). See also his later statements in Erikson and Goldthorpe (1992) and Goldthorpe (2007). I discuss the relationship between these different styles of social mobility research in Savage (1997). See also Friedman and Savage (2018) for a wider discussion of the relationship between conceptions of social mobility and temporality that inform my discussion here.

3. For ease of reading, I am not discussing the technical aspects of Goldthorpe's definition of social fluidity, as "individuals' chances of mobility or immobility considered net of class structural change" (see Bukodi et al. 2017: 842).

4. Goldthorpe et al.'s (1980) classic statement on the significance of distinguishing relative and absolute mobility is well aware that absolute mobility is of greater importance for analyzing "class formation." However, his later work largely eschews an interest in this topic, even though it is of much greater historical importance. See my discussion in Savage (1997).

5. For example, in Spain, Gil-Hernández et al. (2017: 23) note that "both men and women have experienced a significant increase in social fluidity over time. For men, this increase is modest, accounting for a 12% decline in the intergenerational association between the oldest cohort born in the1920s and the youngest cohort in the 1970s. For women, it is substantial, accounting for a 33% decline."

6. But even in the United Kingdom, this issue is contested and should not be assumed to be settled. A lot depends on how robust class categories are for capturing mobility parameters. In the United Kingdom, economists Blanden et al. (2005), who came into prominence in 2005 by claiming that social mobility—measured in their terms by the prospects of children moving into different income groups compared to their parents—has fallen for those born between 1958 and 1970. Erikson and Goldthorpe (2010) repudiated their argument by emphasizing that income data were not as reliable

as that for social class, because these data are harder to measure accurately and because incomes fluctuate more readily than does occupational class. But this defense appears to stack the cards in their own interests (because it is assumed that short-term income fluctuations, which might unsettle their argument, are not to be taken as seriously as the long term stability which might be more evident by using class categories).

7. Their national comparisons are between Australia, the Netherlands, the United Kingdom, the United States, Denmark, Finland, Norway, Poland, France, Spain, Slovenia, Germany, and Italy.

8. In fact, the policing of immigration does also raise issues of class exclusion, given that visa entry is more skewed toward privileged migrants (see, for example, Surak 2020).

9. The following countries are those who have more than 40 percent women in parliament (percentages listed in parentheses): Rwanda (61.30), Bolivia (53.10), Cuba (48.90), Nicaragua (45.70), Sweden (43.60), Mexico (42.60), Finland (42.00), Senegal (41.80), South Africa (41.80), Norway (41.40), and Namibia (41.30).

10. Erola has also pushed this argument though his research on the predictors of social disadvantage (Vauhkonen et al. 2011).

11. There is an obvious parallel with the operation of "power laws" amply discussed in social networks that emphasize nonlinear effects. See, for instance, the summary of Esping Andersen and Wagner (2012: 475): "the importance of non-linearities has been corroborated in inter-generational income mobility studies (Björklund & Jantti, 2009; Couch & Lillard, 2004; Jäntti et al., 2006). These show that parent–child correlations are especially strong at the very top and bottom of the income distribution, but comparatively weak in the middle." And see also Sirniö et al. (2016).

12. Research on educational attainment also demonstrates clearly the specific power of elite universities and schools in bestowing advantages. Jerrim et al. (2015: 30) argue that "while academic achievement in high school is clearly an important mechanism by which high SES (status) families gain an advantage in accessing high status institutions, substantial direct effects of family background nevertheless remain. This suggests that high SES families are able to use their superior resources in multiple ways to gain qualitative advantages within the education system."

13. There is also a slight inverse process of bottom-end outliers, especially with respect to the mean income of graduates. This "bottom-end" stigmatization—which can be directed against racial minorities, migrants, and other disadvantaged groups, is a mirror of the meritocratic reaction against the top end, as some kind of reaction against groups who might also be perceived as not biding by the rules of the meritocratic game can also be expected.

CHAPTER 8. CITIES, ELITES, AND ACCUMULATION

1. *Las Meninas* is iconic in part because of Foucault's (1971) deliberations on it in *The Order of Things* as representing the birth of the modern episteme.

2. The UN World Cities Report (2016) also contains analyses of inequality (though using Gini coefficients) in different cities, which generally supports these impressions: the report notes (table C.1) that the most unequal cities are in South Africa: in Buffalo, Ekurhuleni (East Rand), eThekwini (Durban), Johannesburg, Port Elizabeth and Tshwane (Pretoria).

3. The UN World Cities Report (2016) indicates variation within Asia, with non-Chinese cities being more unequal: "the highest degrees of inequality are found in Hong Kong; Ho Chi Minh City, Viet Nam; and Chiang Mai, Thailand, with Gini coefficients above 0.5" (see their box 4.2).

4. Knight (2017) reports urban Gini coefficients of .33 in 2002 rising to .36 in 2013. This compares with rural Gini coefficients of .35 and .40, and national coefficients of .46 falling slightly to .43 in these same years. Xie and Zhou (2014) demonstrate the unusually marked significance of the urban-rural divide in explaining China's high levels of inequality increase.

5. Davis and Feng (2009: 26) report "that China has shifted from a status-ranked society toward one in which economic assets trump . . . the sharp urban-rural divide has eroded, and for the first time since the mid-1950s, those on the lowest rungs of the urban income ladder stand below those at the top of the rural ladder." Chinese urbanization is proceeding faster than in any other part of the world, with the proportion of urban dwellers rising from 22.87 percent to 51.77 percent between 1985 and 2011.

6. Chetty et al. (2014) located individuals born between 1980 and 1991, and linked their income at age 32 to the pre-tax household income of their parents when they first filed that they had dependent children. In doing so, the researchers were able to systematically determine the prospects of children born in different parts of the United States in moving up or down the income scale compared to their parents in a remarkably granular fashion. Social mobility research conventionally differentiates "outflow" from "inflow." In the former, attention is directed to the prospects of children from different social positions; in the latter, research considers the origins of people in different social locations.

7. An exemplary study using longitudinal data is Gorning and Goebel (2018), who document clear income polarization in German cities, with middle earners becoming less frequent compared to high and low earners.

8. See also Krishna (2013a) on Indian cities. He found "a common verdict of limited and precarious upward mobility. In spite of having lived in this city for multiple generations, the men and women of Bangalore slums make their livings in most part by providing low-skilled services and plying lowskilled trades" (Krishna 2013a: 1015).

9. "Our main result concerning wealth inequality in Sweden is that it appears to have increased since 2007. The recorded rise in the Gini coefficient and top wealth shares is about ten percent, and almost all of this increase occurred around the years of the financial crisis 2008–2009. A decomposition analysis shows that it can be attributed primarily to more unequal holdings of apartments and bank savings" (Lundberg and Waldenstrom 2018: 540).

10. See https://www.topuniversities.com/university-rankings/world-university-rankings/2021.

Chapter 9. The Force of Information and Technology

1. On the relation between technology and power, see Mackenzie and Wajcman (1985), Law and Hassard (1999), and Latour (2005).

2. On the take-up of assembly line methods in the United Kingdom, where there were much stronger craft traditions, see Zeitlin and Herrigel (2000) and Sabel and Zeitlin (1985).

3. This argument has been pursued with respect to motor cars, refrigerators, housing design, and so forth. The case of motor cars, given the early prominence of electrical and steam cars (which were ultimately eclipsed by the internal combustion engine), is especially noteworthy.

4. There are differing interpretations on the extent to which Marx was fundamentally a technological determinist. G. Cohen (1978) makes one of the most powerful statements regarding the power of the forces of production to drive forward social change. There is no doubt that Marx's rendition of the shift from the formal to the real subsumption of labor is wedded to what he saw as the changing relationship between humans and machines.

5. See also Jasanoff's reference to "collectively held, institutionally stabilized, and publicly performed visions of desirable futures, animated by shared understandings of forms of social life and social order attainable through, and supportive of, advances in science and technology" (Jasanoff 2015: 4).

6. See the debate inspired by Habermas on the public sphere, including the digital public sphere (for example, Calhoun 1992).

7. See https://www.transparency.org/news/feature/corruption_and_inequality_how_populists_mislead_people.

8. There is an extensive, indeed exhaustive literature on cultural omnivorousness in cultural sociology. I do not need to review the extensive ins and outs of this debate other than to note that for the reasons explained here, this literature largely supports my claims. Valuable recent reviews are Karademir and Warde (2016) and Gayo (2015), who especially points out the Eurocentric nature of the debate.

9. The failure of more complex visualizations to work effectively on this narrative basis is striking. A good example is the way that social network analysis, which through the deployment of sociograms has been at the forefront of visualizations, has failed to capture such a central role—unless reduced to a simpler principle, such as the "six degrees of separation" made famous by Duncan Watts (2003).

Chapter 10. Reinstating the Time of Politics

1. "The fact that colonists were all European settlers and no native political institutions intervened meant that the principles of British constitutional government flowed steadily into the governance of the colonies. . . . It soon became apparent that if the colonists were to be acknowledged as British subjects with full entitlements to natural and hence legal freedoms, then the modern form of British representative government . . . could hardly be withheld from them. Yet that would require a fundamental resolution of the problem of sovereignty. The contradiction reached a breaking point with the American revolution" (Chatterjee 2012: 93–94).

2. I do not have the scope to go into the extensive debate on the relationship between nationalism and modernity. It is helpfully reviewed in Calhoun (2007).

3. See also Jessop (2016: 32), who also questions the "originary (founding) myth of the Westphalian system."

4. Chatterjee makes a similar point in his call to recognize an "early modernity" before the nation-state.

5. Characteristically, the crucial final part of Churchill's famous "We shall fight on the beaches" speech in 1940 is rarely remembered. It reads "we shall never surrender, and if, which I do not for a moment believe, this island or a large part of it were subjugated and starving, then our Empire beyond the seas, armed and guarded by the British Fleet, would carry on the struggle, until, in God's good time, the New World, with all its power and might, steps forth to the rescue and the liberation of the old." See https://www.presentationmagazine.com/winston-churchill-speech-we-shall-fight-them-on-the-beaches-8003.htm.

6. These ideas about the overload of national state infrastructures have been made in a different register before, notably by Jürgen Habermas and the scholars associated with the Frankfurt School in the 1980s.

7. Here Moore is very similar to much historiography, certainly on Germany, which fixates on the rise of fascism as being the overriding issue.

8. See Thompson's (1965) brilliant reply to Anderson's critique.

9. This is an important feature of the work of Theda Skocpol (1979), which led to the formulation of "state-centered" theories of social change (see Evans et al. 1985).

10. See https://www.brookings.edu/blog/fixgov/2018/12/28/congress-in-2019-the
-2nd-most-educated-and-least-politically-experienced-house-freshman-class/.

11. The Thomsen index is no longer commonly used to measure class voting (see, e.g., Evans 1999) but is retained here for ease of reference.

12. "The political configuration that emerged during the struggle for independence reflected the tendency of various political groups to rally around a dominant party in an effort to defeat a common enemy" (Kuenzi and Lambright 2001: 439).

13. See also Oliver Heath (2016), who has further charted the significance of the class gap in electoral turnout.

14. See, for instance, the studies of Savage et al. (2015) on friendship ties in the United Kingdom. See also the social media and virtuality debate (Boulianne 2015).

15. It is a striking comment that compared to the extensive literature on class and voting, research on the relationship between race, ethnicity and voting is far less extensive, despite considerable evidence that this divide plays a very powerful role.

Chapter 11. What Is to Be Done?

1. The contemporary importance of Cobbett has recently been reasserted by Craig Calhoun (2015: 160). He notes how "Cobbett declaimed against the injustice, corruption, and harm caused by an interlocked system of government and finance that he called The Thing. It was paying for war on credit that first attracted his attention to the large-scale politics of financial abuse; these were soon joined by the issues of paper money and inflation." Calhoun rightly brings out the resonance of these issues today.

2. The six demands were (1) a vote for every man [sic] twenty-one years of age, of sound mind, and not undergoing punishment for a crime; (2) the secret ballot; (3) no property qualification for members of Parliament; (4) payment of members; (5) equal constituencies; and (6) annual Parliamentary elections.

3. The phrase is commonly attributed to John F. Kennedy, who used it in a 1963 speech to combat criticisms that a dam project he was inaugurating was a pork barrel project.

4. On their ability to mislead, see Mazzucato (2018: chapter 3), who traces the changing conventions by which GDP is measured and shows that its recent incarnations depend on a neoclassical vision of value.

5. Nussbaum's (2001) core features are as follows. Being able to live to the end of a human life of normal length; Being able to have good health, adequate nutrition, adequate shelter, opportunities for sexual satisfaction and choice in reproduction, and mobility; Being able to avoid unnecessary and nonbeneficial pain and to have pleasurable experiences; Being able to use the senses, imagine, think, and reason, and to have the educational opportunities necessary to realize these capacities; Being able to have attachments to things and persons outside ourselves; Being able to form a conception of

the good and to engage in critical reflection about the planning of one's own life; Being able to live for and to others, to recognize and show concern for other human beings; Being able to live with concern for and in relation to animals and the world of nature; Being able to laugh, to play, to enjoy recreational activities; Being able to live one's own life and no one else's; enjoying freedom of association and freedom from unwarranted search and seizure.

References

Abbott, Andrew. 1992. "From Causes to Events: Notes on Narrative Positivism." *Sociological Methods & Research* 20(4): 428–455.

———. 2001a. *Time Matters: On Theory and Method*. Chicago: University of Chicago Press.

———. 2001b. *Chaos of Disciplines*. Chicago: University of Chicago Press.

———. 2016. *The Promise of Process—Processual Sociology*. Chicago: University of Chicago Press.

Abrahamian, Atossa Araxia. 2018. "The Inequality Industry." *The Nation*, September 13.

Abrams, Meyer Howard. 1981. *A Glossary of Literary Terms*. New York: Holt, Rinehart and Winston.

Accominotti, Fabien. 2021. *Consecrated: Modern Art in Paris between Revolution and Hierarchy*. Princeton, NJ: Princeton University Press.

Accominotti, Fabien, and D. Tadmon. 2020. "How the Reification of Merit Breeds Inequality: Theory and Experimental Evidence." International Inequalities Institute Working Paper 42. London: London School of Economics.

Adam, Barbara. 1990. *Time and Social Theory*. Cambridge: Polity.

———. 1998. *Timescapes of Modernity: The Environment and Invisible Hazards*. London: Routledge.

———. 2008. "The Timescapes Challenge: Engagement with the Invisible Temporal." In Barbara E. Adam et al., eds., *Researching Lives through Time: Time, Generation and Life Stories*. Timescapes Working Paper Series 1. Leeds: University of Leeds, pp. 7–12.

Adkins, Lisa, M. Cooper, and M. Konings. 2019. "Class in the 21st Century: Asset Inflation and the New Logic of Inequality." In *Environment and Planning: Economy and Space*, in press.

————. 2020. *The Asset Economy.* Chichester: John Wiley and Sons.

Advani, Arun, F. Koenig, L. Pessina, and A. Summers. 2020. "Importing Inequality: Immigration and the Top 1 Percent." LSE Centre for Economic Performance Discussion Paper No. 1717.

Advani, Arun, and Andrew Summers. 2020. *Capital Gains and UK Inequality* (No. 1260). University of Warwick, Department of Economics.

Agamben, Giorgio. 1998. *Homo Sacer: Sovereign Power and Bare Life.* Trans. Daniel Heller-Roazen. Stanford, CA: Stanford University Press.

Albrow, Martin. 1996. *The Global Age: State and Society beyond Modernity.* Cambridge: Polity.

Alpers, Svetlana. 1983. *The Art of Describing: Dutch Art in the Seventeenth Century.* Chicago: University of Chicago Press.

Alvaredo, Facundo, Anthony Atkinson, Lucas Chancel, Thomas Piketty, Emmanuel Saez, and Gabriel Zucman. 2016. "Distributional National Accounts (DINA) Guidelines: Concepts and Methods Used in WID.world." WID.world Working Paper 2.

Alvaredo, Facundo, Lucas Chancel, Thomas Piketty, Emmanuel Saez, and Gabriel Zucman, eds. *World Inequality Report 2018.* Cambridge, MA: Harvard University Press, 2018.

Alvaredo, Facundo, and Leonardo Gasparino. 2015. "Recent Trends in Inequality and Poverty in Developing Countries." In Anthony B. Atkinson and François Bourguignon, eds., *Handbook of Income Distribution,* Vol. 2A. Amsterdam: North-Holland, pp. 697–805.

Amin, Ash. 2007. "Re-thinking the Urban Social." *City* 111: 100–114.

Amin, Ash, and Nigel Thrift. 2002. *Cities: Reimagining the Urban.* Cambridge: Polity Press.

Amin, Samir. 1990. "Colonialism and the Rise of Capitalism: A Comment." *Science and Society* 54(1): 67–72.

Amoore, Louise. 2013. *The Politics of Possibility: Risk and Security beyond Probability.* Durham, NC: Duke University Press.

Anand, Sudhir, and Paul Segal. 2015. "The Global Distribution of Income." In Anthony B. Atkinson and François Bourguignon, eds., *Handbook of Income Distribution,* Vol. 2A. Amsterdam: North-Holland, pp. 937–979.

————. 2017. "Who Are the Global Top 1%?" International Inequality Institute Working Paper 8. London: London School of Economics.

Anderson, Benedict. 1983. *Imagined Communities: Reflections on the Origin and Spread of Nationalism.* London: Verso.

Anderson, Bridget. 2000. *Doing the Dirty Work? The Global Politics of Domestic Labour.* London: Zed Books.

Anderson, Perry. 1964. "Origins of the Present Crisis." *New Left Review* 23(1): 26–53.

Anderson, Perry. 2009. *The New Old World*. London: Verso.

Andreotti, A., P. Le Gales, and F. J. Moreno-Fuentes. 2015. *Globalised Minds, Roots in the City: Urban Upper-Middle Classes in Europe*. Chichester: John Wiley & Sons.

Andreski, S. 1963. "The Military Participation Ratio." *Past & Present* 26(1): 113–114.

Anthias, Floya, and Nira Yuval-Davis. 2005. *Racialized Boundaries: Race, Nation, Gender, Colour and Class and the Anti-racist Struggle*. London: Routledge.

Appadurai, Arjun. 1996. *Modernity at Large: Cultural Dimensions of Globalization*, Vol. 1. Minneapolis: University of Minnesota Press.

Atkinson, Anthony. 1970. "On the Measurement of Inequality." *Journal of Economic Theory* 23: 244–266.

———. 2015. *Inequality: What Can Be Done?* Cambridge, MA: Harvard University Press.

Atkinson, Anthony Barnes, and François Bourguignon. 2000. "Poverty and Inclusion from a World Perspective." In A. B. Atkinson and F. Bourguignon, eds., *Handbook of Income Distribution*. London: Elsevier, pp. 151–64.

———. 2000. *Handbook of Income Distribution*, Vol. 1. Amsterdam: Elsevier Science.

———. 2015. "Introduction: Income Distribution Today." In *Handbook of Income Distribution*, Vol. 2. Amsterdam: North-Holland, xvii–lxiv.

Atkinson, A. B., A. Casarico, and S. Voitchovsky. 2018. "Top Incomes and the Gender Divide." *Journal of Economic Inequality* 16(2): 225–256.

Atkinson, Anthony Barnes, and Allan James Harrison. 1978. *Distribution of Personal Wealth in Britain*. Cambridge: Cambridge University Press.

Atkinson, Anthony Barnes, and Thomas Piketty, eds. 2007. *Top Incomes over the Twentieth Century: A Contrast between European and English-Speaking Countries*. Oxford: Oxford University Press.

Atkinson, A. B., T. Piketty, and E. Saez. 2010. "Top Incomes in the Long Run of History." In Anthony Barnes Atkinson and Thomas Piketty, eds., *Top Incomes: A Global Perspective*. Oxford and New York: Oxford University Press, pp. 664–759.

Atkinson, Will. 2010. *Class, Individualization and Late Modernity: In Search of the Reflexive Worker*. London: Palgrave Macmillan.

———. 2017. *Class in the New Millennium: The Structure, Homologies and Experience of the British Social Space*. London: Routledge.

Atkinson, Will, and Christopher Deeming. 2015. "Class and Cuisine in Contemporary Britain: The Social Space, the Space of Food and Their Homology." *Sociological Review* 63(4): 876–896.

Back, Les. 1996. *New Ethnicities and Urban Cult*. London: Routledge.

———. 2009. "Portrayal and Betrayal: Bourdieu, Photography and Sociological Life." *Sociological Review* 57(3): 471–490.

Ball, Stephen. 2003. *Class Strategies and the Education Market: The Middle Classes and Social Advantage*. London: Routledge.

Bartels, Larry. 2008. *The New Gilded Age: From Unequal Democracy.* Princeton, NJ: Princeton University Press.

Barth, Fredrik. 1998. *Ethnic Groups and Boundaries: The Social Organization of Culture Difference.* Long Grove, IL: Waveland Press.

Bartolini, S. 2000. *The Political Mobilization of the European Left, 1860–1980: The Class Cleavage.* Cambridge: Cambridge University Press.

Bauman, Zygmunt. 1989. *Modernity and the Holocaust.* Ithaca, NY: Cornell University Press.

———. 2000. *Liquid Modernity.* Cambridge: Polity Press.

———. 2007. *Liquid Times: Living in an Age of Uncertainty.* Cambridge: Polity Press.

Bayly, Christopher. 2004. *The Birth of the Modern World, 1780–1914.* Oxford: Blackwell.

Bayly, C. A. 2011. *Recovering Liberties: Indian Thought in the Age of Liberalism and Empire.* Cambridge: Cambridge University Press.

Bear, Laura. 2015. *Navigating Austerity: Currents of Debt along a South Asian River.* Redwood City, CA: Stanford University Press.

Beauvoir, Simone de. (1953) 1989. *The Second Sex.* Trans. and ed. H. M. Parshley. New York: Vintage Books.

Beck, Ulrich. 1992. *Risk Society: Towards a New Modernity.* London: Sage.

Beck, Ulrich, and Elisabeth Beck-Gersheim. 2001. *Individualization: Institutionalized Individualism and Its Social and Political Consequences.* London: Sage.

Beck, U., A. Giddens, and S. Lash, eds. 1994. *Reflexive Modernization.* Cambridge: Polity Press.

Beckert, S. 2015. *Empire of Cotton: A Global History.* New York: Vintage.

Beckfield, Jason. 2010. "The Social Structure of the World Polity." *American Journal of Sociology* 115: 1018–1068.

Beegle, K., L. Christiaensen, A. Dabalen, and I. Gaddis. 2016. *Poverty in a Rising Africa.* Washington, DC: World Bank.

Bell, Daniel. 1973. *The Coming of Post-Industrial Society: A Venture in Social Forecasting.* New York: Basic Books.

Benedetto, G., S. Hix, and N. Mastrorocco. 2020. "The Rise and Fall of Social Democracy, 1918–2017." *American Political Science Review.*

Benjamin, Walter. 2010. *Theses on the Philosophy of History.* In *Illuminations.* London: Penguin.

Bennett, Tony. 2005. "The Historical Universal: The Role of Cultural Value in the Historical Sociology of Pierre Bourdieu." *British Journal of Sociology* 56(1): 141–164.

Bennett, T., M. Savage, E. Silva, A. Warde, M. Gayo-Cal, and D. Wright. 2009. *Culture, Class, Distinction.* London: Routledge.

Berelson, B. R., P. F. Lazarsfeld, and W. N. McPhee. 1954. *Voting: A Study of Opinion Formation in a Presidential Campaign.* Chicago: University of Chicago Press.

Bergson, Henri. 1998. *Creative Evolution*. New York: Dover Publications.

———. 2002. *Henri Bergson: Key Writings*. Ed. Keith Ansell Pearson and John Ó Maoilearca. London: Bloomsbury.

Berman, Marshall. 1983. *All That Is Solid Melts into Air*. London: Verso.

Bhambra, Gurminder. 2007. *Rethinking Modernity: Postcolonialism and the Sociological Imagination*. London: Springer.

———. 2017. "Brexit, Trump, and 'Methodological Whiteness': On the Misrecognition of Race and Class." *British Journal of Sociology* 68: S214–S232.

Bhattacharyya, Gargi. 2018. *Rethinking Racial Capitalism: Questions of Reproduction and Survival*. London: Rowman and Littlefield International.

Billig, Michael. 1995. *Banal Nationalism*. London: Sage.

Björklund, Anders, and Markus Jäntti. 2009. "Intergenerational Income Mobility and the Role of Family Background." In Brian Nolan, Wiemer Salverda, and Timothy M. Smeeding, eds., *Oxford Handbook of Economic Inequality*. Oxford: Oxford University Press, pp. 491–521.

Blackburn, Robin. 1998. *The Making of New World Slavery: From the Baroque to the Modern, 1492–1800*. London: Verso.

———. 2013. *The American Crucible: Slavery, Emancipation and Human Rights*. London: Verso.

Blanden, Jo, A. Goodman, P. Gregg, and S. Machin. 2005. "Changes in Intergenerational Income Mobility in Britain." In Miles Corak, ed., *Generational Income Mobility in North America and Europe*. Cambridge: Cambridge University Press.

Blau, Peter M., and Otis Dudley Duncan. 1967. *The American Occupational Structure*. New York: John Wiley & Sons.

Bobo, Lawrence D. 2011. "Somewhere between Jim Crow & Post-racialism: Reflections on the Racial Divide in America Today." *Daedalus* 140(2): 11–36.

———. 2017. "Racism in Trump's America: Reflections on Culture, Sociology, and the 2016 US Presidential Election." *British Journal of Sociology* 68: S85–S104.

Boltanski, Luc. 2011. *On Critique: A Sociology of Emancipation*. Cambridge: Polity.

Booth, Charles. 1889. *Inquiry into the Life and Labour of the People of London*. London: Macmillan.

Bottero, Wendy. 2019. *A Sense of Inequality*. London: Rowman and Littlefield.

Boulianne, S. 2015. "Social Media Use and Participation: A Meta-analysis of Current Research." *Information, Communication and Society* 18(5): 524–538.

Bourdieu, Pierre. 1979[1984]. *Distinction*. London: Routledge.

Bourdieu, Pierre. 1986. "The Forms of Capital." In J. Richardson, *Handbook of Theory and Research for the Sociology of Education*. Westport, CT: Greenwood, pp. 241–258.

———. 2000. *Pascalian Meditations*. Trans. Robert Rafalko. Cambridge: Polity.

———. 2004. *Science of Science and Reflexivity*. Cambridge: Polity.

———. 2008. *The Bachelors' Ball: The Crisis of Peasant Society in Bearn.* Cambridge: Polity.

Bourdieu, Pierre, A. Accardo, and S. Emanuel. 1999. *The Weight of the World: Social Suffering in Contemporary Society.* Cambridge: Polity.

Bourdieu, Pierre, and Luc Boltanski. 2011. *On Critique: A Sociology of Emancipation.* Cambridge: Polity.

Bourdieu, Pierre, and Marie-Claire Bourdieu. 2004. "The Peasant and Photography." *Ethnography* 54: 601–616.

Bourdieu, Pierre, and Loïs Wacquant. 1999. "On the Cunning of Imperialist Reason." *Theory, Culture & Society* 161: 41–58.

Bourdieu, Pierre, and Shaun Whiteside. 1996. *Photography: A Middle-Brow Art.* Redwood City, CA: Stanford University Press.

Bourguignon, François. 2015. *The Globalization of Inequality.* Trans. Thomas Scott Railton. Princeton, NJ: Princeton University Press.

Bourguignon, François, and Christian Morrison. 2002. "Inequality among World Citizens: 1820–1992." *American Economic Review* 92(4): 727–744.

Boushey, Heather, B. DeLong, and M. Steinbaum. 2017. *After Piketty: The Agenda for Economics and Inequality.* Cambridge, MA: Harvard University Press.

Bradbury, Malcolm, and James MacFarlane. 1976. *Modernism: 1890–1930.* Brighton: Harvester.

Bradley, Harriet. 2014. "Class Descriptors or Class Relations? Thoughts towards a Critique of Savage et al." *Sociology* 48(3): 429–436.

Braer, Curtis, and James Grabb 2001. "Has Voluntary Association Activity Declined? Cross-national Analyses of Fifteen Countries." *Canadian Review of Sociology and Anthropology* 383: 242–274.

Brambor, T., W. R. Clark, and M. Golder. 2006. "Are African Party Systems Different?" *Electoral Studies* 20: 1–9.

Breen, Richard, ed. 2005. *Social Mobility in Europe.* Oxford: Oxford University Press.

Breen, Richard, and Jan O. Jonsson. 2005. "Inequality of Opportunity in Comparative Perspective: Recent Research on Educational Attainment and Social Mobility." *Annual Review of Sociology* 31: 223–243.

Breen, Richard, and Ruud Luijkx. 2004a. "Social Mobility in Europe between 1970 and 2000." In Richard Breen, ed., *Social Mobility in Europe.* Oxford: Oxford University Press, pp. 37–75.

———. 2004b. "Conclusions." In Richard Breen, ed., *Social Mobility in Europe.* Oxford: Oxford University Press, pp. 383–410.

Breen, R., R. Luijkx, W. Müller, and R. Pollak. 2009. "Nonpersistent Inequality in Educational Attainment: Evidence from Eight European Countries." *American Journal of Sociology* 114(5): 1475–1521.

———. 2010. "Long-term Trends in Educational Inequality in Europe: Class Inequalities and Gender Differences." *European Sociological Review* 26(1): 31–48.

Brenner, Neil, and Christian Schmid. 2014. "The 'Urban Age' in Question." *International Journal of Urban and Regional Research* 383: 731–755.

Britten, Nicky, and A. Heath. 1982. "Women, Men and Social Class." In E. Gamarnirov, ed., *Gender, Class and Work*. London: Heinemann.

Brooks, Chas, and J. Manza. 1997. "The Social and Ideological Bases of Middle Class Political Realignment." *American Sociological Review* 62: 191–208.

Brown, Philip, S. Power, G. Tholen, and A. Allouch. 2016. "Credentials, Talent and Cultural Capital: A Comparative Study of Educational Elites in England and France." *British Journal of Sociology of Education* 37(2): 191–211.

Brown, Wendy. 2015. *Undoing the Demos: Neoliberalism's Stealth Revolution*. Cambridge: MIT Press.

Bryant, Joseph M. 1994. "Evidence and Explanation in History and Sociology: Critical Reflections on Goldthorpe's Critique of Historical Sociology." *British Journal of Sociology* 45(1): 3–19.

Brynin, Matthew, and F. Perales. 2016. "Gender Wage Inequality: The De-gendering of the Occupational Structure." *European Sociological Review* 32(1): 162–174.

Bukodi, Erzebet, John Goldthorpe, and Jouni Kuha. 2017. "The Pattern of Social Fluidity within the British Class Structure: A Topological Model." *Journal of the Royal Statistical Society. Series A: Statistics in Society* 180(3): 841–862.

Bukodi, E., J. H. Goldthorpe, L. Waller, and J. Kuha. 2015. "The Mobility Problem in Britain: New Findings from the Analysis of Birth Cohort Data." *British Journal of Sociology* 66(1): 93–117.

Burrows, Roger, and Richard Webber. 2018. *The Predictive Postcode: The Geodemographic Classification of British Society*. London: Sage.

Burt, Ronald. 2009. *Structural Holes: The Social Structure of Competition*. Cambridge, MA: Harvard University Press.

Buscha, F., and P. Sturgis. 2018. "Declining Social Mobility? Evidence from Five Linked Censuses in England and Wales 1971–2011." *The British Journal of Sociology* 69(1): 154–182.

Butler, Tim, with Garry Robson. 2003. *London Calling: The Middle Classes and the Remaking of Inner London*. Oxford: Berg.

Butler, Tim, and Mike Savage, eds. 1995. *Social Change and the Middle Classes*. London: UCL Press.

Calhoun, Craig. 1982. *The Question of Class Struggle: Social Foundations of Popular Radicalism during the Industrial Revolution*. Chicago: University of Chicago Press.

———, ed. 1992. *Habermas and the Public Sphere*. Cambridge, MA: MIT Press.

———. 2002. "The Class Consciousness of Frequent Travelers: Toward a Critique of Actually Existing Cosmopolitanism." *The South Atlantic Quarterly* 101(4): 869–897.

———. 2007. *Nations Matter: Culture, History and the Cosmopolitan Dream*. London: Routledge.

———. 2013. "Occupy Wall Street in Perspective." *British Journal of Sociology* 64(1): 26–38.

———. 2015. "Beyond Left and Right: A Cobbett for Our Time." In James Grande and John Stevenson, eds., *William Cobbett, Romanticism and the Enlightenment: Contexts and Legacy. The Enlightenment World*. London: Routledge, pp. 157–172.

Callon, Michel. 1998. *Laws of the Markets*. Sociological Review Monograph. New York: John Wiley & Sons.

Carnes, Nicholas, and Noam Lupu. 2016a. "Do Voters Dislike Working-Class Candidates? Voter Biases and the Descriptive Underrepresentation of the Working Class." *American Political Science Review*: 823–844.

———. 2016b. "What Good Is a College Degree? Education and Leader Quality Reconsidered." *Journal of Politics* 78(1): 35–49.

Casanova, Pascale. 2008. *The World Republic of Letters*. London: Verso.

Castells, Manuel. 1977. *Is There an Urban Sociology? Theory and Ideology in Urban Sociology. Urban Sociology, Critical Essays*. London: Tavistock.

———. 1996. *The Rise of the Network Society: The Information Age: Economy, Society, and Culture*, Vol. I. Oxford: Blackwell.

———. 1997. *The Power of Identity: The Information Age: Economy, Society, and Culture*, Vol. II. Oxford: Blackwell.

Chakrabarty, Dipesh. 2000. *Rethinking Working-Class History: Bengal, 1890–1940*. Princeton, NJ: Princeton University Press.

———. 2003. "Subaltern Studies and Postcolonial Histories." In Gerard Delanty and Engin Isin, eds., *Handbook of Historical Sociology*. New York: Sage, pp. 191–204.

———. 2005. "Legacies of Bandung: Decolonisation and the Politics of Culture." *Economic and Political Weekly* 40(46): 4812–4818.

———. 2008. *Provincializing Europe: Postcolonial Thought and Historical Difference*. Princeton, NJ: Princeton University Press.

Chan, Jenny. 2014. "Dying for an iPhone: The Labour Struggle of China's New Working Class." *tripleC: Communication, Capitalism & Critique. Open Access Journal for a Global Sustainable Information Society* 12(2).

Chan, Tak Wing. 2018. "Social Mobility and the Well-Being of Individuals." *British Journal of Sociology* 69(1): 183–206.

Chancel, Lucas. 2020. *Unsustainable Inequalities: Social Justice and the Environment*. Cambridge, MA: Harvard University Press.

Chang, Grace. 2000. *Disposable Domestics: Immigrant Women Workers in the Global Economy*. Cambridge, MA: South End Press.

Chase, Malcolm. 2007. *Chartism: A New History*. Manchester: Manchester University Press.

Chatterjee, Partha. 2012. *The Black Hole of Empire: History of a Global Practice of Power*. Princeton, NJ: Princeton University Press.

———. 2017. "Empires, Nations, Peoples: The Imperial Prerogative and Colonial Exceptions." *Thesis Eleven* 13(9): 84–96.

Chaturvedi, V., ed. 2012. *Mapping Subaltern Studies and the Postcolonial (Mappings Series)*. London: Verso.

Chauvel, Louis, Eyal Bar Haim, Anne Hartung, and Emily Murphy. 2021. "Rewealthization in 21st Century Western Countries: The Defining Trend of the Socioeconomic Squeeze of the Middle Class." *The Chinese Journal of Sociology*, in press.

Chen, Shaohua, and Martin Ravaillion. 2013. "More Relatively-Poor People in a Less Absolutely Poor World." *Review of Income and Wealth* 59(1): 1475–1491.

Chetty, R., N. Hendren, P. Kline, and E. Saez. 2014. "Where Is the Land of Opportunity? The Geography of Intergenerational Mobility in the United States." *Quarterly Journal of Economics* 129(4): 1553–1623.

Chibber, V. 2014. *Postcolonial Theory and the Specter of Capital*. London: Verso.

Clark, Timothy James. 1985. *The Painting of Modern Life: Paris in the Art of Manet and His Followers*. London: Thames and Hudson.

Cohen, Ronald. 1978. "Ethnicity: Problem and Focus in Anthropology." *Annual Review of Anthropology* 7: 379–403.

Colley, Linda. 2005. *Britons: Forging the Nation, 1707–1837*. New Haven, CT: Yale University Press.

Corak, Miles. 2013. "Income Inequality, Equality of Opportunity, and Intergenerational Mobility." *Journal of Economic Perspectives* 273: 79–102.

Couch, K., A. Dean, and R. Lillard. 2004. "Nonlinear Patterns of Intergenerational Mobility: Germany and the United States." In Miles Corak, ed., *Generational Income Mobility in North America and Europe*, pp. 190–206.

Coulangeon, Philippe, and Julien Duval, eds. 2014. *The Routledge Companion to Bourdieu's "Distinction."* London: Routledge.

Couldry, Nick, and U. A. Mejias. 2019. "Data Colonialism: Rethinking Big Data's Relation to the Contemporary Subject." *Television and New Media* 20(4): 336–349.

Crenshaw, Kimberlé. 1989. "Demarginalizing the Intersection of Race and Sex: A Black Feminist Critique of Antidiscrimination Doctrine, Feminist Theory and Antiracist Politics." *University of Chicago Legal Forum* (1): 139–167.

Crouch, Colin. 2005. *Post-democracy*. Cambridge: Polity.

———. 2011. *The Strange Non-death of Neo-liberalism*. Hoboken, NJ: John Wiley & Sons.

Cunningham, Neil, and Mike Savage. 2015. "The Secret Garden? Elite Metropolitan Geographies in the Contemporary UK." *Sociological Review* 632: 321–348.

———. 2017. "An Intensifying and Elite City: New Geographies of Social Class and Inequality in Contemporary London." *City* 21(1): 25–46.

Davies, J. B., R. Lluberas, and A. F. Shorrocks. 2017. "Estimating the Level and Distribution of Global Wealth, 2000–2014." *Review of Income and Wealth* 63(4): 731–759.

Davies, William. 2015. *The Happiness Industry: How the Government and Big Business Sold Us Well-Being*. London: Verso.

Davis, Deborah S., and Feng Wang, eds. 2009. *Creating Wealth and Poverty in Postsocialist China*. Redwood City, CA: Stanford University Press.

Delhey, Jan, and Georgi Dragolov. 2013. "Why Inequality Makes Europeans Less Happy: The Role of Distrust, Status Anxiety, and Perceived Conflict." *European Sociological Review* 30(2): 151–165.

Dekker, Paul, and Andries van den Broek. 2005. "Involvement in Voluntary Associations in North America and Western Europe: Trends and Correlates 1981–2000." *Journal of Civil Society* 1(1): 45–59.

Desrosières, Alain. 1998. *The Politics of Large Numbers: A History of Statistical Reasoning*. Cambridge, MA: Harvard University Press.

Devine, F., M. Savage, J. Scott, and R. Crompton, eds. 2005. *Rethinking Class: Culture, Identities and Lifestyles*. Basingstoke, UK: Macmillan International Higher Education.

DiMaggio, Paul, and Toqir Mukhtar. 2004. "Arts Participation as Cultural Capital in the United States, 1982–2002—Signs of Decline?" *Poetics* 322: 169–194.

DiMaggio, Paul, and Walter Powell. 1983. "The Iron Cage Revisited. Institutional Isomorphism and Collective Rationality in Organizational Fields." *American Sociological Review* 48: 147–160.

Dirks, Nicholas. 2001. *Castes of Mind: Colonialism and the Making of Modern India*. Princeton, NJ: Princeton University Press.

Dorling, D., A. Barford, and M. Newman. 2006. "WORLDMAPPER: The World as You've Never Seen It Before." *IEEE Transactions on Visualization and Computer Graphics* 125: 757–764.

Downs, Anthony. 1957. "An Economic Theory of Political Action in a Democracy." *Journal of Political Economy* 65(2): 135–150.

Du Bois, William. 1899. *The Philadelphia Negro: A Social Study*. Philadelphia: University of Pennsylvania Press.

———. 1900. "The Present Outlook for the Darker Races of Mankind." In Eric Sundquist, ed., *The Oxford W.E.B. Du Bois Reader*. Oxford: Oxford University Press, pp. 47–54.

———. 1903. *The Souls of Black Folk*. Chicago: A. C. McClurg & Co.

Duncan, Simon. 2007. "What's the Problem with Teenage Parents? And What's the Problem with Policy? *Critical Social Policy* 27(3): 307–334.

Durkheim, Émile. 1997[1893]. *The Division of Labour in Society*. Trans. W. D. Halls, intro. Lewis A. Coser. New York: Free Press.

Duster, Troy. 2003. *Backdoor to Eugenics*. London: Taylor & Francis.

———. 2015. "A Post-genomic Surprise. The Molecular Reinscription of Race in Science, Law and Medicine." *British Journal of Sociology* 66(1): 1–27.

Easlea, Brian. 1980. *Witch Hunting, Magic and the New Philosophy: An Introduction to Debates of the Scientific Revolution, 1450–1750* (No. 14). Brighton: Harvester Press.

Easterlin, Richard A. 1974. "Does Economic Growth Improve the Human Lot? Some Empirical Evidence." In R. David and R. Reder, eds., *Nations and Households in Economic Growth*. New York: Academic Press, pp. 89–125.

Edgerton, David. 2018. *The Rise and Fall of the British Nation: A Twentieth-Century History*. London: Penguin.

Eisenstadt, Shmuel N. 2000. "Multiple Modernities." *Daedalus* 129(1): 1–29.

Elias, Norbert, and E. Jephcott. 1994. *The Civilizing Process*, Vol. 2. Oxford: Blackwell.

Elyachar, Julia. 2005. *Markets of Dispossession: NGOs, Economic Development, and the State in Cairo*. Durham, NC: Duke University Press.

Emigh, R. J., D. Riley, and P. Ahmed. 2015. "The Racialization of Legal Categories in the First US Census." *Social Science History* 39(4): 485–519.

Erikson, Robert, and John H. Goldthorpe. 1992. *The Constant Flux. A Study of Class Mobility in Industrial Societies*. Oxford: Clarendon Press.

———. 2010. "Has Social Mobility in Britain Decreased? Reconciling Divergent Findings on Income and Class Mobility." *British Journal of Sociology* 61: 211–230.

Erikson, R., M. MacKuen, and J. Stimson. 2002. *The Macro Economy*. New York: Cambridge University Press.

Erola, Jani, S. Jalonen, and H. Lehti. 2016. "Parental Education, Class and Income over Early Life Course and Children's Achievement." *Research in Social Stratification and Mobility* 44: 33–43.

Esping-Andersen, Gøsta. 1990. *The Three Worlds of Welfare Capitalism*. Princeton, NJ: Princeton University Press.

Esping-Andersen, Gøsta, and S. Wagner. 2012. "Asymmetries in the Opportunity Structure. Intergenerational Mobility Trends in Europe." *Research in Social Stratification and Mobility* 30(4): 473–487.

Evans, Geoffrey, ed. 1999. *The End of Class Politics?: Class Voting in Comparative Context*. Oxford: Oxford University Press.

Evans, Geoffrey, and James Tilley. 2016. *The New Politics of Class: The Political Exclusion of the British Working Class*. Oxford: Oxford University Press.

Evans, P., D. Rueschmeyer, and T. Skocpol. 1985. *Bringing the State Back In*. Cambridge: Cambridge University Press.

Fanon, Frantz. 1952. *Black Skin, White Masks*. New York: Grove Press.

Favell, A. 2011. *Eurostars and Eurocities: Free Movement and Mobility in an Integrating Europe*, Vol. 56. Chichester: John Wiley and Sons.

Featherstone, Mike. 1987. "Lifestyle and Consumer Culture." *Theory, Culture & Society* 41: 55–70.

———. 1991. *Consumer Culture and Postmodernism*. London: Sage.

Federici, Siliva. 2004. *Caliban and the Witch: Women, the Body and Primitive Accumulation*. Brooklyn, NY: Autonomedia.

————. 2012. *Revolution at Point Zero: Housework, Reproduction, and Feminist Struggle.* Brooklyn, NY: Common Notions, PM Press.

Ferreira, Frederico H., S. A. Chen, A. Dabalen, Y. Dikhanov, N. Hamadeh, D. Jolliffe, A. Narayan, E. B. Prydz, A. Revenga, P. Sangraula, and U. Serajuddin. 2016. "A Global Count of the Extreme Poor in 2012: Data Issues, Methodology and Initial Results." *Journal of Economic Inequality* 14: 141–172.

Fischer, Claude. 1982. *To Dwell among Friends: Personal Networks in Town and City.* Chicago: University of Chicago Press.

Flemmen, Magne. 2014. "The Politics of the Service Class: The Homology of Positions and Position-Takings." *European Societies* 16(4): 543–569.

Flemmen, Magne, and Johs Hjellbrekke. 2016. "Response: Not So Fast: A Comment on Atkinson and Deeming's 'Class and Cuisine in Contemporary Britain: The Social Space, the Space of Food and Their Homology.'" *Sociological Review* 641: 184–193.

Flemmen, Magne, and Mike Savage. 2017. "The Politics of Nationalism and White Racism in the UK." *British Journal of Sociology* 68: 233–264.

Fligstein, Neil. 2001. "Social Skill and the Theory of Fields." *Sociological Theory* 192: 105–125.

————. 2008. *Euroclash: The EU, European Identity and the Future of Europe.* Oxford: Oxford University Press.

————. 2009. "A New Agenda for Research on the Trajectory of Chinese Capitalism," with Jianjun Zhang. *Management and Organization Review* 7: 39–62.

Fligstein, Neil, and Doug McAdam. 2012. *A Theory of Fields.* Oxford: Oxford University Press.

Foucault, Michel. 1971. *The Order of Things.* London: Tavistock.

————. 1976. *Discipline and Punish.* London: Penguin.

————. 1977. *The History of Sexuality,* Vol 1. London: Penguin.

————. 1997. "Technologies of the Self." In M. Foucault and P. D. Rabinow, eds., *Essential Works of Foucault 1954–1984,* Vol. 1, *Ethics: Subjectivity and Truth.* New York: Penguin, pp. 223–252.

Fourcade, Marion. 2009. *Economists and Societies. Discipline and Profession in the United States, Britain, and France, 1890s to 1990s.* Princeton, NJ: Princeton University Press.

————. 2016. "Ordinalization: Lewis A. Coser Memorial Award for Theoretical Agenda Setting 2014." *Sociological Theory* 34(3): 175–195.

Fourcade, M., and K. Healy. 2013. "Classification Situations: Life-chances in the Neoliberal Era." *Accounting, Organizations and Society* 38(8): 559–572.

Fourcade, M., E. Ollion, and Y. Algan. 2015. "The Superiority of Economists." *Journal of Economic Perspectives* 291: 89–114.

Fourcade-Gourinchas, Marion. 2001. "Politics, Institutional Structures, and the Rise of Economics: A Comparative Study." *Theory and Society* 30(3): 397–447.

Fraser, Nancy. 1995. "From Redistribution to Recognition? Dilemmas of Justice in a 'Post-Socialist' Age." *New Left Review* 212: 68–93.

Friedman, Sam. 2016. "Habitus Clivé and the Emotional Imprint of Social Mobility." *Sociological Review* 64(1): 129–147.

Friedman, Sam, and Daniel Laurison. 2017. "Mind the Gap: Financial London and the Regional Class Pay Gap." *The British Journal of Sociology* 68(3): 474–511.

———. 2020. *The Class Ceiling: Why It Pays to Be Privileged.* Cambridge: Policy Press.

Friedman, Sam, and Mike Savage. 2018. "Time, Accumulation and Trajectory: Bourdieu and Social Mobility." In G. Payne and S. Lawler, eds., *Social Mobility for the 21st Century.* Basingstoke: Macmillan.

Friedman, Sam, M. Savage, L. Hanquinet, and A. Miles. 2015. "Cultural Sociology and New Forms of Distinction." *Poetics:* 1–8.

Fukuyama, Francis. 1992. *The End of History and the Last* Man. New York: Free Press.

Galbraith, John Kenneth. 1958. *The Affluent Society.* Boston: Houghton Mifflin.

Garfinkel, Harold. 1967. *Studies in Ethnomethodology.* New York: Prentice Hall.

Gatrell, Peter. 2019. *The Unsettling of Europe: The Great Migration, 1945 to the Present.* London: Penguin.

Gayo, Modesto. 2015. "A Critique of the Omnivore: From the Origin of the Idea of Omnivorousness to the Latin American Express." In Laurie Hanquinet and Mike Savage, eds., *Routledge International Handbook of the Sociology of Art and Culture.* Abingdon: Routledge, pp. 104–115.

Gershuny, Jay, and Oriel Sullivan. 2019. *What We Really Do All Day: Insights from the Centre for Time Use Research.* London: Penguin.

Ghani, Ashraf, and Clare Lockhart. 2009. *Fixing Failed States: A Framework for Rebuilding a Fractured World.* Oxford: Oxford University Press.

Ghosh, Jayati. 2011. "Dealing with 'the Poor.'" *Development and Change* 42(3): 849–858.

———. 2018. "A Note on Estimating Income Inequality across Countries Using PPP Exchange Rates." *The Economic and Labour Relations Review* 29(1): 24–37.

Gibbons, Michael, ed. 1994. *The New Production of Knowledge: The Dynamics of Science and Research in Contemporary Societies.* London: Sage.

Giddens, Anthony. 1971. *Capitalism and Modern Social Theory: An Analysis of the Writings of Marx, Durkheim and Max Weber.* Cambridge: Cambridge University Press.

———. 1985. *A Contemporary Critique of Historical Materialism,* Vol. 2, *The Nation State and Violence.* Cambridge: Polity.

———. 1990. *The Consequences of Modernity.* Cambridge: Polity.

———. 1991. *Modernity and Self-Identity. Self and Society in the Late Modern Age.* Cambridge: Polity.

———. 1992. *The Transformation of Intimacy: Sexuality, Love and Eroticism in Modern Societies.* Cambridge: Polity.

Gilens, Martin. 2012. *Affluence and Influence: Economic Inequality and Political Power in America.* Princeton, NJ: Princeton University Press.

————. 2015. "Descriptive Representation, Money, and Political Inequality in the United States." *Swiss Political Science Review* 21(2): 222–228.

Gil-Hernández, C. J., I. Marqués-Perales, and S. Fachelli. 2017. "Intergenerational Social Mobility in Spain between 1956 and 2011: The Role of Educational Expansion and Economic Modernization in a Late Industrialized Country." *Research in Social Stratification and Mobility* 51: 14–27.

Gillborn, David. 2005. "Education Policy as an Act of White Supremacy: Whiteness, Critical Race Theory and Education Reform." *Journal of Education Policy* 20(4): 485–505.

Gilroy, Paul. 2004. *After Empire: Melancholia or Convivial Culture?* London: Routledge.

Gini, Corrado. 1912. "Variabilità e mutabilità." In E. Pizetti and T. Salvemini, eds., *Memorie di metodologica statistica.* Rome: Libreria Eredi Virgilio Veschi, Memorie di metodologica statistica.

Gitlin, Todd. 2013. "Reply to Craig Calhoun." *British Journal of Sociology* 64(1): 39–43.

Glass, David Victor. 1954. *Social Mobility in Britain.* New York: Free Press.

Glick Schiller, Nina, and Andreas Wimmer. 2003. "Methodological Nationalism, the Social Sciences, and the Study of Migration: An Essay in Historical Epistemology." *International Migration Review* 37(3): 576–610.

Glucksberg, Luna. 2016. "Gendering the Elites: An Ethnographic Approach to Elite Women's Lives and the Re-production of Inequality." International Inequality Institute Working Paper 7. London: London School of Economics.

Go, Julian. 2008. "Global Fields and Imperial Forms: Field Theory and the British and American Empires." *Sociological Theory* 26(3): 201–229.

————. 2013. "Decolonizing Bourdieu: Colonial and Postcolonial Theory in Pierre Bourdieu's Early Work." *Sociological Theory* 31(1): 49–74.

Go, Julian, and Monika Krause. 2016. "Fielding Transnationalism: An Introduction." *Sociological Review* 64(2): 6–30.

Godechot, Olivier. 2015. "Financialization Is Marketization! A Study on the Respective Impact of Various Dimensions of Financialization on the Increase in Global Inequality." MaxPo Discussion Paper Series 15 / 3. Paris: Max Planck Sciences Po Center on Coping with Instability in Market Societies.

Goetzmann, W., L. Renneboog, and G. Spaenjers. 2011. "Art and Money." *American Economic Review: Papers & Proceedings* 101(3): 222–226.

Goldthorpe, John H. 1981. "The Class Schema of 'Social Mobility and Class Structure in Modern Britain': A Reply to Penn." *Sociology* 15(2): 272–280.

————. 1982. "On the Service Class, Its Formation and Future." In A. Giddens and G. MacKenzie, eds., *Social Class and the Division of Labour.* Cambridge: Cambridge University Press, pp. 162–185.

————. 1983. "Women and Class Analysis: In Defence of the Conventional View." *Sociology* 17(4): 465–488.

———. 2000. *On Sociology: Numbers, Narratives and the Integration of Research and Theory.* Oxford: Oxford University Press.

———. 2009. "Analysing Social Inequality: A Critique of Two Recent Contributions from Economics and Epidemiology." *European Sociological Review* 26(6): 731–744.

———. 2013. "Understanding—and Misunderstanding—Social Mobility in Britain: The Entry of the Economists, the Confusion of Politicians and the Limits of Educational Policy." *Journal of Social Policy* 42(3): 431–450.

———. 2016. *Sociology as a Population Science.* Cambridge: Cambridge University Press.

Goldthorpe, John H., and Catriona Llewellyn, with Clive Payne. 1980. *Social Mobility and Class Structure in Modern Britain.* Oxford: Clarendon Press.

Goldthorpe, John H., David Lockwood, Frank Bechhofer, and Jennifer Platt. 1968a. *The Affluent Worker: Industrial Attitudes and Behaviour.* Cambridge: Cambridge University Press.

———. 1968b. *The Affluent Worker: Political Attitudes and Behavior.* Cambridge: Cambridge University Press.

———. 1969. *The Affluent Worker in the Class Structure,* Vol. 3. Cambridge: Cambridge University Press.

Goldthorpe, John H., and Gordon Marshall. 1992. "The Promising Future of Class Analysis: A Response to Recent Critiques." *Sociology* 263: 381–400.

Gorning, Martin, and Jan Goebel 2018. "Deindustrialisation and the Polarisation of Household Incomes: The Example of Urban Agglomerations in Germany." *Urban Studies* 55(4): 790–806.

Graeber, David. 2008. *Debt: Five Thousand Years.* New York: Melville House.

Graham, Stephen. 2016. *Vertical: The City from Satellites to Bunkers.* London: Verso.

Granovetter, Mark. 1973. "The Strength of Weak Ties." *American Journal of Sociology* 78(6): 1360–1380.

Grau Larsen, Anton, and Christoph Ellersgaard. 2015. "Data Exchange Network: The Danish Elite Network." *Connections* 35(1): 64–68.

Griswold, Wendy. 2011. "Made in America: A Social History of American Culture and Character by Claude S. Fischer." *American Journal of Sociology* 116(5): 1658–1660.

Guldi, Jo, and David Armitage. 2014. *The History Manifesto.* Cambridge: Cambridge University Press.

Hacker, Jacob S., and Paul Pierson. 2010. "Winner-Take-All Politics: Public Policy, Political Organization, and the Precipitous Rise of Top Incomes in the United States." *Politics & Society* 382: 152–204.

Halford, Susan, and Mike Savage. 2017. "Speaking Sociologically with Big Data: Symphonic Social Science and the Future for Big Data Research." *Sociology* 51(6): 1132–1148.

Hall, Peter. 1999. "Social Capital in Britain." *British Journal of Political Science* 29: 417–461.

Hall, Peter A., and David Soskice. 2001. *Varieties of Capitalism: The Institutional Foundations of Comparative Advantage.* New York: Oxford University Press.

Hall, Stuart. 1992. "The West and the Rest: Discourse and Power." *Formations of Modernity:* 275–331.

———. 1996. "New Ethnicities." In David Morely and Kuan-Hsing Chen, eds., *Stuart Hall: Critical Dialogues in Cultural Studies.* London: Routledge, pp. 441–449.

Hall, Suzanne, and Mike Savage. 2015. "Animating the Urban Vortex: New Sociological Urgencies." *International Journal of Urban and Regional Research* 40(1): 82–95.

Halperin, S. 2017. "The Imperial City-State and the National State Form: Reflections on the History of the Contemporary Order." *Thesis Eleven* 139(1): 97–112.

Hammerschmidt, William. 1949. *Whitehead's Philosophy of Time.* New York: Kings Crown Press.

Hanquinet, L., H. Roose, and M. Savage. 2014. "The Eyes of the Beholder: Aesthetic Preferences and the Remaking of Cultural Capital." *Sociology* 48(1): 111–132.

Hanquinet, Laurie, and Mike Savage, eds. 2015. *Routledge International Handbook of the Sociology of Art and Culture.* London: Routledge.

Hardoon, Deborah. 2017. *An Economy for the 99%: It's Time to Build a Human Economy That Benefits Everyone, Not Just the Privileged Few.* Oxfam briefing paper. Boston: Oxfam International.

Hardt, Michael, and Antonio Negri. 2000. *Empire.* Cambridge, MA: Harvard University Press.

———. 2019. "Empire, Twenty Years On." *New Left Review* (120): 67–92.

Harmel, R., and L. Svåsand. 1993. "Party Leadership and Party Institutionalisation: Three Phases of Development." *West European Politics* 16(2): 67–88.

———. 1997. "The Influence of New Parties on Old Parties' Platforms: The Cases of the Progress Parties and Conservative Parties of Denmark and Norway." *Party Politics* 3(3): 315–340.

Harrits, G. S., A. Prieur, L. Rosenlund, and J. Skjott-Larsen. 2009. "Class and Politics in Denmark: Are Both Old and New Politics Structured by Class?" *Scandinavian Political Studies* 33(1): 1–27.

Hartmann, Michael. 2018. "The International Business Elite—Fact or Fiction?" In Olav Korsnes, Johan Heilbron, Johs Hjellbrekke, Felix Bühlmann, and Mike Savage, eds., *New Directions in Elite Studies.* London: Routledge.

Harvey, David. 1975. "The Geography of Capitalist Accumulation: A Reconstruction of the Marxian Theory." *Antipode* 7(2): 9–21.

———. 1982. *The Limits to Capital.* London: Sage.

———. 1985. *Consciousness and the Urban Experience. Studies in the History and Theory of Capitalist Urbanization.* Baltimore: Johns Hopkins University Press.

———. 1989. *The Condition of Post-Modernity.* Oxford: Blackwell.

Healy, Kieran, and James Moody. 2014. "Data Visualization in Sociology." *Annual Review of Sociology* 40: 105–128.

Heath, A. F., and V. Di Stasio. 2019. "Racial Discrimination in Britain, 1969–2017: A Meta-analysis of Field Experiments on Racial Discrimination in the British Labour Market." *British Journal of Sociology* 70(5): 1774–1798.

Heath, Anthony F., Roger Jowell, and John Curtice. 1985. *How Britain Votes*. Oxford: Pergamon.

Heath, Anthony F., and Mike Savage. 1995. "Political Alignment within the Middle Classes, 1972–89." In T. Butler and M. Savage, eds., *Social Change and the Middle Classes*. London: UCL Press, pp. 175–192.

Heath, Oliver. 2016. *Policy Representation, Social Representation and Class Voting in Britain*. London: Royal Holloway, University of London. Available at http://citeseerx.ist.psu.edu/viewdoc/download?doi=10.1.1.678.3983&rep=rep1&type=pdf.

Hecht, Katharina. 2018. *A Relational Analysis of Top Incomes and Wealth: Economic Evaluation, Relative Disadvantage and the Service to Capital*. LSE III Working Paper. London: London School of Economics.

Helman, Gerald B., and Steven R. Ratner. 1992. "Saving Failed States." *Foreign Policy* 89: 3–20.

Hennion, Antoine. 2007. "Those Things That Hold Us Together: Taste and Sociology." *Cultural Sociology* 11: 97–114.

Hickel, Jason. 2017. *The Divide: A Brief Guide to Global Inequality and Its Solutions*. Oxford: William Heinemann.

———. 2020. *Less Is More: How Degrowth Will Save the World*. London: Penguin.

Hillygus, D., and Todd Shields. 2008. *The Persuadable Voter: Wedge Issues in Presidential Campaigns*. Princeton, NJ: Princeton University Press.

Hirschman, Daniel. 2016. "Rediscovering the 1%: Economic Expertise and Inequality Knowledge." *SocArXiv* 13.

Hirschman, Daniel, and E. P. Berman. 2014. "Do Economists Make Policies? On the Political Effects of Economics." *Socio-Economic Review* 12(4): 779–811.

Hjellbrekke, Johs. 2018. *Multiple Correspondence Analysis for the Social Sciences*. London: Routledge.

Hobsbawm, Eric. 1964. *Labouring Men*. London: Weidenfeld and Nicholson.

———. 1981. *Forward March of Labour Halted*. London: Verso.

Hochschild, A. R. 2018. *Strangers in Their Own Land: Anger and Mourning on the American Right*. New York: The New Press.

Hodges, M. 2008. "Rethinking Time's Arrow: Bergson, Deleuze and the Anthropology of Time." *Anthropological Theory* 8(4): 399–429.

Honneth, Axel. 1996. *The Struggle for Recognition: The Moral Grammar of Social Conflicts*. Boston: MIT Press.

Hotelling, Harold. 1929. "Stability in Competition." *Economic Journal* 39(153): 41–57.

Igo, Sarah E. 2007. *The Averaged American: Surveys, Citizens, and the Making of a Mass Public*. Cambridge, MA: Harvard University Press.

Inglehart, Ronald. 1990. *Culture Shift in Advanced Industrial Society*. Princeton, NJ: Princeton University Press.

Ingold, Timothy. 2006. "Against Human Nature." In Diederik Aerts, N. Gontier, and J. P. Van Bendegem, eds., *Evolutionary Epistemology, Language and Culture*. Theory and Decision Library A 39. Dordrecht: Springer.

Irwin, Sarah. 2015. "Class and Comparison: Subjective Social Location and Lay Experiences of Constraint and Mobility." *British Journal of Sociology* 66(2): 259–281.

Iverson, Torben, and David Soskice. 2006. "Electoral Institutions and the Politics of Coalitions: Why Some Democracies Redistribute More than Others." *American Political Science Review* 100(2): 165–181.

———. 2019. *Democracy and Prosperity Reinventing Capitalism through a Turbulent Century*. Princeton, NJ: Princeton University Press.

James, C. L. R. 1938. *Black Jacobins, Touissiant L'Ouverture and the San Domingan Revolution*. London: Secker and Warburg.

Jameson, Fredric. 1993. *Postmodernism: Or the Cultural Logic of Late Capitalism (Poetics of Social Forms)*. London: Verso.

Jäntti, M., B. Bratsberg, K. Røed, O. Raaum, R. Naylor, E. Österbacka, A. Björklund, and T. Eriksson. 2006. "American Exceptionalism in a New Light: A Comparison of Intergenerational Earnings Mobility in the Nordic Countries, the United Kingdom and the United States." Discussion Paper 1938. Forschungsinstitut zur Zukunft der Arbeit (Institute for the Study of Labor). Available at http://ftp.iza.org/dp1938.pdf.

Jasanoff, Sheila. 2015. "Future Imperfect: Science, Technology, and the Imaginations of Modernity." In Sheila Jasanoff and Sang-Hyun Kim, eds., *Dreamscapes of Modernity: Sociotechnical Imaginaries and the Fabrication of Power*. Chicago: University of Chicago Press, pp. 1–33.

Jay, Martin. 1993. *Downcast Eyes: The Denigration of Vision in Twentieth-Century French Thought*. Berkeley: University of California Press.

Jenkins, Henry. 2006. *Convergence Culture: Where Old and New Media Collide*. New York: New York University Press.

Jenkins, Stephen P. 2011. *Changing Fortunes: Income Mobility and Poverty Dynamics in Britain*. Oxford: Oxford University Press.

———. 2016. "The Income Distribution in the UK." In H. Dean and L. Platt, eds., *Social Advantage and Disadvantage*. Oxford: Oxford University Press, pp. 135–160.

Jerrim, J., A. K. Chmielewski, and P. Parker. 2015. "Socioeconomic Inequality in Access to High-Status Colleges: A Cross-Country Comparison." *Research in Social Stratification and Mobility* 42: 20–32.

Jerven, Morten. 2013. *Poor Numbers: How We Are Misled by African Development Statistics and What to Do About It.* Ithaca, NY: Cornell University Press.

Joas, Hans, and Wolfgang Knöbl. 2009. *Social Theory: Twenty Introductory Lectures.* Cambridge: Cambridge University Press.

Jodhka, S. S., B. Rehbein, and J. Souza. 2017. *Inequality in Capitalist Societies.* London: Taylor & Francis.

Jones, G. S. 1983. *Languages of Class: Studies in English Working Class History 1832–1982.* Cambridge: Cambridge University Press.

Joyce, Patrick. 2003. *The Rule of Freedom: Liberalism and the Modern City.* London: Verso.

———. 2013. *The State of Freedom: A Social History of the British State since 1800.* Cambridge: Cambridge University Press.

Karademir, Hazır I., and A. Warde. 2015. "The Cultural Omnivore Thesis: Methodological Aspects of the Debate." In L. Hanquinet and M. Savage, eds., *Routledge International Handbook of the Sociology of Art and Culture.* London: Routledge, pp. 77–89.

Khan, Omar. 2020. *The Colour of Money: Race and Economic Inequality.* London: Runnymede Trust.

Khan, O., and K. Sveinsson. 2015. "Race and Elections." In *Runnymede Perspectives.* London: Runnymede Trust.

Khan, Shamus. 2011. *Privilege—The Making of an Adolescent Elite at St. Paul's School.* Princeton, NJ: Princeton University Press.

Kilmartin, Terence. 1985. *A Guide to Proust.* London: Penguin.

King, D., and P. Le Galès. 2017. "The Three Constituencies of the State: Why the State Has Lost Unifying Energy." *The British Journal of Sociology* 68: S11–S33.

Kitschelt, H. 1994. *The Transformation of European Social Democracy.* Cambridge: Cambridge University Press.

Kleven, H., and C. Landais. 2017. "Gender Inequality and Economic Development: Fertility, Education and Norms." *Economica* 84(334): 180–209.

Kleven, H., C. Landais, J. Posch, A. Steinhauer, and J. Zweimüller. 2019, May. "Child Penalties across Countries: Evidence and Explanations." In *American Economic Association Papers and Proceedings* 109: 122–126.

Knight, Barry. 2017. *Rethinking Poverty: What Makes a Good Society?* Bristol: Policy Press.

Koch, Insa L. 2018. *Personalizing the State: An Anthropology of Law, Politics, and Welfare in Austerity Britain.* Oxford: Oxford University Press.

Koch, Insa, Mark Fransham, Sarah Cant, Jill Ebrey, Luna Glucksberg, and Mike Savage. 2020. "Social Polarisation at the Local Level: A Four-Town Comparative Study on the Challenges of Politicising Inequality in Britain." *Sociology,* in press.

Korsnes, O., J. Heilbron, J. Hjellbrekke, B. Bühlmann, and M. Savage, eds. 2018. *New Directions in Elite Studies.* London: Routledge.

Koselleck, Reinhart. 2004. *Futures Past: On the Semantics of Historical Time.* Trans. and with intro. By Keith Tribe. New York: Columbia University Press.

Krause, M. 2014. *The Good Project: Humanitarian Relief NGOs and the Fragmentation of Reason.* Chicago: University of Chicago Press.

Kriesi, Hanspeter. 1998. "The Transformation of Cleavage Politics. The 1997 Stein Rokkan Lecture." *European Journal of Political Research* 33(2): 165–185.

Krishna, Anirudh. 2013a. "Stuck in Place: Investigating Social Mobility in 14 Bangalore Slums." *Journal of Development Studies* 49(7): 1010–1028.

———. 2013b. "The Spatial Dimension of Inter-Generational Education Achievement in Rural India." *Indian Journal of Human Development* 6(2): 245–266.

Kros, C. 2015. "Rhodes Must Fall: Archives and Counter-archives." *Critical Arts* 29(supp. 1): 150–165.

Krugman, Paul. 2004. *The Great Unraveling: Losing Our Way in the New Century.* W. W. Norton & Company.

Kuenzi, Michelle, and Gina Lambright. 2001. "Party System Institutionalization in 30 African Countries." *Party Politics* 7(4): 437–468.

Kuhn, Thomas 1977. *The Essential Tension: Selected Studies in Scientific Tradition and Change.* Chicago and London: University of Chicago Press.

Kuipers, Giselinde. 2011. "Cultural Globalization as the Emergence of a Transnational Cultural Field: Transnational Television and National Media Landscapes in Four European Countries." *American Behavioral Scientist* 555: 541–557.

Kumar, Krishan. 2010. "Nation-States as Empires, Empires as Nation-States: Two Principles, One Practice?" *Theory and Society* 39(2): 119–143.

———. 2019. *Visions of Empire: How Five Imperial Regimes Shaped the World.* Princeton, NJ: Princeton University Press.

Kumar, Sushil. 1978. "The Concept of Political Development." *Political Studies* 26(4): 423–438.

Lamont, Michèle. 1992. *Money, Morals, and Manners: The Culture of the French and American Upper-Middle Class.* Chicago: University of Chicago Press.

———. 2019. "From 'Having' to 'Being': Self-worth and the Current Crisis of American Society." *British Journal of Sociology* 70(3): 660–707.

Lamont, Michèle, S. Beljean, and P. Chong. 2015. "A Post-Bourdieusian Sociology of Valuation and Evaluation for the Field of Cultural Production." In Laurie Hanquinet and Mike Savage, eds., *Routledge International Handbook of the Sociology of Art and Culture.* New York: Routledge.

Lamont, Michèle, and Virág Molnár. 2002. "The Study of Boundaries in the Social Sciences." *Annual Review of Sociology* 281: 167–195.

Lamont, M., G. M. Silva, J. Welburn, J. Guetzkow, N. Mizrachi, H. Herzog, and E. Reis. 2016. *Getting Respect: Responding to Stigma and Discrimination in the United States, Brazil, and Israel.* Princeton, NJ: Princeton University Press.

Landes, David. 1969. *The Unbound Prometheus.* Cambridge: Cambridge University Press.

Lash, Scott. 2002. *Critique of Information.* London: Sage.

Lash, Scott, and John Urry. 1987. *The End of Organized Capitalism.* Madison: University of Wisconsin Press.

Latour, Bruno. 1982. "Give Me a Laboratory and I Will Move the World." In K. Knorr and M. Mulkay, eds., *Science Observed.* London, Sage, pp. 141–170.

———. 1986. "Visualisation and Cognition: Thinking with Eyes and Hands." In H. Kuklick, ed., *Knowledge and Society Studies in the Sociology of Culture Past and Present,* Vol. 6. Newton, MA: JAI Press, pp. 1–40.

———. 1993. "Ethnography of High-Tech: About the Aramis Case." In Pierre Lemonnier, ed., *Technological Choices—Transformations in Material Culture since the Neolithic.* London: Routledge and Kegan Paul, pp. 372–398.

———. 2005. *Reassembling the Social.* Oxford: Oxford University Press.

———. 2012. *We Have Never Been Modern.* Cambridge, MA: Harvard University Press.

Laurison, Daniel. 2015. "The Willingness to State an Opinion: Inequality, Don't Know Responses, and Political Participation." *Sociological Forum* 30(4): 925–948.

Laurison, Daniel, and Sam Friedman. 2016. "The Class Pay Gap in Higher Professional and Managerial Occupations." *American Sociological Review* 81(4): 668–695.

Law, John, and John Hassard, eds. 1999. *Actor Network Theory and After.* Oxford: Blackwell.

Law, John, Evelyn Ruppert, and Mike Savage. 2011. "The Social Life of Methods." CRESC Working Paper Series. Manchester: University of Manchester.

LeBaron, Frédéric. 2011. "Economists and the Economic Order. The Field of Economists and the Field of Power in France." *European Societies* 31: 91–110.

Le Galès, Patrick. 2002. *European Cities Social Conflicts and Governance.* Oxford: Oxford University Press.

———. 2018. "Urban Political Economy beyond Convergence: Robust but Differentiated Unequal European Cities." In Alberta Andreotti, David Benass, and Yuri Kazepov, eds., *Western Capitalism in Transition.* Manchester: Manchester University Press.

Lenin, Vlaidimyr. 1902. *What Is to Be Done?* Available at https://www.marxists.org/archive/lenin/works/download/what-itd.pdf.

Le Roux, B., H. Rouanet, M. Savage, and A. Warde. 2008. "Class and Cultural Division in the UK." *Sociology* 42(6): 1049–1071.

Lees, L., H. B. Shin, and E. Morales. 2015. *Global Gentrification.* Bristol: Policy.

———. 2016. *Planetary Gentrification.* Cambridge: Polity.

Levitsky, S., and D. Ziblatt. 2018. *How Democracies Die.* Portland, OR: Broadway Books.

Li, Gordon. 2020. "From Parvenu to 'Highbrow' Tastes: The Rise of Cultural Capital in China's Intergenerational Elites." *British Journal of Sociology,* in press.

Li, Y., M. Savage, and A. Pickles. 2003. "Social Capital and Social Exclusion in England and Wales (1972–1999)." *British Journal of Sociology* 54(4): 497–526.

Li, Y., M. Savage, G. Tampubolon, A. Warde, and M. Tomlinson. 2002. "Dynamics of Social Capital: Trends and Turnover in Associational Membership in England and Wales, 1972–1999." *Sociological Research Online* 7(3): 1–17.

Lijphart, Arend. 1979. "Religious vs. Linguistic vs. Class Voting: The 'Crucial Experiment' of Comparing Belgium, Canada, South Africa, and Switzerland." *American Political Science Review* 73(2): 442–458.

Lilla, Mark. 2017. *The Once and Future Liberal: After Identity Politics.* New York: Harper Collins.

Lipset, Seymour Martin, and Stein Rokkan, eds. 1967. *Party Systems and Voter Alignments: Cross-national Perspectives,* Vol. 7. New York: Free Press.

Lloyd, John. 2004. *What the Media Do to Our Politics.* London: Constable & Robinson.

Lockwood, David. 1958. *The Blackcoated Worker: A Study in Class Consciousness.* Oxford: Clarendon.

Loury, Glenn C. 2001. "Politics, Race, and Poverty Research." In S. H. Danziger and R. H. Haveman, eds., *Understanding Poverty.* Cambridge, MA: Harvard University Press, pp. 447–52.

Lundberg, J., and D. Waldenstrom. 2018. "Wealth Inequality in Sweden. What Can We Learn from Capitalized Income Tax Data." *Review of Income and Wealth* 64(3): 517–541.

MacAdam, Doug. 2007. "From Relevance to Irrelevance: The Curious Impact of the Sixties on Public Sociology." In C. Calhoun, ed., *Sociology in America: A History.* Chicago: University of Chicago Press, pp. 411–426.

Mackenzie, Donald A. 1981. *Statistics in Britain, 1865–1930: The Social Construction of Scientific Knowledge.* Edinburgh: Edinburgh University Press.

———. 2005. "How a Superportfolio Emerges: Long-Term Capital Management and the Sociology of Arbitrage." In Karin Knorr Cetina and Alex P. Reda, eds., *The Sociology of Financial Markets.* New York: Oxford University Press, pp. 62–83.

———. 2008. *An Engine, Not a Camera: How Financial Models Shape Markets.* Cambridge, MA: MIT Press.

MacKenzie, Donald A., and Yuval Millo. 2003. "Constructing a Market-Performing Theory: The Historical Sociology of a Financial Derivatives Exchange." *American Journal of Sociology* 109(1): 107–145.

MacKenzie, D. A., F. Muniesa, and L. Siu, eds. 2007. *Do Economists Make Markets? On the Performativity of Economics.* Princeton, NJ: Princeton University Press.

Mackenzie, Donald A., and Judy Wajcman. 1985. *The Social Shaping of Technology.* Milton Keynes and Philadelphia: Open University Press.

Mckenzie, Lisa. 2015. *Getting By: Estates, Class and Culture in Austerity Britain.* London: Polity.

McLaughlin, H., C. Uggen, and A. Blackstone. 2012. "Sexual Harassment, Workplace Authority, and the Paradox of Power." *American Sociological Review* 77(4): 625–647.

Mack, J., and S. Lansley. 1985. *Poor Britain*. London: Allen & Unwin.

Mahoney, James, and Dietrich Rueschemeyer, eds. 2003. *Comparative Historical Analysis in the Social Sciences*. Cambridge: Cambridge University Press.

Majima, Shinobu. 2008. "Fashion and Frequency of Purchase: Womenswear Consumption in Britain, 1961–2001." *Journal of Fashion Marketing and Management* 12(4): 502–517.

Mandel, H., and M. Semyonov. 2016. "Going Back in Time? Gender Differences in Trends and Sources of the Racial Pay Gap, 1970 to 2010." *American Sociological Review* 81(5): 1039–1068.

Mandler, Peter. 2013. *Return from the Natives: How Margaret Mead Won the Second World War and Lost the Cold War*. New Haven, CT: Yale University Press.

———. 2016. "Educating the Nation: III. Social Mobility." *Transactions of the Royal Historical Society* 26: 1–23.

———. 2020. *The Crisis of the Meritocracy: Britain's Transition to Mass Education since the Second World War*. Oxford: Oxford University Press.

Mann, Kirk. 1992. *The Making of an English "Underclass"? The Social Divisions of Welfare and Labour*. Milton Keynes, UK: Open University Press.

Mann, Michael. 2005. *Incoherent Empire*. London: Verso.

———. 2012. *The Sources of Social Power*, Vol. 2, *The Rise of Classes and Nation-States, 1760–1914*. Cambridge: Cambridge University Press.

Marable, Manning. 1983. *How Capitalism Underdeveloped Black America: Problems in Race, Political Economy, and Society*. New York: South End Press.

Mareeva, S. 2020. "Socio-Economic Inequalities in Modern Russia and Their Perception by the Population." *Chinese Journal of Sociology*, in press.

Marshall, Thomas Humphrey. 1951. *Citizenship and Social Class*. Oxford: Oxford University Press.

Martin, John Levi. 2003. "What Is Field Theory?" *American Journal of Sociology* 109(1): 1–49.

———. 2011. *The Explanation of Social Action*. Oxford: Oxford University Press.

Martin, John Levi, and Forest Gregg. 2015. "Was Bourdieu a Field Theorist?" In Mathieu Hilgers and Eric Mangez, eds., *Bourdieu's Theory of Social Fields*. London and New York: Routledge and Taylor & Francis, pp. 39–61.

Martin, J. L., and K. T. Yeung. 2003. "The Use of the Conceptual Category of Race in American Sociology, 1937–99." *Sociological Forum* 18(4): 521–543.

Marx, Karl, and Friedrich Engels. 1969[1848]. "Communist Manifesto." In *Marx / Engels Selected Works*, Vol. 1. Moscow: Progress Publishers, pp. 98–137.

Maskileyson, Dina, and Moshe Semyonov. 2017. "On Race, Ethnicity and on the Economic Cost of Immigration." *Research in Social Stratification and Mobility* 50: 19–28.

Massey, Doreen. 2005. *For Space*. London: Sage.

Massey, Douglas S. 2007. *Categorically Unequal: The American Stratification System*. New York: Russell Sage Foundation.

Mau, Steffen. 2010. *Social Transnationalism: Lifeworlds beyond the Nation-State*. London: Routledge.

Mazzucato, Mariana. 2018. *The Value of Everything*. London: Penguin.

Mbembe, Joseph-Achille. 2003. "Necropolitics." Trans. Libby Meintjes. *Public Culture* 15(1): 11–40.

McClure, Roger. 2005. *The Philosophy of Time: Time before Times*. London: Routledge.

McKibbin, Ross. 1998. *Classes and Cultures: England 1918–1951*. Oxford: Oxford University Press.

Mears, Ashley. 2015. "Working for Free in the VIP: Relational Work and the Production of Consent." *American Sociological Review* 80(6): 1099–1122.

Mears, A. 2020. *Very Important People: Status and Beauty in the Global Party Circuit*. Princeton, NJ: Princeton University Press.

Meghji, A. 2017. "Positionings of the Black Middle-Classes: Understanding Identity Construction beyond Strategic Assimilation." *Ethnic and Racial Studies* 40(6): 1007–1025.

———. 2019. "Encoding and Decoding Black and White Cultural Capitals: Black Middle-Class Experiences." *Cultural Sociology* 13(1): 3–19.

Méndez, Maria Louise, and Modesto Gayo. 2018. *Upper Middle Class Social Reproduction: Wealth, Schooling, and Residential Choice in Chile*. New York: Springer.

Merlau-Ponty, Maurice M. 1989. *Phenomenology of Perception*. London: Palgrave Macmillan.

Meyer, J., J. Boli, G. Thomas, and F. Ramirez. 1997. "World Society and the Nation-State." *American Journal of Sociology* 103(1): 144–181.

Mies, Maria. 1998. *Patriarchy and Accumulation on a World Scale: Women in the International Division of Labour*. London: Palgrave Macmillan.

Mijs, Jonathan J. 2016. "The Unfulfillable Promise of Meritocracy: Three Lessons and Their Implications for Justice in Education." *Social Justice Research* 29(1): 14–34.

———. 2019. "The Paradox of Inequality: Income Inequality and Belief in Meritocracy Go Hand in Hand." *Socio-Economic Review* mwy051. Available at https://doi.org/10.1093/ser/mwy051.

Milanovic, Branko. 2015. "Global Inequality of Opportunity: How Much of Our Income Is Determined by Where We Live?" *Review of Economics and Statistics* 97(2): 452–460.

———. 2016. *Global Inequality: A New Approach for the Age of Globalization*. Cambridge, MA: Harvard University Press.

———. 2019. *Capitalism, Alone: The Future of the System That Rules the World*. Cambridge, MA: Harvard University Press.

Miles, A. 1993. *Social Mobility in Nineteenth- and Early Twentieth-century England.* Basingstoke: Macmillan.

Miliband, R. 1969. *The State in Capitalist Society.* London: Weidenfeld and Nicholson.

Miller, M. K. 2013. "Electoral Authoritarianism and Democracy: A Formal Model of Regime Transitions." *Journal of Theoretical Politics* 25(2): 153–181.

———. 2017. "The Strategic Origins of Electoral Authoritarianism." *British Journal of Political Science* 50: 1–28.

Mills, Colin. 2014. "The Great British Class Fiasco: A Comment on Savage et al." *Sociology* 48(3): 437–444.

Mitchell, Timothy. 2002. *Rule of Experts, Egypt, Techno-Politics, Modernity.* Berkeley: University of California Press.

Moi, Toril. 2017. "Describing My Struggle." *The Point,* December 27.

Moore, Barrington. 1966. *Social Origins of Dictatorship and Democracy.* London: Penguin.

Moretti, Franco. 1999. *Atlas of the European Novel, 1800–1900.* London: Verso.

———. 2007. *The Novel,* Vol. 1, *History, Geography, and Culture.* Princeton, NJ: Princeton University Press.

Morgan, Mary. 2019. "Introduction." In *Charles Booth's Poverty Maps.* London: Thames and Hudson, pp. 20–44.

Mouzelis, Nicos. 1994. "In Defence of 'Grand Historical Sociology.'" *British Journal of Sociology* 45(1): 31–36.

Mozifar, S., J. R. Scarritt, and G. Galaich. 2003. "Electoral Institutions, Ethnopolitical Cleavages and Party Systems in Africa's Emerging Democracies." *American Political Science Review* 97(3): 379–390.

Munn, Nancy. 1992. "The Cultural Anthropology of Time: A Critical Essay." *Annual Review of Anthropology* 21: 93–123.

Nairn, T. 1977. *The Break-Up of Britain: Crisis and Neo-nationalism.* London: New Left Books.

Neve, Christopher. 1990. *Unquiet Landscape: Places and Ideas in 20th Century British Painting.* London: Thames and Hudson.

Nichols, Georgia, and Mike Savage. 2017. "A Social Analysis of an Elite Constellation: The Case of Formula 1." *Theory, Culture & Society* 34(5–6): 201–225.

Nieuwbeerta, P., and N. D. De Graaf. 1999. "Traditional Class Voting in Twenty Postwar Societies." In Geoffrey Evans, ed., *The End of Class Politics.* Oxford: Oxford University Press, pp. 23–56.

Niño-Zarazúa, M., L. Roope, and F. Tarp. 2017. "Global Inequality: Relatively Lower, Absolutely Higher." *Review of Income and Wealth* 63(4): 661–684.

Nussbaum, M. C. 2001. *Women and Human Development: The Capabilities Approach,* Vol. 3. Cambridge: Cambridge University Press.

Nye, David. 1996. *American Technological Sublime.* Cambridge, MA: MIT Press.

Nye, D. E. 2013. *America's Assembly Line.* Boston: MIT Press.

Odusola, A. F., G. A. Cornia, H. Bhorat, and P. Conceição. 2017. *Income Inequality Trends in Sub-Saharan Africa: Divergence, Determinants and Consequences.* Addis Ababa: United Nations Development Programme, Regional Bureau for Africa.

Oesch, Daniel, and Line Rennwald. 2018. "Electoral Competition in Europe's New Tripolar Political Space: Class Voting for the Left, Centre-Right and Radical Right." *European Journal of Political Research* 57(4): 783–807.

Offen, Karen M. 2000. *European Feminisms, 1700–1950: A Political History.* Stanford, CA: Stanford University Press.

Offer, A. 2017. "The Market Turn: From Social Democracy to Market Liberalism." *The Economic History Review* 70(4): 1051–1071.

Ogle, Vanessa. 2017. "Archipelago Capitalism: Tax Havens, Offshore Money, and the State, 1950s–1970s." *The American Historical Review* 122(5): 1431–1458.

Olsen, D. 1988. *The City as a Work of Art.* New Haven, CT: Yale University Press.

O'Neil, Cathy. 2016. *Weapons of Math Destruction: How Big Data Increases Inequality and Threatens Democracy.* Portland, OR: Broadway Books.

Osborne, T., and N. Rose. 1999. "Do the Social Sciences Create Phenomena? The Example of Public Opinion Research." *British Journal of Sociology* 50(3): 367–396.

Oskarson, M. 2005. "Social Structure and Party Choice." In J. Thomassen, ed., *The European Voter: A Comparative Study of Modern Democracies.* Oxford: Oxford University Press, pp. 84–105.

Osterhammel, Jürgen. 2014. *The Transformation of the World: A Global History of the Nineteenth Century.* Princeton, NJ: Princeton University Press.

Pabón, Fabio, Andrés Díaz Murray Leibbrandt, Vimal Ranchhod, and Mike Savage. 2021. "Piketty Comes to South Africa." *British Journal of Sociology,* forthcoming.

Page, Benjamin I., and Robert Y. Shapiro. 1983. "Effects of Public Opinion on Policy." *American Political Science Review* 77(1): 175–190.

Pager, D., and D. S. Pedulla. 2015. "Race, Self-Selection, and the Job Search Process." *American Journal of Sociology* 120(4): 1005–1054.

Parker, Simon. 2004. *Urban Theory & the Urban Experience Encountering the City.* London: Routledge.

Parthasarathi, P. 2011. *Why Europe Grew Rich and Asia Did Not: Global Economic Divergence, 1600–1850.* Cambridge: Cambridge University Press.

Peck, Jamie. 2001. "Neoliberalizing States: Thin Policies / Hard Outcomes. *Progress in Human Geography* 25(3): 445–455.

Pedulla, D. S., and D. Pager. 2019. "Race and Networks in the Job Search Process." *American Sociological Review* 84(6): 983–1012.

Perrons, Diane. 2014. "Gendering Inequality: A Note on Piketty's *Capital in the Twenty-First Century.*" *British Journal of Sociology* 65(4): 667–677.

Persson, Mikael, and Johan Martinsson. 2016. "Patrimonial Economic Voting and Asset Value—New Evidence from Taxation Register Data." *British Journal of Political Science* 480(3): 1–18.

Pfeffer, Fabian, and Nora Waitkus. 2019. "The Wealth Inequality of Nations." The Inequality Lab Discussion Paper 2019-2. www.theinequalitylab.com.

Pfotenhauer, Sebastian, and Sheila Jasanoff. 2017. "Panacea or Diagnosis? Imaginaries of Innovation and the 'MIT Model' in Three Political Cultures." *Social Studies of Science* 47(6): 783–810.

Piachaud, David. 1987. "Problems in the Definition and Measurement of Poverty." *Journal of Social Policy* 16(2): 147–164.

Pierson, Paul. 2004. *Politics in Time: History, Institutions, and Social Analysis.* Princeton, NJ: Princeton University Press.

Piketty, Thomas. 2013. *Capital in the Twenty-First Century.* Cambridge, MA: Harvard University Press.

———. 2015. "An Interview with Thomas Piketty, Paris, July 8, 2015, by Mike Savage." LSE, International Inequalities Institute Working Paper (1).

———. 2020. *Capital and Ideology.* Cambridge, MA: Harvard University Press.

Piketty, Thomas, and Emmanuel Saez. 2003. "Income Inequality in the United States, 1913–1998." *Quarterly Journal of Economics* 118(1): 1–39.

Piketty, T., E. Saez, and G. Zucman. 2017. "Distributional National Accounts: Methods and Estimates for the United States." *Quarterly Journal of Economics* 133(2): 553–609.

Polanyi, K., and R. M. McIver. 1944. *The Great Transformation.* Boston: Beacon Press.

Pomeranz, K. 2009. *The Great Divergence: China, Europe, and the Making of the Modern World Economy.* Princeton, NJ: Princeton University Press.

Poovey, Mary. 1995. *Making a Social Body: British Cultural Formation, 1830–1864.* Chicago: University of Chicago Press.

Porter, Theodor M. 1995. *Trust in Numbers: The Pursuit of Objectivity in Science and Public Life.* Princeton, NJ: Princeton University Press.

Poulantzas, Nikos. 1969. "The Problem of the Capitalist State." *New Left Review* 1(58): 67–78.

———. 1978. *State, Power, Socialism.* London: Verso.

Power, Michael. 1997. *The Audit Society: Rituals of Verification.* Oxford: Oxford University Press.

Power, S., P. Brown, A. Allouch, and G. Tholen. 2013. "Self, Career and Nationhood: The Contrasting Aspirations of British and French Elite Graduates." *British Journal of Sociology* 64(4): 578–596.

Prieur, Annick, and Mike Savage. 2011. "Updating Cultural Capital Theory: A Discussion Based on Studies in Denmark and in Britain." *Poetics* 39(6): 566–580.

———. 2013. "Emerging Forms of Cultural Capital." *European Societies* 1(2): 246–267.

Przeworski, Adam. 1986. *Capitalism and Social Democracy.* Cambridge: Cambridge University Press.

Putnam, Robert D. 2000. *Bowling Alone: The Collapse and Revival of American Community.* New York: Simon & Schuster.

———. 2016. *Our Kids: The American Dream in Crisis.* New York: Simon & Schuster.

Ragin, Charles C. 2014. *The Comparative Method: Moving beyond Qualitative and Quantitative Strategies.* Berkeley: University of California Press.

Ragin, Charles C., and Howard S. Becker, eds. 1992. *What Is a Case? Exploring the Foundations of Social Inquiry.* Cambridge: Cambridge University Press.

Raitano, Michele, and Francesca Vona. 2015. "Measuring the Link between Intergenerational Occupational Mobility and Earnings: Evidence from Eight European Countries." *Journal of Economic Inequality* 13(1): 83–102.

Rancière, Jacques. 2006. *The Politics of Aesthetics.* Trans. Gabriel Rockhill. London: Bloomsbury.

Ravaillon, Martin. 2012. "Poor, or Just Feeling Poor? On Using Subjective Data in Measuring Poverty." Policy Research Working Paper WPS 5968. Washington, DC: World Bank.

Ravallion, M., G. Datt, and D. van de Walle. 1991. "Quantifying Absolute Poverty in the Developing World." *Review of Income and Wealth* 37(4): 345–361.

Ravallion, M., S. Chen, and P. Sangraula. 2009. "Dollar a Day Revisited." *World Bank Economic Review* 23(2): 163–184.

Raworth, Kate. 2017. *Doughnut Economics: Seven Ways to Think like a 21st-century Economist.* New York: Random House.

Reay, Diane. 2001. "Finding or Losing Yourself? Working-Class Relationships to Education." *Journal of Education Policy* 16(4): 333–346.

———. 2018. "Miseducation: Inequality, Education and the Working Classes." *International Studies in Sociology of Education* 27(4): 453–456.

Reay, D., G. Crozier, and J. Clayton. 2010. "'Fitting In' or 'Standing Out': Working-Class Students in UK Higher Education." *British Educational Research Journal* 36(1): 107–124.

Reay, Mike. 2007. "Academic Knowledge and Expert Authority in American Economics." *Sociological Perspectives* 50(1): 101–129.

———. 2012. "The Flexible Unity of Economics." *American Journal of Sociology* 118(1): 45–87.

Recchi, E., A. Favell, A. Apaydin, R. Barbulescu, M. Braun, I. Ciornei, N. Cunningham, J. Díez Medrano, D. Duru, L. Hanquinet, J. Jensen, S. Pötzschke, D. Reimer, J. Salamońska, M. Savage, and A. Varel. 2019. *Everyday Europe: Social Transnationalism in an Unsettled Continent.* Bristol: Policy Press.

Reddy, S. G., and T. Pogge. 2010. "How Not to Count the Poor." In Sudhir Anand, Paul Segal, and Joe Stiglitz, *Debates on the Measurement of Global Poverty.* Oxford: Oxford University Press, pp. 42–85.

Regev, Motti. 1997. "Rock Aesthetics and Musics of the World." *Theory, Culture & Society* 14(3): 125–142.

Reis, E. P., and M. Moore. 2005. *Elite Perceptions of Poverty and Inequality.* London: Zed Books.

Rigby, Elizabeth, and Gerald C. Wright. 2013. "Political Parties and Representation of the Poor in the American States." *American Journal of Political Science* 57(3): 552–565.

Rivera, Lauren A. 2016. *Pedigree: How Elite Students Get Elite Jobs.* Princeton, NJ: Princeton University Press.

Roberts, David. 2011. *The Total Work of Art in European Modernism.* Ithaca, NY: Cornell University Press.

Robertson, Roland. 1992. *Globalization: Social Theory and Global Culture.* London: Sage.

Robinson, Jenny. 2006. "Inventions and Interventions: Transforming Cities—An Introduction." *Urban Studies* 43(2): 251–258.

———. 2011. "Cities in a World of Cities: The Comparative Gesture." *International Journal of Urban and Regional Research* 35(1): 1–23.

———. 2013a. *Ordinary Cities: Between Modernity and Development.* New York: Routledge.

———. 2013b. "The Urban Now: Theorising Cities beyond the New." *European Journal of Cultural Studies* 16: 659–677.

Robinson, Joan. 1952. *The Generalisation of the General Theory, In the Rate of Interest, and Other Essays,* second edition. London: Macmillan.

Rodney, Walter. 1972. *How Europe Underdeveloped Africa.* London: Bogle-L'Ouverture Publications.

Rollock, Nicola. 2014. "Race, Class and 'the Harmony of Dispositions.'" *Sociology* 48(3): 445–451.

Rollock, N., D. Gillborn, C. Vincent, and S. J. Ball. 2014. *The Colour of Class: The Educational Strategies of the Black Middle Classes.* London: Routledge.

Rosa, Hartmut. 1990. *Governing the Soul: The Shaping of the Private Self.* London: Routledge.

———. 2003. "Social Acceleration: Ethical and Political Consequences of a Desynchronized High-Speed Society." *Constellations* 10(1): 3–33.

———. 2013. *Social Acceleration.* New York: Columbia University Press.

Rose, N. 1999. *Powers of Freedom: Reframing Political Thought.* Cambridge: Cambridge University Press.

Rose, Nikolas. 2001. "The Politics of Life Itself." *Theory, Culture & Society* 18(6): 1–30.

Rothstein, Bo. 2011. "Anti-corruption: The Indirect 'Big Bang' Approach." *Review of International Political Economy* 18(2): 228–250.

Rowbotham, Sheila. 1973. *Hidden from History.* London: Pluto Press.

Rowntree, Seebohm. 1901. *Poverty, A Study of Town Life.* New York: H. Fertig.

Roy, Ananya, and Emma Shaw Crane, eds. 2015. *Territories of Poverty: Rethinking North and South*. Athens: University of Georgia Press.

Rundell, J. 2019. "David Roberts: Images of Aesthetic Modernity." *Thesis Eleven* 152(1): 76–86.

Ruppert, Evelin. 2009. "Becoming Peoples: 'Counting Heads in Northern Wilds.'" *Journal of Cultural Economy* 21(2): 11–31.

———. 2011. "Population Objects: Interpassive Subjects." *Sociology* 45(2): 218–233.

Ruskin, J. 1856. *Modern Painters*. London: Smith, Elder and Co.

Sabel, Charles, and Jonathan Zeitlin. 1985. "Historical Alternatives to Mass Production: Politics, Markets and Technology in Nineteenth-Century Industrialization." *Past & Present* 108(1): 133–176.

Sachs, J. D. 2012. "From Millennium Development Goals to Sustainable Development Goals." *The Lancet* 379(9832): 2206–2211.

Saez, Emmanuel, and G. Zucman. 2019. *The Triumph of Injustice: How the Rich Dodge Taxes and How to Make Them Pay*. New York: W. W. Norton & Company.

Said, Edward. 1977. *Orientalism*. London: Penguin.

Samuel, R. 2016. *People's History and Socialist Theory (Routledge Revivals)*. London: Routledge.

Santoro, M., A. Gallelli, and B. Gruning. 2018. "Bourdieu's International Circulation: An Exercise in Intellectual Mapping." In T. Medvetz and J. Sallaz, eds., *The Oxford Handbook of Pierre Bourdieu*. Oxford: Oxford University Press, pp. 21–67.

Sapiro, Gisèle. 2010. "Globalization and Cultural Diversity in the Book Market: The Case of Literary Translations in the US and in France." *Poetics* 38(4): 419–439.

Saunders, Peter. 2010. *Beware False Prophets: Equality, the Good Society and the Spirit Level*. London: Policy Exchange.

Savage, M. 1997. "Social Mobility and the Survey Method: A Critical Analysis." In David Bertaux and Paul Thomson, eds., *Pathways to Social Class: A Qualitative Approach to Social Mobility*. Oxford: Clarendon Press, pp. 299–232.

———. 2000. "Walter Benjamin's Urban Thought." In Mike Crang and N. J. Thrift, eds., *Thinking Space*. London: Routledge, pp. 9–33.

———. 2008. "Elizabeth Bott and the Formation of Modern British Sociology." *Sociological Review* 56(4): 579–605.

———. 2009. "Against Epochalism: An Analysis of Conceptions of Change in British Sociology." *Cultural Sociology* 3(2): 217–238.

———. 2010. *Identities and Social Change in Modern Britain: The Politics of Method*. Oxford: Oxford University Press.

———. 2013. "The 'Social Life of Methods': A Critical Introduction." *Theory, Culture & Society* 30(4): 3–21.

———. 2014. "Piketty's Challenge for Sociology." *British Journal of Sociology* 65(4): 591–606.

———. 2015. "Introduction to Elites: From the 'Problematic of the Proletariat' to a Class Analysis of 'Wealth Elites.'" *Sociological Review* 63(2): 223–239.

———. 2016. "The Fall and Rise of Class Analysis in British Sociology, 1950–2016." *Tempo Social* 28(2): 57–72.

Savage, M., C. Allen, R. Atkinson, R. Burrows, M. L. Méndez, and P. Watt. 2010. "The Politics of Elective Belonging: Focus Article." *Housing, Theory and Society* 27(2): 115–161.

Savage, M., G. Bagnall, and B. Longhurst. 2001. "Ordinary, Ambivalent and Defensive: Class Identities in the Northwest of England." *Sociology* 35(4): 875–892.

———. 2005a. *Globalization and Belonging*. London: Sage.

Savage, Mike, James Barlow, Peter Dickens, and Anthony Fielding. 1992. *Property Bureaucracy & Culture: Middle Class Formation in Contemporary Britain*. London: Routledge.

Savage, Mike, and Roger Burrows. 2007. "The Coming Crisis of Empirical Sociology." *Sociology* 41(5): 885–899.

———. 2009. "Some Further Reflections on the Coming Crisis of Empirical Sociology." *Sociology* 43(4): 765–775.

Savage, M., N. Cunningham, F. Devine, S. Friedman, D. Laurison, L. McKenzie, A. Miles, H. Snee, and M. Taylor. 2015. *Social Class in the 21st Century*. London: Pelican.

Savage, M., N. Cunningham, D. Reimer, and A. Favell. 2019. "Cartographies of Social Transnationalism." In E. Recchi, A. Favell, A. Apaydin, R. Barbulescu, M. Braun, I. Ciornei, N. Cunningham, J. Díez Medrano, D. Duru, L. Hanquinet, J. Jensen, S. Pötzschke, D. Reimer, J. Salamońska, M. Savage, and A. Varel, *Everyday Europe: Social Transnationalism in an Unsettled Continent*. Bristol: Policy Press, pp. 35–60.

Savage, M., F. Devine, N. Cunningham, M. Taylor, Y. Li, J. Hjellbrekke, B. Le Roux, S. Friedman, and A. Miles. 2013. "A New Model of Social Class? Findings from the BBC's Great British Class Survey Experiment." *Sociology* 47(2): 219–250.

Savage, Mike, and Modesto Gayo-Cal. 2011. "Unravelling the Omnivore: A Field Analysis of Contemporary Musical Taste in the United Kingdom." *Poetics* 39(5): 337–357.

Savage, M., L. Hanquinet, N. Cunningham, and J. Hjellbrekke. 2018. "Emerging Cultural Capital in the City: Profiling London and Brussels." *International Journal of Urban and Regional Research* 42(1): 138–149.

Savage, Mike, and Cynthia Meersohn. 2021. "The Politics of the Excluded: Abjection and Reconciliation amongst the British Precariat." *Chinese Journal of Sociology*, in press.

Savage, Mike, and Elisabeth B. Silva. 2013. "Field Analysis in Cultural Sociology." *Cultural Sociology* 7(2): 111–126.

Savage, M., and A. Warde. 1993. *Urban Sociology, Capitalism and Modernity*. Basingstoke: Macmillan.

Savage, M., A. Warde, and F. Devine. 2005b. "Capitals, Assets, and Resources: Some Critical Issues 1." *British Journal of Sociology* 56(1): 31–47.

Savage, M., A. Warde, and K. Ward. 2003. *Urban Sociology, Capitalism and Modernity.* London: Palgrave Macmillan.

Savage, M., and K. Williams. 2008. "Elites: Remembered in Capitalism and Forgotten by Social Sciences." *The Sociological Review* 56(Suppl. 1): 1–24.

Scheidel, Walter. 2018. *The Great Leveler: Violence and the History of Inequality from the Stone Age to the Twenty-First Century,* Vol. 74. Princeton, NJ: Princeton University Press.

Scheve, K., and D. Stasavage. 2017. "Wealth Inequality and Democracy." *Annual Review of Political Science* 20: 451–468.

Schimpfössl, E. 2018. *Rich Russians: From Oligarchs to Bourgeoisie.* Oxford: Oxford University Press.

Schmutz, Vaughan. 2009. "Social and Symbolic Boundaries in Newspaper Coverage of Music, 1955–2005: Gender and Genre in the US, France, Germany, and the Netherlands." *Poetics* 37: 298–314.

Scott, Joan Walloch. 2019. *Sex and Secularism.* Princeton, NJ: Princeton University Press.

Sen, Amartya. 1983. "Poor, Relatively Speaking." *Oxford Economic Papers* 35(2): 153–169.

———. 1985. "A Sociological Approach to the Measurement of Poverty: A Reply to Professor Peter Townsend." *Oxford Economic Papers* 37(4): 669–676.

———. 1990. "More than 100 Million Women Are Missing." *New York Review of Books* 37(20): 61–66.

———. 1992. *Inequality Re-examined.* Oxford: Clarendon Press.

———. 2009. *The Idea of Justice.* Cambridge, MA: Harvard University Press.

Seymour, Anne. 2009. "Foreword." In R. Long, *Walking the Line.* London: Thames and Hudson.

Shapiro, T. M. 2017. *Toxic Inequality: How America's Wealth Gap Destroys Mobility, Deepens the Racial Divide, and Threatens Our Future.* New York: Basic Books.

Simone, Abdul Malik. 2004. *For the City Yet to Come: Urban Life in Four African Cities.* Durham, NC: Duke University Press.

———. 2009. *City Life from Jakarta to Dakar: Movements at the Crossroads.* New York; London: Routledge.

Sherman, Rachel. 2019. *Uneasy Street: The Anxieties of Affluence.* Princeton, NJ: Princeton University Press.

Simson, Rebecca. 2018. "Mapping Recent Inequality Trends in Developing Countries." LSE International Inequality Institute Working Paper 24: 2–54.

Simson, R., and M. Savage. 2020. "The Global Significance of National Inequality Decline." *Third World Quarterly* 41(1): 20–41.

Sinclair, Iain. 2003. *Lights Out for the Territory.* London: Penguin.

Sirniö, O., P. Martikainen, and T. M. Kauppinen. 2016. "Entering the Highest and the Lowest Incomes: Intergenerational Determinants and Early-Adulthood Transitions." *Research in Social Stratification and Mobility* 44: 77–90.

Skeggs, Beverley. 1997. *Formations of Class and Gender*. London: Sage.

Skocpol, Theda. 1979. *States and Social Revolutions*. Cambridge: Cambridge University Press.

Skocpol, Theda, and Margaret Somers. 1980. "The Uses of Comparative History in Macrosocial Inquiry." *Comparative Studies in Society and History* 22(2): 174–197.

Slater, Don. 2014. *New Media, Development and Globalization: Making Connections in the Global South*. New York: John Wiley & Sons.

Smidt, Corwin D. 2017. "Polarization and the Decline of the American Floating Voter." *American Journal of Political Science* 61(2): 365–381.

Soja, Edward. 1989. *Postmodern Geographies: The Reassertion of Space in Critical Social Theory*. London: Verso.

Soskice, David. 2014. "Capital in the Twenty-First Century: A Critique." *British Journal of Sociology* 65(4): 650–666.

Southerton, D., W. Olsen, A. Warde, and S. L. Cheng. 2012. "Practices and Trajectories: A Comparative Analysis of Reading in France, Norway, the Netherlands, the UK and the USA." *Journal of Consumer Culture* 12(3): 237–262.

Standing, G. 2017. *Basic Income: And How We Can Make It Happen*. London: Penguin UK.

Stanworth, Michelle. 1984. "Women and Class Analysis: A Reply to John Goldthorpe." *Sociology* 18(2): 159–170.

Steinmetz, G. 2005. "Return to Empire: The New US Imperialism in Comparative Historical Perspective." *Sociological Theory* 23(4): 339–367.

Steinmetz, G., ed. 2013. *Sociology and Empire: The Imperial Entanglements of a Discipline*. Durham, NC: Duke University Press.

Stengers, Isabelle. 2011. *Cosmopolitics II*. Trans. Bononno. Minneapolis: University of Minnesota Press.

Stiglitz, Joseph. 2011. "Of the 1%, by the 1%, for the 1%." *Vanity Fair* 11(64): 156–111.

Stiglitz, J. E., and L. J. Bilmes. 2012. "The 1 Percent's Problem." *Vanity Fair* . https://www.vanityfair.com/news/2012/05/joseph-stiglitz-the-price-on -inequality.

Strathern, Marilyn. 2000a. "Abstraction and Decontextualisation: An Anthropological Comment." *Cambridge Anthropology* 22: 52–66.

———. 2000b. "The Tyranny of Transparency." *British Educational Research Journal* 26(3): 309–321.

Stedman Jones, Gareth. 1971. *Outcast London*. London: Penguin.

———. 1984. *Languages of Class: Studies in English Working Class History, 1832–1982*. Cambridge: Cambridge University Press.

———. 2016. *Karl Marx: Greatness and Illusion*. London: Penguin.

Streeck, Wolfgang. 2014. "How Will Capitalism End?" *New Left Review* 87: 35–64.

Surak, K. 2020. "Millionaire Mobility and the Sale of Citizenship." *Journal of Ethnic and Migration Studies*, pp. 1–24.

Szreter, Simon. 2002. *Fertility, Class and Gender in Britain, 1860–1940*, Vol. 27. Cambridge: Cambridge University Press.

Taylor, Charles. 2004. *Modern Social Imaginaries*. Durham, NC: Duke University Press.

Therborn, G. 2013. *The Killing Fields of Inequality*. Cambridge: Polity.

Thompson, E. P. 1956. *William Morris: Romantic to Revolutionary*. London: Merlin Press.

———. 1963. *The Making of the English Working Class*. London: Penguin.

———. 1965. "The Peculiarities of the English." *Socialist Register*, pp. 311–362.

———. 1994. *Witness against the Beast: William Blake and the Moral Law*. Cambridge: Cambridge University Press.

Thrift, Nigel J. 2003. *Knowing Capitalism*. London: Sage

Thrift, Nigel J., and Ash Amin. 2002. *Cities: Reimagining the Urban*. London: Sage.

Tilly, Charles. 1999. *Durable Inequality*. Berkeley: University of California Press.

Todd, Selina. 2014. *The People: The Rise and Fall of the Working Class, 1910–2010*. New York: Hachette.

Toft, Maren. 2018. "Upper-Class Trajectories: Capital-Specific Pathways to Power." *Socio-Economic Review* doi: 10.1093/ser/mwx034.

Tooze, Adam. 2018. *Crashed: How a Decade of Financial Crises Changed the World*. New York: Penguin.

Townsend, Peter. 1979. *Poverty in the United Kingdom*. London: Allen Lane and Penguin.

Tufte, Edward Rolf. 2001. *The Visual Display of Quantitative Information*, Vol. 2. Cheshire, CT: Graphics Press.

———. 2006. *Beautiful Evidence*. Cheshire, CT: Graphics Press.

Tufte, Edward Rolf, N. H. Goeler, and R. Benson. 1990. *Envisioning Information*, Vol. 126. Cheshire, CT: Graphics Press.

Turok, Ivan, and Jackie Borel-Saladin. 2018. "The Theory and Reality of Urban Slums: Pathways-out-of-Poverty or Cul-de-Sacs?" *Urban Studies* 55(4): 767–789.

Tyler, I. 2013. *Revolting Subjects: Social Abjection and Resistance in Neoliberal Britain*. London: Zed Books.

———. 2020. *The Stigma Machine*. London: Zed Books.

UN World Cities Report. 2016. *UN Habitat*. Available at http://wcr.unhabitat.org/.

UNESCO. 2000. *World Culture Report 2000*. New York: UNESCO.

Upton-Hansen, Chris. 2018. "The Financialization of Art: A Sociological Encounter." PhD dissertation, London School of Economics and Political Science, London.

Urry, John. 2000. "Mobile Sociology." *British Journal of Sociology* 51(1): 185–203.

Uslaner, Eric M. 2008. *Corruption, Inequality, and the Rule of Law: The Bulging Pocket Makes the Easy Life*. Cambridge: Cambridge University Press.

———. 2010. *The Moral Foundations of Trust*. Cambridge: Cambridge University Press.

Vanderbroek, Dieter. 2018. "Toward a European Social Topography: The Contemporary Relevance of Pierre Bourdieu's Concept of 'Social Space.'" *European Societies* 20(3): 359–374.

Vauhkonen, T., J. Kallio, T. M. Kauppinen, and J. Erola. 2017. "Intergenerational Accumulation of Social Disadvantages across Generations in Young Adulthood." *Research in Social Stratification and Mobility* 48: 42–52.

Wahrman, D. 2004. *The Making of the Modern Self: Identity and Culture in Eighteenth Century England.* New Haven, CT: Yale University Press.

Walks, Alan. 2016. "Homeownership, Asset Based Welfare and the Neighbourhood Segregaton of Wealth." *Housing Studies* 31(7): 755–784.

Wallerstein, Immanuel. 2000. *The Essential Wallerstein.* New York: New Press.

Warde, Alan. 2005. "Consumption and Theories of Practice." *Journal of Consumer Culture* 52: 131–153.

———. 2011. "Cultural Hostility Re-considered." *Cultural Sociology* 53: 341–366.

Warde, A., D. Wright, and M. Gayo-Cal. 2007. "Understanding Cultural Omnivorousness: Or, the Myth of the Cultural Omnivore." *Cultural Sociology* 12: 143–164.

Watts, Duncan J. 2003. *Six Degrees: The Science of a Connected Age.* New York: Norton.

Webster, F. 2014. *Theories of the Information Society.* 4th ed. London: Routledge.

Weeden, Kim A., and David B. Grusky. 2004. "Are There Any Big Classes at All?" *Research in Social Stratification and Mobility* 22: 3–56.

———. 2005. "The Case for a New Class Map." *American Journal of Sociology* 111(1): 141–121.

———. 2012. "The Three Worlds of Inequality." *American Journal of Sociology* 117(6): 1723–1785.

WEF. 2017. *Global Risk Report.* Geneva: World Economic Forum.

Wetzstein, Steffen. 2017. "The Global Urban Housing Affordability Crisis." *Urban Studies* 54(14): 3159–3177.

White, Harrison. 1992. *Identity and Control: How Social Formations Emerge.* Princeton, NJ: Princeton University Press.

Williams, Eric. 2014[1950]. *Capitalism and Slavery.* Chapel Hill: University of North Carolina Press.

Wilkinson, Richard G., and Kate E. Pickett. 2008. "Income Inequality and Social Gradients in Mortality." *American Journal of Public Health* 98(4): 699–704.

———. 2010. *The Spirit Level: Why More Equal Societies Almost Always Do Better.* London: Allen Lane.

———. 2019. *The Inner Level: How More Equal Societies Reduce Stress, Restore Sanity, and Improve Everyone's Wellbeing.* London: Allen Lane.

Williams, Eric. 2014. *Capitalism and Slavery.* Chapel Hill, NC: University of North Carolina Press.

Williams, Raymond. 1983. *Keywords: A Vocabulary of Culture and Society.* Waukegan, IL: Fontana Press.

Wimmer, Andreas. 2017. "Power and Pride. National Identity and Ethnopolitical
    Inequality around the World." *World Politics* 69(4): 605–639.

Wimmer, Andreas, and Yuval Feinstein. 2010. "The Rise of the Nation-State across the
    World, 1816 to 2001." *American Sociological Review* 75(5): 764–790.

Wimmer, Andreas, and Brian Min. 2006. "From Empire to Nation-State: Explaining
    Wars in the Modern World, 1816–2001." *American Sociological Review* 71(6):
    867–897.

Witz, Anne. 1992. *Professions and Patriarchy*. London: Routledge.

Woodward, Susan L. 2017. *The Ideology of Failed States: Why Interventions Fail*. Cam-
    bridge: Cambridge University Press.

Wright, Noah. 2015. "Data Visualization in Capital in the 21st Century." *World* 5: 54–72.

Xie, Yu, and Xiang Zhou. 2014. "Income Inequality in Today's China." *Proceedings of
    the National Academy of Sciences* 111(19): 6928–6933.

Yuval-Davis, N. 1993. "Gender and Nation." *Ethnic and Racial Studies* 16(4): 621–632.

Zaller, John. 2004. "Floating Voters in U.S. Presidential Elections, 1948–2000." In
    Willem E. Saris and Paul Sniderman, eds., *Studies in Public Opinion: Attitudes,
    Nonattitudes, Measurement Error, and Change*. Princeton, NJ: Princeton University
    Press.

Zeitlin, Jonathan, and Gary Herrigel, eds. 2000. *Americanization and Its Limits.
    Reworking US Technology and Management in Post-War Europe and Japan*. New
    York: Oxford University Press.

Zucman, G. 2015. *The Hidden Wealth of Nations: The Scourge of Tax Havens*. Chicago:
    University of Chicago Press.

Zukin, Sharon. 2010. *The Naked City: The Death and Life of Authentic Urban Places*. New
    York: Oxford University Press.

Zweig, Ferdynand. 1961. *The Worker in an Affluent Society: Family Life and Industry*.
    London: Heinemann.

Acknowledgments

I humbly acknowledge all the support and assistance that helped shape this work into the book it has become. In a very real sense I could only have written this book from the vantage point of working at the London School of Economics (LSE), which I joined in 2012. My experiences as the head of the Department of Sociology (2013–2016) and as director of the International Inequalities Institute (2015–2020) have been ethnographically central to the argument I relate in this book. I have seen at first hand how debates about inequality have played out at this remarkable institution, among academics, students, and the wider public. My initial years at the LSE made me hugely aware of the astonishing and energizing power of the inequality discourse itself, even in a risk-averse, conservative environment. In a few short years between 2008 and 2014, the topic of inequality became central to academic and public debate, subsuming issues of class, gender, and race into an over-arching bleak prognosis of increasing economic inequality. Thomas Piketty's *Capital in the Twenty-First Century* played an inspiring role. I still remember the remarkable moment shortly after the publication of Piketty's magnum opus in 2014 when, as head of the Department of Sociology, I attended a meeting of other LSE department heads. Waiting for the meeting to begin, rather than do the usual moaning about resource and planning constraints, for a few brief moments, several department heads put aside their territorial battles to offer their takes on Piketty's book. Some of them, alongside other LSE colleagues, contributed to a special issue of the *British Journal of Sociology* (2015) on this theme. This moment of intellectual luminescence was short-lived, but it imprinted indelibly on my mind. The topic of inequality was opening up new intellectual horizons.

It was out of this sense of possibility and the breaking down of boundaries that the LSE formed the International Inequalities Institute (III) in 2015, as a result of major lobbying from colleagues across the institution. This book draws on the resources and networks that the III, as an interdepartmental institute concerned with inequality issues, has fostered, and it grew organically out of the teaching, research, and conversations that the III has hosted; indeed, without the III, this book would not, and could not, have been written. The III succeeded in winning interdisciplinary funding for PhD students, nurtured a masters course in Inequalities and Social Science (one of the first in the world to address inequality as an interdisciplinary issue), and has hosted innumerable events and seminars. In 2017, Atlantic Philanthropies invested a generous sum to create the Atlantic Fellows Programme in Social and Economic Equity (AFSEE). AFSEE is a twenty-year program that supports Fellows, especially from the global south, to study at the III. I thank the board of Atlantic Philanthropies, and especially its chief executive, Chris Oechsli, for supporting our work and keeping faith with us. I have learned so much from my colleagues, who have invested so much time and energy in the III. First and foremost, I acknowledge the late John Hills, surely the United Kingdom's leading social policy commentator on inequality issues, who was originally the co-director-in-charge of the III, and who brought his extensive experience, collegiality, and gravitas to the III's early years. Nicola Lacey (from the Law Department) and David Soskice (from the Government Department) threw themselves into the III with remarkable generosity and enthusiasm, taking on major teaching responsibilities—especially for our doctoral students—far beyond any call of duty. Above all, Niki and David embraced the vision for interdisciplinary and big-picture thinking that the III has prized, which I hope this book reflects, even if from my own sociological perspective. I have worked with a great group of postdocs and research staff—Mark Fransham, Luna Glucksberg, Jonathan Mijs, Tahnee Ooms, Aaron Reeves, Nora Waitkus, and Susanne Wessendorf—some of whose work I draw on at various points in this book.

I also thank Armine Ishkanian, who has taken on the directorship of the III's Atlantic Fellows Programme for Social and Economic Equity with gusto. Liza Ryan has been a wonderful manager of the III, and Francisco Ferreira has taken on the directorship of the III with great energy and responsibility. I also thank Meliz Ahmet and Asmaa Akhtar from the III/AFSEE team in particular for their support. Beyond this core group is a much larger set of LSE colleagues who have thrown themselves into the inequality arena and from whom I have learned. I cannot list all of them, but must name Poornima Paidipaty (who was a great teacher in the master's program in Inequalities and Social Science); Tim Allen (International Development and Africa Centre); Gareth Jones (Geography and Environment, and Latin American and Caribbean Centre); Laura Bear, Katy Gardner, and Alpa Shah (Anthropology Department); Simon Hix (Government Department), Naila Kabeer (Gender and International Development); Nick Couldry, Ellen Helsper, and Seeta Ganhadaragan (Media and Communications Department); Insa Koch and Andy Summers (Law); Neil Lee (Geography and Environment); Diane Perrons (Gender); and Tim Besley and Camille Landais (Economics). Paul Segal, an III affiliate based at Kings College London, has also been a terrific interlocutor.

As well as the LSE faculty, I acknowledge the students from whom I have learned so much. Very early on, I came to realize that students would not necessarily understand or even know British reference points, and that it was crucial to teach in a way that recognized the sheer diversity of the student body. It also became clear that the astonishing energy and enthusiasm of LSE students, both graduates and undergraduates, provide great resources to "think big." I could not have written this book without this stimulus.

I have numerous debts to many colleagues and friends outside the LSE. I thank Ettore Recchi, Laurie Hanquinet, Adrian Favell, David Reimer, Juan Diaz Medrano, Niall Cunningham, and my other collaborators for their work on the European Union–funded "Europeanization of Everyday Life" project, which I draw on in Chapter 5. It has been a great privilege to work with Rebecca Simson, whose research on global inequality trends informs Chapter 5, and Katharina Hecht, who assisted with Chapter 7. I have also been hugely fortunate in engaging with inspiring academics who have visited the III, including Modesto Gayo and Maria Luisa Mendez (Center for Social Cohesion and Conflict Studies, Santiago, Chile), Thomas Piketty (Paris School of Economics), Branko Milanovic (City University of New York), and Kirsten Sehnbruch (initially from COES, Chile, who is now a colleague at the LSE). Alan Hirsch and Murray Leibbrandt have been wonderful hosts during my several visits to the University of Cape Town.

The arguments in this book are in many ways a working-through of those that were developed at the Centre for Socio-Cultural Change (CRESC), where I worked between 2004 and 2010, and I thank my colleagues at the University of Manchester and the Open University, who played a wonderful role in making CRESC an inspiring platform. In particular, I thank Tony Bennett, Karel Williams, Josine Opmeer, Andy Miles, Evelyn Ruppert, and John Law. They helped to develop interest in the sociology of elites, in new forms of cultural capital and distinction, and in the "social life of methods" perspective, all of which are points of departure for the arguments in this book (for example, see Savage and Williams 2008; Bennett et al. 2009; Law et al. 2011; and Savage 2013).

I also thank colleagues and friends from my home discipline of sociology. My book takes up reflections about the nature of sociological expertise that have preoccupied me for a long time (see notably Savage and Burrows 2007 and Savage 2010). Since the LSE's foundation in the early twentieth century, the tradition of sociology at the school has been a macro-oriented form of "grand historical sociology." This approach fell from grace in the later twentieth century, when sociology became more empirically oriented (see my own account in Savage 2010) and it is with a degree of surprise that I can now see that I am renewing this project.

This has been an exciting (though at times lonely) path to tread, and I thank numerous colleagues who have offered guidance. Over the past fifteen years, I have benefited hugely from working with collaborators elsewhere in Europe committed to renewing sociological research repertoires for looking at inequality in heterodox ways. In particular, I mention Johs Hjellbrekke (Bergen, Norway), who introduced me to geometric data analysis; Annick Prieur (Aalborg, Denmark), who led the remarkable Social and Cultural Differentiation research network; Marianne Nordli Hansen, who invited me to visit Oslo where I gave the first presentation of the key ideas here; Patrick Le Gales (Sciences Po, Paris), who pushed me to think further about cities and social inequality; Ettore Recchi (also Sciences Po), who led the EUCROSS project, which I draw on in this book; and Laurie Hanquinet, whom I first met when she was a PhD student in Brussels, who later became a colleague at the University of York, and whose sensitive cultural sociology has been a model. Michele Lamont (Harvard) has been a wonderful interlocutor and advocate at too many venues to mention. In the United Kingdom, I especially thank Andrew Miles (Manchester), who (like me) is a historian turned sociologist with the distinct sensibility this brings with it; and Susan Halford (Bristol), who has shown how sociologists can succeed when they use their skills and creativity to drive interdisciplinary agendas, most notably with her research on web science. Sarah Cant's passion for sociology has been a constant inspiration. More broadly, the amazing Great British Class Survey team (Niall Cunningham, Fiona Devine, Sam Friedman, Daniel Laurison, Lisa Mckenzie, Andrew Miles, Helene Snee, and Paul Wakeling) has shown how sociologists can take the initiative. In particular, the LSE trio of Daniel, Lisa, and Sam were wonderful colleagues and have given much advice and support along the way. I have benefited from working with terrific and supportive colleagues in LSE sociology, from whom I have learned a lot, including Fabien Accominotti, Carrie Friese, Suzi Hall, Monika Krause, and Charis Thompson—as well as Sam Friedman, mentioned above. Some amazing LSE sociology PhD students working specifically on inequality topics—including Katharina Hecht, Kristina Kolbe, Gordon Li, Dan McArthur, Georgia Nichols, Emma Taylor, and Chris Upton-Hansen, whose work I refer to in this book—have been of enormous assistance. I also thank my many other colleagues in LSE sociology who have given support to me as I was writing.

It has been a pleasure to work with the outstanding team at Harvard University Press, especially Ian Malcolm, who has shown an unwavering faith and confidence in my project since he commissioned it, and Olivia Woods for her editorial support. I also thank Aimee Nazroo and Kristina Kolbe for their editorial assistance in the later stages of preparing this manuscript, as well as Elisabeth Schimpfoessl, who explained how I needed to improve the titles of my chapters. Elisabeth Schimpfoessl, Fabien Accominotti, Susan Halford, Johs Hjellbrekke, Katharina Hecht, Ettore Recchi, Jason Hickel, Paul Segal, Bev Skeggs, and Sam Friedman have kindly commented on parts of the book. Miles Corak, Niall Cunningham, Katharina Hecht, Simon Hix, Johnny Miller, Paul Segal, Rebecca Simson, the Equality Trust, and the Pew Foundation have assisted with the figures. I particularly thank Patrick Le Gales and Michelle Lamont for (anonymously) reading the initial submission of this manuscript in such an encouraging, perceptive, and insightful way and for encouraging me to develop unfinished arguments.

During the course of writing this book, I have relied on the support of several close friends and family, whose counsel and advice, sometimes during trying times, have been invaluable. In no particular order (well, in alphabetical order), I thank Andy, Bardy, Cristiana, Georgia, Johs, Jon and Mark, and Sarah and Susan. I hope this book has been worth the wait and endurance!

I end these acknowledgments on a personal note. On numerous occasions, I have been overcome with the sheer impossibility of writing this book—as if inequality had opened up a Pandora's box of issues that were ultimately overwhelming. Such is the sheer sophistication and also specialization of research in the social sciences that the project of effectively synthesizing work from different disciplines and research traditions is daunting enough. Of even more concern is my anglocentrism and lack of detailed knowledge of trends and trajectories in vast arenas of the globe. However, when these doubts nagged—which was often—I was also beset by the stronger feeling that some attempt at this kind of sociological synthesis had to be undertaken. Economists were leading the way by charting inequality trends using ambitious new data sets, measurement tools, and theoretical insights. But (with the greatest respect), economists are not always best placed to recognize the tissue of social and cultural relations that also needs to be brought to the table. It is vital for sociologists to rise to the challenge of offering their interpretations of social change. This is my attempt. Limited though it undoubtedly is, if it is a spur to others to write better accounts, then I will have served a purpose.

This book is dedicated to my son Bardy, who is studying to become an engineer. I hope it sheds light on the world he will inherit and help to improve. And also to Georgia, who was skeptical about Bourdieu, and insisted that I should pay more attention to time.

Index